ALONG THE TIGRIS

ALONG THE TIGRIS

THE 101ST AIRBORNE DIVISION IN OPERATION IRAQI FREEDOM

February 2003 to March 2004

Thomas L. Day

Schiffer Military History
Atglen, PA

Book design by Robert Biondi.

Copyright © 2007 by Thomas L. Day.
Library of Congress Catalog Number: 2006933297.

Printed in China.
ISBN: 978-0-7643-2620-2

We are always looking for people to write books on new and related subjects. If you have an idea for a book, please contact us at the address below.

Published by Schiffer Publishing Ltd.
4880 Lower Valley Road
Atglen, PA 19310
Phone: (610) 593-1777
FAX: (610) 593-2002
E-mail: Info@schifferbooks.com.
Visit our web site at: www.schifferbooks.com
Please write for a free catalog.
This book may be purchased from the publisher.
Please include $3.95 postage.
Try your bookstore first.

In Europe, Schiffer books are distributed by:
Bushwood Books
6 Marksbury Ave.
Kew Gardens, Surrey TW9 4JF
England
Phone: 44 (0)20 8392-8585
FAX: 44 (0)20 8392-9876
E-mail: info@bushwoodbooks.co.uk
www.bushwoodbooks.co.uk
Free postage in the UK. Europe: air mail at cost.
Try your bookstore first.

PREFACE

Along the Tigris is a memoir of a division at war, from the private with less than a year in the Army to a general with 30. It's about the 20,000 soldiers who served with the 101st Airborne Division during the course of Operation Iraqi Freedom, and it's about the sixty-one who did not make it home. War for the 101st Airborne Division began on March 20, 2003. On the battlefields of Iraq, the soldiers of the famed "Screaming Eagles" would put cities like An Najaf, Karbala, Al Hillah, and Baghdad in the same breath as the sacred grounds of Jamestown, Gettysburg, and Normandy. But war for the 101st Airborne did not end after the defeat of Iraqi dictator Saddam Hussein. For nine months, the 101st Airborne was tasked to rebuild a broken society in northern Iraq and a city named Mosul. The unique mission was as dynamic and difficult as any the venerable division had ever faced. The soldiers to take on that mission were as determined and stalwart as any force on earth.

Division soldiers from top to bottom were interviewed for *Along the Tigris*, including the division's commanding general and all three infantry brigade commanders. The purpose of *Along the Tigris* is to provide both an historical documentation of the division's deployment in support of Operation Iraqi Freedom, as well as a narrative of the personal stories behind the headlines.

Much of the "post-May 1" material is taken from the pages of the *Iraqi Destiny*, a newsletter produced and electronically distributed by the 101st Airborne Division

Public Affairs Office with the 40th Public Affairs Detachment and the 22nd Mobile Public Affairs Detachment (Fort Bragg, N.C.). The *Iraqi Destiny* was produced both as a product for soldiers to keep informed on the division's missions and for families in the United States to know what their loved ones were doing in Iraq. The mission of the *Iraqi Destiny* mirrors the mission of *Along the Tigris*.

CONTENTS

INTRODUCTION

They are celebrated at every street corner in America. Their popularity transcends politics, ethnic and religious divides, social divides – in fact, sometimes it seems like they are really the only thing that can unite America. Some young men and women have chosen to join them; others chosen just to admire them. Country music artists have written Top 40 hits about them. They have appeared on the cover of magazines like movie stars. They get discounts at restaurants. Friends fight one another for the right to buy them drinks. To some, they can walk on water. When introduced to an American soldier, Americans often respond with a simple and genuine, "thank you."

Now get to know the men and women underneath the uniform. Some soldiers went to Iraq, took care of business and came home eager and ready to resume life as normal. Others came back lonely, confused, and utterly oblivious to anyone who considered them "heroes." They were shot at, they received emails from home with bad news they could nothing about, and they had their dreams of going home pushed further and further away like some kind of cruel game. They ate meals that were prepared and packaged months, even years ago. They went weeks without showering. They lost friends and family – both from separation and from combat.

And they dethroned a murderous dictator. They reached out to a people who had never known the gift of freedom, even reaching out to some who never desired it. They won over friends and allies and destroyed their enemies. They found family where they never thought they would. From packs of young men and women from differing backgrounds – so much so that unit cohesion might seem impossible – came a fighting force unparalleled in military history. An American soldier is no one thing. Ask a soldier why he or she joined, you could get a different answer for each and every one. But all who serve, wittingly or unwittingly, do so with their trust in the man or woman to their left and right, driven by the fear of letting their buddies down. The decision to invade Iraq was perhaps the most fateful in recent American history, and now the men and women of the American military fight to decide its ultimate conclusion.

Behind the headlines of Operation Iraqi Freedom, the first major armed conflict of the 21st century lays the heart and soul of the American workingman and woman. From the eighteen-year old private to the four-star commanding general of the Iraq theater, in good and in bad, there is a story in every soldier and there is a story in every unit. The 101st Airborne Division came to Kuwait in February of 2003 with ruthless Iraqi dictator Saddam Hussein still in power in Iraq. By the time the division went home, they would start the rebuilding of war-torn nation.

In between was a narrative of grand strategies, complex command decisions, deadly battle engagements, and the memories of the men and women who served with the division. It's a story about love and pain, bravery and sacrifice, tragedy and victory, from Fort Campbell, Ky., to Kuwait, through the toughest battles in the blitz of Baghdad, to a place called Nineveh, the capital of the Assyrian empire aggrandized in the biblical gospels of Luke and Matthew. What the soldiers who served with the 101st in Iraq will remember their tour by is unique to each and every soldier. But for a year, the soldiers of 101st Airborne collectively etched their legacy in the annals of the Army's 227-year history, not with mythological superhumans, but with soldiers from the big city streets to the Midwest farm towns.

More than 20,000 soldiers would earn the venerable 101st Airborne Division combat patch in Iraq, denoting that they had served with the division in combat. The price of that honor would be high, even for the soldiers who never saw a tracer bullet whiz by their ears. It's a story that would not have a storybook ending, but the work and the sacrifices made by the soldiers of the 101st Airborne Division during their 2003-2004 deployment will not soon be forgotten.

For Ben and Maggie Smith, the memories began in flight school at Fort Rucker, Ala., where Ben first noticed Maggie during weekend a game of Frisbee football and had eyed her ever since. He was smitten early on. Maggie had noticed him too, but for all the wrong reasons. "Big Ben," as his friends called him, had earned an early reputation as a goofball in class. Maggie had earned a reputation as just the opposite.

Ben came to West Point after completing a tour in South Korea as an enlisted man. Whenever anyone asked where he went to college, the humble Ben always replied "a small community college on the east coast." Maggie had been a prior enlisted soldier too, serving a four-year enlistment before earning her commission through the Reserve Officer Training Corps (ROTC) at her hometown Colorado State University. Their career paths in the military were about all they shared in common when they first met. Ben, simply put, was a farm boy. He reminded Maggie even a bit of Forrest Gump before they met. He had grown up on a pig farm in Swinky, Mo., and would speak volumes about his farm if anyone ever asked him about it. At one point, during training, Ben felt behooved to make a very important announcement. "I have something to get out in the open. I know you all have been talking behind my back, and I think it's finally time for me to come out in the open about this." Maggie and the rest of the class, including the instructors, wondered where Ben was going with this. "Yes it's true, my brother is on the cover of Successful Farming Magazine, and ladies, he is single." Out of his flight bag, Ben pulled out a cover of the magazine, and sure enough his brother Sam graced the cover.

If he hadn't captured Maggie's attention by that point, he would for certain when he started sitting next to her in class. "How old are you, Maggie?" he asked in middle of a lecture.

Annoyed, Maggie whispered, "twenty-nine," and returned her focus to the instructor.

"Twenty-nine?" Ben almost jumped out of his seat, incredulous that she was two years older than him. "You must use Oil of Olay." Maggie was not amused, but yes, she did in fact use Oil of Olay. Ben continued listing cosmetic and hygiene products that he thought she used, guessing correctly on everything but her toothpaste. She tried her best to follow the lecture, but Ben had a way about him that just demanded her attention. By the end of class Maggie had actually warmed up to this strange country boy, though she wondered if he had been going through her trash. She didn't know it at the time, but Ben had earlier managed to steal her number off an instructor's phone roster. He called days later only after finding the necessary courage. Their phone conversations lasted for hours, sometimes leaving little time for studying, but Maggie rejected every last attempt from Ben to take her out on a date. Maybe she was playing hard to get or maybe she was still a bit concerned about dating a man who was raised with pigs, but she could go out with him among other friends acting as a buffer zone. Ben, as Maggie would later find out, simply did not lose. He found ways to win at everything: bingo, cards, raffles, even video games – it was magical. Now he was determined to win her heart. Ben wouldn't lose at that game either.

His talents at a Fort Rucker karaoke bar were certainly not what eventually won her over (and didn't win too many people in the bar either), but Maggie had a great time their first night out. She didn't even notice her other friends. From that night on, Ben was all she thought about outside of school. The two were still nominally friends until Ben showed up unexpectedly on her front doorstep with flowers. "Wow, since when do friends bring friends *flowers*?"

"What, don't you know that Wednesdays are Flower Days? Everyone knows that," Ben replied. The two were no longer friends, both knew. They were falling in love. From that point on, every Wednesday became Flower Day for the couple. Even on the busiest Wednesday's, Ben would always find a way to deliver flowers to Maggie.

It was the pigs, not the flowers, which would eventually seal the deal for Ben. He took the woman that would be his wife to meet the people who would be her in-laws, Bill and Kathy Smith, as well as his five siblings, Margie, Leo, Mary, Sally, and of course, the cover boy himself, Sam. The family took in Maggie as one of their own. She instantly felt like she belonged. To her surprise, all of the purportedly simple farmers were in fact college graduates. Ben had been one of the first to actually leave the small town; most of them just wouldn't and two of them, Mary and Sally, actually built homes on the farm with their husbands. Maggie never considered herself a small town girl before, but she instantly fell in love with Swinky just as she had for Ben's family. On Sundays, the town's church packed them in for morning services. "The Dugout" was known for packing them in for happy hour; Ben, Maggie, and local friends would rarely miss a chance to grab a cold beer and play shuffleboard at the local bar. Coming back from Swinky, Maggie knew she had found the man she wanted to spend the rest of her life with.

A month later, Ben came to Maggie's apartment to watch a movie with a pizza and a six-pack, inexplicably wrapped in newspaper. Nestled in the six-pack was a ring box, an engagement ring Maggie would find after she unwrapped the newspaper. "Maggie, will you marry me?" he asked as she opened the box.

Gladly but, as she said, "this has to be the worst marriage proposal in the world." The engagement came on a Thursday, which instantly became Proposal Day for the couple. From that point on, every Thursday, Ben would find new and innovative ways to propose to Maggie.

Unlike some military marriages, Ben and Maggie did not have to get married in haste for any reason. They didn't have to stop by the Post Chapel for a "Shotgun" marriage to avoid separate duty assignments. Ben and Maggie were both assigned to Fort Campbell with the 101st Airborne Division after flight school. Both were assigned to the 101st Aviation Brigade, which meant that in the event of a deployment, both would likely stay or go together. With no need then to get married just to force the Army to send them to the same post, Ben and Maggie waited for two years to get married. September 14, 2002, a year and three days after the attacks on the World Trade Center and the Pentagon, Captains Ben and Maggie Smith were married at the Smith family farm in an area far away from the pigs. It was a ceremony that an outsider would never guess involved two Army officers. No dress blues or Army greens were seen anywhere in the crowd dominated by service members. The reception was held at the local Knights of Columbus. Ben and Maggie were introduced as bride and groom for the first time, just as the day took a turn for the worse. With the lights dimmed and nineties cult-hit "I'm Too Sexy" setting the tone, Ben unintentionally stepped on the back of Maggie's dress, leaving the train on the ground. It would be a small blemish on a perfect day for Ben and Maggie.

Their honeymoon was in Aruba, their first of two trips in the next year to a hot, sandy "get-away." In the day, they sunbathed on the beach. As the sun went down, they gambled. When they won, they spent their winnings on dinner and entertainment, and entertainment for Ben meant karaoke. Holding one last note for over a minute, Ben came home one night from "Carlos & Charlie's" with the coveted singing award. Maggie, not to be outdone, won the "Mexican Bandito Calling Contest." Walking back to their hotel that night, the two were cheered like rock stars by a busload of partygoers who had seen their talents.

The party couldn't last forever though, and when they returned to Fort Campbell the next week, they returned to a post preparing for war. Going back to work after vacation can be tough for anyone, but for Ben and Maggie, going back to work meant coming back to reality. They were almost certainly going to be off to war before they really had a chance to enjoy being married. Such was the life of a soldier in the post-September 11 world.

A war without a manual. Soldiers are trained to fight and win wars – that's their job. They were not, however, told how to fight and win the peace. Sergeants and lieutenants are not trained to rebuild a dilapidated health clinic. Officers, no matter how senior, do not receive training during normal military exercises on how to run a city council. Not even generals are supposed to know how to govern one of the world's most volatile provinces. But when handed a mission, no matter how daunting, good soldiers "soldier on" and good units learn, adapt, and accomplish the mission.

Semper Gumbi. "Always Flexible." Overthrow the Iraqi dictator, reestablish order, build the foundations for a functioning democracy, defeat an armed insurgency and do all of this without any similar precedent in American history. Do all of this without a plan for success. That would be the mission handed to the 101st Airborne Division during its twelve months in Iraq, one of the world's fiercely nationalistic and militarized countries, from late February 2003 to early March of 2004. It would be mission impossible for lesser soldiers, and to find answers to questions, they would need to look no further than themselves, because answers weren't going to come from anywhere else.

Understanding the uniqueness of the 101st Airborne's actions in Iraq begins with the legacy of the 35th President of the United States, John Fitzgerald Kennedy, and his vision for a modern Army for a modern battlefield. It would not be a stretch to say that the 101st's tour in Iraq began inside the famed Michie Stadium at West Point during the graduation ceremony of the United States Military Academy Class of 1961. It was there that Kennedy issued a challenge. A President known for his vision, Kennedy laid out an image of an American Army so ahead of his time that it would take more than a generation to see its realization. It was a challenge to the Army and its soldiers to "understand the importance of military power and also the limits of military power." The Army, in the post-World War II generation, would be forced to fight battles on non-linear battlefields. Their enemies would be unconventional. Their missions would require "traditional" forces to take on "less traditional roles":

> "Whatever your position, the scope of your decisions will not be confined to the traditional tenets of military competence and training. You will need to

know and understand not only the foreign policy of the United States but the foreign policy of all countries scattered around the world that 20 years ago were the most distant names to us. You will give orders in different tongues and read maps by different systems. You will be involved in economic judgments which most economists would hesitate to make. In many countries, your posture and performance will provide the local population with the only evidence of what our country is really like. In other countries, your military mission, its advice and action, will play a key role in determining whether those people will remain free."

In his address, he referenced recent and ongoing missions in Malaya, Greece, the Philippines, Algeria, Cuba and, finally, Indochina. "This is another type of war, new in its intensity, ancient in its origin. War by guerillas, subversives, insurgents, assassins, war by ambush instead of by combat; by infiltration instead of aggression."

Kennedy had laid out a new Army for the new kind of conflicts America would face: terrorism, guerilla warfare, and nation building in the face of armed insurgents. To fight and win, Kennedy needed officers who knew diplomacy, economics, and geography. Facing an Army resistant to reeducating itself, Kennedy's vision would be a source of constant struggle between Camelot and the Pentagon.

Inside the White House, the President's vision found a more receptive audience. "What are we doing about guerilla warfare?" was reportedly the first question he posed his aides after his inauguration. Ted Sorensen, one of Kennedy's closest advisors, helped pen the 1961 speech to West Point. He had been with the President during his days in the Senate and came to the White House with Kennedy as his most trusted advisor. Forty years later, the Kennedy legacy endures under the stewarding of Sorensen, who continues to write arguments from his office in New York City about his former boss. Through Vietnam, the end of the Cold War and September 11, Sorensen has seen the Kennedy Presidency flourish into a legacy that stands with some of America's greatest presidents. "(Kennedy) recognized that the United States fighting communism on a global scale in those days, mostly the competition was not military, it was political and economic, it was ideological and diplomatic. He knew the military had to be thinking along those lines as well," Sorensen remembered.

The Army was slow but ultimately tepidly responsive to Kennedy's call for change. Within the first two years of Kennedy's 1961 inaugural, Gen. Maxwell Taylor (a former 101st commander) chaired two committees, both including Attorney General Robert F. Kennedy, that researched ways of preparing the military for a battle against an insurgent force. But the Taylor committees failed to establish a clear doctrine on combating insurgencies. In the end – and the end came after Vietnam – the Army remained recalcitrant towards the idea of turning focus away from conventional warfare.

At the time of Kennedy's West Point speech, America was leading itself, albeit unknowingly, into the longest major conflict in American history. From the White House, the Kennedy administration could see the pitfalls of putting combat divisions in Indochina. So could Sorensen. "We were facing guerillas, and guerillas depend of the support of the country side. And Kennedy was having difficulty with the South Vietnamese government in adopting the reforms he knew they were going to have to adopt if they were ever going to get the support of the country side." Kennedy never got the support he needed from the South Vietnamese. After his death, the "advisors" he sent into the country rapidly blossomed into a 500,000 troop strength level in America's most unpopular war.

The President, even from his days in the Senate, didn't believe in fighting against armed nationalists. To avoid war with those kinds of enemies, according to Sorensen, the military had to know how to win the peace. "They would need more than traditional military skills to serve their country's interests in a comprehensive fashion. They would find themselves on occasion as negotiators, as peacemakers, as nation builders, making economic decisions for a community or a village – trying to make decisions with the knowledge of the history of ethnic divisions, religious divisions. Those are all the problems that the U.S. military in the field are going to be facing increasingly. He knew that back then."

But the Army couldn't, wouldn't. Several Army field manuals were written on combating insurgent forces, the last of which written in 1967. It remained on the shelf as the 101st Airborne Division staged in Kuwait on March 19, 2003. No field manual on combating an insurgent force had ever been updated since the Vietnam War.

Every 101st Airborne soldier is well versed in the words of Maj. Gen. William C. Lee, the father of the Airborne, as he introduced the 101st Airborne Division. "(The 101st) has no history, but we have a rendezvous with destiny," the first

Screaming Eagle commander told his division on its first day of activation in 1942. Lee's words could not have been more accurate. The 101st Airborne has fought in nearly every American foreign war, from the beaches of Normandy to the deserts of Kuwait. The division took pride where some soldiers in Vietnam couldn't with its unofficial motto, "First in, last out!"

The 101st Airborne Division was activated on August 16, 1942, after the 82nd Division (itself reactivated March 25, 1942) was sub-divided in two into what now are the 101st and the 82nd Airborne Division in Fort Bragg, N.C. The following two years would be a marathon of jump training, 25-mile road marches and very little rest – much of which has been celebrated in the HBO mini-series "Band of Brothers."

The concept of dropping fighters deep behind enemy lines can be traced back to American Brig. Gen. William Mitchell, who championed the idea as a way of breaking the trench-warfare stalemate during World War I. The idea couldn't come to fruition before the allied victory, but the foundation had been laid for airborne training during the build-up to the next Great War.

A test platoon of airborne troops was trained at Fort Benning, Ga., in the summer of 1940 under the direction of then Lt. Col. William Lee. The platoon's success in its initial jump before a group of high-ranking officers spawned the activation of the 501st Parachute Regiment. The importance of airborne strength and the ability to drop fighters deep behind enemy lines was later postulated emphatically to American commanders after the Nazis defeated Dutch defenses in Crete with relative ease, using a small airborne force.

Further expansion of the American airborne force had already been in the works, but the preparations were galvanized after the Nazi dominance of Crete. In the aftermath, the U.S. Department of Defense quickly drew up plans for a larger airborne force of their own – a force that would develop and expand into the Army's first "specialty" divisions.

The division was baptized by fire on June 5, 1944, on the beaches of Normandy. 6,600 parachutists from the division took part in the D-Day invasion, including Lt. Frank Lillyman, who was the first American to drop land in Normandy at 12:15 a.m. Under the command of Maj. Gen. Maxwell Taylor, the 101st led from the front and cleared the way for the 4th Infantry Division at Utah Beach. After the German defeat at Normandy, the 101st defeated Nazi forces in the town of Carentan and took part in the doomed Operation Market Garden before returning to England to regroup.

The division's next mission would set the stage for its most glorious chapter. The 101st had been ordered to man the supply transportation route through the town of Bastogne. There the Germans surrounded the division. The German commander demanded the division's surrender, to which acting division commander Brig.Gen. Anthony McAuliffe had a simple, one word response: "Nuts!"

Undersupplied and extremely cold, the division withheld Nazi attacks for ten days before reinforcements, under the command of Lt.Gen. George S. Patton, broke through the enemy line and reestablished supply routes. Not one soldier who fought with the division has ever acknowledged the need for Patton's reinforcements.

In the months that followed, the division broke through the Rhine and defeated the Nazi's at Berchtesgarden before being deactivated on November 30, 1945. The division finally went home after nearly a year and a half of training and fighting in Europe.

Eleven years later, the 101st was reactivated on September 21, 1956, at their new home of Fort Campbell, Ky. As a new, modern combat division, the 101st made Fort Campbell and the nearby Clarksville, Tenn., their training home. It has been their training home ever since.

Vietnam would be the division's next rendezvous. The 327th Infantry Regiment, the division's First Brigade, was deployed to Vietnam in July of 1965 – "First in … " The rest of the division followed in December, 1967. The division fought in fifteen campaigns, thwarted the movement of more than 2,000 tons of rice to the enemy and killed more than 800 enemy soldiers during the VC's "Tet Offensive." In 1968, the division for the first time utilized helicopters to attack the enemy as an "Air Mobile" division. Its success would change the 101st Airborne Division forever. On April 6, 1972, Vice President Spiro Agnew and Army Chief of Staff Gen. William Westmoreland, himself a former 101st Airborne commanding general, welcomed the division colors home after five years in Vietnam – " … Last out."

The 101st would get a facelift when it returned from Vietnam. Armed with new technologies in aviation, the doctrine of penetrating enemy positions from behind enemy lines would be modified a bit. The Huey and then the Cobra attack helicopters provided the division the capability to more rapidly attack an enemy. The 101st became the first division of its kind in world history, an "Air Assault" division. The new 101st Airborne Division (Air Assault) would provide corps level commanders with unprecedented maneuverability and agility – with the ability to repel in the battle – perfect for modern battlefields.

In August of 1991, the 101st Airborne Division was among the first deployed to Saudi Arabia after the launch of Operation Desert Shield. It would be the first opportunity to test their abilities in combat as an entire air assault division. Following Iraqi President Saddam Hussein's invasion of Kuwait, U.S. President George H.W. Bush demanded the unconditional withdrawal of Iraqi forces. When negotiations between U.S. Secretary of State James Baker and Iraqi minister Tariq Aziz broke down, "Operation Desert Shield" became "Operation Desert Storm" on January 17, 1991. The thirty-nine day air campaign cleared the way for a 100-hour ground campaign. The 101st would go deep into Iraq in providing the instrumental left-flank, forcing the near immediate surrender of Saddam's forces with not one 101st Airborne Division life lost. American troops would remain in Kuwait long after Saddam's surrender, with good reason: it would not be the 101st Airborne Division's last rendezvous with "The Bastard of Baghdad."

Military conflicts in Haiti, Somalia, Bosnia, and Serbia were all fought with the help of 101st Airborne soldiers. The division's Third Brigade landed in Afghanistan in November of 2001, following the horrific September 11 terrorist attacks. With their complement of CH-47 Chinook, UH-60 Blackhawk and AH-64 Apache helicopters, the "Rakkassans," so-named by locals during post-World War II occupation duty in Japan, joined in the American response. The brigade participated in Operation Anaconda in the fall of 2002, thwarting crucial supplies and escape routes for Taliban and Al Qaeda militant forces and keeping Osama bin Laden and his top lieutenants constantly on the run.

Through it all, the valor and dedication of the soldiers of the 101st Airborne Division have remained constant. With the exception of the Korean War, 101st soldiers have participated in every major and nearly every minor American military conflict in the post-World War II era. And when the soldiers of the 101st Airborne Division have fought, they have fought with an old friend on their shoulders.

The roots of the Screaming Eagle patch, made famous on the beaches of Normandy, are seeded with a union brigade during the Civil War. The 8th Wisconsin Regiment fought for and beside their beloved mascot: a live American eagle they took into battle. The eagle who the 8th Wisconsin Regiment soldiers said "screamed into battle" would take on the name of America's greatest president, "Old Abe." Old Abe was even wounded twice by confederate gunfire and one confederate general offered a reward for his capture or head. When Pvt. Jesse M. Willis won a contest to name the newly activated 101st Airborne the "Eagle Division," the 101st borrowed from the Wisconsin soldiers and "Old Abe" for their unit patch. Bastogne hero Brig.Gen. McAuliffe added the "Airborne" tab shortly before arriving with the division for his tour as Assistant Division Commander.

The history of the 101st Airborne Division is as proud as the soldiers who wear the Screaming Eagle patch. Its traditions and the Screaming Eagle trademark are as recognizable to anyone who has served in the United States Army as the New York Yankee pinstripes are too any young boy who ever picked up a baseball glove. Simply put, to fight with the 101st Airborne Division is what any young soldier who appreciated the Army would ever want. The Screaming Eagle patch is more than a badge of honor, it's the privilege of carrying on a tradition unlike any the Army has ever known.

And if "Old Abe" can be seen as the Yankee Pinstripes of the Army, for a general officer, the honor of being given the 101st colors is tantamount to having your bust on a plaque in Yankee Stadium's monument park. The lineage that starts with William C. Lee continues through Taylor (who later became Kennedy's Chairmen of the Joint Chiefs of Staff), Vietnam commander William Westmoreland, Army Chief of Staff John Wickham, and a constellation of others who would become three and four-star generals. In 2003, Maj. Gen. David H. Petraeus was added to the lineage, commanding the 101st during the first year of Operation Iraqi Freedom. Petraeus took command of the division in the summer of 2002 from Maj. Gen. Dick Cody as the division's Third Brigade was returning from a tour in Afghanistan. Cody was an infectious personality who had endeared himself to his more than 16,000 soldiers. The new "CG" would take command as a bit of an enigma to his troopers, many of whom missed their former commander – who reported to the Pentagon shortly after leaving the 101st. In a division defined by "muddy boot grunts," Petraeus' resume had some strange entries. He had, to be sure, served with the 101st as a lieutenant colonel, commanding the Third Battalion, 187th Infantry Regiment and later serving in the prestigious Division G-3 position. And he had commanded a brigade in the 101st's rival, the 82nd Airborne Division, where he'd later served as assistant division commander for operations. (Petraeus would become acting commander of the 82nd for a month, making him the first and only man to command both the 82nd and 101st Airborne Divisions.) In truth, he'd been an infantry wizard most of his career. But he also had an academic background that wowed some of his new subordinates and left some others scratching their heads. Petraeus had finished near the top of his class at West Point and was first in the Command and General Staff College Class of 1983 (only the second captain to earn that distinction; all the rest were majors). But it was his academic background that stood out from other general officers in the Army, earning his Ph.D. in 1987 from Princeton University in international relations. He had subsequently taught economics and international relations at West Point, and he had written or edited a number of books and articles. Instead of attending one of the military's war colleges, he had completed a fellowship at Georgetown University. In short, his civilian education read like that of a college professor. But this wasn't the Ivy League, it was the 101st Airborne Division.

There was something else a bit odd about the new commanding general. On Petraeus' collar were two stars, on his chest an Expert Infantryman Badge, master parachutist wings, and the Air Assault badge, and on his left shoulder above the "Screaming Eagle" patch was the coveted Ranger tab. But on his right shoulder, where soldiers wear the patch of the unit with which they served in combat, was nothing. In the Army's preeminent division, Petraeus arrived with the 101st with a Ph.D. but no combat patch. He was, when he arrived at Fort Campbell, simply put, more revered more for his brain than his brawn in a division synonymous with Army combat power – a division that at one point, before modesty set in, had erected a sign near the main gate to Fort Campbell that proclaimed it was the "World's best, most powerful division."

Then his soldiers looked a little closer.

Petraeus' career had taken him through many of the most pivotal missions of the Reagan and Clinton eras, the most accomplished units in the Army, and even two emergency rooms. In 1970, just after the nadir of the Vietnam War, he gained admission to the United States Military Academy. He had grown up just seven miles from the academy and, in spite of popular sentiment at the time, he held West Pointers and soldiers as heroes during a time when those wearing the uniform were held in the same esteem as bank robbers in much of America. He grew up with dreams of walking through West Point's famed Thayer Gates in his dress gray uniform at a time when soldiers in uniform were regularly spit on at airports in America. Plebe David Petraeus, or "Peaches" (his boyhood nickname), raised his right hand to become a cadet at a time when young men of his talents balked at the thought of joining the Army. "It was a challenge and I've always been one to look for challenges," Petraeus remembered.

Any challenges Petraeus took as a cadet, he met. Petraeus consistently excelled – academically, athletically, and militarily – playing intercollegiate soccer and competing in the Eastern Intercollegiate Ski Championships, achieving "Starman" status (for being in the top 5% of his class), and earning the coveted rank of "Cadet Captain" his final year. But it was on a blind date for an Army football game that his early courage really shone through. His date that afternoon was more than just a pretty girl on campus for the weekend. She turned out to be Holly Knowlton, daughter of Lt. Gen. William Knowlton, the West Point superintendent. "It was not the most comfortable situation," Petraeus recalled, noting that he'd felt a bit "set up" when he found out who he was escorting.

"At that time," he remembered, "there were two ways cadets reacted to the idea of dating the 'Supe's' daughter. A few were eager for such an opportunity because they wanted to curry favor with the boss, but most didn't want to do it in a million years because they didn't want to be within a country mile of the top brass, even as much as this particular Supe was admired." Petraeus recounted that he was solidly in the second category. The plan he devised, on learning the identity of his date, was to go to the game, take her out to dinner with another couple, and take her back home "as quickly as would be socially acceptable." It didn't quite work out that way. Holly turned out to be funloving and more than Petraeus' intellectual equal, and the two had a great time that night. Petraeus, though still uncomfortable with the idea of seeing the boss' daughter, threw caution to the wind and continued to date her. They managed to keep it quiet for a while, but the two soon fell in love, and the word got around. Plenty of ribbing from his classmates inevitably followed; nonetheless, they got engaged shortly before Petraeus graduated and were married at the West Point Chapel a month later.

Having been shielded from the Army's dark days during his four years at West Point, 2nd Lt. Petraeus entered an Army that had serious challenges. It was, as Army Chief of Staff Gen. Edward C. Myer later described it, a "hollow Army." Petraeus, however, saw relatively little of that part of the Army: as a result of his class standing, he got the most sought-after unit in the army for his first assignment – a tour with the First Battalion, 509th Airborne Battalion Combat Team in Vicenza, Italy. As Petraeus remembered, "It was a great unit and seemed to have had its pick of many of the great Airborne Ranger troopers doing an overseas tour." He thoroughly enjoyed the assignment, deploying for NATO exercises to Turkey, the UK, Belgium, and Germany, traveling with Holly throughout Europe, and earning French and British jump wings.

It was no wonder that Petraeus sought that assignment. He'd chosen Infantry as his branch before his commissioning in 1974, and there was then, and has been nothing else for Petraeus in the Army since. The infantry, like basketball for Michael Jordan, was what he woke up for in the morning as a lieutenant, and it was what he loved all the way through his command of the 101st.

He started strong and never slowed. He was an Honor Graduate of his Infantry Officer Basic Course and then finished first in his Ranger school class. His career had few "breather" assignments for an infantryman. In addition to his tour as a lieutenant with the airborne battalion in Italy, he served with the 24th Infantry Division (Mechanized) as a captain, with the 3d Infantry Division as a major, with the 101st as a lieutenant colonel, and with the 82nd Airborne Division as a colonel and brigadier general. The infantry was his passion, even on the day after which he almost didn't wake up at all.

It happened at close range in 1991. Then-Lt. Col. Petraeus took an accidentally fired M-16 round through the chest while watching his soldiers conducting a live fire exercise at Fort Campbell. The round hit just inches from his heart. Lying in the grass of the post he would later command, Petraeus' life was in the hands of his battalion's medics. Kneeling at his side was Brig.Gen. Jack Keane, the 101st's assistant division commander, who was watching the exercise with Petraeus. (Keane would later command the Division and retire with four stars after serving as the Acting Chief of Staff of the Army). Keane stayed with Petraeus throughout the subsequent ten hours, through a MEDEVAC helicopter flight to the Fort Campbell medical center, during emergency insertion of a chest tube there, for an onward flight to Nashville's Vanderbilt University Medical Center, and until Petraeus was out of the operating room and in the intensive care unit – by which time Holly had arrived at the Center as well.

The surgeon at Vanderbilt was Bill Frist, one of the nation's preeminent thoracic surgeons, who would later became Sen. Bill Frist and eventually Senate Majority Leader Frist. Petraeus lost a small part of his lung as a result of the shooting, but would survive. He later credited Frist with saving his life.

The 1991 experience would not be his last brush with death. The collapse of the nose of his skydiving canopy during freefall parachuting at a drop zone near Fort Bragg, North Carolina in September 2000 was another close encounter for Petraeus. The accident left his pelvis shattered and required major surgery at Fort Bragg's medical center. Incredibly, Petraeus would come out of the two experiences stronger and faster, albeit a half-inch shorter on one side. A lean 5'10" and 153 pounds, he ranked with the most physically fit soldiers in the 101st when he took command of the division. In fact, two years after fracturing his pelvis, as the division commander, Petraeus finished the annual "Army 10-miler" race in Washington in an exceptional sixty-three minutes and forty-six seconds, by far the fastest time of any general officer in the race. His drive and competitive spirit would serve him well when the division had to confront countless post-liberation challenges in northern Iraq.

He was, it seemed, destined for this job at this moment. Petraeus took the 101st colors as the division was beginning to anticipate deployment orders for the looming showdown with Saddam. The most storied and capable division in the Army needed a ready commander for what would become its fourth full division deployment in its storied six decades. The Screaming Eagles got just such a commander in Petraeus.

Despite the lack of a combat patch, Petraeus was hardly a neophyte to contingency operations when the 101st arrived in theatre. He had seen a year in Bosnia, a short stint in Panama during operations in El Salvador, and a tour in Haiti – operations in which he oversaw both nation-building and, in the case of Bosnia, counter-terrorist and war criminal apprehension operations, as well. Those who watched him in those operations saw the innovativeness, drive, tactical savvy, and leadership qualities that would become clear to all in Iraq. He had also served as the executive officer for Gen. Hugh Shelton, chairman of the Joint Chiefs of Staff, from 1999-2001, a period that included the Kosovo campaign and attacks on Iraq and Afghanistan. And he'd done a brief stint in Kuwait while assigned to the 82nd Airborne as a brigadier general. In retrospect, his academic background, his operational deployments, and his time in the Chairman's office had made him uniquely well qualified for the challenges with which the 101st would have to deal in northern Iraq.

For the officers reared in the post-Vietnam era, the war on terrorism and the Iraq war were their time to help prove the Army's might once again. In the aftermath of Vietnam, they had rebuilt an Army. They had cleaned out the drug dealers and violent criminals who polluted the corps. They took the kids who enlisted in the Carter and Reagan years, shaped them into proud men and women, and prepared for the Cold War battlefield, only to see the battlefield change with the fall of the Berlin Wall. Now the men and women of the new Army found itself fighting on the post-September 11 battlefield. For Petraeus, it was a chance to show America what the Army had learned in a generation and why it could be proud of its Army once again.

His most formative experience would come in Haiti as a lieutenant colonel. He had been studying Haiti during a fellowship at Georgetown and was preparing to assist the National Security Council staff in a "lessons learned" effort. Midway through the year, he received a phone call from Maj. Gen. Joseph Kinzer, the newly selected United Nations Mission in Haiti Force commander, who asked Petraeus, "How would you like to do Haiti, rather than study Haiti?" Petraeus jumped at the chance and became Kinzer's chief of operations. In Haiti, Petraeus would get a crash course on nation building, the practice of which he pursued further during a year in Bosnia from 2000 to 2001. "Haiti was also a great experience in coalition operations," he would later recall. "Obviously it was heavy on peacekeeping and light on anything resembling combat, although there were engagements in which soldiers were wounded and lots of moments of high adventure. Still, it was very much nation building and, in a sense, we were running the country, as there was little or no government to speak of during the time I was there."

A decade later, he would find himself in a similar mission as anarchy descended on post-liberation Iraq. Many in Washington had expected a short war and an even shorter trip home. Few in Washington had anticipated, going into Iraq, the need for the 101st and other combat divisions to not only help fight and win the war, but to have to fight even harder to win the peace. The 101st Airborne Division was not "a stabilization force" as soldiers used that term, and thus most hoped that there would be no need for the division to stick around for a long time after Saddam was toppled. The "Screaming Eagles" expected to be in the vanguard of the push toward Baghdad, and then hoped to head back to the home. Few expected Iraq to be their home for the next year in a deployment that would stretch from February 2003 to early March 2004. And even fewer expected to be engaged in a war that would be long from over when the division finally flew back to Kentucky.

While most generals etch their names in the history books in the field of fire, Petraeus achieved Army immortality after the 101st Airborne helped complete the overthrow of Saddam and set up shop in the northern Iraq city of Mosul – the capital of the province in Iraq that most of the division would call home for nearly a year.

Where Patton earned mythical status on the snowy battlefields of Holland and Luxembourg, the name "Petraeus" will be celebrated for actions in a much different action: "The Battle of the Bucks." The 101st Airborne Division in Iraq would fight with tremendous initiative and innovativeness with money as much as with guns. And if the Petraeus and the 101st will be remembered for "The Battle of the Bucks," no one could have been better than a former economics professor at West Point to lead the charge. "Money is ammunition in this war," Petraeus often stated to those who asked what the Division needed, and he fought hard to get all the dollars he could for his subordinate commanders during the Division's 10-month stint in Northern Iraq. The 101st Airborne Division commanding general also became a fixture on Iraqi radio and television, in meetings of northern Iraq political leaders, and on the streets of Mosul and the other cities of the vast region for which he was responsible. It often seemed that he was waging a political battle as much an armed one. His somewhat novel approach to combat would make him a fixture on all the networks back home too. By the time he returned to Fort Campbell, Maj. Gen. Petraeus had become the most talked about commander in the Army.

CHAPTER 1

THE NEXT RENDEZVOUS

Major Gen. David Petraeus had his team in front of him as he walked into his daily battle update brief – or "BUB" – at the Fort Campbell post headquarters one bitterly cold February evening. War was on the doorstep, he knew, but the party couldn't start without him and his division. In January, Petraeus and the division staff had taken part in computer "war games" in Germany with the U.S. Army's V Corps, the outfit that would command all Army elements in the Iraq war. It was a digital dry run – commanders from all the other U.S. Army units likely to participate in the Iraq blitzkrieg were there as well. It was also a show of force. Saddam Hussein needed to abandon the banned weapons arsenal the Bush administration believed he had or the next time, there would be no games. Petraeus landed from Germany jet-lagged but more determined than ever to make sure his division was ready for the deployment orders he was certain would ultimately come. (While still in Germany, Petraeus ordered one-hundred division helicopters to fly to Jacksonville, Fla., the port of debarkation for Kuwait, on what was officially termed a "cross-country flight training exercise.")

His first command staff meeting after landing in Nashville would be a long one. Assembled in the room were commanders of many of the division's major units and Petraeus' most trusted advisors. They rose to attention when he walked into the room. "Good evening, air assault! Have a seat." The 101st Airborne Division's cast of characters would change before the curtains closed, but as the division prepared for war, the group that would lead the division at the outset of the deployment was nothing short of the Army's finest. His top two officers were both West Pointers. Brigadier Gen. Benjamin C. Freakley, a former rugby player at West Point and avatar of everything that is the infantry, would be Petraeus' number two as assistant division commander for operations, or "The O." The assistant division commander for support, "The S," was career aviator Brig. Gen. Edward J. Sinclair.

Command Sgt. Maj. Marvin L. Hill, the division's top enlisted soldier, had the remarkable ability of projecting himself to near omnipotence and omniscience throughout this division – for better or worse. In a division of more than 15,000 soldiers, it's difficult to corral every last one of your enlisted subordinates. Hill managed. He was the quintessential non-commissioned officer: a tough, rigid and inspiring career enlisted soldier who always led from the front. Petraeus' guidance to him had been simple: "Help me expand my impact and my situational awareness."

Petraeus' chief of staff, Col. Thomas J. Schoenbeck, had previously commanded the division's First Brigade before jumping to division headquarters. 101st Airborne soldiers likely will remember Schoenbeck for his massive, concrete frame – he had been a wide receiver in college, not a cadet. Breaking with the division's West Point tradition, Schoenbeck was the only officer of the 101st division command staff at the time who did not graduate from the U.S. Military Academy. Schoenbeck enlisted in 1975 after college, and then finished Officer Candidate School two years later.

The three infantry brigades were commanded by the same commanders for the entire tour in Iraq. Schoenbeck's First Brigade successor, Col. Ben Hodges, had been a battalion commander and executive officer with the division before taking the 327th Infantry Regiment post. It was his fourth tour at Fort Campbell – he had been with the 101st as a captain, a major, a lieutenant colonel and now as a "full bird." Colonel Joseph Anderson, the Second Brigade commander, quietly nicknamed "Big Joe" by his lower enlisted soldiers (or "Smokin' Joe," by those who witnessed the rare occasions on which he demonstrated the full range of emotions), was easily identifiable from anywhere in the room with his cartoon-like deep voice. The "Rakkassans" were commanded by the affable but intense Col. Michael Linnington, who took command of the Third Brigade in middle of their combat tour in Afghanistan. Linnington would be charged with the unenviable task of holding his brigade together as a majority of his soldiers were serving their second tour in as many years.

The division's combat support assets, the 101st Corps Support Group and the 101st Division Support Command (DISCOM), were commanded by Col. Gerald Dolinish and Col. James Rogers, respectively. The 101st Division Artillery (DIVARTY) was commanded by Col. William Greer, who would later make history in May of 2003 when he commissioned his son who had just graduated from West Point from Iraq via satellite.

The "air" in air assault was provided by the division's two aviation brigades – the 101st and 159th Aviation Brigades. These two brigades gave the 101st vastly more helicopters than any other division in the U.S. Army – and more than the entire British Army. As one company of Chinooks was still in Afghanistan, "only" 254 of the Division's aircraft were ready to be deployed. The 101st Aviation Brigade was under the command of Col. Gregory Gass, an attack helicopter guru. Colonel William Forrester, a former special operations aviator, was in command of the 159th.

They were the best of the best. Colonels and sergeant majors don't come to the 101st Airborne Division because they want to wear the Screaming Eagle patch. They have to earn it. Every good soldier, after all, would join the 101st Airborne Division if they could. This was no ordinary division in no ordinary time. Petraeus took a seat with his staff and took in the usual slide show presentations – my brigade is doing this, we are this far in the load-out, we will be doing this next week, these are the outstanding issues. It was all so monotonous before it became so pertinent. The time was rapidly approaching when these seemingly insignificant numbers would be put to the test – and all in the room knew it. "Where are we on the ammo?" Petraeus asked in no uncertain terms. "What is the ship schedule?" "Where are we on the rail schedule?" "What's the latest on the truck schedule?" It went on and on, with everyone keenly aware that time was running out. Despite the usual attempts at jocularity, the tension was palpable. Nobody, least of all Petraeus, was bored at this meeting. This was the real deal, an intense endeavor for which those in the room had trained for decades, and they knew it was show time.

For the families, the orders had been around the corner, literally weeks or even days away, for four months. Soldiers and loved ones had celebrated weekends throughout the holidays and through the winter, like the next week would bring the news that would inevitably come: the men and women of the 101st Airborne Division were going to the Middle East to fight in war. The anticipation was palpable.

The local and national media too was expecting an eminent deployment order from the Pentagon for the U.S. Central Command area of operation. Increased activity of the division's helicopters the morning of February 4 had fueled presumptuous speculation that the division had received the orders. Soldiers driving to their morning physical training formations would hear the gossip on the Clarksville morning radio programs. Two days later, on Thursday, February 6, the wait was over. Months of speculation and expectation ended with one simple press release from the Fort Campbell Public Affairs Office at 2 p.m. central standard time.

FOR IMMEDIATE RELEASE 03-022
FORT CAMPBELL, Ky., February 6, 2003. - The 101st Airborne Division (Air Assault) and associated units stationed at Fort Campbell, Kentucky, have received orders to deploy to the U.S. Central Command area of operations (AOR) to support possible future operations in the global war on terrorism. The specifics of any such operations are not known at this time.

If David H. Petraeus ever had a rendezvous with destiny, it was for certain fulfilled when the division received deployment orders. While not specified in the press release, the destination was well known to the 101st soldiers. They were going to Kuwait. The "dep orders" came as a surprise to no one in the division and signaled President Bush's intent to the rest of America. The 101st was the last piece of the puzzle; with the division ready to go in Kuwait, America was ready for war.

For nearly a month, the division loaded vehicles, helicopters and storage units onto trains en route to Jacksonville, Fla. There the massive equipment would be shrink-wrapped in plastic, like a toy, and shipped to Kuwait City. Picking up an entire division and moving more than 15,000 soldiers half way across the world takes time.

The usual green camouflage uniforms would not suffice for this mission. Lines at the Clarksville tailor shops stretched out the door as soldiers scrambled to get the Screaming Eagle patch, the Colors, "U.S. Army," their last name and their training badges sewn on their desert uniforms. If the lines were just too long, some lucky soldiers had a backup plan. The Screaming Eagles' wives never had it tougher than the weeks following the deployment orders.

Realizing what the Pentagon knew for months, that the 101st was in fact the last piece of the puzzle, national and local media flooded to Fort Campbell. The usually routine task of driving a humvee onto a train car became an event, with media from as far as Germany there to witness. Only war could bring the worlds of CNN and Clarksville, Tenn., together. The Clarksville community had done this before of course. For many of the soldiers of the 101st, this had almost become routine. Soldiers from the Seventh Battalion of the 101st Aviation Regiment had returned from six months in Afghanistan just days before the division was told it was going to Kuwait. The 7-101 soldiers had just four days leave before they needed to pack up to jump the Atlantic again.

In spite of the grim news, the developments had come as a relief for most 101st Airborne soldiers. The local schools, the Fort Campbell Family Readiness Center, the local banks and the 101st families had prepared for the orders. Now was the time to put their plans into action. Life would continue for the Fort Campbell community, no schools were cancelled, but for the soldiers, the starting gates opened. The next day, Friday the seventh, would mark the beginning of a two-week sprint for the division's soldiers. The division's massive and abundant equipment had to be loaded onto trains due for Jacksonville. From Florida, they would be loaded up onto a boat due for the Persian Gulf. In Kuwait City, the equipment would arrive at their new home. Like nearly every task the 101st does, there wasn't a whole lot of time. The first of eight trains left at 7 p.m. that night.

For the motorpools, the work days became especially taxing. Specialist Nick Degreek, twenty-one, a power generator mechanic, had enlisted for this. His wife Jessica, his high school sweetheart from Montana, had enlisted in her own right when she married him when the two were nineteen years old. The Degreeks had one two-year-old daughter, McKenzie, when daddy had to leave to go fight the bad guys. "My wife was angry, she never understood the military," Degreek later recalled. Jessica was one of many 101st spouses strapped with single parent responsibilities when the head of the household said goodbye. Specialist Degreek would miss a lot in Iraq, including McKenzie's third birthday. "(McKenzie) didn't understand anything. She just knew daddy was going to work for a very long time."

For Degreek and his motorpool comrades, the weeks following the deployment orders would be especially taxing. Every vehicle and generator under Degreek's section had to be inspected before being loaded up onto the trains. "The coffee and Copenhagen were flowing ... We worked our asses off."

Fifteen-hour days were the easy days; twenty-hour days were not uncommon. Compounding difficulties was the cold. The winter of 2003 was uncommonly frigid for Fort Campbell. The first day of deployment preparations were done through a snowstorm, totaling no more than one or two inches, that closed the post's schools. Of greater concern for the division was the ice that delayed the uploading of equipment. That night, Feb. 7, Degreek worked outside until after 2 a.m.

Major Gen. Petreaus knew he could not afford any more delays. At the division's daily Battle Update Brief for Feb. 7, he stressed the need for "a safe, but sustainable" pace after one soldier was injured uploading equipment. The second train left the next morning.

For Third Brigade, the rush to war could have been demoralizing. It was not. Putting their war face on for the second time in a year, they prepared to move into Kuwait with as much spring in their step as any other 101st Airborne unit. Their toughness was a credit to their commander, a former math teacher.

Colonel Michael Linnington had missed his chance in 1991 to fight in the first Gulf War. Linnington, much to his disappointment, was standing in front of a blackboard teaching calculus as Operation Desert Shield turned into Operation Desert Storm on Jan. 17, 1991. He thought he had missed his only chance to serve in combat, but that was not the case. On June 5, 2002, Linnington took command of the distinguished Third Brigade, the Rakkassans, in Afghanistan. He had only arrived two days earlier at Fort Campbell when Maj. Gen. Dick Cody, then the 101st Airborne Division commander, picked him up and delivered him to his new brigade. Linnington did not even have time to unpack his boxes at his new home.

The next ten months that followed would be about as fast and furious as ten months possibly could be for an infantry brigade. In August, the brigade returned home, only to face the realization that their stay at Fort Campbell would be short lived. There would be little time to rest. Much of the fall months were spent in the field and the month of November were spent at the Joint Readiness Training Center at Fort Irwin, California. "Really the training for the Third Brigade soldiers never stopped," Linnington said.

In February, with the rest of the division, the Rakkassan soldiers learned that they would be on their way back to the Middle East. The deployment orders could have paralyzed lesser soldiers.

Sergeant First Class Rick Johanningsmeier, a platoon leader for Third Brigade, was not formally introduced to his new squad leader until he picked him up out of the Montgomery County Jail after a "hell raising" evening. "Nice to meet you sergeant, I'm Troy Jenkins," he introduced himself, not even trying to suppress the grin on his face. He didn't exactly make the best first impression on his new squad leader. The Rakkassan's finest have never been known for their high standards of decorum out of uniform, but this had crossed the line. Making formal introductions outside the police station is just not a culmination of a routine evening, even for the infantry. But such was the case for Johanningsmeier, or "Sergeant Jo," and Jenkins.

In the car, Johanningsmeier did not press the evening's activities too much; it would be a subject to be breached on Monday he figured. He was not upset; that would have been a bit hypocritical, after all. The two mostly used the opportunity to get acquainted. He found out a good deal about Jenkins on the drive home.

Jenkins, Sergeant Jo quickly learned, was a family man, in spite of his undomesticated nature on the weekends. He was a young man, twenty-four, who acted his age when he could. But those times were few and far between. He was a father. Jenkins struck a balance between weekend family time with his two sons, Triesten and Brandon, and weekend debaucheries with his infantry family. Triesten and Brandon always had priority. Johanningsmeier was convinced by the time he dropped Jenkins at his house that his new NCO cared about nothing more than his two sons. Time was precious with Triesten and Brandon, especially after he came home after six months in Afghanistan with Third Brigade. Triesten was three and Brandon was born just before he went off to Afghanistan. He was a genuinely dedicated father, Johanningsmeier immediately sensed from Jenkins. He was also fearless soldier, in and out of uniform, as Johanningsmeier later found out.

Jenkins left Afghanistan with a Purple Heart after a firefight that left a bullet wound in his right arm. It was a scar he carried around proudly and wasn't shy about showing it to his buddies. Jenkins had been put in but not approved for a Silver Star – but awards meant very little to him. Knowing that Triesten and Brandon were nearly left without a father after that experience, Jenkins dedicated himself to making himself the best daddy he could be. That's what was important. His time in the military was about to expire anyway; he was scheduled to be a civilian by the summer of 2003. He didn't know what he wanted to do after be left the military, but he knew where he wanted to go. After he was done, he decided, he wanted to move to California and either go back to school or become a policeman.

Sergeant Jenkins had fallen in love with the Golden State when he was Sgt. Jenkins of the United States Marine Corps. Just two days after he had finished his enlistment with the Corps, he reenlisted, this time as a soldier. His time as a soldier in garrison was short lived before he was off to Afghanistan. Just three months after he got back from Operation Anaconda, he was back in Desert Camouflage Uniforms, on his way to Kuwait. Facing another extended period of time away from his sons, his misery was transparent. "He knew it was his job," Johanningsmeier remembered. "Everyone was a little skeptical, but coming back from a six-month deployment and then going to Iraq, c'mon." Like every soldier in Third Brigade who left a family behind in the Spring of 2002, just to deploy again in the Winter of 2003, Jenkins struggled with shielding his private pain while maintaining his focus. This was going to be war, after all.

But there was someone who he couldn't shield anything from. Her name was Becky Weiss. She saw the side of Troy nobody else ever saw; that's the way he wanted it.

The sparks began to fly one night at Kickers – Clarksville's most popular country line dancing club – but not without a bit of charm on Troy's part. Becky had every reason to view the crowd of single men looking her direction with skepticism. There were plenty of them, some with a bit more social grace than others, she could see. Troy, even at 6' 6", could do nothing to capture her attention among the group of bachelors. But Troy Jenkins was anything but timid. So with nothing to lose, he gave it his best shot.

"Can I borrow this chair?"

"Sure," Becky politely answered, giving a haphazard smile. "Oh you've gotta be kidding me, another guy with more one liners," she transparently thought to herself.

It was an inauspicious beginning; the blonde beauty queen was clearly not interested in making his company, he could tell already. But Troy was unfazed. Without a fear in the world, he pressed on. "Can I sit by you?"

He was attractive, Becky admitted to herself. He certainly wasn't one to give up, that's for certain. "That's fine," she answered in her sweet Kentucky accent.

"I'm not from the area. My buddies brought me here. Where else is there to go in this town to have a good time?" It was a desperate attempt by Troy to get his new acquaintance to open up a bit.

"I don't know, you probably need to ask someone else. I'm not from around here either," Becky replied, still unresponsive. This may be a lost cause, Troy thought. But with friends watching, he wasn't about to walk away with his head down.

"I just got back from Afghanistan." And with that, Troy had just confirmed what Becky had suspected: he was another "Joe" in a bar where nobody has any kind of facial hair below the lip. "I'm Troy."

"Hi, I'm Becky." Unwillingly or not, Becky would never shake the persistent Troy that night. And at one point during their conversation, Troy's trifling eventually broke down Becky's barriers. Once that happened, she knew she had found a friend. They talked about everything – family, music, war and love. Becky and Troy had a lot in common, they found out that night. She was a social worker who dealt with disadvantaged kids in the area. At twenty-seven, Becky was an older woman. She grew up in a remote area of Kentucky, gone to college and dedicated her life to helping kids. Becky was more than just an attractive blonde and Troy, much to her surprise, was more than just a bugaboo at a bar.

The two even talked openly about a subject that neither one had talked openly about to another person before that night. Both Troy and Becky were trying to recover from recent heartbreaks. Becky had just broken up with her boyfriend of five years, the man she thought she was going to marry. Troy had come home from Afghanistan to an unfaithful wife. He decided to file for a divorce as soon as he got home, and he wanted to take the kids with him. The two were almost mirror images of one another. They both were trying their best to forget.

Before the bell was rung for last call, Becky gave Troy her phone number, something she had never done for another guy before. She didn't think he'd actually call, but she was wrong. The next day, breaking all rules and regulations for swinging bachelors, Troy called and asked her to dinner. Becky half thought he was a romantic, half thought he was a psycho, but she accepted his invitation without a second thought.

Becky was terrified of getting involved with Troy. She didn't know the man that well, after all, and she didn't want to make a fool out of herself. What was this guy in for? But the more and more she talked to him and got to know him, the more and more she trusted him. She lived about an hour outside of Clarksville, but that was no worry for Troy. Whenever he could, he drove up to see Becky, who was then living with her parents after moving out of the home she shared with her ex-boyfriend. Sometimes Troy wouldn't even give her prior notice. He would just show up. Becky loved his spontaneity. Nobody could make Becky lighten up like Troy. He didn't have a fear in the world. He didn't even fear telling her "I love you" on the phone.

On the weekends, when his wife took the kids, Becky would take Troy to the Kentucky Lake just to be alone and talk. They enjoyed going back to Kickers every once in a while, but they enjoyed being away from the crowd more than anything. Becky let her guard down with Troy. She trusted him. Becky even cooked for him. The rail-thin man she had met at Kickers had gained a few pounds since. Every once in a while Troy would even talk about his ex-wife, something that was a bit of a taboo subject early in the relationship. Becky knew how much it hurt for him to go through the divorce, knowing how difficult it was going to be on the boys. Troy, however, was never vindictive towards the woman who left him when he was at war. Whenever she came up in a conversation, Troy just talked about how good of a mother she was for Triesten and Brandon. Becky never once heard him say anything bad about her. Besides, Troy knew, she was in the past.

"Have you ever loved someone?" Troy asked Becky one night at the lake. He knew the answer was yes, but he wanted to see where he stood. "No, I mean really loved someone?"

Becky just smiled. "Yes, Troy, I have really loved someone."

"Well, are you with him now?" Suddenly, Troy's meaningless I love you's became a bit more serious.

Becky was a country girl, but she at least got a newspaper delivered to her doorstep in the morning. She new what the cloud in her sunny day was going to be. With each passing day, President Bush had made it clearer and clearer that America was going to war with Saddam Hussein. On October 8, the commander-in-chief took to the airwaves from Cincinnati to outline the threat posed by Saddam and what he was prepared to do about it. Becky was watching with keen interest. "Eleven years ago, as a condition for ending the Persian Gulf War, the Iraqi regime was required to destroy its weapons of mass destruction, to cease all development of such weapons and to stop all support for terrorist groups. The Iraqi regime has violated all of those obligations. It possesses chemical and biological weapons. It is seeking nuclear weapons. It has given shelter and support to terrorism and practices terror against its own people." Bush had made his intentions for regime change in Iraq clear, and it was clear what that would mean for the soldiers who would administer Bush's policies.

"Some have argued that confronting the threat from Iraq could detract from the war against terror. To the contrary, confronting the threat posed by Iraq is crucial to winning the war on terror."

Confronting the threat meant war. Wars are fought by warfighters and Troy was with the 101st Airborne Division. There could be no war in Iraq without the Screaming Eagles. There were so many reasons Troy didn't want to leave, but he felt a sense of duty, not only to his country but also to his sons. "I have to go," he told the morose Becky. "I don't want my boys to have to deal with this. I don't want Triesten and Brandon fighting a war I should have fought myself."

"Please don't go," she pleaded. "Just tell him you can't. You can go AWOL." She was kidding, of course. Troy had brought the kind of stability in her life that she hadn't had since she left her ex-boyfriend of five years. Now Troy and that stability were about to go away. All Troy could tell her is that he had to go. He couldn't even assure her that he was coming back home. Troy was in the infantry with the 101st. He would see combat, there was little doubt about that. And when the bullets started to fly, Troy wasn't about to run and hide.

After the deployment orders came, the division established a Soldier Readiness Program at the Dreyer Field House on post. As if on an assembly line, soldiers would tackle financial and legal issues, including the dreaded anthrax and smallpox immunizations. President Bush on January 30 directed specified federal employees, including all military personnel destined for the U.S. Central Command area of operation, to receive the smallpox vaccine. Bush rolled up his sleeves and received the vaccine himself. If the commander-in-chief could do it, so could the soldiers, and got it they did without fear. Receiving the smallpox vaccine was no pleasure, especially for those who had received it before. Soldiers who had never previously received the vaccine were given three shots; those who had received fifteen.

The vaccine was given on the right or left shoulder. Married soldiers and soldiers who had recently and fortuitously received tattoos were exempt from the vaccine, for the time being. Just before they got on the plane, they would receive the vaccine. Soldiers who got it over with at Fort Campbell came home, looked at their shoulder, and saw what could only be described as a burgeoning horror show. That was if the vaccine worked. If it did work, the area the vaccine was given to would break into a grotesque rash that would linger for weeks, even months.

After that was completed, the soldiers needed to pack. They had to pack light. One bag, the "A" bag, was designated for items that soldiers would need when they landed. Sleeping units, an extra uniform, poncho-liners (named "woobies," which doubled as blankets), socks and underwear were earmarked for this bag. Ruck sacks were jammed with flack vests, chemical masks and chemical uniforms, called "JSLIST's" for Joint Service Lightweight Integrated Suit Technology. Additional tactical gear was crammed in, as units and soldiers saw fit. Alleviating some pack-rat concerns, the JSLIST's were vacuumed sealed in green packages, labeled with a "W" for woodland, and brown pages labeled "D" for desert. Both the A-bags and the Ruck-sacks were carried with the soldiers onto the airplane en route to Kuwait. Weapons too had to be carried onto the plane with the bolt removed in order to calm the stewardesses.

Unit "quadcons" – a military term for the storage containers – were packed mostly with portable tents, cots, chairs, camouflage netting and soldier's "B" bags. B-bags were loaded with items soldiers did not figure to use in the initial days in Kuwait – wet weather boots, for example. Personal items, like a photo album or a book, often made its way into the B-bag. The quadcons would travel on the boats crawling across the Atlantic, most of which would not arrive at the Kuwait City port until weeks after the majority of the division took its places in Kuwait.

On the quaint Calloway Drive, just behind the Clarksville Police Station, a soldier had packed his bags and was due by the hour to join the rest of the 801st Main Support Battalion before flying to Kuwait. Sergeant First Class Hector Jusino had seen just about all a soldier could ever see in his career. A native of Puerto Rico, Jusino broke out of the chains of poverty, paying his way through college and graduating from American University of Puerto Rico with a degree in Political Science in 1979. He didn't intend to become a soldier, it just happened. Jusino was a counselor for a U.S. Federal Government youth program for the sexually abused before joining the Army. In 1981, the harsh realities of President Ronald Reagan's cuts in social programs hit Jusino hard. He found himself out of a job for more than a year when Reagan cut the counseling program as part of his immediate federal government downsizing.

Out of work, Jusino turned to Uncle Sam and enlisted as a missile repairman. For more than two decades, that's what he was. It had been a long way to this moment, Jusino thought, but this was it. He was eligible for retirement two years ago, but then the World Trade Center had collapsed and America found itself at war. He had begged to get out of a rotation to the Korean Peninsula to go to war with the 101st. Jusino wasn't just patriotic in his heart – he put his American pride into action. It may have been en vogue to fly the Colors on your doorstep after September 11, but Jusino drove a pickup truck with no less than a half-dozen patriotic bumper stickers long before America came under attack.

Now he was off to war. He was not in a line unit, he would be back home sooner or later he knew, but he still had a job to do. He was focused. His wife knew him well enough to sense his detachment from the family as he prepared to leave them for the Middle East.

The Jusinos' love story began after Hector had been on convalescent leave for sixty days, recovering from surgery. As a single sergeant E-5 in Fulda, Germany, Jusino had made a weekend ritual out of hanging out at his apartment with friends and, as he put it, "doing things that single guys do." Having been socially paralyzed for two months, Jusino didn't need too much cajoling on the part of his friends to go out to the "Hispanic Night" party at the post's NCO club. With few social environments in the Army where Jusino could be around other Hispanics, this was sure to be a good time. And it would be.

On the other side of the room was a local college student who felt more than a bit out of place. Christine was a part-time tour guide for American soldiers looking to know the local sites. She spoke fluent English but little Spanish. It was her curiosity that drew her here this evening. With most soldier parties involving many German traditions she already knew quite well – mainly beer and embarrassing episodes caused by beer – she wanted to see how the other "Joes" lived. After all, not every American soldier spends their weekends "doing things that single guys do," right?

With her white blonde hair and cover girl smile, Christine caught the attention of more than a few swingers that evening. Hector, finding his own good time standing in the corner of the room and doing his best to remain inconspicuous, was not likely to stop Christine in her tracks that evening. But his stoic charm had connected with this beautiful blonde somehow, and Christine maneuvered through the crowd and approached the man who would change her life forever.

"Do you know how to dance to this music?" she asked in her exotic German accent.

Aghast, staring at what had to be the most beautiful woman he had ever met, Hector could only muster a swift, one-word response. "Yes."

"Could you teach me? Would you dance with me?" With that, Hector's evening, and his life, had begun anew. They would marry less than a year later. Reluctant to leave her life in Germany to follow her new husband to his next assignment, Fort Lewis, Wash., Christine resigned herself to her life as an Army wife. Fourteen years and two daughters later, Sgt. First Class Hector Jusino was leaving for his last deployment, rounding third base and heading home after a twenty-three year career in the Army.

The Jusinos had found a home in Clarksville. She found a good job working for the local hospital. The kids liked the area. They had good neighbors and good friends. Hector and Christine had even agreed to stay when he retired, assuming he could find a job in the area when he came back. She had followed him everywhere, even Korea. As Sgt. First Class Jusino's career reached a crescendo in this his last war, Christine's sacrifices were about to come to an end.

On Friday, February 21, the 101st Airborne Division guidon was cased for movement to Kuwait. Several days later, Maj. Gen. Petraeus left Fort Campbell en route for Kuwait with his staff. Brigadier Gen. Freakley took over the division's deployment operations. For most soldiers that would be the last weekend they would have with their families; most commanders left them alone and ordered them just to have a good time. The Clarksville and Nashville nightspots were alive with single Screaming Eagles enjoying their last social outings. All bartenders within a one-hour driving distance had an extremely busy weekend. The married soldiers and soldiers with children were, for the most part, a little more domesticated.

The final hours for soldiers and their families were anticlimactic for some, unbearable for others. Having braced for the day for several months, the day just came and went, the memories followed. Families were often given their final goodbyes at unit headquarters, not at the Fort Campbell airport terminal. Once separated from their families, the soldiers had only each other in their final hours on American soil.

With nine-year old Annika and six-year old Melissa, Sgt. First Class Jusino said goodbye as a family. The distant Hector confused the emotional Christine. "You are about to leave your wife and two kids for war. Aren't you feeling anything right now?" she thought to herself. Of course she couldn't tell him how upset she was, not then. All she could do was be supportive. That's what she had done for the last fourteen years and she wasn't going to stop now.

"Hey, I'll see you in a couple of months," Jusino told his family, wryly. It was a moment that tied a knot in Christine's stomach as she kissed her husband goodbye and watched him disappear.

It didn't get any easier for Becky Weiss. When the deployment orders came, all Becky could do was try to stay strong. She was less than successful. That final weekend, Troy spent his time with his kids and Becky stayed away. She wanted Troy all to herself that weekend, but she knew Triesten and Brandon were more important. So she waited and called after Troy had put the boys to bed. As he always had been with Becky, Troy was an open book. This time though, he was a bit too candid about his emotions on the eve of his second deployment in one year. Becky was panicking and Troy just couldn't bring himself to say what Becky needed him to say, not this time.

"You know, I'm not coming back on this one." Becky just froze, unable to even muster an immediate response. After a few seconds of dead silence, she shook her head in frustration. How could he say such a thing?

"Troy, don't, just don't. You can't think like that. You have your boys you've got to take care of. You can't think negative ... " Becky was prepared to lecture him all night, but Troy stopped her.

"I want you to know that no matter what happens, I love you." No matter what the previous trifling I love you's meant, this one was for real. Becky knew Troy was not just kidding around this time. She wasn't either.

"Troy, I love you too," Becky told him for the first time. She started to cry, and the usually fortified Troy showed his emotions too on the other end of the phone line. The two talked once the next day before Troy left for Kuwait. Still uncertain of what her role was, she promised to be as supportive as possible and to write as often as she could. Troy didn't know what would come next either. When he saw her again, would he sweep Becky off her feet to California to start a new life together, or would she just walk away when he was gone, just like his last love?

Manifesting the plane could often take hours. Soldiers didn't get a whole lot of sleep the last day at Fort Campbell. Those who did manage got an early introduction to "field sleeping," including the practice of using one's Kevlar helmet as a pillow. Soldiers with families were exempt from the Smallpox vaccine – until now. Other vaccines that soldiers missed were given just before loading the plane. Local church and support groups had tables with grocery store novels and Bibles, to go with some much needed coffee.

Roll call was given during the last formation and then it was time. Officers and senior noncommissioned officers were given first class; the junior enlisted had crammed into coach. It would be a twenty-hour flight with a layover at an Air

Force installation in Germany. The ultimate destination would not come until at least a day after take off with an eight-hour time difference between Eastern Standard Time and Kuwait time. The junior enlistee's knees would feel like hell by the time the planes touched down in Kuwait City.

Rein Mein Air Force Base outside of Frankfurt would host the soldiers, usually for only a couple of hours, while the planes refueled. Nobody would be amused by the noticeable and outdated "Welcome Home" signs posted in the terminal. Equally as irritating were the soldiers and airmen hanging around in the area in green uniforms. Few troops based in Germany had received deployment orders, and for the Air Force troops who did receive orders, they would not be gone for long. The standard U.S. Air Force deployment runs a maximum of four months.

Soldiers lucky enough to sit on the outside seats, near the window, could get to see the city lights of London, the coast of France, and even the vastness of Cairo on the way to Kuwait. For the soldiers who had never been outside the United States, this would be quite a trip. It was far less a thrill for those who had, especially those who had been outside the U.S. recently – like to Afghanistan. The trip half-way across the globe felt like just that for all the soldiers when they touched down at the Kuwait International Airport. The seasonably mild temperatures of Kuwait contrasted quite nicely for soldiers dealing with temperatures often not even reaching above the freezing level at Fort Campbell just days before. The climate change would be swift and subtle in a number of ways they wouldn't soon take for granted. The soldiers would not see green grass for several months.

Camp Wolf would introduce the soldiers to the Middle East, where the soldiers would be held, sometimes for days, as they "in-processed." Upon arrival, the soldiers were taken directly to a tent, where the staff would greet the newcomers with a sardonic "Welcome to Kuwait" and go over combat allowances and camp policies. Then they were guided to a holding tent, where they would stay for as long as it took to catch a ride on a local bus with a local bus driver. Sometimes that would take days. When the rides did arrive, soldiers packed into the buses with their "full battle rattle" and enjoyed the tour of the vast Kuwaiti desert. After an hour and a half, lights would appear in the horizon if someone were particularly attentive. Those lights would be their new home.

For most of the 101st Airborne Division, their new homes would either be Camp Pennsylvania, Camp New Jersey, Camp New York, Camp Thunder or Camp Udairi – none of which more hospitable or even livable than the other. The camps were nothing more than a patch of desert consisting of one small Post Exchange shop for toiletries, magazines and junk food, a phone center and a cafeteria. Few of the living tents were large enough to comfortably hold all of the new soldiers. Both the PX and the cafeteria were a minimum forty-five minute wait, which paled in comparison to the two to three hour wait to call home at the phone center.

Specialist Degreek, having just arrived at Camp New Jersey at the end of February, braved the line for one last chance to call home. After a few minutes of hanging up and picking up the phone in an attempt to get a connection, he finally did and dialed home and talked to his wife Jessica, who was waiting for her husband's phone call. "Honey, I have some news," she told her husband. Degreek's wife was pregnant with their second child.

On Sunday, March 9, the final soldiers from the division took off from Fort Campbell. They arrived at Camp Wolf the next day. National Guardsmen and reservists would man some of the posts vacated by deployed soldiers at Fort Campbell. Any visitor could see the 101st Airborne Division soldiers had moved out by a simple glance at the Fort Campbell grounds. Motorpools, once packed with humvees and military vehicles, were bumper to bumper with civilian cars, SUV's and pickup trucks. Nobody had any problems taking a morning drive around post. There were no more morning runners or unit marches to stop traffic.

The 101st Airborne Division's next rendezvous with destiny had arrived.

CHAPTER 2

CROSSING THE BERM

Camp rules, extending to every camp in Kuwait, dictated that every soldier carry his or her pro-mask whenever leaving the unit tents. Cigarette breaks, showers, and friendly strolls around the camp – wherever any soldier of any rank went, the pro-mask followed. Unit baseball games were even played with a green bag on every player's hip. There were no exceptions to the rule. Weapons could be stored at a secured place, the pro-masks couldn't go anywhere.

The first weeks in Kuwait were a training marathon, and the focal point was the chemical and biological threat posed when the soldiers crossed the border. Army doctrine teaches soldiers to be able to don the mask and seal the airway within eight seconds of an alert. Chemical and biological alerts are given three ways: calling "Gas, Gas! Gas!", a continuous beeping of horns, or by tapping one's shoulders like a basketball player calling a twenty-second timeout. Every soldier was well versed in Army NBC (for Nuclear, Biological, Chemical) doctrine by the time they arrived in Kuwait. If they weren't, they would be.

The frightening possibility of a chemical or biological attack in Baghdad had kept commanders and noncommissioned officers up at night for months. Everyone knew the dangers. To graduate Basic Training, soldiers first must complete the "NBC" course, geared at teaching soldiers how to react to a NBC attack. Included in the instruction is the dreaded "Gas Chamber," where soldiers pull off their masks in a room clouded in potent tear gas and shout their name, rank and social security number. Soldiers leave the chamber with their eyes burning and mucus pouring out of their noses – but always recovered once they got out in the fresh air. Baghdad was to be the real thing.

Soldiers were expected to be able to react instinctively to a chemical or biological attack. With constant attack drills, they would meet that expectation.

January 1 was the deadline for the soldiers of the 2-327th Infantry Regiment to be trained the ins and outs of their chemical suits at Fort Campbell, including how to drink, urinate, defecate and perform in combat with the masks and suits on. Not an easy task, especially in temperatures exceeding one-hundred degrees, which is what was expected by the time the soldiers went to war. The MOPP suits, for Mission Oriented Protective Posture, were lined with charcoal and unbearably hot even at room temperature.

Captain Richard Morgan, the 2-327th Infantry Regiment chemical officer, was tasked with getting his battalion ready for a combat in an NBC environment by the due date. "These aren't the guys who are going to be afraid of anything, but they do have concerns," Morgan explained. "Fear? No. Apprehension? Yes. Uneasiness? Yes."

To start, the soldiers went back to the chamber. Soldiers were picked at random to play the roles of casualties for mass casualty exercise, a chilling but not so remote possibility. Soldiers were taught how to give other soldiers and themselves direct aid with their atropine kits, designed to save lives if attacked with a biological weapons. Companies, platoons and squads would have to be certified in every category.

Conventional battle tactics would have to be modified. Morgan worked to break the infantry soldiers' knee-jerk reactions to fit the NBC battlefield the battalion figured to be fighting in once they pushed into Baghdad. "Every infantry soldier has had it drummed into their heads – when you take fire, you turn to the direction of the fire and lay down a base of fire. The first element is going to get down on the ground in the prone and lay down the base of fire. They've been taught that from day one."

In a chemical attack, the technique would have to be adjusted. "In an NBC environment, what you've just done is contaminated your knee." In this scenario, the soldiers in the first element, kneeling in the prone firing position, would have to lift their knees inches off the ground while returning fire.

The training continued past the first of the year and into Kuwait. The 2-327th soldiers were given additional mass casualty and mass evacuation exercises. Mass hydration in the desert sun was emphasized; the weather and the desert sun were only going to get hotter. Water would not be scarce. Palates of bottled water contracted locally and through Saudi Arabia would were piled up in small mountains, all within walking distance of every tent. Soldiers were trained until Army doctrine of how to react to an NBC attack became like second nature. Daily alarms would go off around lunch time to check for soldier readiness, at which point, every soldier would reach into their bag at their hips and don their masks – or face the wrath of the nearest sergeant major. Most just popped their mask on and continued doing what they were doing.

The 2-327th Infantry, also known as "No Slack," lived up to their name with their commitment to NBC training. They had to. Their determination came from the top, Lt. Col. Christopher Hughes, a commander who also embodied his battalions' moniker. Hughes was a son of a career Air Force enlisted man, who made a second career as a chiropractor after retirement. After high school, he decided to follow his father's footsteps into the military, enrolling in the Army Reserve Officer Training Corps program at Northwest Missouri State University. While many of the future battalion commanders of the 101st were parading in their dress whites on the fields of West Point, Hughes had made the tiny school his own launching pad towards infantry greatness.

NWMSU was also the launching pad for his marriage to his college sweetheart Margerite. She came with a friend to a dorm party Hughes was hosting. She left having just met the love of her life. They got married right out of college. Three kids later, the oldest one on her way to college in 2003, Chris and Margerite were still going strong. For the Hughes, it was not the first tour with the 101st, but it was the first with the Screaming Eagles during war. In 1990, just before his Delta Company, 1-327th Infantry and the division deployed to Saudi Arabia, Capt. Hughes was kicked back to the Joint Readiness Training Center at Camp Champion, Ca. (later renamed Fort Irwin). He left the 101st kicking and screaming. Like everyone at Fort Irwin, Hughes filed his DA-4187 form to get transferred to the Gulf and away from the sidelines. It was a futile effort, for him and all of the Fort Irwin soldiers looking for a way out. The Army had worked for most of the late 1980's trying to stand up the JRTC program – it wasn't about to dismantle the project so people like Hughes could get a piece of the action. He accepted his role and watched CNN during the 1991 war with Saddam.

The 2003 war would be different. Hughes had learned a great deal in the field under a simulated condition at JRTC. A decade after his tour there, he was eager

45

to teach what he had learned at Camp Champion to his "No Slack" soldiers at Fort Campbell. For example, soldiers in the field during training exercises would have no contact with their families: no cell phones, no email, nothing. It wasn't that Hughes was cold hearted – he wanted to call his wife and kids too – but cell phones and email are nowhere to be found during the real thing, after all. "Soldiers truly believed that when they were in a field exercise they should be able to pop out their cell phones and call their wives at three o'clock in the morning and tell her how he was doing during the exercise," Hughes recalled. "They had not experienced that in their lives, not being connected to their families and visa versa. We had to wean them of that kind of ability to communicate."

Training was important to Hughes, as much as any battalion commander. He wanted to make certain his battalion was as ready as it could possibly be if deployment orders came, and on Sept. 11, 2001, he knew they would come eventually. As the morning frenzy of September 11 was being situated at Fort Campbell, his 2-327th soldiers were guarding the post with locked and loaded weapons. There was little that was certain for the 101st and Lt. Col. Hughes that day, but everyone in the military knew that the peacetime era had just ended. September 11 took his training schedule and sent it through the shredder. "Obviously at that point we knew something was going to happen soon."

For the "No Slack" soldiers and families, uncertainty was the only constant in the fall of 2001. Hughes had been told to get ready to move, then told to stand down twice before it was certain that the unit would not go to Afghanistan. With the First and Second battalions of the 187th Infantry Regiment already in theatre, it was decided that the Rakkassan's third battalion would complete the trio. Hughes' 2-327th would not get the chance to support Operation Enduring Freedom, a disappointment to some. "If anything it helped us with our system to get ready for OIF," Hughes said.

And ready they were in February of 2003. Hughes had made certain that the families would be as informed as he was before the deployment. He also made certain that there were no false hopes. "Once we cross the border, you will be lucky if you even get a letter in the first forty-five to sixty days," he told a class at the Fort Campbell Family Readiness Center. He wasn't talking about just his soldiers. This was the truth that Margerite was going to have to face also.

The 2-327th was scheduled to fly out March 1. Hughes had drawn a line in the sand at his own battalion headquarters. Once the battalion left for the Campbell Airfield, they had to leave their families behind. When the plane took off, it was time to get your game face on, which Hughes himself learned was an easier task in theory than in practice. Sitting in his office until after midnight, Hughes spent his last hours with his family fighting back tears. Looking at his oldest son Patrick, he knew then how averse he was to taking the Hughes military tradition into a third generation.

Once in Kuwait, Hughes and "No Slack" were ready, and as predicted, contact with family back home was sparse. The lines at the phone center were long, very long. Those who did brave the lines waited at a minimum, even in the wee hours of the morning, for two to three hours. Many times the wait was ultimately futile. The satellite connection linking soldiers with their loved ones at home was undependable. Soldiers were allotted fifteen minutes to get a connection. The process of hanging up and picking up the phone, hoping for a dial tone, was enough to make even the most mild-tempered soldier red in the face. Half the world away from their families, the inability to even say one last "I Love You" was the ultimate slap in the face to the soldiers who were weeks away from war. Hughes' admonition to his soldiers became a hard to swallow truth.

By March 11, the units had taken their positions in Kuwait. Camp New Jersey would act as the division's main command point. Third Brigade, 101st Airborne Division Headquarters and Headquarters Company, the 2-320th Field Artillery Regiment, the 626th Forward Support Battalion, the 63rd Chemical Brigade Headquarters, and the 1-377 Field Artillery Regiment (attached to the 101st from Fort Bragg, N.C.) would colocate at Camp New Jersey with Maj. Gen. Petraeus and his command staff.

Second Brigade would fall in Camp New York with the 526th Fire Support Battalion, 1-320th Field Artillery, and the 2-63rd Chemical Brigade. Camp Pennsylvania hosted First Brigade, 2-320th Field Artillery, 426th Forward Support Battalion, 801st Main Support Battalion, and the 1-63rd Chemical Brigade. The Division-Rear element, commanded by Brig. Gen. Sinclair, set up at Camp Udairi with the Division Support Command and the 101st Aviation Regiment. The 159th Aviation Regiment, composed mostly of Apache helicopters, landed at Camp Thunder. All of the camps were located in relatively close territory, with Camps New York, New Jersey, Pennsylvania and Udairi practically within walking distance of one another. The placement of the units was by design: the elements assembled in Kuwait would, for the most part, act with and support one another once the orders came down to move into Iraq.

Units continued with field training exercises and unit certifications in Kuwait. Personnel recovery procedures were rehearsed in the event of a downed pilot. Soldiers only laughed when explosions loud and thunderous enough to break glass were heard throughout the camps. The 101st Division Artillery Regiment was calibrating its weapons.

Soldiers and commanders had to adjust their internal clocks once again after gaining eight hours when they jumped the Atlantic Ocean. As soon as the division arrived in Kuwait, commanders started operating on "Zulu" time, oriented on the International Date Line. For example, if it was 10:00 A.M. Kuwait time, it was 0700 Zulu time.

March 17 would be circled on every commander's calendar. If Saddam Hussein would not comply with United Nations Resolution 1441 by St. Patrick's Day, American troops would move into Iraq on President Bush's orders. The long wait for war, particularly for the 3rd Infantry Division, who had been in Iraq for more than six months, would be over. The soldiers had trained for this for months and the moment was fast approaching.

For the 101st Airborne, the moment was too fast in approaching. With days to go before the American forces were to be unleashed, the 101st Airborne Division simply did not have their equipment ready. As of March 12, all three combat brigades had reported to Petraeus that they were in "Black" status, not combat ready. Only two of the 101st Aviation Regiment's Apache battalions had reported that they were "Green," ready to go. The last boats would likely not arrive until after the March 17 deadline. How then would the 101st Airborne Division, likely one of the combat divisions to cross behind the 3rd Infantry Division, ride into battle without its horses?

"We really cut it really close in terms of when our equipment arrived and when we had it in operational capability and able to fight," Col. Linnington, the Third Brigade commander recalled. Third Brigade, ready to cross into Iraq, waited with sweaty palms as their equipment rolled into Kuwait. Most of the Third Brigade equipment came in the first two boats. Unfortunately, all of it was supposed to be on boats one and two. When boats three and four came in, both thankfully carrying Linnington's AT4 Shoulder Fired Missile systems, his brigade scrambled to get them to the right units. "The equipment came in, in some cases, even hours before we needed to load up our equipment and get across the border."

On March 17, the fifteen-year anniversary of Iraq's chemical attacks on its own Kurdish people in the northern region during the Iraq-Iran war, Saddam Hussein had still not surrendered his weapons of mass destruction the Bush administration insisted he possessed. That night, President Bush spoke live to the nation to prepare America for war. A proposed U.N. resolution, authorizing force to disarm Saddam, would be withdrawn and American forces would move into Iraq with "a coalition of the willing." He spoke for fourteen minutes in the White House Cross Hall, contrasting with every one of his modern predecessors, who nearly always used the Oval Office to speak to the nation during such historic occasions.

"Saddam Hussein and his sons must leave Iraq within forty-eight hours. Their refusal to do so will result in military conflict, commenced at a time of our choosing," the President told the nation and the world, ending nearly a year of diplomatic efforts by the administration and the United Nations. "This is not a question of authority; it's a question of will."

The President spoke during prime time, 8:00 Eastern Standard Time, when most of America could and would watch. The Americans who would decide the fate of his decision lined along the Kuwaiti border were, for the most part, asleep. The local time there was 4:00 a.m. Some woke up hoping to watch the speech at the recreation tents, the only place with a television, but they were closed. The address that launched America into war days later would be blacked out from the soldiers who would fight it.

With little doubt that war was just days away, concerns surrounding the division's readiness plagued the 101st command staff. The Infantry brigades were short critical TOW (Tube-launched, Optically tracked, Wire-guided missile) missiles, vital in potential urban combat, and the 159th Aviation Regiment was missing necessary 2.75MM Flechette rockets that had been relocated to a Corps air aviation unit. With the division's supply battle chief impatiently waiting for the rockets to arrive from Fort Benning, Ga., all the division could do was sweat the clock.

Colonel Joseph Anderson was sweating through his shirt. His brigade was the last of the three infantry brigades to get their equipment on the boats back at Fort Campbell. If the war was going to start on the 17th, Anderson's brigade could be watching the first week of the war from Kuwait. There was no guarantee the war was going to last a week.

The 3rd Infantry Division, primed and ready along the Iraq-Kuwait border, would go first. Their task was to clear the way for the 101st Airborne Division in the initial stages of the war on the way to Baghdad. The 101st Airborne Division would follow the 3rd Infantry on the ground and through the air, establishing massive forward operating bases off the main route every one-hundred miles or so, at which it would refuel and rearm its attack and assault helicopters. This would enable the division to conduct deep attack operations on the flank and in front of the 3rd Infantry.

Meanwhile, the First Marine Expeditionary Unit would move towards Baghdad from the southeastern approaches. The British forces and American Special Forces would move quickly to secure Saddam's southern oil fields before he could command his ready units to burn them – as he did in 1991.

The anticipation for war had reached a boiling point during the final hours of March 19. The first 101st soldiers across would be the First and Second Battalions of the 187th Infantry Regiment (Third Brigade). They would follow the 3rd Infantry Division's lead units, who were expected to destroy any resistance from the Iraqi Border Guards with little resistance. Nearly two-hundred Rakkasan vehicles would constitute the lead 101st force, carrying Col. Linnington and Command Sgt. Maj. Hill into the country. The two Rakkasan battalions would be followed by the "Eagle Forward" team, a forward command post to which Freakley would fly to once it had found its position. Petraeus would follow once its tents and communication systems were established.

The Eagle Forward elements, on the eve of war, had a full slate that day preparing and rehearsing for their Ground Attack Convoy into Iraq. For nearly a year, the Eagle Forward team went through exercise after exercise prior to its debut. The concept was this: quickly establish a forward operating base for the division deep in Iraqi territory from which attack helicopters and ground forces could stage. The team was a marriage of mostly of communication soldiers and brigade liaisons, created to enable the Division to have two command posts that could perform all the functions needed to support Petraeus. They would oversee the close fight, plan and execute attack helicopter operations well behind enemy lines, plan and resource the future fight. Their first duty would be to establish communications once they reached their first objective: Forward Area Arming and Refueling Point "Shell," where the Eagle Forward Attack Command Post (ACP) would make home during the first days of the war.

The name FARP Shell, as with other planned refueling points like FARP Exxon, came from an oil company by the same name. Similarly, initial forward ground objectives, like Objective Raiders and Objective Rams, were named after NFL football teams. If America was going to go to war, it wasn't going without its sense of irony.

Third Brigade's First and Second battalions was to move into the area by convoy and the Eagle Forward convoy would follow. Third Battalion was to be attached to the 3rd Infantry Division once they linked up with the rest of the brigade at FARP Shell. The addition of a 101st Airborne Division battalion figured to give 3rd ID unique light infantry capabilities for a mechanized division. The Eagle Forward's battle command and control point was to command the Third Brigade operations during forward engagements. The Division-Main element, a much more "heavy" element, would trace and pass the Eagle Forward post in later days and eventually establish at FARP Exxon.

15,857 soldiers either wearing a Screaming Eagle patch or attached to those who did were deployed and in Kuwait as of March 19. That night, at what was the Morale, Welfare and Recreation tent, Petraeus, Freakley and all of the Third Brigade commanders and much of the Eagle Forward battle staff met for their nightly "Rock Drill." Whenever and wherever Third Brigade went, the Eagle Forward team would follow as its command post.

At the Rock Drill the CG stressed the need to positively identify targets before engagement and avoiding the use of artillery in the cities unless it was absolutely necessary. "We did not want to cause needless collateral damage," Petraeus recalled. "We were sensitive to the fact that we didn't want to save a city by destroying it. What we wanted to do was liberate a city with as little collateral damage as possible while still killing or capturing the bad guys and keeping casualties to our soldiers to an absolute minimum. There's a great deal of balance of judgment that goes into that." For the three infantry brigade commanders – Col. Ben Hodges, Col. Joe Anderson and Col. Michael Linnington – the judgments were going to fall squarely on them and their battalion commanders. In the post-Vietnam Army, field grade commanders were expected to be more competent in battle than ever. Hodges, Anderson, and Linnington would not disappoint.

Also on Petraeus' mind was the ability to communicate with his ground convoy commanders and their ability to navigate and operate independently. With prolonged communication blackouts likely, field commanders would need to know exactly where they were and where they were going in the vast desolation of southern Iraq. Each commander had to know how to read his map and his "plugger," which gave commanders their exact grid locations on the Global Positioning System.

Capt. Ben Smith had received dispensation from his weekly "Flower Day" responsibilities when he and his wife, Capt. Maggie Smith, arrived in Kuwait. Flowers don't grow very often in sand, they figured. That was why Maggie was so aghast when her husband showed up at her tent on Wednesday, March 12, with a fistful of flowers. He later managed to find a pot of coffee and a party hat, both not easy to find in the Kuwaiti desert, for Maggie's 32nd Birthday. The time in Kuwait was the first time in their marriage that the two had to live separately, if even just on different sides of Camp Udairi. Two weeks earlier, as the two were walking out of their house for the last time, Ben had told his wife, "we are so lucky to have an extended honeymoon in a distant and exotic country." In truth, the two had talked before flying to Kuwait about the need to not "flaunt" their proximity with one another, knowing that other soldiers with spouses weren't so fortunate. When they arrived in Kuwait it became apparent that there would be no need to worry about seeing each other too much. They had jobs and their jobs were to fly.

On March 15, Maggie's birds finally arrived, giving all of the 9-101st Aviation officers a chance to exhale. Wasting no time, she and the other pilots boarded a bus en route to the harbor. Flying a Blackhawk helicopter after its rotor blades have been reassembled is always a bit unnerving, but landing it in the desert, as Maggie found out that day, is enough to give a healthy young woman premature gray hairs. The flight over Kuwait City and the Persian Gulf was uneventful. The descent down to the landing zone, known as "Thunder 1," was much more dramatic. For Smith and her copilot, the excitement began when the lead aircraft descended into the parking area for her battalion, leading the convoy blindly into the landing zone. Maggie followed right beside the lead aircraft. Smith had never been taught in flight school how to land a helicopter in a cloud of dust; she would learn quickly. At one-hundred feet, Maggie lost the first aircraft. "Hey, where'd chalk one go?" she asked her copilot. He was just as blank. It would get worse as they descended. At fifty feet, they became less concerned about where the other aircraft went as the cloud of dust enveloped them. "Hey, where'd the ground go?" Taking a deep breath, they dropped down the final fifty feet praying for the best.

By the grace of God, Maggie and her copilot caught sight of the ground at about ten feet and recovered quickly enough to make a safe landing. As the dust settled, literally, on her introduction to desert flying, Maggie saw pieces of military equipment that had emerged from the desert floor. "Thunder 1" was more than just a decorative name for a patch of desert for helicopters to land on, it was also the sight of a major battle during the first Gulf War.

It was a story that got a chuckle out of Ben and nearly a heart attack out of Maggie. Ben had miraculously at times found ways to make his way over to Maggie's tent to sneak a quick hug from his wife. He wasn't going to be able to do that too much longer. Once the war started, they were going their separate ways, both knew. Ben worked with the 5-101st Aviation tactical operations center as a trusted advisor to Lt. Col. Laura Richardson, the 5-101st commander best known at that point for gracing the cover of *Time* magazine weeks earlier in a feature titled "When Mom Goes To War." Ben immediately impressed Richardson, a naturally warm person but stalwart commander. Every day he would rush around his battalion, gathering flight information from pilots and presenting Richardson with the day's mission details. He was essentially her secretary, but someone had to do it, and the most dependable junior officer in the battalion was perfect for the job. Maggie was assigned as the Forward Area Arming and Refueling Point officer in Charge. Her job was to make sure the battalion and other 101st elements were not moving into battle without fuel and ammo. "No fuel or ammo, no warfare," she explained to her family in a letter home. "I do believe that our astounding infantry could walk to Baghdad and kick ass with nothing more than a Gerber pocket knife, but it sure preserves combat power to give them a ride and a loaded M-16 rifle."

Fortunate to be within the same brigade, they were not going to be so fortunate to know what each other was doing at any given moment, or even any given day. If their battalion convoys were attacked, Ben could not be around to protect Maggie or the other way around. It was a difficult separation that could be worse if one had been back at Fort Campbell. The two met for the last time before the sun went down on March 19. They hadn't been able to watch television, but they didn't need to watch Fox News to know what was about to happen the next day. Ben after all had personally met Geraldo Rivera, a Fox News embedded reporter, days earlier.

Ben and Maggie went to an area where nobody could find them. The two didn't have much time, but they had much to talk about. They talked about what was on their minds: what they were going to do once they got back home. At the top of Ben's "to do" list was starting a family. When they got home, both planned on applying for the Aviation Captains Career Course in Fort Rucker, Ala., where they first met. "We're not leaving Fort Rucker until one of us is knocked up," Ben joked.

Maggie, accustomed to her husband's sense of humor, just laughed. She had no arguments. Motherhood was something she was ready for. They talked about family, how they felt about what they were about to do, and they talked about their future beyond the war they were about to fight.

Before most of the division even woke up on the morning of March 20, the war had started. At 4 p.m. Eastern Standard Time, CIA Director George Tenet briefed President Bush in the Oval Office on real time intelligence on a meeting between Saddam, his two most powerful sons Uday and Qusay, and other high level Ba'ath Party officials in Baghdad. Bush authorized the operation on the spot. In what became the opening act and most spectacular scene of the war, two Air Force F-117 Stealth bombers dropped a barrage of "bunker buster" bombs on the regime target. The strike, if successful, would hit the regime at its core and effectively end the war against Saddam before it really even began. The Iraqi Republican Guard, the force the Pentagon believed to be most loyal to Saddam, would fold knowing their leader and rallying cause had just been killed, so the logic went. In the following days it became clear that the targets escaped.

"Shock and awe" is how the Pentagon had termed how the first engagements in the war would reverberate around the world – and indeed the fireworks of Day 1 left little doubt how shocking and awesome American airpower really was going to be in Iraq. Sixty U.S. Navy Cruise guided missiles pelted regime targets in Baghdad the first night, shaking the Iraqi capital but leaving civilian infrastructure untouched. "Our military capabilities are so devastating and precise that we can destroy an Iraqi tank under a bridge without damaging the bridge," Secretary of Defense Rumsfeld pronounced during one of his daily noon press briefings. Normal life, as much as it could have, resumed the next morning in Baghdad. Only regime targets had been destroyed during the initial air missions, the Pentagon insisted.

Unlike the first Gulf War, where the ground war followed a thirty-nine day air war, the ground war was to start immediately after opening air operations. It was "go time" for the 101st Airborne Division. Theatrics for Petraeus didn't seem prudent at that moment, even if it were his military career at a crescendo. The

101st commander didn't bother giving his division a Knute Rockne-esque pre-game speech. The 101st Airborne Division soldiers didn't need it. In a brief, cogent message for his troops, he got on the radio, saluted his soldiers and went to work. "Guidons, guidons. This is Eagle 6. The 101st Airborne Division's next rendezvous with destiny is north to Baghdad. God's speed, Air Assault – Out."

Brigadier Gen. Freakley and the Eagle Forward convoy were slated to leave the next day, March 22, but the earlier than planned Air Force mission had hastened that plan. Sergeant Maj. Hector Torres, like Paul Revere in Lexington and Concord in 1769, called his soldiers to arms from their uneasy slumber that morning. No rehearsals, this was the real deal.

The Eagle Forward vehicles lined up in Camp New Jersey, received their last briefing from Freakley and their leaders, and prepared to move out around midday, 1230 Zulu (3:30 p.m.). True to form, an NBC alarm sounded and the soldiers calmly put on their masks. It was only when two PATRIOT guided missiles blasted into the sky to intercept the Iraqi SCUD missile attack that the soldiers realized the alarm was genuine – Kuwait was under attack. The PATRIOT guided missiles intercepted the SCUDs and "all clear" was given fifteen minutes later. The coalition forces in Kuwait came under a SCUD attack again later in the day, again successfully intercepted.

At 1100 Zulu (2:00 P.M.), the 1-187th Infantry Regiment, carrying maintenance supplies for the convoy route to FARP Shell, departed Camp New Jersey. An hour later, the 2-187th Infantry followed. Their destination was Tactical Assembly Area Carla, the front porch to the Iraqi border, where they would link up with the Eagle Forward post before moving into Iraq. The Eagle Forward convoy, carrying a load of equipment that would assemble the division's forward command post, left Camp New Jersey at 4:00 p.m. as the sun was starting to set on D-Day plus one.

As the forward elements were readying to charge into Iraq, back at the D-Main, still holed up at Camp New Jersey, Petraeus' prayers were starting to be answered. The USNS Pillilaau had docked at the Kuwait City port and crucial supplies were on their way to the infantry brigades. The TOWs and 2.75MM Flechette rockets had also arrived from Fort Benning. The 318th Psychological Operations Company, a reserve unit based out of St. Louis, had started to arrive at Camp Wolf and would be ready to move in three to five days. The 318th PSYOPS team would be tasked with moving into cities with bullhorns and leaflets ahead of the division, urging locals not to fight the incoming forces.

But vital supplies for the 101st remained absent and the caged lions remained under lock-and-key, able only to watch the war developments on CNN. Both the First and Second Brigades were still in the black status, unable to move into battle until their equipment arrived from the Kuwait. The "just-in-time deployments," as the 101st command staff had facetiously referred to their predicament as, were for some units not in time at all. Second Brigade had welcomed the bulk of their vehicles and ammunition the day that the 3rd Infantry Division had crossed into Kuwait.

"We massed every asset we had, used all of our trucks, and the only way we got our stuff up there is run a red-ball express back and forth from the port to Camp New York," recalled Second Brigade commander, Col. Joe Anderson. For three days, Second Brigade enlisted soldiers drove from one side of Kuwait to the other, sleeping so little that it's a wonder nobody fell asleep behind the wheel. "The only reason we survived," Anderson said, "is because every swinging truck we had was committed to doing runs down there."

The Bastogne commander, Hodges, gave his soldiers an irrational ninety-six hour time limit, four days, in which his equipment had to be unloaded off of the ships, packed at Camp Pennsylvania and ready to move. He later termed it a "stretch objective." Nobody in his brigade actually expected the equipment to be unloaded, transported across Kuwait and assembled in such a short time – but it couldn't be too much longer if First Brigade was going to be ready for war when the President was.

The Iraqi defenses had entrenched themselves in plenty of time for the U.S.-led invasion. In February, Saddam had divided his Army into four Corps, with the Iraqi III Corps in Southern Iraq nearest the border. The IV Corps would fall behind the III Corps, the I Corps would guard Baghdad and Saddam's northern flank and the II Corps, commanded by Qusai Hussein, would position around South Baghdad.

The III Corps' defenses would provide the early indicator of how and even if Saddam's Army was going to fight the U.S. led invaders. The only thing the division wasn't sure of was if the III Corps was going to come south and defend the borders or if they were going to say in the urban areas. It was becoming apparent in the early intelligence reports that they were going to fight in the cities.

As the Iraqi III Corps' armor fell into An Najaf and An Nasariyah, the G-2, or intelligence, officers noticed something else: they weren't wearing any protective chemical suits, an early indication that they did not plan to use any chemical or biological weapons. As the Eagle Forward convoy was crossing the Iraqi border, it became apparent that they were not going to be hit with a chemical or biological attack in the south. None of the Iraqi forward units were armed with chemical and biological munitions. Nobody breathed a sigh of relief. Major Gen. Petraeus had expected, not feared, that Saddam would use chemical weapons. The time he thought would come after the 3rd Infantry Division crossed the Karbala Gap, a choke point for V Corps on the road to Baghdad. The 101st too could come through the Karbala Gap; the 101st too had to be ready.

Day one of Operation Iraqi Freedom had provided several opening day highlights for coalition forces. The First Marine Expeditionary Unit and British forces had quickly secured the city of Umm Qasr, a port city a short distance from the Persian Gulf, and had defeated Iraqi defenses surrounding the Ramallah oil fields. The 3rd Infantry Division had rolled into Iraq with little resistance from the Iraqi border guards, as expected. The only thing that could stop the American-led push towards Baghdad on the first day was the inclement weather that cancelled scheduled 3rd ID deep attacks.

At 2118 Zulu the next day, March 21, the 101st Airborne Division joined the fight as the Third Brigade convoys crossed "the berm" and into Iraq. As expected, the first Screaming Eagles encountered no enemy contact as they moved into enemy territory.

The first enemy contact for the 101st, as it turned out, would be at Camp Pennsylvania.

Lieutenant Col. Christopher Hughes had been caught off guard when a SCUD alarm went off just before midnight the night of March 22. With his battalion readying to cross into Iraq, he could have been excused if his mind was fluttering when the by-then routine alarm sounded. He had gotten complacent. When the alarm went off, he ran out to the bunker in shorts and a t-shirt and his mask on. His subordinates, deftly aware that their commander needed to get in contact with the division headquarters, grabbed his radio and chased after him into the bunker. It was standard operating procedure for Hughes to carry a radio into the bunker, but by the time his radio got to him, the night was about to take a turn that was anything but standard.

"Sir, here, something's going on at brigade." Hughes could hardly hear through his mask, so he took his mask off to talk on the radio, thinking correctly that the SCUD alarm was not an issue. Using his call sign, he searched for someone who knew what was happening.

"This is No Slack 6, over."

On the other side was Sgt. Maj. Bart Womack. "We are under attack, the brigade (headquarters) is under attack. We got small arms fire and explosions."

Hughes looked back at the other soldiers, momentarily confused. How could the brigade headquarters be under attack, we're in Kuwait? "All clear, get your damn masks off. Something's going on at the brigade," Hughes told his soldiers. Pulling his sergeant major aside, he gave explicit instructions to secure the brigade headquarters area while he went with a radioman to his battalion command post to check on what was going on.

Major Kyle Warren, the brigade's top intelligence officer, was the first to respond to Hughes' inquiries. "Where's Bastogne 6," he asked Warren, referring to Col. Ben Hodges, First Brigade commander. Hodges had been hurt in the attack, he was told. Hughes immediately took the radio and paged Hodges three times without a response. With Hodges out, possibly dead, he called every station on the net. "Ok, I have no comms with Bastogne 6, we're under attack by some unknown force. Send forces to that area and secure your footprints. Send some guys out to the berm and confirm that the guards on the berm are ok. Get your night vision goggles out and identify and acquire targets.

"I'm taking command of the brigade."

Hodges was not dead when Hughes took command of Bastogne, but he did have a deep cut on his harm. After a few minutes of investigative reporting on Hughes' part, the real Bastogne 6 came on the radio. "Bastogne 6, are you injured?" Hughes asked.

"Well, I got knocked on my ass, but I'm ok now – over." What a relief it was to hear his gentle Florida accent. Hodges was back in charge. Now it was time to figure out what the hell just happened. Only one man knew for certain.

"Sir," First Lt. John Evangelest approached Hughes with one of his NCOs in tow, "we're missing a man. His name is Sergeant Akbar. We think he's behind this."

"Why would you think that?" Hughes was incredulous.

"Well sir, he was pulling guard on our equipment and we had drawn our ammunition today. He relieved the guards and told them to go back so he could be there by himself. We went back to the vehicles where he was on guard and we found six empty grenade canisters."

Hughes did ask any more questions after that explanation. He got back on the radio, paging every station on the network. "Everyone be on the lookout for a Sergeant Akbar, he has at least six hand grenades."

Sergeant Asan Akbar, an NCO with the 326th Engineering Battalion, was known throughout his company as unpredictable and undependable. He had little credibility with his subordinates and several of his superiors had tried to block his deployment. In a letter to his mother, Akbar had complained, "nobody in my platoon likes me." And he was right. Whether it was because of his un-Army like nature or his faith, Akbar had few friends in his unit. He later contended that it was the latter reason. Akbar was a Muslim with deep objections towards an American-led coalition invading an Islamic country. His uneasiness was compounded by several offensive comments he later claimed he had overheard from soldiers in his unit, no doubt directing their anti-Islamic venom towards Akbar.

On March 22, Akbar became more than just an outcast. During the SCUD alarm, he executed the plan he presumably had plotted for some time. With six grenades in his pro-mask case, Akbar ran to three tents, including the First Brigade command staff's tent, and pitched live grenades in each. During the ensuing confusion, Akbar locked and loaded his M-4 rifle and shot Maj. Kenneth Romaine through both hands and Capt. Chris Seifert in the chest, both from short range. Seifert died minutes later. Fourteen soldiers, including Col. Ben Hodges, Akbar's brigade commander, were injured. Another soldier, Maj. Gregory Stone, would die two days later from wounds suffered in the grenade attack. Seifert would be the first 101st Airborne Division soldier to lose his life in Operation Iraqi Freedom.

Hodges was still incredulous moments after the attacks. He had been sleeping on the floor of his tent when Womack woke him up. "Sir, you've got to get out of here," Womack told his commander. Hodges grabbed his 9mm pistol and loaded a magazine just as Akbar threw one phosphorous grenade and another frag grenade towards his brigade commander. The explosion laid Hodges flat on his back. In a stroke of fate, a box that Womack had left inside the tent absorbed most of the blast. If the box had not been in the way, Hodges may never have gotten up. Instead of a potentially fatal injury, Hodges had only been cut on his arm. Through the smoke, he managed to low crawl his way to the apocalyptic scene outside the commander's tent. Once outside, ignoring his own wounds, Hodges ran from tent to tent to assess the situation.

Just moments before his own death, Seifert had told Hodges "my back hurts" as several medics huddled around. He was still coherent, remarkably, and Hodges assumed Seifert would survive his wounds. Using a flashlight he had grabbed from one of his soldiers, Hodges peered inside an adjacent tent. There he saw

Romaine laid out with both hands "looking like a dog had just chewed them up." Romaine did survive his wounds, but was sent back home days later.

The attacker was on the loose for about an hour before the search team located its man. An hour after the attack, Akbar was found underneath a bunker, face down in the desert sand – broken, guilty, unapologetic.

Camp Pennsylvania was the site of another tragic fratricide incident that night. Already a bit frisky, a soldier with Lt. Col. Hughes' security element had yelled "RPG" – for Rocket Propelled Grenade – after a Camp Pennsylvania Patriot launched a missile into the sky. The rest of the group reacted as if the unsuspecting soldier was actually telling the truth; Hughes just chuckled. "That aint no fuckin' RPG guys, but you may want to put your masks on." Before they had a chance to follow Hughes' instructions, an explosion rocked the compound. Hughes pirouetted like a figure skater to see what had just happened. What he saw was a flashing light in the sky. It was like a Fourth of July fireworks show, but this was nothing worth celebrating. A British Tornado fighter jet was shot down accidentally by an American Patriot battery. The aircraft exploded over the Kuwait night sky and descended like a shooting star in slow motion while the soldiers at the compound watched, horrified.

Few could sleep after that night of calamity. Hughes did not even try. At one point, Hughes found Bastogne 6 doing a television interview with his arm in a sling from the grenade attack. "This," he said to himself, "is not a good idea." Hodges, he figured, may still be in shock. Stopping the interview mid-sentence, he politely pulled Hodges away from the cameras and impolitely chastised the camera crews for taking advantage of the shaken old man.

Hughes later caught up with Maj. Gen. Petraeus, who was rallying the troops as best he could. "Chris, the most important thing we can do at this point is get this brigade across the berm and get it out of here." From that point on, there was no discussion about anything other than getting Bastogne into Iraq.

Naval and Air Force operations, aimed directly at enemy command and control centers, had rained Tomahawk missiles and Joint Direct Attack Munition (JDAM) bombs on targets in Baghdad, Mosul, Kirkuk and Karbala – Saddam's theatre command and control center – during the first days of combat operations. The "Command Based Operations," a favorite battle tactic of Air Force and Navy brass alike, had taken an early and large bite out of Saddam's military communications infrastructure. Iraqi air defenses were defenseless. As Secretary of Defense Donald Rumsfeld cogently put it during an afternoon press conference, "it's domination. They have not put up a single aircraft."

Also targeted for the initial air armadas were Iraqi Republican Guard elements circled around Baghdad. On one night, March 21-22, 1,500 coalition sorties hit more than a 1,000 targets. Six-hundred cruise missiles were launched that same night. The effect was a rapidly denigrating enemy defense around the Iraqi capital and the Iraqi dictator.

After numerous delays and vehicle breakdowns, the FARP Shell and Eagle Forward convoys arrived at Attack Position Terri in the early morning hours and, after some short rest, began setting up shop. The planned thirty-six hour convoy went more than twenty hours longer than expected. The slow movement had complicated plans for a V corps deep attack the next night, March 23. Petraeus, concerned that the refueling point would not be ready in time, ordered the establishment of FARP Shell become a top priority.

The 101st CG decided, during a 1500 Zulu briefing to his command staff, that the 101st Aviation Regiment would immediately move with their AH-64 Apache helicopters to FARP Shell. Petraeus needed the Apaches to support the planned Corps deep attack. He was also worried that if the 101st Aviation didn't arrive soon enough, they would encounter incapacitating weather and sandstorms. As if commanded by the heavens above, the pilots moved up and out in a near flash of an instant.

Meanwhile, the 3rd Infantry Division continued to encounter tougher than expected fighting against the Ba'ath militia and the "Fedayeen" entrenched around the city of An Nasariyah. The Pentagon and V Corps' intelligence officers did not expect the Fedayeen and the Ba'ath militia to be as loyal as they had been in the opening days of the war. Saddam's Iraqi Republican Guard, his most elite fighting force entrenched around Baghdad, was expected to fight far more decisively once the Iraqi forces in the south folded. When forces in An Nasariyah did not fold as predicted, the global media sensed a bit of coalition frustration.

In truth, it was difficult for the coalition commanders to hide much from the media, especially with the 101st. Virtually every major American media source was represented with the 101st Airborne Division under the "media embed" system, the brainchild of Pentagon Public Affairs Chief Victoria Clarke. Reporters embedded with units and traveled along as if one of the soldiers and broadcasted the coalition's every move, down to the company level, live to the world. It was a dangerous position for both the soldiers and the media. No journalists would be permitted to carry a weapon, only their cameras and notepads, as they covered the war on the front lines. Journalists were even issued Kevlar helmets, flak-vests with protective plates, and pro-masks – this was a made-for-TV war and they were there as it happened.

Rich Atkinson of *The Washington Post*, and Jim Dwyer, of *The New York Times*, received the star treatment from the 101st command staff. The two star journalists were given unprecedented access to the 101st Airborne Division command staff during combat operations. Both Atkinson and Dwyer sat in on countess division briefings with a notepad and pen. Both shared a tent, alone, with Brig. Gen. Freakley and traveled with the assistant division commander during combat operations. Army public affairs doctrine instructed that embedded journalists be accommodated like a Major in uniform. Atkinson and Dwyer were promoted far higher than an O-4, though both handled themselves quite adroitly in their new, distinctly un-New York or Washington-like field conditions. Dwyer even shaved his full beard before the movement into Iraq and kept clean shaving every day while with the division.

For Atkinson, the opportunity to write about the U.S. Army in combat was not a novelty. Atkinson had one Pulitzer Prize for his series of articles profiling the United States Military Academy's class of 1966 (mentioned several times in Atkinson's book is the class valedictorian and young cadet who would eventually command the Allied NATO Forces in Kosovo in 1999, Wesley Clark). He later penned "An Army at Dawn," a chronicle of the African theatre of World War II, which was nominated for another Pulitzer at the time Atkinson left Washington for the Middle East.

Atkinson won that second Pulitzer, he found out about the honor while with the 101st in Iraq.

By March 23, the third day of combat operations, it was clear the Fedayeen forces in An Nasariyah were going to resist the coalition until the last man standing. Marines with the 1st MEF had reported several false surrenders as well as men recklessly attacking American armor with AK-47s, knowing their mission would ultimately end in their own deaths. The Republican Guard's 14th Mechanized Brigade of the Republican Guard's Medina Division had dispersed around the Southern Iraq front, putting up significant resistance in the city of Basra. Intel reports had also indicated that the 14th Brigade had moved armor and six mortar carriers into the Karbala Gap, aimed at plugging the coalition's movement towards Baghdad. The 3rd Infantry Division was fighting deep inside Iraq and supply lines were beginning to stretch their limits.

The stretched supply lines meant longer, more vulnerable convoys. Never was that so apparent and so tragic than the disaster of the 507th Maintenance Company. Their movement into Iraq started at Camp Virginia. They were a support unit attached to V Corps and, in truth, few were qualified for combat. This was not a front line unit, by definition. But on March 23, their status as a support unit would have little significance. As the Army always teaches, no matter what your Military Operational Skill – or MOS – when the bullets start flying, you're infantry.

And the bullets did start flying when the convoy took a wrong turn into an area outside of An Nasiria that had not been cleared of enemy personnel. According to a U.S. Army report issued months after the attack, the unit was at the rear of a 600-vehicle convoy that had been moving continuously, with little to no sleep, for sixty to seventy hours. When the unit commander had moved so far outside the convoy route that they lost communications with the rest of the convoy, the unit drifted right into an ambush in the heart of An Nasariyah. Fedayeen forces, many of whom were dressed in civilian clothes, fired at the convoy from both sides of the street, and the convoy shot right back. Fighting their way out of the ambush against a larger force, the unit "performed admirably," according to the Army report. But in the end, eleven soldiers were killed by enemy fire and seven were taken as prisoners. It was perhaps the low point for the coalition in the initial push to Baghdad.

The 507th disaster was another indication of the surprisingly high resistance from the Fedayeen. The irregular forces were putting a monkey wrench in the coalition's war strategies. The coalition had to deal with another block in the road to Baghdad: sandstorms. The division had experienced the desert's fury in all it might in Kuwait. Several late-night sandstorms had nearly leveled living tents. The dust had paralyzed equipment. High winds and punishing sandstorms had persisted through the launch of Operation Iraqi Freedom and now the weather was beginning to paralyze missions, particularly for aviation. During the worst of the sandstorms, visibility was no further than five inches. (During one especially violent sandstorm, Petraeus and aides had to find the battle command point using a Global Position System "plugger" when the tent was in fact only a couple hundred meters away.)

The 101st Aviation Regiment, having successfully moved air assets from Camp Udairi to FARP Shell, was raring for a March 24 deep attack on the 14th Brigade elements positioned in the Karbala Gap. That morning, Petraeus issued a "weather hold" until the weather cleared. The weather would never clear that evening and the mission was cancelled due to high winds. 101st Aviation ground assets continued to move into Iraq in the mean time.

Entering day four of Operation Iraqi Freedom, much of the 101st remained in Kuwait, readying to move into battle. By far the most effective method of movement, given the incessant dust storms, was on the ground. First Brigade had continued to prepare for movement into the vicinity of FARP Shell to isolate the enemy in An Najaf. Second Brigade, using three UH-60 Blackhawk helicopters, dispatched several teams to pull local security around stranded convoys and escorted supplies to FARP Exxon. The Third Brigade elements pulling security around FARP Shell and FARP Exxon continued to do their mission. Few 101st Screaming Eagles had participated in major combat operations in the first days, with the exception of the FARP Shell and Eagle Forward movement and the 101st Military Police, who ran fuel supply missions in support of 3rd Infantry.

The Eagle Forward team, ready for work, took command responsibilities for the forward fight on March 24, as planned. Brigadier Gen. Freakley was already in place, and when Maj. Gen. Petraeus arrived later that morning, the Eagle Forward ACP became the Division's main command post. Eagle Forward had the responsibility to continuously update the remaining elements in Kuwait, but the ball was now in their court. The rest of the division was not scheduled to move into Iraq until March 31.

Meanwhile, unbeknownst to many of 101st soldiers in Kuwait and Iraq, the 507th Maintenance Company disaster had been broadcasted to the American public by the enemy captors. The Iraqi forces had released videotape of the 507th Maintenance Company captured soldiers and several dead bodies being beaten. The footage became an instant fixture on the news channels running 24-hour live coverage of the war. Shocking to many Americans was that two soldiers taken prisoner, Pfc. Jessica Lynch and Spc. Shoshanna Johnson, were women.

Enemy tactics on the ground were getting increasingly unconventional and dangerous to civilians and civilian infrastructure. Coalition aircraft had received several incidents of small arms fire directed from small villages and parks. Schools and hospitals were being used as command and ammunition supply points. Enemy troops were being transported, out of uniform, in civilian vehicles.

The coalition had believed that Saddam Hussein's elite Iraqi Republican Guard would put up the strongest fight as the Marines and V Corps approached Baghdad. Few expected to face much enemy resistance before crossing the Karbala Gap. What had unfolded in the first few days of the war was exactly the opposite of what was expected of the enemy. "Clearly the Ba'ath militia and the Fedayeen became the enemy that fought and resisted most fiercely, whereas the other expected enemy, the Republican Guard, really was not materializing in large numbers – though there were some engagements with their elements," Maj. Gen. Petraeus recalled. The response was to fight the enemy where they stood. The coalition was not going straight to Baghdad as they had hoped.

More encouraging news came from the Kuwait City port. For the first time, all 101st Airborne Division units reported in "Green" status for readiness. The entire division could exhale.

After the 101st Aviation Regiment, First Brigade and the 101st command staff consolidated at FARP Shell, the necessary elements were in place for the planned March 27 deep attack on the 14th Mechanized Brigade of the Medina Division. Weather would be the key – the necessary aviation elements would have to be grounded if the sandstorms continued – and they storms would continue. The sand was not the only difficulty 101st aviation assets were facing. Congested routes slowed the ground supply convoys, carrying 250,000 gallons of fuel. The weather and other troubles had forced the delay of planned 101st missions by two to three days. Thinking ahead of the weather, Petraeus decided to consolidate much of his early forward assets at FARP Shell and prepare for longer than expected ground movements. Air assaulting assets deep into enemy territory was simply not going to be possible for the time being.

The uncertainties of air travel plagued the 101st's early missions. The Medina Division deep attack was originally planned to be completed days earlier. Instead, the 101st Apache pilots were riding out the sandstorms using their aircraft to take refuge from the storms. The 101st commanders knew time was being lost. Iraqi forces were reinforcing the 14th Mechanized to block off Highway 9, a main entrance into Baghdad.

For the soldiers, the sand was making life imperiously difficult. The soldiers who had crossed into Kuwait had no access to showers. There weren't enough Q-tips to clean the sand out of soldier's ears. A small snowstorm of sand was accumulating inside the tents. Cleaning the computers inside the Eagle Forward and D-Main tactical operations centers became an hourly issue. By the time the storm cleared, nearly four days of division operations, from March 23 to March 27, had been cancelled, delayed, or severely hindered.

All was hardly lost for the coalition. By March 26, the 173rd Airborne Brigade had taken an airfield north of Baghdad in the only combat jump of the Iraq war. They would provide the northern front that the 4th Infantry Division could not. Left back at Fort Hood, Texas, the 4th ID would not participate in the push to Baghdad after the Turkish government had rebuffed final attempts to stage the division along their Iraq border. Where diplomacy failed, the coalition's air power compensated. With an eye towards post-war stability and support operations, the Air Force and Navy Command Based Operations had been remarkably successful in taking out Saddam's military communications without damaging the Iraqi infrastructure, i.e. water, electricity and major highways. The post-Saddam government was also a concern. More than 500 regime buildings, vital to standing up the next administration, were off targets for Navy and Air Force sorties. Rumsfeld's declaration of the American ability to "destroy an Iraqi tank under a bridge without damaging the bridge" was being showcased.

While the air missions were successful in taking out communications with field-grade commanders, they did not aim to destroy Saddam's line of communication with the people of Iraq. The only information on the ongoing war the people were receiving was what Saddam was feeding them through the regime-dominated television and radio stations – the coalition could not broadcast messages throughout the country. Iraqis, based on the information they were receiving, were beginning to question coalition resolve to defeat Saddam's regime. That was exactly how Saddam wanted it.

The March 23rd Akbar attack had shocked every Bastogne and 101st soldier but served also to galvanize the brigade into battle. Many of the officers hurt that night by the Akbar attack were back at work very quickly with a stack of maps planning the next day's entry into Iraq. Nothing was going to change. First Brigade was going to cross the berm March 25. The attack had destroyed the brigade guidon, killed two officers and forced five others back home, but couldn't touch the Bastogne fighting spirit. "I was very proud of how well we responded and got after work. I was exceptionally proud," Hodges remembered. "That's our Army culture. Whatever the challenges are, you have to do your mission. You get trained on that from day one of basic training."

On March 25, forward elements of First Brigade crossed into Iraq with a 459-vehicle convoy with 1,056 soldiers destined for FARP Shell. In the lead was Col. Ben Hodges, leading his brigade into battle just four days after losing two of his soldiers in an attack launched by another of his soldiers. The Bastogne Brigade comeback was complete. Who better to lead the First Brigade at that moment than Hodges? It was his third tour with Bastogne. In total, Hodges was in his seventh year with the brigade. Now he was at the helm in the brigade's most crucial moment since Vietnam.

Waiting for Col. Hodges and First Brigade outside of An Najaf were elements of the 3rd Infantry Division, commanded by Maj. Gen. Buford Blount. With their M-1 Abrams and Bradley tanks, the 3rd ID had isolated the main approaches into the city. Now the 101st Airborne Division was going to join in the fight, although it was unclear what the division's role would be.

CHAPTER 3

DECISIVE OPERATIONS

The first weekend of war ended on an inauspicious note for the coalition. The March 23rd deep attack by the 11th Attack Helicopter Regiment's Apache helicopters against the Medina Division ended with one aircraft shot down. Their mission was to start clearing the Karbala Gap, a potential choke point for coalition forces along Highway 8 leading into Baghdad. The armada met a swarm of anti-aircraft fire from enemy elements buried deep inside the developed areas between Karbala and Al Hillah. Nearly every helicopter that flew the mission sustained some battle damage. The two pilots forced down·in the attack, Chief Warrant Officer 2 Ronald D. Young and Chief Warrant Officer 2 David S. Williams, were taken prisoner. Their images days later were broadcasted on Iraqi TV.

For the aviators, a face was now on the enemy. They had air defense capabilities, as primitive as they were. The aviation commanders immediately went to the drawing boards, revamping everything that had been postulated in their initial Intelligence Preparations of the Battlefield (IPB). Flying away from densely populated urbanized areas, where the enemy had been hiding, became a top concern. The Fedayeen had fired at the 11th Helicopter Regiment out of windows with Rocket Propelled Grenades. Ever vigilant of civilian casualties, it was not worth blowing up a building to kill one enemy combatant.

The next morning, in an After Action Report, or AAR, with the 101st commanders, Col. Bill Wolf, the 11th Helicopter Regiment commander, spelled out what the 101st was likely to face in the division's planned deep attack later that night in the same target area. Wolf's pilots had seen an elaborate network of visual observers, using cell phones from the avenues of approach to call in air defense attacks. Once the Apaches crossed over one built up area, the entire town's electricity cut off for several seconds, a way of winking at the ground air defenses. When the power came back on, the bullets and rocket propelled grenades started flying towards the 11th AHR Apaches.

It was a pithy discourse between the two Apache regiment commanders, Wolf and Col. Gregory Gass, 101st Aviation Regiment commander. That night, the 101st Apaches were going to fire its first shots of the war. They had received orders from V Corps the previous night to hit targets around the Karbala Gap. As the sun went down over the Eagle Forward command post, the anticipation reached tropospheric levels. "I hope you have the coffee hot," Col. Michael Linnington told the guard duty as he walked into the command tent. It was going to be a long night. After the 11th Helicopter Regiment troubles, this was an uneasy introduction to Operation Iraqi Freedom for the 101st Airborne.

Armed with much better intelligence on the enemy defenses and routes planned to avoid built-up areas, Col. Gregory Gass, the 101st Aviation Regiment commander came into the first night attack cautiously confident. The 11th Helicopter Regiment's troubles did not change his plan of attack for that night, only tweaked it a bit. What worried Gass more than the enemy's unorthodox battle tactics was the forecast for that night. "It was real dark. There was no illumination. I don't think there was anybody who didn't have some reservation." Gass was as uneasy as an aviation commander could be, riding in his command and control Blackhawk helicopter.

The 11th AHR's attack came in from the east towards the objective; the 101st Aviation's movement came from the north. The cell phone visual observers didn't cause any problems for Gass' Apaches that night. "The concept was to attack with one battalion minus from the south in a feint, while a second battalion (main effort) ingressed over Lake Karbala attacking from the north into the enemy's rear," Gass said of the attack. Coming from the south, Gass' second battalion would fly close enough to be let the enemy gunmen know they were coming to town, then disengage. First battalion would then fire from the west, using the Lake Karbala as a buffer zone between the Apaches and the enemy fire. The 101st Aviation Regiment pilots had an evening of target practice. Forty Apaches fought in the deep attack in the Karbala Gap area, two pilots in each. That night, the 101st Aviation pilots remembered why they became an Apache pilot in the first place. The pilots manning the Apache Longbow model, a 1999 update of the 1984 Alpha Model Apache, put on an especially spectacular show. Their aircraft were just another testament to how absurdly overmatched the Iraqi Republican Guard was against the American superior battlefield technology. About half of the Longbows came to Iraq equipped with Fire-Controlled Radar system, enabling pilots to acquire a target, fire and turn to the next target without following the Hellfire Missile through to its target. The Fire-Controlled Radar system ensured pin-point accuracy after the rockets had been fired, as opposed to the 1984 Alpha Model Apache, which could lock onto a target and fire only with laser guided missiles. In comparison, the 1984 model would seem outdated. On the battlefield, the two models were indistinguishable to the hapless Iraqi Republican Guard air defenses.

Gass' Second Battalion was only the second outfit in the entire Army to fly with the Apache Longbows. It had wowed the division when the aircraft arrived on post months after the Longbow had been introduced. Its first major league combat experience came in Iraq, where the Longbow picked up where it left off against the primitive air defenses. Having not picked up one hit from enemy radar during the deep attack, Gass and Petraeus decided that the Apaches had fought in their last night operation for the time being. With the ability to identify and strike a target from up to seven kilometers away during the daylight hours, knowing that the enemy defending that target could not get the Apache in range until it was literally on top of them, fighting at night posed an unnecessary risk.

The Apache pilots came back to FARP Shell knowing they had completed a very successful mission. They were right. The division assessed the battle damage at about 50 vehicles and an unknown but significant number of enemy personnel and equipment. "It was a great mission. It worked exactly as Army doctrine is supposed to work," Gass recalled. "Nothing is textbook, but that came pretty close to it."

The earlier 11th Helicopter Regiment's troubles had revalidated Petreaus' concerns about using the Apaches and Blackhawks in deep attacks on urban areas. The 101st routes were always, as Petraeus put it, "out over the deserts and then coming in," leaving little time for the enemy air defense artillery to respond to the attack. Petraeus and Gass made certain also to package close air support from the Air Force and a ready Downed Aircraft Recovery Team whenever the Apaches went into the skies. All of the adjustments made after the After Action Report with Col. Bill Wolf had worked to near perfection. "Colonel (Gregory) Gass and his team used the tactics very successfully," Petraeus recalled. When the mission ended, not one aircraft was lost from enemy fire during the attack, though two were lost from the dust. One Apache crashed on take off, another Apache crashed after the mission, a crash landing after the pilots lost all visibility fifty feet from the ground. One pilot suffered a broken leg from the landing, the only serious injury from the mission.

At a military hospital in An Nasariyah, a mile down the road from where her convoy had been ambushed days earlier, Pfc. Jessica Lynch laid unconscious in the uneasy care of an Iraqi medical corps brigadier general. Unbeknownst to her, Spc. Lori Piestewa had earlier died in the same hospital after being rushed into care by local police. Lynch and Piestewa were best friends.

The general's name was Adnan Mushafafawi. He was the enemy, but it was Mushafafawi who would save Lynch's life. "If we had left her without treatment, she would have died," he later told *The Washington Post*. In truth, even with treatment, her fate was uncertain. As Lynch slept, Mushafafawi and his staff set several fractures she had suffered in a severe Humvee accident during the attack. It was not the kind of care she likely came to know in her hometown of Palestine, W. Va., but she left with splints and plaster casts on her wounds. She later briefly regained consciousness, but fell out of it before she was transferred to Saddam Hussein Hospital on the other end of the city. Even months later, Lynch could not recall being taken prisoner. The three hours after the humvee crash remained blank in Lynch's mind. This much is known about the first few days of her stay at Saddam Hussein Hospital: an Iraqi intelligence officer was posted outside her door as she slept.

She later awoke for good as her conditioned improved. Heavily sedated, Lynch asked the hospital staff if they were going to torture her for intelligence. Around one-hundred Iraqi soldiers were being treated along side Lynch at the hospital, but the answer to her question would ultimately be no. Acting on intelligence indirectly provided by the hospital, U.S. Special Forces' elite Task Force 20, raided the site looking for Lynch on April 1. It made for wonderful theatre, broadcasted on television just hours after the mission was accomplished. It was also wholly unnecessary. Iraqi defenses around the hospital had abandoned post earlier that morning, though the U.S. Special Forces team had to enter the building erroring on the side of caution. The Special Forces team never fired a shot, and in retrospect, could have walked into the hospital and asked for Lynch by name at the receptionists desk.

It had been falsely reported by a number of national news sources that Lynch had shot and killed several of her attackers with her M-16 rifle. Her weapon in fact jammed and she never fired a shot. It had also been reported that Lynch had been sexually assaulted by her captures. Either because of privacy concerns or lack of memory, Lynch never confirmed those reports. Even as her mythological tale of heroism was still developing, the truth slowly emerged, still Lynch became a household name. In July, she returned to West Virginia a hero, complete with a good old-fashioned small-town parade. "For a long time, I had no idea so many people knew I had been missing, but I read thousands of letters, many of them from children who offered messages of hope and faith," she told the gathering media.

The biggest bugaboo for Petraeus and the 101st pilots continued to be dust, even after the sandstorms had settled. The issue became especially troublesome outside of An Najaf. "It was an enormous problem for us. It was something we had expected, we were keenly aware of the challenges the dust would pose, but they were even greater than we expected." Targets on the ground were virtually invisible to the helicopters. "It just wasn't worth it," the CG recalled. Taking off and landing, particularly for the Apaches at night, became nearly impossible. "The night takeoff and landing challenges, due to the dust, were also so enormous that we did adapt big time in that area."

One aviator who knew all about the difficulties of taking off and landing in the desert, Capt. Maggie Smith, was still in Kuwait as of March 26, much to her surprise. So too was her husband, Capt. Ben Smith. The two met early in the morning for what they knew would be the last time before they crossed into Iraq. Maggie and her platoon had orders to prepare Second Brigade's for its assault into Iraq. The mission was to drop Second Brigade 465 kilometers into the battle for An Najaf. More than fifty helicopters were going to be used in the assault that would land Strike Brigade north of the city. Maggie would be responsible for fueling all of the aircraft. That meant that she would not have any time from that point on to wonder over to Ben's area for another visit. In spite of that, she wasn't sorry for the change. Most of her first week of war was spent helping embedded journalists figure out their chemical gear.

After her usual MRE lunch, Maggie scrambled from helicopter to helicopter, making sure all were ready to go. Somewhere in middle of the head-spinning chaos, she took a moment to take in what she was witnessing. The helicopters had lined up one-by-one for the infantry to load in and take off that night. It was the kind of image the Army should use in its recruiting commercials. In her eight years in uniform, it was one of the most amazing scenes she had seen in the Army. More than a thousand soldiers waiting on the flight line with stalwart determination beaming from their eyes, raring for combat. She was no more proud to wear the American flag than at that one moment.

Then Geraldo Rivera showed up.

Rivera was on his way to FARP Shell to link up with Col. Michael Linnington and Third Brigade. Given the star treatment that only Rick Atkinson and Jim Dwyer could beat, Rivera was authorized his own transportation from Kuwait to Shell with one condition: "you may not release any operational information prior to its execution."

Rivera arrived with Third Brigade in time to do a live Sunday show for Fox News. Before he went live to the air, Rivera met with the Rakkassan soldiers he was now embedded with. To his credit, Rivera was less concerned with the colonels and the generals than he was with the sergeants and lieutenants. That was who he set out to interview as soon as he arrived with the Rakkassans. Many soldiers, through Rivera and Fox News, got the chance to talk to their families back home. "He did a very positive piece on our guys and what we were doing," Col. Michael Linnington recalled. Rivera did get around to meeting the commander, and Linnington came away immediately impressed with the television news superstar.

Linnington wasn't around when Rivera went live on Fox News that Sunday. If he had been, the Rakkassan commander might have stopped Rivera from doing what he ultimately did to infuriate the Pentagon. Kneeling on the desert floor, with the cameras rolling, Rivera illustrated with his pointer finger in the sand where the 101st was and what they were about to do. In effect, he was releasing operational information prior to its execution. The Pentagon brass was watching, although they couldn't believe their eyes. Major Hugh Cate, 101st Airborne Division Public Affairs commander, was told to send Rivera back to Kuwait almost before the Fox News cameras turned off.

"I didn't think it was a big deal and I frankly didn't think he should have been chastised for it," Linnington said. "It was common knowledge where the 101st was."

Regardless of what Linnington thought, the Pentagon had their way. Four days after Rivera had promised not to tell the world about future 101st Airborne operations, he was back in Kuwait, removed from Iraq for telling the world about future 101st operations. An annoyed Capt. Maggie Smith was detailed to watch Rivera and his Fox News crew as their helicopter refueled at Camp Udairi before taking them back to Kuwait City. Her job was to make sure they didn't wander off anywhere and she was under no obligation to be courteous. Maggie greeted the 101st's new least-favorite person by stopping her humvee inches from Rivera's knees as he climbed off the aircraft. Rivera's crew had started to unload their equipment when Maggie made her not-so-polite introduction. "Gentlemen, don't even bother, you will be leaving momentarily."

The media embed system – at least in one isolated incident – had backfired badly for the 101st Airborne. For Geraldo and the 101st, the marriage of journalists and soldiers would come to an ignominious end, but only momentarily. Remarkably, Rivera managed to explain himself well enough that he was given another chance. In Kuwait, Rivera got re-vetted and linked up with Third Brigade seven days after the illustration in the sand incident.

First Brigade was initially scripted to isolate enemy forces inside An Najaf and prevent any encroachment of the 3rd Infantry Division supply route along Highway 8. Second Brigade would isolate the city from the north, and on the 28th of March, they landed in country at Kifl, assaulting their First and Third battalions into the area. Colonel Joe Anderson and his Second "Strike" Brigade landed on the northern approaches in what would be the largest air assault into enemy territory of the war. They would set up around the town of Kifl, blocking off the north. Wasting no time, they set up an immediate assembly area west of the Euphrates River. They also wasted no time in gaining key morale supplies from an abandoned Kufa-Cola factory. Whatever soda had not already been raided by the 3rd ID was cleared by the Second Brigade soldiers. In the end, a $15,000 claim was given by the 101st Airborne Staff Judge Advocate. Of course Strike Brigade was tasked to do more than drink soda. Once they set up shop, Col. Anderson was given the mission to relieve the First Brigade of the 3rd Infantry Division as they moved north. The rest of their division would follow after Hodges and First Brigade got entrenched. To their credit, they had stayed in the area long enough to clear the area of most, but not all of the enemy personnel outside the city before moving up towards their next battle. Anderson and his brigade quickly got postured before the 3rd Infantry tank elements were let go. In Kifl, Anderson met up and assumed command over the 2-70th Armor Regiment (minus one company given to Hodges), giving him much needed tanks for the fight in An Najaf.

March 29th, things started to heat up. As the line units were up against sniper fire and RPGs around Anderson's perimeter, the Second Brigade staff was working on the orders for the next day. "We air assaulted elements all over the place," Anderson would later recall. Their primary mission was to block off the escape routes and squeeze Fedayeen elements looking to live another day. The noose was going to get tighter. The secondary task was to secure the communication routes and supply routes along Highway 8 for the Baghdad-bound 3rd Infantry Division. Anderson's First and Third Battalions again were ordered to team up again to take key bridges leading in, and out, of the city. A number his companies had already begun setting up blocking positions and vehicle checkpoints on Highway 8 before the sun went down. The Strike commander knew the Fedayeen would try to bring suicide bombers to the fight.

From the south, it was going to be up to Col. Ben Hodges and his First Brigade to take the battle of An Najaf right to the enemy. The idea of simply isolating the city left Hodges uneasy. The brigade intelligence officers were beginning to hear reports of Fedayeen forces compelling locals to repel the coalition with the alternative of death. Ever cognizant of the Shiite skepticism from the 1991 Gulf War, Hodges wanted to make sure there was no doubt of the coalition's intent to protect the Shiites from further slaughter at the hands of Saddam and his loyalists.

The early war plan for Lt. Col. Chris Hughes and No Slack was to air assault just to the east of An Najaf, and secure a major road and five bridges leading into the city. Once the 2-327th had completed their mission, 3-7th Cavalry of the 3rd Infantry Division could move in. The rest of First Brigade would seize other inroads to An Najaf for 3rd ID, titled Objective Bears. The hope was that the Iraqi Medina Division would pull forces out of Karbala to meet the 3rd ID tanks. If that happened, the Air Force could watch the Medina armor move from position to position and pick them off for sport. If they failed, the 2-327th would have to be ready for one helluva fight. The last thing Hughes wanted was his battalion's light infantry going up against tanks outside the city. He made sure he secured all of his TOW and Javelin missiles just in case that happened.

In An Najaf, coalition technology would again help define the battlefield. A program called Blue Force Tracker enabled Petraeus and his staff to pinpoint 3rd ID locations down to the company level, find them, and relieve them in place. It was a digital map laid out by satellite imagery that connected all coalition forces in a virtually unprecedented intra-force network. For the 101st and Petraeus, it made the tasks of finding units quicker and safer. "That was where Blue Force Tracker really came in handy because all you needed to do was dial in the descriptor of the unit you were relieving," Petraeus remarked. "You'd just put the unit in there, find the icon and drive right to them. You could even send them a message that said, 'Hey, we're on our way, don't shoot us up.'"

Fratricide from 3rd ID was not a preeminent worry as Bastogne sat outside An Najaf. Along Highway 8, just to the east, First Brigade could start to see civilization for the first time since they crossed into Iraq. The buildings in the distance were a welcome sight in a way, but civilization, of course, was their next rendezvous with destiny. It had taken the brigade two and a half days, through the most wretched sandstorms the deserts had to offer, just to reach the city. 3-7th Cavalry of the 3rd ID was waiting; Hughes and No Slack were going to relieve them with the mission of protecting the fuel and supply train into An Najaf. The 3rd Infantry was occupying positions outside the city when Bastogne Brigade approached. They were to isolate An Najaf until the 101st could relieve them at a few locations, then move in. The Fedayeen, V Corps figured, was going to try to attack the supply routes outside the city once they saw how overmatched they were by the 3rd ID Abrams and Bradleys. Bastogne Brigade was to make certain they weren't successful.

In command of the operation was Col. David Perkins, the Second Brigade, 3rd ID commander, who briefed Hughes and Lt. Col. Marcus DeOliviera on what he wanted now that his attack elements were in place. DeOliviera and his First Battalion would relieve the 3rd ID elements covering checkpoint Charlie, a highway leading into the city from the south. Then he turned to Hughes. "Lieutenant Colonel Hughes, you're going to replace Lieutenant Colonel Ingram here," Perkins said as he pointed at his map. He pointed to west An Najaf where Lt. Col. Jeff Ingram, commander of the 2-70th Armored Brigade, was located. There was no time for trifling either. Hughes, DeOliviera and their battalions moved with a purpose to their objectives, though the movement would take around fifteen hours. The relief in place was completed in the early morning hours.

Bastogne Brigade was tasked with blocking all approaches leading into the city from the south and west; Second Brigade would block the city from the north. Colonel Linnington and Third Brigade would guard the supply routes west of An Najaf and south of Karbala. Colonel Hodges concerns were in the western part of the city, where two major roads led from the west into the southern end of the city without a coalition presence. Both roads were left uncovered by 3rd ID when

Bastogne Brigade arrived. The Bastogne commander had only two of his own battalions to cover the entire area, which meant he would have to designate a smaller force at checkpoints than what he really wanted. To compensate, he ordered Hughes to leave his Bravo Company with DeOliviera to set up checkpoints on both roads, then take the rest of his battalion and block the two roads coming from the west to the south. It was a stretch of his assets, but Hughes would make it work.

The remaining elements of Second Battalion went with Hughes to cover the objective. What they found was a pretty desert horizon but no enemy personnel. Hodges called and told Hughes he was on his way. There was going to be a change in plans. Hughes picked out a spot on the west side of the city, where one of his roads began, to link up.

The two led their convoys to a remote village, with a canal and actual green trees amongst a sea of desert. It was a nice spot to have a talk, Hughes figured. Hodges jumped out of his vehicle and Hughes gave him a swift salute. It was dinnertime and both were starving, so they grabbed a couple of MREs and went trotted toward a nearby canal to discuss what would happen next. A fragmented order was going to come down from V Corps. It would be up to them to win An Najaf. After first receiving and order to isolate Najaf, Petraeus had convinced Lt. Gen. William Wallace, the V Corps commander, to send the 101st in to clear the city. "We might as well find out if we can take these guys in a city," Petraeus told his boss. Wallace agreed and afforded Bastogne a tank battalion in support, but the rest of 3rd ID was going to move up north. First Battalion would lead the main effort; No Slack would follow in the rear.

"Do you want to fight the enemy or do you want to fight the graphics?" Hodges asked Hughes rhetorically. It was a reference to the all talk and no action role Bastogne Brigade had been playing up to that point. Sitting on a dike, watching an Iraqi fisherman catch minnows in the canal, Col. Ben Hodges answered his own question. "There's nothing going on here. Let's go fight the enemy." Hughes couldn't agree more. Third Infantry had successfully isolated the Fedayeen inside the city. Any attempts to ambush supply routes along Highway 8 had been thwarted long before they reached the First Brigade position.

Hughes was instructed to grab his Bravo Company back from DeOliviera and isolate the city from the west. It would be another fifteen-hour movement, but once they were in place, there would be no sitting around listening to noisy crickets.

The new plan meant that the Second Battalion would likely attack the city on the ground in their vehicles. Hughes had designed his truckloads to be able to fight from their humvees in the event that his battalion would ride into battle in their vehicles – not drop into battle in an air assault from the skies.

On March 30, No Slack got their orders. "No Slack 6, when are you going to attack?" Hodges asked Hughes on the radio.

"Is this a coordinated attack?" Hughes replied. Hodges said it wasn't, meaning he was free to attack whenever he wanted. Hughes opted for mid-afternoon the next day. He wanted to attack with the sun to his back. They were to come from the west, launching their operation after First Battalion commenced its attack from the south. Colonel Joseph Anderson and Strike Brigade would continue to attack into the city from the north and northeast, blitzing into the city from three entry points, closing off escape routes for Fedayeen elements looking to fight American troops another day. Anderson's First Battalion would come into the city on the city's major highway and would be the brigade's main effort. His Second Battalion was to swarm the bridge entering the city, patrol the area along the river and a nearby town to the east. Theirs would mostly be a supporting role. Second Brigade's Third Battalion would secure the center sector of the city.

The next morning, a swarm of OH-58 Kiowas and AH-64 Apaches woke up any citizens of An Najaf who decided to sleep in that morning. For Hughes, the target objective was a Fedayeen-held escarpment on the southwestern side of the city, known as Objective Fox. Destroying the Fedayeen positions on Objective Fox would open up entry points into the city for First Battalion. It would also help identify the likely enemy response before the real ground assault began.

What had been observed, both by the 3rd Infantry Division and by initial First Brigade intelligence reports, was that the Fedayeen had been using holy sites in An Najaf to launch attacks on the coalition. No doubt they were astutely aware that the Americans were not eager to destroy Mosques, even if that meant taking casualties. The battle of An Najaf for coalition field commanders was like walking barefoot on broken glass. Shi'ia Muslims constituted sixty percent of the Iraqi population, and An Najaf contained the holiest site for Shi'ia Islam: the Imam Ali Mosque, commonly known as the Golden Mosque of Ali for its brilliant golden dome. Gaining the support of the Shi'ia dominated southern region was crucial to winning the peace in An Najaf. The political objective was every bit as important as the military one in An Najaf, and Hughes knew it.

Seizing the political objective for Hughes and the coalition meant one thing, winning the support of the Grand Ayatollah Sayyad Ali Husayni Sistani. The most revered of the just thirteen grand ayatollahs in Shi'ia Islam, Sistani had been confined for eight years in an An Najaf compound after an assassination attempt on him in 1996. The Mosque – burial site of the son-in-law of Prophet Muhammad, Ali ibn Abi Talib, who was stabbed to death in 661 A.D. – was the most sacred of grounds for Sistani and his minions. A Special Forces team who had been operating in the city briefed Hughes about the mission and made one point above all other messages: do not shoot, scratch, touch the Mosque. That would not be easy. The Mosque was located in the middle of Objective Fox, a 2-327th objective. For Hughes to use his artillery and air power, they would have to be precise. Offending Grand Ayatollah Sistani would be disastrous.

From the west into the southern region of the city, Hughes' Delta Company was observing the enemy escarpment from a fortified support-by-fire position. With the helicopters flying overhead and a 2-70th Armored Regiment tank platoon rolling towards their position, the Fedayeen element entrenched in a thickly vegetated area revealed their position on a ridge. Hughes approached a Delta Company platoon leader. "Your mission," he told the lieutenant, "is to go to the base of that escarpment and be a shit magnet. I want you to go down there and draw fire and while you're drawing fire, I'll bring the full weight of the artillery battery, the 2-17th Cavalry, Delta Company, and every piece of close air support I can bring in. I'm not trying to hurt you. I know you can survive whatever they bring at you." War can provide some tense moments, but this moment for Hughes was as dramatic as any this war could provide. With everyone set, the platoon approached the ridge practically in the shadow of the Golden Mosque.

It didn't take long for Hughes to see that his reconnaissance by fire mission was working. The Fedayeen had taken his invitation to fire at his lead element, but couldn't pinpoint their locations because the sun was blocking their shots. Hughes' tactic of attacking with the sun to his back was paying off. Now artillery and close air support was going to initiate the rest.

The artillery went first. Hughes covered his ears when a supporting howitzer fired the first shot, then gasped when he saw where the projectile was heading. "What part of don't shoot at the fuckin' Mosque didn't you understand?" he bellowed at his Fire Support Officer, or FSO. The round had hit the nearby ridge and made the Golden Mosque of Ali disappear in a cloud of sand. For what seemed like a lifetime, Hughes and his commanders held their breaths, speechless, while the cloud dissipated. Only when they could see that the Mosque was in fact unscratched could Hughes and his FSO breath easier. "OK men, no more artillery on that ridge," Hughes told his subordinates.

He didn't waste anytime after the artillery scare to release the hounds on the Fedayeen escarpment. Not even a minute into the fight, the TOW missile gunners were identifying and shooting at targets – many of which were fortified mortar positions. In just three and a half hours, Hughes' Delta Company would shoot fifty-six TOW missiles at the Fedayeen escarpment. With all the firepower in his battalion, Hughes found his most lethal weapon when a brazen former Iraqi soldier embedded with his battalion tugged on his sleeve with a helpful suggestion. "In fifteen minutes, the people of An Najaf are going to go to the Mosques to pray," he told him.

Hughes was initially unconcerned. "Step away from the commander," he thought to himself. Then he took a minute to give the idea a second thought. If he laid down his arms long enough for the people to go to the Mosques, what a powerful message that would send to the people and to Ayatollah Sistani. "Cease fire for fifteen minutes. Stand by," he ordered on the radio. Instantly the guns went quiet. A minute later, he got back on the radio and ordered all elements fighting in the city to fall back so the streets could be clear enough for the locals to go to their Mosques. Then he grabbed his linguist. "I want you to get on the speakerphone and tell them four things. One, we aren't here to steal your religion from you. Two, you are free to go to your Mosques. Three, we're here to release you from Saddam Hussein and four, we don't want to hurt the people of An Najaf." It was a gamble for certain. The remaining elements of the Fedayeen were on the run, but to give them fifteen minutes to regroup could backfire, Hughes knew. He knew too that sitting in that golden Mosque was Grand Ayatollah Sistani, hearing his message loud and clear.

"Sir, look at that," said one of Hughes' staff officers. He peered up at the ridge that had just moments ago been a target and saw a stream of white. Immediately he grabbed his binoculars to get a closer look. Hundreds of An Najaf locals had taken to the streets with white flags of surrender.

The white flags were not being waved by the Fedayeen, so the battle of An Najaf continued after the momentary tranquility. As a way of warning the locals to get back into their homes, Hughes' had his artillery fire an innocuous smoke round into the city. As luck would have it, the round landed in a school being used as an ammunition supply point. The school caught fire and the supply point was destroyed. Fortuitously, Hughes had just scored a major blow to the Fedayeen without really even trying. The battle was back on.

Anderson's march into An Najaf had also been fruitful. Several minefields on the outskirts of the town and along the highway had been found without incident. All of the schools encountered by Anderson's brigade in An Najaf – twenty-four in total – turned up weapons caches.

In the skies was the cavalry. A century and a half ago, the cavalry rode into battle on their horses. In 2003, the saddle was on the seat of an OH-58 Kiowa helicopter. An aircraft so small that, minus the rotors and the tail, could fit comfortably into a two-car garage, the Kiowa has unparalleled vertical capabilities. Its ceiling is 19,000 feet, nearly twice the height that the Blackhawk is capable of flying at, yet it also has the ability to hover so low to the ground that it can practically blend into traffic. Its purpose is to observe an enemy from such a distance that enemy air defenses are incapacitated, but that never meant the Kiowa pilots couldn't have a little fun.

First Lt. Monica Strye had grown tired of pulling security around FARP Shell. She had been tasked to fill the holes in the perimeter that the undermanned Rakkassans couldn't plug. The wall of sandstorms had grounded any other air activity for Strye and the 2-17th Cavalry Regiment. Day 1 of the battle of An Najaf was a chance for her and her crew to enter the fight. She had worked too hard at Fort Campbell to just pull security missions.

Lieutenant Col. Stephen Schiller, 2-17th Cavalry commander, had been ruthless in training his pilots and crew chiefs for combat at Fort Campbell. "He was extremely battle focused," Strye recalled. "We flew all of our tactical flights in full body armor and MOPP suits, just to get used to the weight." With An Najaf in full view, Strye knew why her commander was so demanding. This was the moment and she was ready. The objective for her was "Dog East" and "Dog West" (as in Bulldog East and West, the First Brigade mascot). She was told the objective was a military compound the division knew was in the southern region of An Najaf. Another Kiowa team would cover another militarized area, a cemetery the Fedayeen had used to stage troops. The Kiowa teams' mission was to get a real time view of the battlefield back to Hodges and the division headquarters. As Bastogne's First and Second Battalions moved about the city, so too did the Fedayeen. Strye and her Kiowa team were to track their movements and call in artillery fire if needed.

Strye was the air mission commander for her team, consisting of herself, her right-seat pilot Chief Warrant Officer 3 James Carter, and Chief Warrant Officer 4 Tim Merrel leading the other Kiowa with Chief Warrant Officer 2 Mike Blaze. The targeted military compound consisted of about fourteen or fifteen buildings with a small airfield in the north area of the objective. The target was easily visible from the air, satellite imagery had shown, with a chain-linked fence and barbed wire cordoning off the area. As the thinking went, if the coalition could seize the compound without destroying it, the compound could be used after the end of the war. Because of that, the objective would be handed down to First Brigade, not the Air Force and their 1,000-ton bombs.

Strye's team would be a third eye as First Brigade went into the objective. If personnel went in and out of the compound, Strye's team would get the word back to the First Brigade commanders.

From the air, the first thing Strye noticed was a hill on the south end of the compound with trees, perfect for concealed defenses around the objective. As expected, as she approached, her team saw mortar positions nestled in the foliage. What she didn't see were enemy soldiers around the position. The team needed to make contact with personnel in the area, she knew. With approaching ground infantry, there could be no surprises. Her aircraft orbited the objective, hoping to incite some kind of contact with whatever enemy personnel were in the area. Nobody responded. Then she saw the infantry on its way, and stepped back. Strye's team took a figure-eight formation, allowing her and her team to keep an eye on the objective without loosing vision at any point. On the ground, First Battalion fired an artillery round into a three-story building believed to be an enemy compound, blowing a hole through its side. After the smoke cleared, Strye saw what they had hit and chuckled. The building they had hit was an enemy ammunition supply point; the munitions blocked their entry into the compound. Approaching infantry would see missiles, mines, grenades, an assortment of unexploded ordinances that would make any further encroachment impossible. Simply put, First Battalion had not done themselves much of a favor.

Strye knew the downfalls of using a figure-eight flying pattern: lower air speed and predictability for enemy personnel. Shortly after the ammunition point was engaged, the enemy on the ground took advantage of the figure-eight's tactical pitfalls. "Hey JC, get out of there. You're getting fired at," Chief Warrant Officer 4 Tim Merrel warned Strye and her copilot, Chief Warrant Officer 3 James Carter. The mortars on the ground had come alive. Strye looked to her left and saw clouds of smoke, close enough to her bird that she knew she needed to break the formation. The enemy was launching mortars into the air, hoping that one would hit. None did. Picking up the air speed, the team started flying around the compound in an erratic, arbitrary pattern. The mortars stopped firing. Strye and her team stayed in the air, undaunted by the mortar attack. Only until she started to run out of fuel did the team turn around and head back. At that point, the infantry had found a way into the compound and had cleared their way through the first five buildings.

The gunfire ebbed as the sun went down for Strike Brigade. "The larger challenge was crowd control. As we cleared the streets, people came out of their homes in jubilation," Anderson remembered. His concern was innocent bloodshed – Fedayeen forces had used civilian shields during their fight in the northern entry points of An Najaf, including shooting right over the heads of local non-combatants. "(The locals) were everywhere and it became increasingly more difficult to separate them from us."

The next day, however, Anderson would march out of An Najaf, executing a planned "relief in place" with Col. Hodges and drive on north. It would become First Brigade's fight.

To further advance into the city, the 2-327th also had to clear a minefield that blocked their entry. The locals had told the soldiers exactly where the mines were; division explosive ordnance assets took the matter from there. That night, after finding a couple of schools where no classes had been conducted in weeks anyway, Hughes and the battalion found a home for the night. They wouldn't get much sleep, but their first night in An Najaf was spent with a roof over their heads and a nice, warm MRE.

CIA and Special Forces were working with three emissaries to contact Grand Ayatollah Sistani, Hughes was told that night. Determined to make sure Sistani and the locals knew his intentions, Hughes tasked an entire company to work humanitarian assistance into An Najaf. When they found out the city needed water, a thousand gallons of water were delivered into the city as requested. Another company was going from school to school, clearing ammunition left by the Fedayeen. At one school, a Second Battalion soldier found an elaborate map drawn in the sand, pinpointing where all of the ammunition dumps were located. That made things a bit easier. Over the next several days, No Slack and supporting units would discover that the Saddam Fedayeen and Ba'ath Militia had stockpiled ammunition and weapons in virtually every one of the dozens of schools in this city of some 500,000. But the endgame, Hughes knew, was with the Grand Ayatollah Sistani. If he issued a declaration to stop fighting the coalition, or a "fatwa," An Najaf would be clear. The rest of the Shiite south would likely join in support. To do that, Hughes told the emissaries that he wanted to meet Sistani personally.

The next day, day two, Hughes would break ground with Sistani. Two of the emissaries the CIA and Special Forces were working with were in fact nobodies, with no more ties to Grand Ayatollah Sistani than Hughes' next-door neighbor. One man was legitimate. The CIA and Special Forces had been in contact with an Ayatollah from Iran whose father was Sistani's predecessor. Through him, the coalition had been able to talk to the Ayatollah, but it was Hughes who endeared himself the most to Sistani. "He liked your words, he liked your actions," the new emissary relayed to Hughes. Now Sistani wanted to meet him. He was apparently flattered that the coalition would come to him and was more than willing to talk to Hughes. The messages Hughes had broadcasted when his battalion first entered the city also impressed the Grand Ayatollah. But if the No Slack commander wanted to speak with Sistani, he was going to have to walk up to the Mosque and knock on the door, literally.

Hughes received a cram session on how to approach the Grand Ayatollah. "How do you meet an Ayatollah?" he blankly asked the emissary. "Do you bow? Do you kneel? Do you kiss his ring?" He was told to bow and strike his heart as he said to Sistani, "Allah be praised." Don't try to shake his hand, he was warned. One issue that would create some problems was his weapon and gear. He could not even think of wearing them into the Golden Mosque of Ali. That would mean a lieutenant colonel walking around in an active war zone armed with nothing more than his faith. It was a chance he was going to have to take, Hughes knew. Sistani told his former student that he wanted his Mosque to be secured by Hughes' unit before he could meet Hughes. The 1996 assassination attempt had made Sistani wary of everyone in every situation.

The fight had changed even before Hughes could meet Sistani. First Lt. Monica Strye had begun to see clearer skies from her Kiowa pilot seat. Direct from her battalion commander, she was given a grid for her and her team to find and destroy. It was an artillery battery, again staged in a wooded area for concealment. The challenge was to come into the city from such an approach that the battery, if they were still able to man their artillery pieces, would not be able to see Strye's approach in time to do anything about it. Fearless but still mindful of her experiences from the previous day's work, Strye locked into the objective from the western approaches. This day there would be no drama, at least none of the kind she saw on day two of the battle of An Najaf. The artillery battery had abandoned post. Strye counted the artillery pieces on the ground, around a dozen tubes, and promptly lit them up. Throughout the city, the people of An Najaf had begun to see the futility of fighting the coalition. On several occasions, low-flying 2-17th Cavalry pilots would peek outside their window and see locals pointing at the few remaining enemy targets.

With the tactical objectives in the city under coalition control, the infantry on the ground had also started to take a change of approach. With an eye towards the post-war occupation, they were tasked with clean up duty. "We were looking for caches and, at that point, anyone with a weapon," remembered Capt. Joe Kuchan, a 1-327th company commander who led the initial incursion into the city from the south.

Sparse fighting remained on April 3. Hughes' meeting with Grand Ayatollah Sistani would be a pivotal moment. It would also be a first step for the entire coalition towards winning the support of the people of Iraq. The weight of the coalition was on Lt. Col. Hughes' shoulders as he approached the Golden Road to the Mosque of Ali, a street that was not paved with gold but did in fact lead to the Golden Mosque of Ali.

Hughes was very concerned about how the surrounding community would respond to an American soldier walking into the Mosque. He had met Sistani's demands that he secure the area before meeting him, but that would hold little weight with some locals. Hughes could see the images, and distortions, on Al Jazeera already. Was the coalition coming to arrest the Grand Ayatollah? Indeed, a crowd had already formed around the Mosque when the convoy arrived. The soldiers immediately dismounted their vehicles with their weapons locked and loaded. The emissary rushed towards the crowd, doing his best to explain that the soldiers had been invited to the scene and were not here to apprehend the Grand Ayatollah Sistani. Several unruly citizens weren't listening. A number of Sistani's students in white turbans rushed from the Mosque to talk to the crowd to cooperate the story. Some still weren't listening.

"My god," Hughes thought as he approached the ornate Mosque, "this is like the Wizard of Oz." For the people of An Najaf, the analogy was also significant, although few in the city had likely ever seen Judy Garland in her ruby-glass slippers. For almost a decade, Sistani was never seen or much heard from by the people who lionized him. In fact, if Sistani actually walked through the streets of the city, it's likely that many locals would have just walked by him without giving the Grand Ayatollah a second glance. His name was a myth but his face was never seen. As he stepped out of his passengers seat, Hughes grasped that he was about to meet a man and see a face that the entire southern region of Iraq could only dream of standing before.

Outside, the word had almost instantaneously spread around town that an American was meeting with Sistani in the Golden Mosque of Ali. Locals sprinted through the streets to catch a glimpse of this mythological figure. Hundreds of students rushed out of the Mosque to talk to the locals, assuring them that Hughes was invited. But sure enough, what had started as a few curious people quickly grew into a mob outside the Mosque. Hughes would later learn that several extremists, possibly Fedayeen, had jumped into the crowd and shouted, "He's going to kill the Grand Ayatollah." Soon men were arguing with one another with steam coming out of their ears. Nobody seemed to know for certain what was going on. For the soldiers pulling security, they had a problem on their hands. Some in the crowd had even started to throw objects at the soldiers, one of which nailed Hughes in the back. Wisely, he stopped in his tracks and told the emissary that he'd be right back.

Hughes ran back to his humvee and grabbed the radio to report the situation. He was upset but he didn't think forcing the crowd to shut up would be very effective. Hughes chose not to control the mob with the standard four S's: shout, show (your weapon and the intent to use it), shove (push the mob away), and finally, shoot. Instead, he decided to take a more diplomatic approach. "Guys, take a knee," he told his soldiers. Dumfounded, several soldiers looked at their battalion commander like he was joking. "Take a knee and point your weapon to the ground." Hughes had again employed the ultimate weapon against the Fedayeen elements in An Najaf. He simply reached out his hand to those who weren't certain about the coalition's intentions. "Ok, I want everyone to smile. Smile men, smile. They have to know we've been invited." His soldiers realized his thinking and executed his orders with the best Hollywood grins they could muster.

The crowd slowly went silent. Holding their uneasy but convincing smiles, the soldiers were getting their message across. Most of the crowd that had thought the patrol was on its way to apprehend Sistani now understood the real intentions.

Then an extremist from inside the crowd again hit some buttons and got people talking again. Few were listening, but a group of fanatics again took to throwing objects at the soldiers. Hughes went back to his vehicle and got on a speaker to shout out orders to his troops. "I want everyone to stand up and back off. This is just a misunderstanding." He was also talking to anyone in the crowd who spoke English, for certain.

The meeting with Sistani would have to be cancelled. He could not leave his soldiers in a potentially explosive situation. Hughes ordered his troops to get up and walk away with their backs turned to the crowd. Again, Sistani was watching and again, actions spoke louder than words. That night, without ever meeting with a coalition soldier, Sistani issued the fatwa. It was a call for his followers to "not interfere" with the coalition, falling short of a call for support. Nonetheless, the fatwa ended the resistance in An Najaf. The coalition had taken the city and Hughes was the hero.

After Col. Joe Anderson and his Second Brigade had cleared the northern part of An Najaf long enough for Hodges' First Brigade to occupy the southeastern part of city, he and one of his Strike Brigade elements marched forward towards their second ground engagement of the war. The city was Al Hillah and on April 3, they advanced on Iraqi defenses postured in the city.

On the southern approaches to Al Hillah, the coalition continued to have its way with the overwhelmed Iraqi Republican Guard. Along Highway 8, Second Brigade and the 2-70th Armored Regiment came face-to-face with an Republican Guard battalion – dug in and augmented with tanks, artillery and air defense. It was a firefight that lasted most of the day and cost the division its first soldier, Spc. Brandon Rowe, who was shot by an enemy sniper. "We had limited advances that were given to us by V Corps – don't go beyond this gridline," Col. Anderson said. "So we only penetrated the southern portion of Hillah, but it was a hell of a firefight." From the V Corps level, the mission Anderson was handed was nothing more than a demonstration. It was to be a feint to focus enemy attention away from the 3rd Infantry Division, planning an attack on the Karbala Gap the next day, where the coalition had expected one of the largest, bloodiest battles in the war. The enemy took the trap without a second thought. Seeing the column roll towards Hillah created the false impression that the lead elements into Al Hillah were going to come from the south. It was a ruse. The Iraqi Republican Guard forces rushed towards the column as the 3rd Infantry Division moved through the

Karbala Gap. Like a badly fooled poker player, the Iraqi forces jumped at the Second Brigade convoy as the 3rd Infantry tanks attacked the next day.

As the infantry fought deep inside Iraq, the Division-Main compound finally uprooted from Camp New Jersey and set up just beyond a spectacular Iraqi ridge north of An Najaf and south of Karbala in time for the latest battle. Karbala would be the next objective. Many of Saddam's forces were using Karbala as a command point. The Karbala Gap, the coalition had figured, was the most opportune objective for Saddam's forces to choke the coalition advance to Baghdad. The victory at An Najaf would have to be celebrated another day.

The mission for the 101st Airborne had taken another direction during the battle for An Najaf. As the fight unfolded, V Corps Commander Lt. Gen. William Wallace ordered Petraeus to use his light infantry capabilities to fight the enemy from the front with one arm and clear the rear area routes with the other arm. The official orders came days later. First Brigade would be responsible for clearing the main supply route leading from the southern Iraqi town of Samawah to Baghdad once they coalition was ready to enter into the Iraqi capital. With the supply lines increasingly stretched, vulnerable, and under attack, the rear 101st Airborne elements held the balance of the 3rd ID's movements in their hands. It was a critical move that would effectively keep the 101st out of the first days of the battle for Baghdad. "That was a decision that was made when we realized the critical importance of dealing with the Ba'ath party militia and the Fedayeen," Petraeus said. Gulf War II had become a non-linear war. As V Corps and the First Marine Expeditionary Unit pushed Saddam's defenses into the Iraq capital, irregular forces from behind the line had refused to accept their own defeat.

CHAPTER 4

. VICTORY

In Karbala, the great battle that the division expected would never pan out. "We expected to find a large number of Republican Guard in Karbala with our Apaches," according to Maj. Gen. Petraeus. "Instead of destroying hundreds of armored vehicles, which you might do with a really successful deep attack of more than two full Apache battalions, we got around forty or fifty." The rest of the enemy equipment, as it turned out, had already been destroyed by air operations a week earlier or deserted. The division had been running daylight reconnaissance missions after its first assault on the Karbala Gap – sometimes as close as five kilometers from the enemy positions – with no resistance.

"Man, I think we can operate during the day," a grinning Lt. Gen. William Wallace had told Petraeus in response to the coalition target practice. In fact, many of the positions were abandoned by a paralyzed enemy. With an empty-net goal, the 101st destroyed most of two divisions' worth of tanks, personnel carriers, artillery pieces, air defense systems and weapons caches. Most enemy personnel in the Karbala Gap had just melted away back into civilian life. "They really knew that if they were going to hang around the Karbala Gap for too much longer, they were going to get smoked," Petraeus remembered. The onslaught of destruction left the Karbala Gap virtually clear. "They just melted away. There was no fight to speak of." The 3rd Infantry just sailed right through after an engagement at a bridge leading into the city; the 101st would follow without serious difficulties.

The remaining fight to clear the enemy in the city of Karbala – a city of some half a million people – would be left for Col. Joe Anderson. Second Brigade got into attack position on April 4 outside Karbala, again relieving elements of the 3rd Infantry at locations outside the city. The tactical operations center on day one was another abandoned school. To that point, nobody had actually operated inside the city, but the 3rd Infantry Division did run their tanks through a part of Karbala, shooting up some enemy targets before returning to their headquarters, a practice some of the 101st division officers termed "drive-by shootings."

Anderson met with the Third Brigade scout elements in the morning. Hoping for an extensive briefing on the enemy, he instead got a bunch of educated guesses. "All we knew is what I surmised," Anderson said. "We attacked where I would defend it. That's how we developed our air assault plan." On April 5th, it would rain Strike Brigade soldiers in Karbala. All three battalions would land on key objectives on the outside neighborhoods of the city, all at the same time, and attack inward. The 2-70th Armor tanks, attached to Second Brigade from First Brigade a day earlier, would provide the hammer with Anderson's Third Battalion in what figured to be a quick, devastating attack.

But like most battles, the plan would change. A 3rd Infantry Division commander had strongly advised Anderson not to drive the tanks into the city. Anderson thought the enemy stronghold was on the west side of the city. The 3rd Infantry commanders were certain the targets Anderson was looking for were further inward. In a tactical move that Anderson would later regret, he left his 2-70th anvil to fight alone from the northeast, bringing the fight directly into the city with his helicopters and rifle infantry. If he had it to do over again, he recalled, he would have dropped all of the tanks directly where he thought the enemy center of mass was located. Only Company C from the 1-41st Infantry, a mechanized element from Fort Riley, Kansas, would support Third Battalion.

The bullets started flying just before lunchtime. The enemy, as Anderson later found out, was completely erased of any Iraqi Republican Guard elements. Ba'ath party militia and the Fedayeen fighters were in position when the helicopters started circling the city, but the fiercest resistance would come from an Army who had little loyalty to Saddam Hussein at all. "They were predominately Syrian foreign fighters … we never found an Iraqi Republican Guard guy there," Anderson said.

Pilots from the 101st Aviation Regiment effectively began the battle by calling in an avalanche of artillery fire from above on a number of "stubborn" targets inside Karbala. One heavily fortified building, holding a large element of Fedayeen forces, was reduced to rubble with a number of enemy personnel inside. Colonel Gregory Gass and his pilots could follow the ground movement of Fedayeen forces like rooks on a chessboard. Pin-point accuracy and quick communication to ground forces again proved the division's greatest asset.

The 101st Aviation Regiment's Third Battalion operated outside the city, destroying any Fedayeen forces trying to flee the city and decimating enemy equipment staged outside Karbala. The former mission was hardly problematic. Most of the enemy forces had abandoned their armored vehicles before they ever posed a threat to the 101st Airborne ground forces. Rather than wait for enemy personnel to scramble back to their fighting positions, Gass had his pilots destroy more than 100 armored vehicles.

Anderson's First Battalion was charged with the southeast section of the city, going straight towards the heart of Karbala after landing in the drop zone just outside the southeastern approaches. The northeast charge would come from the 2-70th tanks with 2-502nd Infantry Regiment assaulting in from the southwest. A couple of hours into the attack, all three elements had begun to coalesce in the center of the city without much resistance. The enemy had fortified the northwest approaches into the city, exactly where the 3-502nd Infantry Regiment was air assaulting and exactly where Anderson thought the enemy center of mass would be.

The battalion landed about 1,500 meters outside of the city at about 11:00 a.m. local time (Anderson never used Zulu time and was scolded several times by Petraeus for his refusal to do so). The 1-41st tanks were waiting on the drop zone when they arrived. The 2-17th Cavalry Regiment again provided the initial blow from the skies, but they were receiving fire as well as giving it. The infantry watched the Kiowas started taking RPG fire, concentrated around one area. As they approached, they spotted a courtyard that was the source of the enemy fire. The quick solution was obvious. Lieutenant Col. Christopher M. Holden, Third Battalion commander, called in a Joint Direct Attack Munition (JDAM) to destroy the location.

As they waited for the rockets to red glare, a Third Battalion infantry squad spotted a nearby truck with several men, out of uniform, unloading a mortar tube. Too shocked to react instantly, a gunner standing behind a Mrk .19 Grenade Launcher took a second to lick his lips before lighting up the truck, and the men. Then the wait was over. From the heavens, the JDAM landed right on target.

Most of the 3-502nd soldiers couldn't see the missile land, but they sure felt the explosion. So too could the enemy. The irregular Fedayeen forces, as it turned out, had used the location as a command and control point.

Having lost many of their field grade commanders, the Fedayeen scattered towards the western approaches, meeting the tanks and 3-502nd Infantry in a dash towards death. The coalition was ready. The tanks already had a foothold in the city and destroyed the approaching enemy as they came. All was not a total success for the 1-41st Infantry during the battle. One Bradley fighting vehicle was hit from an enemy mortar and seven soldiers had to evacuate the tank. As they fled, an automatic weapon position from the second floor of a close-by building started firing. One 1-41st Mechanized Regiment soldier was hit. He was the only coalition fatality of the battle of Karbala. An estimated 150 enemy soldiers were killed during the 3-502nd attack into the city.

The battle of Karbala effectively ended when 3-502nd Infantry Regiment and the 1-41st controlled every enemy stronghold in the northwest quadrant of the city. The enemy had collapsed in that region of the city. The next day they cleared the city block for block and linked up with the rest of Second Brigade. Then Anderson and Strike Brigade starting preparing for their next assignment.

Al Hillah was the next stop on the 101st's drive to Baghdad. Colonel Michael Linnington and his Third Brigade would lead the charge from the west, supported by the 2-70th Armor Brigade. Lieutenant Col. Christopher Hughes and his 2-327th Infantry Regiment, attached to Third Brigade, would attack from the south. Second Brigade would provide a second front of support and Gass' Apaches would provide fire support from above. For the Rakkassans, it would be their Operation Iraqi Freedom debut in combat. Linnington and his brigade had been tasked to that point with manning fixed security points and protecting supply lines. Incredibly, the battle of Al Hillah would also in many ways be the Iraqi Republican Guard's introduction. To that point, after the U.S. Navy and Air Force operations had taken apart the IRG division by division, no regular forces had been able to mount a defensive against the American-led coalition.

Linnington, perhaps the division's best battle tactician, wanted to take the battle to the enemy without "rushing infantrymen into the fight, potentially with armored formations." His battle plan scripted the Day 1 of the battle for Al Hillah for knocking out enemy targets with close air support and artillery – or "predatory fires," as Linnington put it. The targets were a Republican Guard headquarters and several military complexes the brigade intelligence officers had located in the city. The plan called for Rakkassan Infantry to follow into the city through the holes in the enemy defenses created by the early engagements. "I wanted to make sure that we got as much information as we could and attack with precision where we needed to attack," Linnington said. Also on his mind: collateral damage. Linnington knew, as Hughes had already known from An Najaf, that the battle wouldn't be over until the local populace welcomed the new sheriff in town. Al Hillah was a city of several hundred thousand people, according to coalition estimates, and nobody thought it would fall easily.

The Linnington battle plan would be orchestrated like a dream. As he watched from outside the city, the Apaches, Kiowas and his artillery assets lit up the targets with pinpoint precision. The Iraqi Republican Guard abandoned the targets by the time the sun came up the next morning.

Back to flying at night again, the 101st Aviation Apaches had no repeat problems with dust and identifying targets. They did find out early that the Iraqi Republican Guard's air defenses were a bit more elaborate than firing small arms from villages, albeit they were hardly above using civilians as shields. In spite of their ignominious decimation in Al Hillah, the IRG had been able to cause some headaches for the 101st helicopters. Eight hits, none serious, were reported to Gass. The somewhat functional equipment the IRG had deployed from Baghdad was able to keep pace with the 101st Apaches, if only for a short time. What they had been able to do, in the end, was inflict a small wound on Gass compared to the paralyzing effect of the 101st's superior firepower. Most of the Iraqi Republican Guards artillery and anti-aircraft arsenal as well as manned machine-gun positions were destroyed by the end of the night.

Two of the helicopters hit during the battle were back to the fight the next morning; only one helicopter was sent back to Kuwait, but it too could be flown without any trouble.

The early coalition successes did not mean the IRG abandoned the fight entirely, not yet. Linnington's 1-187th Infantry and the attached 2-70th Armor led the push into the city from the west the next day. After the barrage from the previous night, nobody from brigade intelligence had a clear idea of what to expect from the Iraqi Republican Guard. This much was clear: there was certain to be more irregular forces employing militarily ridiculous tactics. The enemy would continue to hide among villages, blending among unconcerned villagers, as they had done during the 11th Attack Helicopter Regiment attack two weeks earlier. Linnington could also expect more attempts at suicide bombings at control points, as the coalition had continually faced since crossing into Iraq.

Linnington's push into the western quadrant of the city began as a scenic tour of what the predatory fires had done to the enemy the night before. The division commander was also in tow. Whatever fight was left in the Iraqi Republican Guard had gone up in flames. They found burned out buildings, they found decimated tanks and vehicles, and they found uniforms left at the side of the road. They also found a city ready to rebuild – literally. The 1-187th led convoy came to a stop when they reached an impassible bridge, blocked because it was undergoing renovations. The construction crew had abandoned the project after the war started. As the commander's figured out how they were going to get around the obstacle, they found themselves in an ambush.

Delta Company was in the front, Alpha Company followed behind. In the very last vehicle – a five-ton cargo truck – was Sgt. First Class Joe Montoya. A few vehicles ahead was another platoon sergeant, Sgt. First Class Raymond Dakos. At the very front of the 12-vehicle Company A convoy was First Lt. Paul Moriarti, the company executive officer. The three needed to huddle, so Dakos and Montoya walked towards their lieutenant as their company commander, Capt. Marc Cloutier, got on the radio to figure out what was going on. "We got some UXOs on the far side of the bridge," Montoya and Dakos overheard. The Alpha Company convoy had spotted some unexploded ordinances, likely left from the coalition's artillery fire the previous night. Nobody in Delta Company thought anything of it.

The crackling of machine gun fire is what grabbed their attention. It came from a thicket to the right of the convoy, so the soldiers scurried behind their vehicles and pointed their weapons at the source. All went silent.

Montoya, looking straight at his company commander, flagged Cloutier from several vehicles ahead. "What do you need, sir?" What he needed, Cloutier told him, was a team to go into the thicket and find the bastards who just shot at the convoy. Montoya and Dakos weren't about to let anybody else lead that charge. "Sir, can I throw a grenade in there first?"

"Go ahead, good idea." From his hip pouch, Montoya grabbed one out, removed the pin, and fired one right into the bushes about 20 yards from his position. The blast was enough to end the game of hide and seek. Weapon in hand, a man emerged from the thicket, unharmed. Dakos was skeptical. There couldn't have been one man in that thicket, he figured. Gripping his M4 Carbine a little tighter, aiming it right at the man, he kept focused on the situation. His deft handling of the bogus surrender saved at least one of his soldier's lives.

There was indeed another man in the bushes, and he emerged with his armed cocked ready to throw a grenade as his partner continued his subterfuge. Dakos, acting as if seeing the developments in slow motion, pushed a nearby specialist out of the way, aimed his weapon at the grenadier and fired right on target. The grenade never got out of his hand. Then the other man picked up his weapon ready to fire back at Dakos. Dakos was quicker to the draw.

The Montoya-Dakos team went into the thicket, weapons on semi, and cleared the area. There was nothing more. Another clearing mission in the nearby grain silo compound turned up a couple of men who had shot at the convoy earlier, but they managed to run away. Later, an abandoned five feet deep bunker was found around the area, signaling that the Iraqi Republican Guard had indeed intended to put up a stand near the bridge.

The volley of fire continued up ahead. From the other side of the road, the Delta Company convoy started to receive fire from a wooded area, with Col. Michael Linnington and Command Sgt. Maj. Iuniasolua Savusa, the brigade sergeant major, riding along. Savusa, with a cigar in his mouth, immediately took charge, ordering his soldiers to take cover behind the berm that ran along the road. When he heard a grenade explode, Savusa spun around and fearlessly ran towards a sand-bunker from which the RPG had apparently come. "Who has a grenade?" the fearless Savusa asked his soldiers. In one motion, Savusa took the grenade from one assenting soldier, pulled the pin and pitched it into the bunker. Two enemy soldiers lay dead after the cloud of sand subsided. Savusa's heroism earned him headlines from coast-to-coast in the United States.

Montoya was later honored with the Bronze Star with a "V" device for Valor for his actions during the engagement. Dakos earned the Silver Star, the only soldier in the battalion to come home with the honor. Savusa was also honored with the Bronze Star with a "V."

The firefight had lasted more than an hour. Even soldiers in Petraeus' security element had joined in the firefight. Rick Atkinson, trialing the 101st commander with a pen and a notepad, looked at Petraeus in astonishment. "You're going to get yourself killed."

The series of engagements at the bridge were the only serious enemy contact the Rakkassans faced during the battle. A day later Cloutier was told that two men running out of the compound were shot by a couple of Kiowas. Once any remaining enemy elements were cleared, the Rakkassans continued into Al Hillah. They were greeted with smiles and hand waves but no further enemy resistance.

Hughes' movement into Al Hillah came from the South. For the "No Slack" commander, the battle got off to a shaky beginning. Hughes and his staff were never told about Anderson's engagement, and No Slack partitioned its Company D to seize the same objective that had been cleared of any enemy presence. Once the D-Main command center straightened out the confusion, Hughes called the company back into its attacking position. His objectives were first to seize the University, then forward to the United Nations Oil for Food warehouse, called Objective (Detroit) Lions. Before day one was finished, Hughes and his battalion had control of both without much enemy resistance. Company A staged at the university that night. Company C, commanded by Capt. Mathew Konz, racked at the UN warehouse. They could rest well that night, but the relative docility of the enemy that day would not foretell their capitulation the next morning.

Day 2 began when an attached tank company from the 2-70th Armor took off in the lead for No Slack, with Companies B, C, and A following up Highway 8 in that order. Company B pulled ahead of the convoy and acted as the main maneuver element for Hughes, but it was Company C that found itself pulling most of the load. Their tale began after their convoy pulled into another set of abandoned warehouses, these ones storing an abundance of paper and rugs. The scene was like a prison, with high, brick walls surrounding the areas with Highway 8 running through the two compounds. It was an easily securable place to run the company out of, but behind one of the buildings was a site that Konz knew he had to keep an eye on: a large weapons factory. At the corners of both compounds, he put Squad Automatic Weapon (SAW) gunners with their eyes opened wide before he left with one of his platoons back to the battalion headquarters.

As he left, First Lt. Leo Barron, an Officer Candidate School graduate with a master's degree in military history, took charge of the remaining elements of the company. He would get to see first hand that day exactly what he had only read about in school. His baptism by fire as a junior officer began when two of his First Platoon SAW gunners, manning the southwest corner position, saw something they shouldn't have. "Hey sir, looks like we got a couple of guys with AK's." Following the Four S's – Shout, Show, Shove, and Shoot – Barron ordered the gunners to curtly get the guy's attention. "Put down your weapons!" Of course nobody expected the men to actually speak English, but you didn't have to know

Above: Three 101st Airborne Division pilots on the eve of battle, waiting to cross into Iraq. (Photo by 101st Airborne Division Public Affairs)

Right: A game of softball as 101st soldiers wait in Kuwait for the orders to cross into Iraq. (Photo by Spc. Josh Risner)

In Kuwait, two soldiers "field shaving" without running water, a mirror, and certainly no aftershave lotion. (Photo by 101st Airborne Division Public Affairs)

President George W. Bush alerts the nation that Saddam Hussein and his two sons have forty-eight hours to leave the country. "Failure to do so will result in military conflict." (White House photo)

As the 101st Airborne Division moves forward into Iraq, the 101st mobile command facility is rigged and airlifted into Iraq. (Photo by 101st Airborne Division Public Affairs)

Three First Brigade officers say goodbye to one of their own, Capt. Christopher Seifert, who died at the hands of one their own, Sgt. Asan Akbar. (Photo by 101st Airborne Division Public Affairs)

Major Gen. David H. Petraeus and Brig. Gen. Ben Freakley in the D-Main command facility during a deep attack on the Karbala Gap. (Photo by Sgt. Thomas Day)

The division's number 1, Maj. Gen. Petraeus, talks with his assistant division commander of operations, Brig. Gen. Ben Freakley, during a deep attack on the Karbala Gap. (Photo by Sgt. Thomas Day)

The 101st Airborne Division D-Main war room during a deep attack on Karbala, with Maj. Gen. David H. Petraeus in command. (Photo by Sgt. Thomas Day)

The 101st Airborne Division D-Main war room, with Maj. Gen. David H. Petraeus in command. (Photo by Sgt. Thomas Day)

The 101st's 1 and 2 – Maj. Gen. David H. Petraeus and Brig. Gen. Ben Freakley on the road to Baghdad. (Photo by 101st Airborne Division Public Affairs)

A Third Infantry Division Abrams tank rolls north towards Baghdad. (Photo by Sgt. Thomas Day)

An attack on a school that the Iraqi military used as a command center and a weapons cache point. (Photo by 101st Airborne Division Public Affairs)

A soldier prepares to mount a CH-47 Chinook helicopter for movement into Baghdad. (Photo by Sgt. Thomas Day)

A field nap with a group of 101st soldiers. (Photo by 101st Airborne Division Public Affairs)

Major Paul Fitzpatrick surveys Saddam Hussein's Mosul palace as a potential new home of the 101st Airborne Division's command staff. Later in the day, Fitzpatrick advised Maj. Gen. Petraeus to commander the palace, a recommendation Petraeus swiftly followed. (Photo by Sgt. Thomas Day)

A group of 101st soldiers survey the new home of the division headquarters, Saddam Hussein's Mosul palace. (Photo by 101st Airborne Division Public Affairs)

Specialist Roth Quedrau, 801st Main Soldier Support Battalion, 101st Airborne Division (Air Assault), sets a basketball net for the Mosul gymnasium. The 801st is renovating the facility that was destroyed by looters. (Photo by Sgt. Thomas Day, 40th Public Affairs Detachment)

Left: Captains Ben and Maggie Smith at their 2002 wedding. Right: Captains Maggie and Ben Smith at the Quyarrah Airfield. (Photos provided by Maggie Smith)

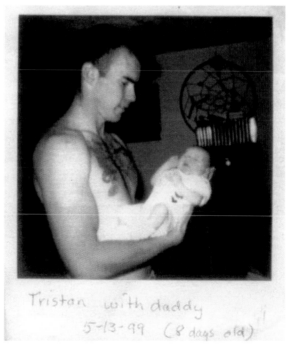

Tristan with daddy
5-13-99 (8 days old)

Troy Jenkins with his newborn son. (Photo provided by the Jenkins family)

Major Gen. David H. Petraeus, 101st Airborne Division (Air Assault) commanding general, thanks a soldier from the 2-44th Air Defense Artillery Regiment for his part in training a company of Iraqi Civil Defense Corps soldiers. (Photo by Sgt. Thomas Day, 40th Public Affairs Detachment)

Above: Specialist Blake L. Selesnew of the 51st Chemical Company surveys what was believed to be a nerve agent, later determined to be a pesticide. (Photo by Sgt. Thomas Day).

Top right: Major Gen. David H. Petraeus, 101st Airborne Division (Air Assault) commanding general, escorts L. Paul Bremer, head of the Coalition Provisional Authority, to meetings inside a 101st Airborne compound in Mosul. (Photo by Sgt. Thomas Day, 40th Public Affairs Detachment)

Right: Major Gen. David H. Petraeus with a group of Iraqi city council members and religious leaders. (Photo by 101st Airborne Division Public Affairs)

Right: A meter just outside the 7-101st Aviation Regiment's sleeping tents counts the days Company B has been deployed supporting Operation Enduring Freedom and Operation Iraqi Freedom. (Photo by Sgt. Thomas Day, 40th Public Affairs Detachment)

Below: A 101st patrol stops on the way to Mosul as a convoy of helicopters flies by. (Photo by 101st Airborne Division Public Affairs)

A 101st patrol marches down a muddy street. (Photo by 101st Airborne Division Public Affairs)

Above: A 101st patrol in Mosul. (Photo by 101st Airborne Division Public Affairs)

Right: One of the six members of the recently elected Tal Afar city council swears into office at city hall. The Tal Afar election was one of only three fully democratic elections that have been held in Iraq, along with Sinjar and Avgani. (Photo by Spc. Chris Jones, 40th PAD)

Right: Nineveh Province Governor Ghanim al-Basso. (Photo by 101st Airborne Division Public Affairs)

Below: A First Brigade patrol in the small Northern Iraq town of al-Hawd. (Photo by Sgt. Thomas Day)

Right: Major Gen. David H. Petraeus, commander of the 101st Airborne Division, and members of the Mosul City Council tour a cement factory in Sinjar, the largest in Iraq. (Photo by 101st Airborne Division public affairs)

Below: Command Sgt. Maj. Iuniasolua Savusa, the Third Brigade Rakkassans top enlisted soldier, directs traffic at a Tal Afar intersection. In an area bereft of civil authority in the aftermath of the invasion, simple policing tasks like directing traffic often fell on soldiers, albeit far more junior soldiers than Suvusa. (Photo by 101st Airborne Division Public Affairs)

Lieutenant Col. Christopher Holden, a battalion commander for Col. Joe Anderson, with an injured Iraqi boy. (Photo by Spc. Blake Kent)

Major Gen. David H. Petraeus gives a talk to his senior officers and non-commissioned officers at the Quyarrah Airfield. (Photo by 101st Airborne Division Public Affairs)

Right: It is back to school for the children of Mosul, Iraq. The children begin this school year in a newly renovated building though, and also have computers to learn on. The reconstruction work was done by the 8-101st Aviation Brigade, 101st Abn. Div. (AAslt.) and the donations of computers and school supplies came from U.S. companies. (Photo by Spc. Blake Kent)

Below: The young women of the Tall Kayf Secondary School for Girls celebrate the reopening of their school after a 101st Airborne Division (Air Assault) $13,000 reconstruction project. (Photo by Sgt. Thomas Day, 40th Public Affairs Detachment)

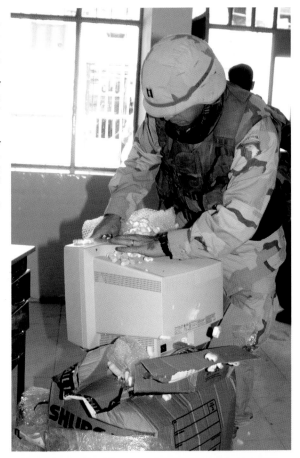

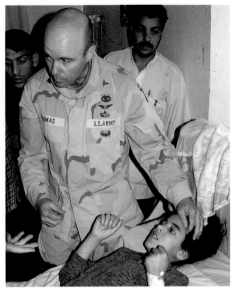

Above: Two players one from the 'Screaming Eagles' team and one from the Sharafeya team battle it out for the soccer ball in the final game of the season. The 'Screaming Eagles' won the game 2-1. (photo by Spc. Mary Rose Xenikakis)

Top right: Lieutenant Col. Richard Thomas, the division surgeon, looks over a injured Iraqi child hurt during a June riot in Mosul. (Photo by 101st Airborne Division Public Affairs)

Right: Major Gen. David H. Petraeus, 101st Airborne Division (Air Assault) commanding general, and Ghanim al-Basso, Interim Mayor of Mosul, fill up on oil from the Kisik Oil Refinery. The oil refinery was not even functional before 101st soldiers helped rebuild the facility with local contractors. (Photo by Sgt. Thomas Day, 40th Public Affairs Detachment)

Major Gen. David H. Petraeus, 101st Airborne Division (Air Assault) commanding general, tours the Quyarrah Oil Refinery with Saleh Ahmed (right), who maintained the facility for seventeen years after it was shut down during the Iran-Iraq war. (Photo by Sgt. Thomas Day, 40th Public Affairs Detachment)

The attack that killed HVT #2 and #3. (Photo by Sgt. Robert Woodward)

A 101st soldier mans a .50 caliber weapon during a night patrol. (Photo by 101st Airborne Division Public Affairs)

A 101st soldier on a patrol in Mosul. (Photo by Spc. Chris Jones)

Soldiers break in to a barracks room at a suspected terrorist training camp. (Photo by Spc. Chris Jones)

Sergeant Maj. James Pleamons with his newest reenlistee, Sgt. Claudia Tapia. The 101st bucked expectations in Iraq, exceeding reenlistment quotas in a combat tour. (Photo by Sgt. Thomas Day)

158 soldiers from the 101st Airborne Division (Air Assault) raise their right hands as they take their re-enlistment oath during an Independence Day celebration at a former Saddam Hussein palace where the Division Main Element is located in Mosul, Iraq during Operation Iraqi Freedom on July 4th, 2003. (U. S. Army Photo by Sgt. Michael Bracken)

Specialist Booby Cobert of Casper, Ala., of the 1-94th Field Artillery Regiment (Fort Bragg, N.C.), helps load 1.2 Billion Dinars into a couple of trucks en route to two banks in Mosul. (Sgt. Thomas Day, 40th Public Affairs Detachment)

158 soldiers from the 101st Airborne Division (Air Assault) salute as the fifty states and their date of entry into the Union are read during their re-enlistment ceremony at an Independance Day celebration at a palace where the Division Main Element is located in Mosul, Iraq during Operation Iraqi Freedom on July 4th, 2003. (U. S. Army Photo by Sgt. Michael Bracken)

Secondary students from Mosul take their yearly final examination in Islamic studies. Examinations for Mosul students started July 5 and will continue until the end of the month. (Photo by Sgt. Thomas Day, 40th Public Affairs Detachment)

An Iraqi Civil Defense Corps formation salutes during the playing of the Iraqi National Anthem. (Photo by Sgt. Thomas Day, 40th Public Affairs Detachment)

The Joint Iraqi Security Company poses with Maj. Gen. David H. Petraeus. (Photo by Pfc. James Matise, 101st Airborne Division Public Affairs)

The Kurdish Peshmerga platoon of the newly formed Joint Iraqi Security Company marches to class. (Photo by Pfc. James Matise, 101st Airborne Division public affairs)

Left: Acting Secretary of the Army Les Brownlee speaks with 101st Airborne Division (Air Assault) soldiers Thursday at the 101st Division/Main element. (Photo by Sgt. Thomas Day, 40th Public Affairs Detachment) Center and right: Mosul Interim Mayor Ghanim al-Basso kicks-off construction on a new wing to the al-Khansa all-girls high school in Mosul. (Photo by Sgt. Thomas Day, 40th Public Affairs Detachment)

A little elbow grease got the Qayyarah Oil Refinery running again. (Photo by 101st Airborne Division public affairs)

Right: Colonel Joseph Anderson, commander, 502nd Infantry Regiment, 101st Airborne Division (Air Assault) speaks at the opening ceremony of the Mosul Public Safety Academy. (Photo by 101st Airborne Division Public Affairs)

Below: Defense Secretary Donald Rumsfeld during a visit to Mosul. (Photo by Sgt. Robert Woodward)

Above: Brigadier Gen. Frank Helmick, Mosul Deputy Mayor Khasro Ghoran (center), and Trevor Flugge (left), the CPA senior agricultural advisor, watch as Dr. Sawsan lil-Sharify, Iraqi deputy minister of agriculture speaks during an agriculture symposium at Mosul University Monday. (Photo by Sgt. Thomas Day, 40th Public Affairs Detachment)

Right: Sergeant Sean Driscoll of Clarksville, Tenn., 926th Engineering Battalion, examines a package with one of hydro pumps for a Mosul Dam Lake irrigation system. (Photo by Sgt. Thomas Day, 40th Public Affairs Detachment)

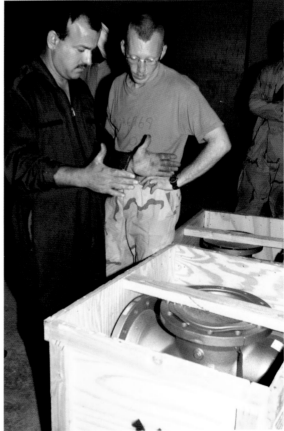

A 101st soldier loads up a commandeered Iraqi munition. The 101st aggressively sought weapons caches left by the Iraqi army as soon as the division arrived in Nineveh. (Photo by 101st Airborne Division Public Affairs)

Major Gen. David H. Petraeus, 101st Airborne Division (Air Assault) commander, speaks at the opening ceremony of the Samer Ames Eagle Support Cafe at the Division Rear military compound. The facility, which took 10 weeks to construct, had a gift and jewelry shop, a shopping market, a restaurant and an Internet room. (Photo by Spc. Chris Jones, 40th PAD)

A 101st element loads up commandeered Iraqi munitions. (Photo by 101st Airborne Division Public Affairs)

The two-year anniversary of September 11, 2001, is marked at the D-Main palace. (Photo by Sgt. Robert Woodward)

The Saddam Hussein dinar is retired for good as any remaining bills are died in red ink to denote their worthlessness. (Photo by Spc. Chris Jones)

Right: Actor Bruce Willis performs with his blues band in Tal Afar. (Photo by Sgt. Thomas Day)

Below: Actor Bruce Willis peers out a CH-47 Blackhawk helicopter before taking off for Tal Afar from the Mosul Airfield. (Photo by Sgt. Thomas Day)

Major Gen. David H. Petraeus, commander, 101st Airborne Division (Air Assault) speaks to a crowd during the 716th Military Police Battalion assumption of command ceremony where Lt. Col. Ashton L. Hayes took control of the battalion after the death of former commander Lt. Col. Kim S. Orlando Oct. 16 in Karbala. (Photo by Spc. Chris Jones, 40th PAD)

Major Gen. David H. Petraeus with Lt. Col. Ashton Hayes during Hayes' assumption of command ceremony following the death of Lt. Col. Kim Orlando, the 716th Military Police Battalion commander. (Photo by Sgt. Robert Woodward)

Above: Lieutenant Col. Linda Richardson, 5-101st Aviation Regiment commander, speaks during the memorial ceremony for her four soldiers who died in a UH-60 Blackhawk crash in Tikrit, Nov. 7. (Photo by Sgt. Thomas Day, 40th Public Affairs Detachment)

Right: A 101st Airborne Division chaplain looks over the aftermath of the divisions' worst day in Iraq. (Photo by Spc. Chris Jones)

The morning after seventeen 101st soldiers were lost in a two-helicopter collision in Mosul. (Photo by Spc. Chris Jones)

Major Gen. David H. Petraeus, 101st Airborne Division (Air Assault) commanding general, presents a challenge coin posthumously to Sgt. Michael S. Hancock, 1-320th Field Artillery Regiment, who died on October 24 during a mission. (Photo by Sgt. Thomas Day, 40th Public Affairs Detachment)

Lieutenant Col. Richard Carlson and Capt. Sung Kim, Carlson's battalion chaplain, remember Staff Sgt. Morgan D. Kennon during a memorial ceremony. (Photo by Sgt. Robert Woodward)

Hundreds of soldiers paid their final tributes to Command Sgt. Maj. Jerry Wilson, command sergeant major of the 502nd, and Wilson's driver, Spc. Rel Ravago, at the soldiers' memorial ceremony here Wednesday. Wilson and Ravago were killed in an ambush Nov. 23. Photo by Spc. Chris Jones, 40th PAD

Colonel Joseph Anderson (left) comforts a soldier during a memorial ceremony for his longtime deputy and confidant. (Photo by Spc. Chris Jones, 40th PAD)

Staff Sgt. Scott Benge speaks at the memorial ceremony at the Division Main compound in Mosul. (Photo by Spc. Chris Jones, 40th PAD)

Maj. Gen. David H. Petraeus looks over an entry point of the Syrian-Iraqi border, manned by a company of First Brigade soldiers. (Photo by 101st Airborne Division public affairs)

A cargo truck crosses the Iran-Iraq border into Iraq as a mural of two ruling Iranian clerics greets incomers going the other way. (Photo by Sgt. Thomas Day, 40th Public Affairs Detachment)

This castle, overlooking a main entry point of the Iran-Iraq border, served as home for a 101st Airborne long range surveillance team looking to train Iraqi guards and plug the leaks of Al Qaeda-sponsored terrorists coming into the country. (Photo by Sgt. Thomas Day)

Captain Thomas Hough talks with Special Agents Larry O'Donnell and Alan Sperling of the U.S. Customs Office on a hilltop overlooking the Iran-Iraq entry point. (Photo by Sgt. Thomas Day, 40th Public Affairs Detachment)

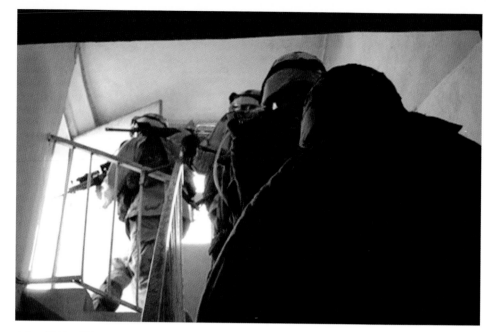

A June 2003 raid into a suspected enemy home. "Cordon and Knock" raids were exactly as the term implied. Infantry units would surround a home, knock on the door, and explain why they needed to search a home before actually entering. (Photo by U.S. Combat Camera)

Six 101st Airborne Division (Air Assault) soldiers vie for the title of Best Costume at the Quyarrah Halloween 10k Race. Cpl. Jason Walters (far right) of Dayton, Ohio, 6-101st Aviation Regiment, won the contest with his elaborate clown suit. (Photo by Sgt. Thomas Day, 40th Public Affairs Detachment)

The deployed version of Fort Campbell's Air Assault School. (Photo by 101st Airborne Division public affairs) (U.S. Army)

A moment of excitement at the Command Sgt. Maj. Marvin Hill-sponsored "Boxing Smoker." Hill practically played the role of Don King (who helped finance the event but did not attend), using the opportunity for 101st soldiers to box one another as a morale booster. (Photo by Spc. Chris Jones)

Two soldiers duke it out in the second round of a boxing match at the Boxing Smoker, where soldiers fight soldiers. (Photo by Spc. Chris Jones)

The head chef at the D-Main palace dining facility stands proudly by his Christmas cake before the holiday celebration. (Photo by 101st Airborne Public Affairs)

Below: Major Gen. David H. Petraeus, 101st Airborne Division (Air Assault) commanding general, speaks to a group of soldiers as he opens up the new M-4 firing range at the 3rd Brigade, 101st Airborne headquarters in Tal Afar. The range was deticated to three soldiers, Sgt. Justin Garvey, Sgt. Jason Jordan, and Sgt. Troy Jenkins, who have died with the "Rakkasans" during Operation Iraqi Freedom. (Photo by Sgt. Thomas Day, 40th Public Affairs Detachment).

Right: A 101st Airborne Division soldier saves a dog from drowning down a Northern Iraq canal. The photo, taken by Sgt. Robert Woodward of the 101st Airborne Division Public Affairs Office, was widely published back in the United States. (U.S. Army)

Right: A Mosul youth sports his new jacket, donated to him from the 2-44th Air Defense Artillery's "Operation Santa Strike." (Photo by Sgt. Thomas Day, 40th Public Affairs Detachment)

Below: Specialist Eric Voss of Halstead, Kan., 482nd Engineering Firefighters (Kansas Reserve), with his three top firefighters: Mohammed Aziz, Raed Ganim Jassim (Honor Graduate) and Sami Hammadali Hamad. (Photo by Sgt. Thomas Day, 40th Public Affairs Detachment)

the language to understand the message. Barron climbed up a ladder to the top of the wall to see what was going on. The two men indeed were carrying AK-47s, and continued to carry their weapons, as if they heard nothing and they were doing nothing wrong. "Hey you, stop … stop!"

Their final admonition was ignored, and as the two men turned towards Barron and his two gunners, it was time to skip two of the four S's and just shoot. As the two men fired careless pop-shots at the compound, Barron took out his own nine millimeter and fired back. Somehow the two men managed to jump in their getaway car and move out of range before Barron and his gunners hit their targets. They would be back. Barron didn't see much, but he saw how the men had managed to pack into a white four-door junkyard car with three other men already inside. They were headed south, towards the battalion command center, with the weapons factory and an apartment building obstructing his view beyond about one-hundred yards. Barron got on the radio and alerted everyone listening on the network about the white car.

On the other side of the road, with Second Platoon, First Lt. Joe Florszac got on the radio to page Barron. He had seen the vehicle too. The white junkyard car whipping around the corner from around weapons factory – that, he told Barron, was the car he was looking for. "Yeah," Florszac said, "that is definitely the car."

Barron had no reason to doubt him, but he wasn't certain. When faced with the decision of to kill or not to kill, Barron needed to be certain. There were thousands of white junkyard cars in this country, he thought. The car wasn't slowing down. He needed to decide now. "Open fire," he told the two platoons on the radio. "Open fire!" And so they did. From the two walls, shooting down at the vehicle, at least one man in the passenger's seat was hit and dropped limp on the dashboard. Others were likely killed too, but Barron couldn't make out the others through the blood on the windows. The car slowed down, almost to a stop, and Infantry soldiers from both compounds rush towards the compound with their weapons up and pointed towards the vehicle. Nobody in the vehicle ever fired back. Barron couldn't even see a weapon in the vehicle. The driver, seemingly unhurt, locked eyes with approaching infantry and slammed the gas. Barron told his soldiers to hold their fire this time.

It was a feeling that tied Barron's stomach in knots. Had he, or hadn't he, just ordered the deaths of innocent civilians. Minutes later, Konz arrived back at the compound. "Sir, the vehicle is heading north," Barron told his commander, pointing north towards where the 2-70th tanks were staged. They knew what to look for, Konz thought. Besides, they wouldn't have time to worry about it.

The "prison" walls surrounding the two warehouses provided Konz protection and concealment from everything – everything except that largely abandoned apartment building behind the weapons factory. He had only been back from the No Slack headquarters for about five minutes. His company hadn't even caught its breath from engaging the white car. It wasn't the most opportune time for the company to start taking fire, but that was the case when the familiar sound of small arms fire started coming from the top floor of the apartment building.

Barron, still uncertain about the earlier engagement, took the company's First and Third Platoon into the building. Vehicles with mounted .50 Calibers followed towards the building. It was going to be a stubborn target, and Konz alerted the No Slack command center and hinted they may need air support if the enemy forces in the building refused to come out alive. From the top of the walls, the gunners could see that there were more than just a few unruly insurgents moving around up there. Apaches were on their way.

Searching the building room by room, the team found three men, later identified as Syrians whose business was just to kill Americans. They didn't put up much of a fight when they were found, but the upstairs element still was far from laying down their arms. Rather than needlessly risk the rifle team by ordering them upstairs, Konz started pounding the building with mortars. Barron's team made certain to abandon the building before they had a fratricide incident. The mortars were precise, but still, they shot back. Then the Apaches arrived. One rocket after another had failed to quiet the target. Practically the entire division's capability to destroy a fixed target had succeeding in reducing the building to a skeleton of its former self, but had failed to kill the men in the building.

Konz had reached his tolerance level. So too had Hughes. The solution was an Air Force strike. Through the blue Iraq skies, flying at lightening speed, a British Tornado fighter jet arrived just in time. "Here it comes," Konz warned his soldiers. Down it came – a 500-pound bomb right on the money. Suddenly, all went quiet. Inside the building, there were no survivors. The building itself had been pulverized into a cloud of dust. That was the last Charlie Company heard from the enemy that day.

The rest of Charlie Company's stay at the warehouses was spent clearing the immediate area. The blast heard around Al Hillah was enough to keep the remaining enemy presence on ice. Third Brigade was on its way from the west. Lieutenant Col. Chip Preysler led the 2-187th Infantry with the rest of Third Brigade following behind. He and Hughes would link up after seizing their objectives. Together, their battalions would seize the remaining parts of Al Hillah and clear the city, block by block.

For Lt. Barron, the culmination of this episode of war would come only when his company commander pulled him aside. Konz had just got off the radio with some forward elements that had pulled over the bullet riddled white car. In the trunk was a load of AK-47s. Indeed, Barron had ordered the shooting of the enemy, not the innocent. His conscious was cleared.

The next day, Preysler and his battalion were gone. Hughes had spoke to the Third Brigade command staff the day before, drawing up plans to move out and push up north. Now the Rakkassans were gone and No Slack was stranded. Before Hughes knew what had happened, Maj. Gen. David Petraeus pulled into his compound. "I'm giving you Hillah, take charge of this. First Brigade's being chopped up to the 82nd, but you hold Hillah." Petraeus did not have time to explain the how's and why's. "Chris, it's your town."

Hughes was being assigned the eastern corner of the Karbala-Al Hillah-An Najaf triangle that was left for Bastogne brigade and the 82nd Airborne's 3-325th Infantry Regiment. Lieutenant Col. Marcus DeOliviera and his 1-327th Infantry Regiment manned An Najaf; Lt. Col. John Castle and his 82nd Airborne troopers took Karbala. Third Battalion, attached to Linnington and Third Brigade, continued up towards Baghdad. The elements left to the triangle were not going to fight in any more battles in this war. They were left to start rebuilding the cities they had just defeated and to clear the way for the Hajj, a sacrosanct Muslim pilgrimage to Mecca that had been obstructed for three decades under Saddam Hussein's government. For the Shi'ia sect of Iraq that had questioned America's resolve to defeat Saddam after Gulf War I, when President George H. W. Bush decided not to attack into Baghdad after the 1991 liberation of Kuwait, the coalition protection of the Hajj sent a clear political message.

In An Najaf, a suspected chemical weapons site believed to be storing small amounts of mustard gas failed to materialize. Five soldiers were evacuated from the site after experiencing nausea, vomiting and burning skin. First Brigade, as sympathetic as they were to their ailing soldiers, couldn't help but celebrate the suspected smoking gun. It was not to be. A Brigade chemical team deployed immediately to the site and came back with a negative reading. The substance was later believed to be just a pesticide. Several other false alarms would follow, many leading to more common pesticides.

Petraeus had expected, not feared, that Saddam would use chemical weapons. He thought the moment would come after the 3rd Infantry Division crossed the Karbala Gap, a choke point for V Corps along Highway 8, or on the outskirts of the Baghdad. The coalition was past the Karbala Gap and was approaching the Iraqi capital. Yet no chemical munitions had been moved to any forward units. On April 3, Petraeus gave the OK for the division to lose its MOPP suits and go back to wearing the regular Desert Camouflage Uniforms. No 101st soldier ever had to dawn his or her mask for an actual chemical attack.

Linnington's Third Brigade was only in Al Hillah for two days. The division needed to move quickly, the fight for Baghdad had begun. The brigade was ordered to set up at an airfield in Iskandiriyah, then prepare for an air assault into South Baghdad. The airfield was formerly occupied by the dilapidated Iraqi Air Force and secured by the 3rd Infantry Division before the 101st arrived. A mural of a grinning Saddam Hussein welcomed the Rakkassans to their new home. By morning, that mural would be removed and replaced by the Rakkassan patented Torie logo.

The Eagle Forward team followed Third Brigade into the airfield. Days later, the D-Rear elements, commanded by Brig. Gen. Edward Sinclair, joined them. Petraeus and Second Brigade too were on their way. The Iskandiriyah Airfield had become the Screaming Eagles new, consolidated home. Aviation pilots and crews had reached the Iskandiriyah Airfield hungry for dust-free landing zone to stage their helicopters. Instead, they got more nightmares. "It was as dusty or dustier as (FARP) Shell," Col. Gregory Gass later complained.

On the way to Iskandiriyah, Petraeus was cheered like a king. Not because he was the division's top soldier – the locals had no idea – but because he, like every other 101st soldier, was wearing an American flag. It was a sure sign that the war was about to come to a victorious end. The local people would never have the courage to come out of their homes and cheer the invading force unless they knew there would be no repercussions from the former regime. The show of support for the division commander was tantamount to a victory lap in a NASCAR race. But, Petraeus knew, the war was not over yet.

It was becoming apparent that the Ba'ath Party militia and the Fedayeen elements had put up a stronger fight in An Najaf than the Iraqi Republican Guard was ever going to put up in Baghdad, that the CG had realized. It was a reality that had refuted every prediction by every general officer in the coalition. Quite simply, the coalition had expected to roll through Southern Iraq directly to Baghdad without much resistance. Once that happened, the coalition would have to fight block by block in Baghdad with the fiercely loyal Iraqi Republican Guard. Instead what happened was exactly the opposite. Air Force operations had destroyed much of the Republican Guard, division by division. The 101st Airborne had even destroyed two division's worth of equipment with deep Apache attacks, according to estimates. By the time V Corps and the Marines were approaching Baghdad, the Iraqi Republican Guard was left in ruins with little will to fight.

Lieutenant Gen. William Wallace had observed to Rick Atkinson that "the enemy we're fighting against is different than the one we'd war-gamed against," during the battle of An Najaf. The comment was published in the next day's *Washington Post,* and caused consternation from the Bush administration. Wallace was later told to keep away from the media for a little while by CFLCC Commander Lt. Gen. David McKiernan. But what Wallace was trying to articulate though wasn't anything that every V Corps field commander hadn't noticed already, certainly not Petraeus.

"Clearly, the Ba'ath militia and the Fedayeen became the enemy that fought and resisted most fiercely, whereas the other expected enemy, the Republican Guards really did not materialize, except in a few locations." Before the approach to Baghdad, Second Brigade's feint into South Al Hillah was the first and only large-scale engagement with any Iraqi Republican Guard elements. "Other than that, I am not aware of the Republican Guard fighting as a coherent force anywhere else in the V Corps area." The surprise resistance from the paramilitary forces meant that instead of making a B-line straight for Baghdad, V Corps would have to fight in the southern cities where had few expected to fight. For the 101st, it also meant supporting the 3rd Infantry Division's movement with deep Apache attacks well in advance of the 101st's own movement.

Only one battle remained for the 101st: Baghdad. By April 4, the 3rd Infantry Division cavalry seized the Saddam Hussein International Airport, renaming it the Baghdad International Airport. Both the 3rd Infantry Division and the First Marine Expeditionary Force had begun cordoning off the city and moving in towards key objectives. The Marines had begun moving into the eastern approaches of Baghdad as the 64th Armored Brigade prepared to roll in from the west.

The coalition was on Saddam's doorstep. Everybody could sense the regime's imminent doom. Everybody but a doggedly recalcitrant man by the name of

Mohammed Saeed al-Sahaf, the Iraqi Minister of Information who quickly became known as "Baghdad Bob." With V Corps and the Marines closing in on Baghdad, Baghdad Bob insisted that the coalition was not even in control of Umm Qasr, a city taken weeks earlier. Of Pfc. Jessica Lynch, the information minister claimed she was being "treated" when the coalition forces "took her" from the An Nasariyah hospital. Finally, for Baghdad Bob's final act, al-Sahaf claimed the coalition was "not even (within) 100 miles" of Baghdad with the grumbling of American tanks shaking the ground he stood on. "They are not in any place. They hold no place in Iraq. This is an illusion."

Sadly for Baghdad Bob, it was no illusion and it was no joke. The first nail in the coffin of the regime came on April 5. The previous night, Col. David Perkins, took what became certainly the most daring adventure of the war. At sun up, he ordered his 1-64th Armored Battalion commander, Lt. Col. Eric Swartz, to roll straight towards the Saddam International Airport to link up with the 3rd ID forces in the airport. To that point, Perkins had so little intelligence on the airport's defenses that he could not even tell Swartz what size a unit he would be going against – much less enemy battle tactics and capabilities. It had the potential to be a suicide walk, Swartz thought. He even initially thought his commander was joking. "No, I need you to do this," Perkins replied, according to one embedded correspondent's report. "Momentum," Perkins remembered later, "was the key."

The attack would be launched from Objective Saints and would ultimately finish right back where it started. The 3rd ID tanks would run through the city, destroy some targets and return to their starting points – the drive-by shootings the 101st officers so detested. The blitz into the Saddam Airport was not intended to hold ground but to weaken the enemy and clear Highway 8 leading into the objective. It would also have the effect of taking a big chunk out of the city while debunking Baghdad Bob's fiction for the entire city to see firsthand. Holding ground would be for the infantry; Perkins just wanted to put the dagger in the heart of the regime.

As planned, the 1-64th Armored Regiment moved out at daybreak. Not until the tanks rolled at "O-Dark Thirty" did Perkins see how surprised the Iraqi soldiers were. The enemy was caught sleeping – literally. As the tanks rolled by, the confused Iraqi Republican Guard watched, wondering what the heck just happened. At one point, a 1-64th Armor platoon arrested an Iraqi brigadier general walking casually to work. The Iraqis had actually believed Baghdad Bob – they thought the coalition really was more than 100 miles outside the city.

The ones who did fight could only fight flat-footed. The 3rd ID artillery would pave the way, launching strikes at enemy roadblocks transparently located where they could choke the coalition's entry into the regime district. Every M-1 Abrams Tank in the 1-64th came back with at least a few battle scars, but with the exception of one, all tanks were ready to go for the next Thunder Run. The first blitz into the airport had given the 3rd Infantry commanders an idea of how defeated the Baghdad defenses had become. It had started to become apparent that the Iraqi will to fight had collapsed in Baghdad, but they knew the fight wasn't over yet. The next Thunder Run, aimed right into the downtown regime district, was to be a stake in the heart of the regime, both in a tactical and figurative sense.

After returning to Objective Saints, Perkins teamed up his 1-64th with his 4-64th Armored Regiment for the final door slammer on Operation Iraqi Freedom. On the evening of April 6th, with the terrain mapped out in front of him, Perkins drew a straight line from Saints to the regime district located along the Tigris River. The objectives for the tank battalions would have to be spacious for the Abrams and Bradleys to maneuver. Alleyways, for example, were to be avoided. Another concern of Perkins was to control the lines of supply and communication. To fail to do so would in effect throw 900 soldiers into a fight, alone, in a city of nearly seven million. It was a Mogadishu-like scenario Perkins wanted nothing of. Fuel could be an Achilles' heel. The Abrams, Perkins knew, could only hold eight hours of fuel. The lane to the regime district was Highway 8. The choke and ambush points were certain to be three underpasses, titled Objective Larry, Moe, and Curly. That was the scenario Perkins presented to Swartz, 4-64th commander Lt. Col. Flip Decamp, and 3-15th Infantry Regiment commander Lt. Col. Steven Twitty.

Twitty's 3-15th was tasked with holding the Three Stooges objectives while the tank battalions moved towards the regime district. Perkins had the option of sending the 3-15th ahead of the tank battalions to clear the choke points. He chose to lead with the tanks. By sending the 1-64th and 4-64th first, a potential drawn out battle with 3-15th could be avoided. The tanks would be freed up to sweep through the objectives quickly before handing over the objectives to 3-15th – a drive-by shooting with a follow up force to hold ground.

If everything went as planned, decision time for Perkins would come at hour four. If Twitty's 3-15th could not defeat the resistance that was certain to come, Perkins was not about to leave his tanks without fuel, stranded in Baghdad. The commander was ready, if need be, to cut his losses and call his tanks back to base for another day. Nobody wanted that to happen. Baghdad Bob had continued taking to the airwaves with his claim that the April 5 Thunder Run had been defeated by the Iraqis. Perkins, his commanders and his soldiers weren't about to go back to Objective Saints without putting an end to Baghdad Bob's act.

The morning of April 7 began inauspiciously. The brigade headquarters at Saints had been hit with an enemy mortar killing five soldiers. It was tragic setback but not one that would delay the planned operation. The tanks rolled as the sun came up, again catching the Iraqi defenses by surprise. Locals on the rooftops cheered as the Iraqi soldiers ran towards the convoy, inviting their own certain and violent deaths at the hands of the 3rd ID Abrams tanks. The Thunder Run had become quite a spectator's sport, with Baghdad citizens cheering like rowdy football fans.

After the tanks rolled through the underpasses, the 3-15th Infantry jumped on Objectives Larry, Moe, and Curly. As hour four approached, he radioed Lt. Col. Swartz for a report. "Tactically, we have a lot of the key objectives," he was told – meaning the open areas where his tanks were less vulnerable were all secured. "Everything is going as planned." He got a similar response from Decamp. For Twitty however, things were not going as planned. In fact, things were starting to heat up.

The enemy had counterattacked after the tanks passed by. For every one platoon holding the objectives, Twitty estimated for Perkins that the enemy had attacked with more than 300 soldiers. "Sir, right now the road is not secure. I can't secure the highways anytime soon." Decision time had arrived for the commander. Without the Three Stooges objectives secured, it would be unwise if not impossible to run his highly vulnerable supply trucks into the forward objectives for fuel and ammo resupply. They would be mobile bombs. The supply trucks would give the enemy a target in which to take out an entire American squad with one single RPG round. If Perkins called the tanks back, he could get them back to Objective Saints without any of his Abrams running out of fuel. He would avoid leaving the tanks stranded inside of Baghdad – the Mogadishu scenario. It would also mean a victory for the enemy and Baghdad Bob. Nobody was prepared to accept that.

Calling all stations on the net, Perkins ordered his Abrams to shut down their engines as the Bradley tanks patrolled the streets. It would buy the 3-15th more time to defeat the counter attack and give the supply trucks time to move. "Sir," it was Twitty again, "we've just been hit. We're really getting hammered." Perkins would later learn that two of his soldiers were killed in the enemy counterattack at the Three Stooges objectives. It was getting worse at Objective Moe, where Twitty had only an hour's worth of ammo. It was time to move.

Perkins came back on the radio and ordered his tanks to get in the left hand lane, allowing the supply trucks to move in the right lane and top off their fuel. The Hemmit supply trucks would have to shoot their way to the objectives. With soldiers on one side of the trucks shooting at the enemy with their M-16s, soldiers on the other side would pick up ammo and load up the 3-15th Infantry underneath the fusillade. Incredibly, at all three objectives, not one coalition soldier was killed. Their Hemmits had taken a beating but the soldiers continued to the tanks. Again, one side of the trucks would provide cover fire while the soldiers on the other side would fuel the Abrams and Bradleys. Again, not one soldier was lost. When the supply trucks returned, each and every one of the trucks had been hit with enemy fire. The trucks and the soldiers in the trucks had moved through Baghdad with flat tires and shattered windows. Perkins asked a specialist from one of the Hemmit trucks how he could have done what he did in Baghdad? "Well sir, we knew this fuel needed to get into the city. We just stuck our M-16s out the windows and hauled ass."

The supply shot in the arm was enough to propel the 1-64th and 4-64th Armor into the final objective: the regime district. Perkins' bold movement into the regime district came short of destroying the Iraqi resistance in Baghdad, but the outcome of this war was no longer in doubt on April 7. Saddam was no longer sitting on this throne and Baghdad Bob had shut up.

Chief Warrant Officers Ronald Young Jr. and David Williams, two 11th Attack Helicopter Regiment pilots shot down in a deep attack over the Karbala Gap, had earned an early redeployment home. After their capture by Iraqi forces, their uncertain faces broadcasted all over the world, attempts to free Young and Williams during a March 25 three-hour firefight had failed. In Young's hometown of Lithia Springs, Ga., Ronald Young Sr. could only pray for his son's safe return, which at that point looked uncertain at best. Family friends and concerned locals flooded the family with their own prayers and support. The local jail sent a group on inmates to erect a flagpole in front of the Young's house, where one family friend inscribed, "United We Stand, CWO2 Ron Young, POW 3-24-03" in the wet cement.

For a week, the two POWs were held blindfolded in a Baghdad prison, listening to coalition bombings with the reality that they could be sitting in middle of a target. As ground forces closed in on the Iraqi capital, the Iraqis moved Young and Williams in an ambulance through a firefight with U.S. Marines in East Baghdad. Again, Young and Williams could only listen as they moved right through the crossfire. They would eventually be thrown in a house, under tight surveillance. A Marine commander, acting on a tip from a local, uncovered the house not long after. "Get down on the ground!" Young and Williams were still blindfolded, but they were wise enough to know that those commands were not coming from their Iraqi captors. Within weeks, they would be on their way back to Fort Hood, Texas, with five other POWs from the 50th maintenance Company, Spc. Shoshanna Johnson included.

The fight for Baghdad had indeed been decided, but it was not over. Baghdad needed to be occupied before the coalition could claim victory in Iraq. Waiting for the orders, Second and Third Brigade were ready to take control where the 3rd Infantry Division and the First Marine Expeditionary Force could not. Formed up in a seemingly endless line along the Iskandiriyah Airfield strip, the 101st Aviation Regiment Blackhawks were ready to deliver the infantry into battle once again. The 101st Airborne Division was assigned most of South Baghdad. Second Brigade's objective would be everything west from Highway 8. Third Brigade would take a zone east of Highway 8 and take back its Third Battalion, who was already operating in the city. The mission was not expected to be heavy in combat, but the weapons were locked and loaded. The 3-7th Cavalry Regiment, a 3rd Infantry asset, had already swept the area, but it had not occupied and cleared the area.

On April 10, the air assault into Baghdad began. The objectives were heavily populated neighborhoods away from the downtown "money" regime targets. Packed into the helicopters like a Jack-in-the-Box, the infantry soldiers could start seeing the city gradually approach under the Baghdad sun. It had no high-rise towers – Baghdad held nothing in common with New York City – but it was expansive. Any commander flying over the city could see how difficult clearing Baghdad block by block was going to be. For every soldier in the 101st Airborne Division, the 3rd Infantry Division and the First Marine Expeditionary Force operating in Baghdad after the helicopters landed, nearly a hundred civilians in Baghdad were walking the streets. Many of them, the coalition knew, were enemy soldiers disguised as civilians.

Colonel Michael Linnington did not expect a great deal of resistance before his planned air assault of two of his battalions into South Baghdad. His expectations were accurate.

Hundreds of enemy soldiers had massed around the eastern entry of the Saddam International Airport. With infrared vision, Col. Linnington's 3-187th Infantry could see the enemy positions as clear as day and destroyed the defense line with TOW missile after TOW missile. Superior coalition battlefield technology had made the engagement like target practice.

In the air, First Lt. Monica Strye's trigger finger felt the affects of the operational condition change. Having identified an unmanned enemy artillery piece in South Baghdad, Strye asked the 3-7th Cavalry headquarters if she could destroy the target. Acting on orders from V Corps, the answer she got was a quick, "no." The division could not afford to cause any more collateral damage. The objective would have to be cleared, without an explosion, on the ground.

Security and Stabilization Operations, or SASO, had begun for the 101st Airborne Division.

"We're going up towards the Syrian border," Sgt. Maj. Hector Torres had told his Eagle Forward soldiers. "It's going to be a two-day GAC (Ground Attack Convoy)." Few accepted the news with any amount of excitement.

On April 18, Lt. Gen. William Wallace paid another visit to the 101st Airborne Division and Maj. Gen. Petraeus. In what would be his last visit to the division in Baghdad, Wallace was presented a gold-plated AK-47 the division had seized in Baghdad. The weapon was tantamount to a victory cigar for Wallace. His tour with V Corps would soon be over and he would be out of country. The 101st Airborne Division would not. The 101st command staff had started preparing to move from Baghdad suspecting the capital would not be home for too much longer. V Corps was slated to take everything north of Baghdad; the First Marine Expeditionary Force would take everything south. Wallace had come with the news: the 101st Airborne had better be ready to move north, way north. The city was Mosul, historically the "capital" of northern Iraq.

To the 101st's south – in the heart of what came to be known as the "Sunni Triangle" – would be the 4th Infantry Division, which had arrived in Kuwait several weeks earlier and immediately headed north. The two divisions had crossed paths in Baghdad on April 14. The Fourth Infantry Division was destined for the city of Tikrit – the birthplace and hometown of Saddam Hussein. In Baghdad, the 3rd Infantry Division would stay in place. Having been in theatre for more than six months waiting in Kuwait, most 3rd ID soldiers expected to be on their way home before or shortly after Memorial Day.

Spirits were high. The coalition had won. Saddam no longer held power in Iraq. In 21 days, the two corps force had steamrolled through Iraq and taken a city of 7 million people. It was a show of force that left no doubt that the American military was the greatest fighting force in the history of modern warfare. The swift defeat of Saddam's forces was the work of a military that could seemingly accomplish any mission, no matter what the given political milieu. Quite simply, it was the work of a military in a hurry, in more ways than one. The goal was to fight and win a war. Done. Now the goal was to find a way home. The 101st was heading the wrong direction on that front. All redeployment operations were to run through Kuwait.

As the 101st Eagle Forward lined up at the Iskandiriyah Airfield to move north, Brigadier Gen. Ben Freakley huddled his team. The Eagle Forward group had become like family. Freakley was the proud patriarch, but he was still wearing a five-pointed star on his Kevlar helmet. Addressing the soldiers as "a band of brothers and sisters," the division's number two officer could sense a certain level of complacency and he wasn't happy about it. "From this general officer to you," he started, "this war isn't over yet." He continued, "It's like in football, if you stop running on a play before the whistle has blown, you're going get leveled. Well, I haven't heard the whistle blow yet."

War for Sgt. Troy Jenkins was remarkably unexciting for the first week. In Kuwait, Sgt. First Class Rick Johanningsmeier decided he needed to play both the role of platoon sergeant and friend to Jenkins. He decided to push Jenkins back to the rear as the 3-187th Infantry pushed across the border with the 3rd Infantry Division. Jenkins would drive a humvee in support of the front line, not with the front line in combat. "Listen, you only got a short time left," Sergeant Jo told him. "I don't need you making mistakes and getting yourself hurt out there." He was bluntly telling Jenkins that he thought he could be a liability. He was vulnerable to lose focus. His divorce was going to proceed as his company pushed toward Baghdad. If anyone needed to be kicked back, it was Jenkins.

With his company first sergeant firmly behind Johanningsmeier's decision, Jenkins knew that fighting the move to Headquarters Company was futile, but he tried anyway. "You only got a little time left," Sergeant Jo firmly told his defiant NCO. "I don't need you out there. Keep doing what you're doing." Jenkins was assigned to the most dilapidated vehicle the unit had. It was an archaic humvee that would need extra special attention if it were to make it through the deserts of

Iraq. Dutifully but somberly, he accepted his new assignment. It wasn't like he had a choice.

By the time he reached Baghdad in April, Jenkins' thirst for combat could have been quenched already. An earlier incident happened when Jenkins, sitting behind the wheel of his humvee, reacted to an ambush of RPG and small arms fire on his convoy. Jenkins did what he was trained to do: he slammed the gas pedal and got out of the kill zone. He had been shot at before and he knew how to react. So did the men in the Delta Platoon vehicles with mounted Mk. 19 grenade launchers and .50 Caliber weapons – they moved towards the enemy team and eliminated the threat and without casualties. Meanwhile, as the convoy moved at top speed on the desert sand, just above sixty miles an hour, Jenkins had just about got out of the kill zone when things got odd. In a vehicle up ahead, an unfortunate specialist fell out of his open-door vehicle without his weapon and was stranded in a cloud of dust when Jenkins' vehicle slammed the brakes. With no available seating for the soldier, Jenkins gave him one option: "Get on the hood." Still a bit confused, the stranded soldier did what he was told and held on for his life. Jenkins made no compromises on speed and the specialist got the thrill ride of a lifetime.

While the incident provided a helluva story to tell his buddies, he still missed being with his platoon. The division operating in Baghdad and Jenkins was on the shelf while his men fight the war. Facing an entire war from the sideline, he panicked. Headquarters life had lent itself to little combat, and with Saddam apparently finished, he felt like he had missed the opportunity to be a part of the war with his infantry brothers. He had already missed the attack on Al Hilla, Baghdad and Saddam International Airport. Whatever fighting was left, Jenkins was determined to be a part of it. So brazenly, after three weeks of doing what he was told, he started begging and pleading and with Sergeant Jo to go along with the patrols. Finally, Johanningsmeier relented.

Much to Jenkins' delight, the bell hadn't rung on the war, not yet. Pentagon Press Secretary Victoria Clarke had repeatedly insisted in the immediate aftermath of the fall of Baghdad that combat operations were still ongoing, in spite of the apparent downfall of Saddam Hussein. "Baghdad," she told the Pentagon press corps "is still a very dangerous place." After battles in Najaf, Karbala and Al Hilla, the relative ease the coalition had breezed through Baghdad had taken the global media by surprise.

Establishing a presence became crucial to finding any remaining enemy elements in the city, determining key infrastructure needs and, as the 101st put it, "wining the hearts and minds" of the new, free Iraq. Sergeant First Class Pete Johanningsmeier had got an early start on the last objective by the second week in April. Trying his best not to compromise the infantry doctrine of maintaining 360 degrees of visibility during foot patrols, Sergeant Jo found himself and his soldiers swarmed by friendly, or at least curious, citizens of Baghdad during presence patrols. They would get close and they would try their best to ask lots of questions, only muted by their inabilities to speak English. Some offered cigarettes; others offered American soldiers their daughters' hand in marriage. A few offered intelligence on enemy elements and positions. One man, a Kurd who did speak fairly fluent English, had his wife serve food to Johanningsmeier and his soldiers as they passed by his house. It was one of the friendliest gestures a soldier who had eaten nothing but MREs for six weeks could ever receive.

UXOs had littered Baghdad from both the American and Iraqi militaries. "They were everywhere," Col. Michael Linnington remembered. Soldiers on patrol had to walk with one eye forward and one eye to the ground.

It was like a six-year old on Christmas morning, only with a more adult flare, when Sgt. Jenkins woke up to go on his first patrol with his platoon. "Doc, Doc," Jenkins said as he not-so-gently woke up the platoon medic, Spc. Pete "Doc" Tenorio. Taking a deep breath and rubbing the haze from his eyes, Tenorio arose from his slumber with Jenkins' back end in his face. "Something's wrong with my ass." Everyone in the tent was watching. Even Tenorio was laughing.

Raring to go with his M-4 rifle gripped so tight his fingertips were as white as cotton, Jenkins finally got his chance to march with Bravo Company on April 16 in Al Jihad. It was another presence patrol with a focus on looking for UXOs around Baghdad. Enemy contact was not likely, according to division intelligence, but Jenkins wasn't too disappointed. All that mattered was that he finally got his wish and got out of Headquarters Company, at least for one day. But just before Johanningsmeier was about to give his pre-action brief, he grabbed Jenkins to rain on this parade a bit. "Hey Sergeant Jenkins, if you're going, you're going to carry the radio."

"Yeah, sure, no problem Sergeant," he instinctively responded. It was not a duty he had expected or in any way desired. He would be at the rear of the patrol with his weapon often slung on his back. The radio operator can be compared to the quarterback in football: he's the man who the men up front in the trenches protect. Jenkins was no white-shirt quarterback.

Standing in a gaggle oriented around Johanningsmeier, the platoon was told about what to look for on patrol. Coalition artillery had rained projectiles all over the neighborhood they were about to cover. Many "duds" had not detonated but were still considered very dangerous. Already at that point, several incidents had been reported in Baghdad on local civilians picking up grenades or anti-personnel mines, just to have the ordinances explode in their hands. It would be a problem that the coalition would have to tackle for months in the aftermath of the war. Psychological operations and public affairs teams were running all-out operations to inform the local populace about the dangers of UXOs. Some just didn't get the message, and many of them were young children.

The platoon would be divided into squads who would fan out to cover the area and rendezvous at two Al Jihad intersections. Delta vehicles, with mounted .50 Caliber rifles would follow along for fire support, just in case they needed it. Sergeant Jo went over every potential situation his soldiers could face. On top of the usual contact with the enemy drills, Johanningsmeier made sure everyone knew what to do if the patrol came upon an unexploded ordinance. In the event of a local carrying a UXO up to a soldier, for example, the soldier would step away and calmly explain to the person that the "thing" they're holding is an explosive and needed to be gently set down on the ground. "Number one, stop the person bringing the UXO to you. Point you're weapon if you need to, get them to stop and everyone in the patrol back off!" Once that situation was diffused, Sgt. Jenkins would be the one to call in for an explosive ordinance team to either explode the ordinance on the spot or take it back to be destroyed away from the city. Sergeant Jo hadn't lost anyone. Every soldier's head was in the game. So with his soldiers on the same page, the platoon sounded off with a loud, thunderous "Air Assault" and headed out.

Before the battle for Baghdad, Iraqi anti-aircraft pieces had established defenses in and around street intersections in Baghdad, making problematic targets for American artillery in high traffic areas. The Al Jihad district was an especially high traffic area. Risks for civilian casualties were high during the push into Baghdad and remained high with artillery duds littered around the Baghdad streets. Coalition forces had yet to run a presence patrol in the area Bravo Company was about to tour on April 16. It would be up to the Rakkassans to sift through the crowds and clean up the UXOs in the area. The crowds were an X-factor too.

While the division soldiers had been for the most part cheered in their way into Baghdad, days earlier Johanningsmeier was not as celebrated when he pulled a reconnaissance mission in the neighborhood. Sergeant Jo and a small convoy had rolled through the area, where they were greeted with a luke-warm response at best.

Jenkins was told about the overzealous locals getting in the way of the patrol, and it didn't take long for him to see what the other soldiers in Bravo Company were talking about. "One thing you may have to do is push them away. Make sure you keep that 360 degrees," Johanningsmeier had admonished his soldiers before the patrol. The neighborhood had no electricity or running water and the locals were not shy about bringing their grievances to the soldiers on patrol, which at their level was futile. Jenkins, or anyone not a field grade or general officer, could do nothing about the situation at that point. But on and on they went, sometimes screaming with frustration, and all Jenkins could do is look blankly at his linguist, who was doing his best at taking the heat. The efforts to "win the hearts and minds" of the people of Baghdad were starting to go sour with the adults. With the kids however, the Americans were still heroes, even if their parents were skeptical. Doc Tenorio, a kid lover, seemed more than happy to take on the kids if the rest of the patrol wanted nothing to do with them. That idea didn't square with Jenkins. "Doc," he hollered to his only medic in the squad, "get back in middle of the fuckin' patrol."

Sergeant Jo spent most of the patrol in an Iraqi ambulance; the division had quickly contracted their services for the coalition. He shadowed the patrol from the ambulance with a convoy of empty troop carriers behind him as his first squad covered one area and his second squad, with Sgt. Jenkins, covered another. Both squads would move out to about two kilometers and circle back in. "The UXOs were all over the place. Everything had been dropped in that area, in the schools, around the Mosques. One time we picked up around ten of them inside a school and the school yard," Johanningsmeier recalled months later. To his surprise, this patrol had gone without much incident as the ambulance weaved its way through traffic to pick up the first squad at the designated rendezvous site. They had done what they needed to do, played nice with the locals. With the first squad on board, Johanningsmeier led the convoy to meet the second squad. They were late. Looking at his watch, then peering impatiently out the window, Johanningsmeier noticed that the crowds of people had begun rushing towards something that had piqued their interests. Before he could collect his thoughts long enough to worry, Sgt.

Stephen Day, another radioman for second squad, hailed his platoon leader. There had been an explosion. "We got a man down, over." Johanningsmeier didn't wait for details. He grabbed his lieutenant and sprinted to the location.

He didn't know what had happened, even if it was an American who was down. It took about a minute to run to the site and push his way through the crowd, but once he saw what had happened, he had answers. A UXO had exploded, the man down was indeed an American soldier and that soldier was Sgt. Troy Jenkins.

Specialist "Doc" Tenorio had immediately gone to work on Jenkins. There were others who were injured, including Pvt. Javier Zoquier, who lost several of his teeth from more than fifty feet. Jenkins was the most serious. His left leg and hand were gone into a pool of blood. Jenkins was still alive, but he had gone into shock. Staring at the sky, unable to see what had been done, Jenkins sensed he was in trouble. His head was racing at one-hundred miles an hour. "Doc, give me some morphine." An obvious request. Tenorio quickly gave him what he needed.

Doc Tenorio knew when he was working on Jenkins that he was looking at the man who may have just saved his life. He had been to the right of the patrol when he heard Jenkins scream for him. Instinctively, Tenorio rushed towards Jenkins. There, a group of four girls had approached Jenkins with what he knew to be an American cluster bomb. Looking down at the girls who barely came up to his waist, he reacted by reaching down for the ordinance with his left hand as he pushed Tenorio away with his right. Just at the point when both Jenkins and the girl were touching the bomb, it exploded. On top of the other soldiers who were hurt, two of the girls who approached him with the UXO were killed instantly; a third would die later that day at the hospital. The explosion went to Jenkins left. If the blast had gone to Jenkins' right, Tenorio and maybe Jenkins' himself would have been killed instantly.

Tenorio kept the conversation with Jenkins going as he administered emergency first aid. He was not going to make it if the bleeding continued, so Tenorio tied a ratchet strap around his leg as tight as he could get it. Air Medical Evacuation (MEDEVAC) could not land in the area and Jenkins needed to get moving out of the area quickly. A humvee ambulance convoy was called to the scene, a much slower option than an Air MEDEVAC. For Tenorio, the convoy seemed to take so long that it was like it was coming from Kuwait. In actuality it took about ten minutes. The other soldiers in the platoon, including Sgt. Day, pulled security around the scene, keeping the curious locals away. Day had taken shrapnel in his legs and his face from the explosion. Johanningsmeier dropped his rucksack and joined the perimeter.

The most important person in the world in that moment was Doc Tenorio. His leaders would later commend him for his work that day, but Tenorio and Jenkins knew the odds.

Jenkins was carried into the ambulance and evacuated to a secure area where two Blackhawk helicopters were waiting. Johanningsmeier went with him. "Was there anyone else that was hurt?" Sergeant Jo knew the answer was yes.

"No, Jenkins, everyone's fine. Sergeant Day took some shrapnel, but he's going to OK."

"What happened?" Jenkins asked. His skin was cool and sweaty and his face was as white as a ghost. Jenkins was going to pass out if Johanningsmeier couldn't keep him talking, but he didn't want to answer the question. What he wanted was for Jenkins to talk about things that made him happy. That was an easy one. Sergeant Jo shrugged off the question and asked him, "I wonder what Triesten and Brandon are doing right now?" Jenkins expended every ounce of strength he had left just to smile.

"Sergeant, make sure my boys are OK." He turned away to look at the Iraqi sky out of the window. Troy Jenkins was half the world away from his boys, but at that moment, it was like they were both lying right next to him.

"You're going to be OK, Troy. C'mon now." Neither men were emotional by nature, but Johanningsmeier was no granite statue either.

Jenkins was drowned in morphine, which is why Johanningsmeier didn't think much of his next comment. "Sergeant, I'm sorry I messed up." Johanningsmeier had indeed given explicit instructions on how to approach an UXO, and if Jenkins had reacted as he was trained to react, he would not have been injured as badly as he was. He also would have watched as a cluster bomb destroyed all four girls and likely Doc Tenorio. That was his choice. In the blink of an instant, Jenkins chose to sacrifice himself to save his brother in arms and a young girl he never met.

At the crux of the decision were his sons, who would grow up knowing their father was a hero, but would indeed grow up watching their crippled dad or would not even see their dad at all. And then there was the woman he loved, Becky Weiss. In watching the 10:00 news while talking on the phone with a friend,

Becky caught a glimpse of the footage from the explosion. The broadcasted war had come to her living room. She didn't think twice about the images until she heard the name "Jenkins." The conversation stopped in its tracks. Incredibly, the televised war had managed to catch footage of the wounded Troy as he was loaded up on the humvee ambulance in Baghdad. The knot in the pit of her stomach told her all she needed to know. "It's him, I know it. I can just feel it," she told her friend. Her friend tried to convince her she was being irrational, but Becky couldn't shake the feeling that the soldier she just saw on TV was the man who had told her "I love you" on the phone weeks earlier. All night she flipped through the channels, anxious to see the footage again.

What she had seen was the last Becky would ever see of Troy alive. Sgt. Troy Jenkins died on April 22 in intensive care in a military hospital in Germany.

CHAPTER 5

THE GREAT BEGINNING

The official orders came down from V Corps and were released to the division on April 20. The division titled the movement, "Operation Eagle Victory." Not much was known at the command level initially about Mosul. Did the division need to attack the city or just ride into town and get to work rebuilding the city? That was the question Col. Joseph Anderson would need to answer. On Easter Sunday, Anderson drove north up to Mosul with much of his brigade command staff. They spent the first night in Tikrit and drove the last leg of the trip the next day. Petraeus had ordered his Second Brigade commander to scout out the area and report back to him. He needed to know where to set up bases. He needed to know where the problematic areas were. What needed to be fixed? Where could the 101st just leave the area and its people to its own devices?

Seated in his humvee, Anderson pulled into Mosul before lunchtime and started making the rounds after slam-dunking an MRE. He saw what had been reported – lawlessness, looting, and businesses that had locked their doors and hibernated during the war. "The number one cause of destruction," Anderson said, "was looting, not the war … everything was closed and ransacked." Somewhat to his surprise, Anderson never encountered resistance. Not one shot was fired at the convoy or by the convoy. For the war-tested commander, the feeling of not being shot at came as an oddity. After fighting in every city the 101st had fought in for a month, it was kind of nice to enter a city without having to first destroy a battalion or two of enemy fighters.

He had found a number of areas that would be perfect for compounds and command points, one he fell in love with at first sight. Along the Tigris River was a military compound perfect for the Second Brigade headquarters. Anderson knew he had to grab the compound before one of his rival commanders took it first.

Anderson reported back to the CG that night and advised that the division not attack into the city. Petraeus heeded his advice. For the time being, the Mosul Airport and adjacent airfield was the division command post in the city. The facility had been used primarily by the Iraqi military. The next day, Anderson had his battalion commanders saddled up on the 101st Aviation Regiment Blackhawks and air assaulted his entire brigade by nightfall. It was the new "longest air assault in 101st History."

Before Anderson arrived, the Eagle Forward team had set up shop in a former Iraqi officers club, looted clean. The 101st Airborne Division's Rendezvous with Destiny had taken the Screaming Eagles from Kuwait to Najaf, Al Hillah to Karbala, Baghdad and now the keystone of northern Iraq. Mosul was about to become home.

The movement north to Mosul provided the 101st Airborne Division soldiers with the first opportunity to see something few had seen since they left Fort Campbell: dirt and green grass. The sands of the southern deserts gradually disappeared as the 101st moved up Highway 1. Almost like another country in itself, the northern Iraq landscape bared little resemblance to the southern region. A perceptive soldier might have noticed that the temperature seemed to drop a bit. The sight of sheep and sheepherders replaced the camels that seemed to outnumber the people in the south. It was like a transatlantic flight for soldiers accustomed to cleaning sand out of their ears and noses for nearly two months. Sandstorms were hardly going to be a problem anymore.

Mosul and the northern region were as close to home as the real thing as anyone was ever going to see in Iraq. From Kuwait to Mosul, the 101st Airborne had fought through the fiercest battles of the war, the most punishing sandstorms, and moved through cities that would become household words during post-war operations: Tikrit, Iskandiriyah, Baghdad. With the war over, and the chaos of battle in the division's rear-view mirror, Mosul was going to be a novel but somewhat welcome sight. The new scenery was a nice change, but it only whetted the appetite for soldiers to redeploy.

The orders were to go north to Mosul, a city more than twice the size of Nashville, and take over the four provinces of Nineveh, Dohuk, Erbil and

Silomania. The mission would be to restore basic services to the region. No time frame was given, and no plans for redeployment were issued. That didn't stop the low-level speculation. Rumors circulated that the CG was given the option by the Pentagon to redeploy by the end of the month and he rebuffed the offer. Petraeus was even clandestinely given the name "General Betray-us" by some of his frustrated soldiers. It was the kind of irrational fiction that can only be written by soldiers eager to go home after war.

With the objective accomplished, the truth was that nobody knew what to expect in Mosul, but that didn't stop some from speculating and fantasizing. The 101st Airborne Division had never been used as a stabilization force before, they were in Iraq to fight a war and the war was over. Officers of the 2-320th Field Artillery Regiment put together a pool on what date their unit would arrive back at Fort Campbell. Most put their money on dates in June and July. One soldier, Capt. Dion Milliner, hedged his bet on March of 2004. Everyone in his unit thought he was out of his mind.

The 101st was not the first on the scene in Mosul. A small element of the 26th Marine Expeditionary Unit was occupying the city, staging at a Mosul Airfield that they now shared with the 101st. Only the small Marine element that had entered the area from a ship on the Mediterranean Sea had manned the second largest city in Iraq. Combined Air Force and U.S. Special Forces missions had defeated Saddam's forces with relative ease in Mosul, with the help of Kurdish militia forces who called themselves "The Peshmerga," (a term translated as "those who face death") and with the help of a number of civilian and military leaders eager to avoid bloodshed. Undermanned, the small Marine force had occupied the city after Saddam's forces were driven out, with little authoritative control. One confrontation with an unruly crowd had left more than a dozen locals dead, leaving the 101st with a strike against them when the division moved in.

Mosul was a stronghold of the former regime with a sizable population of former Iraqi soldiers. More than 1,100 retired generals lived in the area. The 101st needed to get back on track in winning the hearts and minds of the local populace. What could also give the 101st problems, Petraeus knew, were the interethnic rivalries within the region. "We knew it was going to be a real challenge up there. It's a very ethnically diverse population. They have a Sunni-Arab majority but a very sizable Kurdish minority, a smaller but important Christian minority, a Turkmen minority, some Shi'ia, some cross cutting elements of tribes, political parties, and technocratic groups."

The Marines had used the air base as a consolidation point and the terminal as a roof over their heads. When the Eagle Forward team arrived, the Marines wasted no time in packing their bags. They started redeploying home before the entire 101st Airborne Division arrived in the city.

As the Marines set sail on their way back to the United States, the 101st started planting their roots. A building that was once an officer's club for the Iraqi army became the new Eagle Forward post. The division discovered that the northern region was rich with what the 101st needed, beginning with the airport. The Mosul Airport runway was long enough for a C-130 cargo aircraft to land and take off, with still enough room at the airfield to hold the division's arsenal of Blackhawks, Chinooks, Apaches and Kiowas.

Mosul was a unique town in Iraq. Bisected by the Tigris River, the city's nighttime skyline could leave anyone wondering how such a beautiful place could have so many problems. Mosul was a city at high noon. When the division found the city in April, few shops were open, schools were empty and the people were still uneasy about leaving their homes. The Saddam Bridge, which would not be named after the disposed dictator for long, rarely had more than one or two cars passing through at any given time – an unthinkable thought after the city woke up from its slumber.

One explanation for the state of fear in Mosul was the state of anarchy and chaos that followed the defeat of Saddam's forces. Banks, government buildings, hotels, oil refineries, and anything that had any connection with the former regime, were so thoroughly looted that almost anything that could be was carried, detached and hauled away. The Marine element was woefully insufficient to stop it. Everything from couches to toilet seats were subject to mobs of people who wanted everything they could get their hands on. They destroyed anything they couldn't loot. No symbol of the former regime was as detested as Saddam Hussein's Mosul palace, an awesome monument to Saddam's opulence. Built in 1992, shortly after the first Gulf War, the palace rested on a hill that overlooked the city, visible from nearly every neighborhood in Mosul – certainly by design. A statue of a fist with a missile sitting on the knuckles, located in the middle of the street that passed through the property, was a not so subtle reminder of Saddam's military stranglehold on his people. The palace's strategic importance for the regime was obvious. It created a feeling of Ba'ath Party omnipotence despite the fact that Saddam Hussein was rumored to have only once visited the palace and didn't even stay the night.

The fall of Saddam meant for the first time the citizens of Mosul could see what was behind the walls that surrounded the main palace. It was an opportunity that few missed. Everything that could be stolen was taken off. The palace had become such an attraction that street vendors had set up shop at the scene.

Major Paul Fitzpatrick, 101st Airborne Division headquarters commandant, was tasked with scoping out possible sites for the Division-Main compound on April 22. Among the possible locations: A barren patch of land across from the Saddam Bridge, a deserted factory, and Saddam's Mosul palace. The obvious favorite among the division staff was the palace. Visions of a gold plated nirvana filled the heads of the imaginative officers.

When Fitzpatrick and his driver found the palace, the building was little more than a shadow of its former self. The looting had stripped it bare. With nothing left to take after the first few days, the looters managed to breakup parts of the marble floors for souvenirs. The palace walls became a forum for vandals to discuss the U.S. led invasion. In Arabic, one local had written, "Where are you Mr. Saddam?" Another wrote "No USA" in English.

Fitzpatrick and his driver instantly became celebrities when he arrived. A crowd of thousands flocked towards his vehicle. Fitzpatrick was all alone in the estate. At one point, the headquarters commandant stood at a second floor balcony, overlooking the crowd and his vehicle, and waved to the masses like the palace's former owner. The gesture elicited a response that would have made a rock star or a politician blush. Fitzpatrick had found the new home for the D-Main. The crowd had charmed him, but he knew the fun couldn't last if the division was going to quickly establish law and order in the city. That night the decision was made. Second Brigade secured the area days later and the Mosul residents lost their new palatial playground.

At nearly the exact moment that Fitzpatrick stood before the thousands of fawning locals, the man who would really be king landed in Mosul. Major Gen. Petraeus arrived in the city on April 22nd, when he immediately got to work on his first priority, meeting local leaders. He wanted a local government assembled and elected in some kind of democratic process as soon as possible. In no other large city were other divisions even thinking about a local government; Petraeus was thinking about it and wanted it done in the matter of a couple of weeks. "We did nothing but that for ten days," he noted. The CG and a small team worked doggedly to set up a convention. They planned it for May 5, where every faction of the region would be equally represented in the process, culminating with the election of an interim mayor of Mosul and governor of the Nineveh province. The dialogue was not likely to be cordial: five different men claimed to be the rightful governor of the Nineveh province.

Only one could be king. In the days leading up to the election, a working group of representatives from each constituency of the region laid out the ground rules for the election process. After a week of non-stop deliberation, it was agreed that the mayor would be a Sunni Arab, the vice mayor would be a Kurd, and one assistant mayor each would come from the Assyrian-Christian and Turkmen sects. The agreed conditions helped to quell the expected mob-scene on May 5. The setting was a former Ba'ath Party Social Club – an ironic place for the summit that would determine the Ba'ath Party's successors in Nineveh. Two-hundred and thirty two delegates packed the hall. After hours of sparring, a 24-member interim city council was produced. Like the crafting of legislation on Capitol Hill, some came away happy, others didn't. They broke for lunch a few hours late, some too sick to their stomachs to eat. Then it was time to elect the governor. One man stood out in the crowd. Ghanim al-Basso, like Petraeus, had been a two-star general. His military career was truncated after Al-Basso's brother and uncle were brutally murdered by Saddam's hitmen after a 1993 plot to overthrow his regime had been uncovered.

The ballots had been tallied before mid-afternoon and Petraeus was told the winner. Ghanim al-Basso was the new interim governor of Nineveh and mayor of Mosul. In winning the election, al-Basso became the first legitimately elected official in Iraq since 1968. "By being here today, you are participating in the birth of the democratic process in Iraq," Petraeus told the city council. The election marked what would be a start of a partnership and a friendship between the two generals. Twice a week at City Hall, Petraeus and al-Basso would sit side by side for the governing council meetings. Any measure supported by al-Basso would need a two-thirds majority of the council. Petraeus knew that al-Basso, with all of his strengths, was a project. Petraeus would be his mentor and his partner. He would not be his boss. While Petraeus consulted al-Basso on important decisions, he never compelled the government one way or the other. Gradually, as conditions allowed, the 101st and Petraeus would transfer responsibility to al-Basso and his government. In the meantime, Petraeus would do all that he could to help the new governor and the new government to succeed. "Your success is our success," he often told the province council.

In Mosul, Petraeus had his chance to reach the level of the pantheon of general officers who came before him. "I remember someone asked me in Mosul if Macarthur was your role model for what you doing. My gosh, Macarthur remade a country, he rebuilt Japan and reestablished every one of its institutions. I'd never have thought that what we were doing was in any way analogous to his incredible achievement." But Petraeus knew, in Japan, Macarthur had the foundations of a democracy that Iraq didn't have. When the coalition crossed into Iraq in March, more than thirty percent of Iraq could not read, including more than half of the country's women. To begin the healing and rebuilding process in Iraq, Petraeus called to mind the work of America's mayor, the 2001 *Time* magazine Person of the Year. "I was thinking more along the lines of a Rudy Guiliani."

The tactics Guiliani used in New York still had particular significance in the city that now belonged to Petraeus. "Straightening out the city pothole by pothole," was the idea for the 101st commander. Rebuilding the Mosul police was a start, but only that. Petraeus wanted to change what he saw as a deeply imbued lack of respect for the rule of law. To do that, he turned to the lessons learned from Guiliani. Harkening on similar initiatives the former New York mayor launched in his eight years in the Gracie Mansion, Petraeus and his team sought ways to foster a strict rule of law and encourage pride in the city of Mosul. What was once acceptable, even encouraged, was now illegal. No better example of the new law of the land was provided than Petraeus' "Operation Tom Sawyer." "Sawyer," which took its name from the Mark Twain classic in which Tom inspired his friends to whitewash a sizable fence, would officially take to the streets later in the summer, aimed at painting over city walls that had been covered in graffiti. It was a page taken right out of Guiliani's book – literally. "The idea of sweating the small stuff applies not only to crime but to any challenge a manager faces," Guiliani wrote in his 2002 best-seller *Leadership*. "Graffiti (provided) another good illustration of the concept."

The Guiliani turnaround was remarkable, but the New York-Mosul analogy had its limits. After all, few criminals from any of the five boroughs would dare fire an AK-47 round in the air with expectations of impunity. In Mosul, it was different. Citizens of Mosul squeezed their firearms almost like they never expected gravity to bring down what they fired up. The coalition's introduction to Iraq's odd sense of firearm safety was no more evident than on April 28, Saddam Hussein's sixty-sixth birthday. Nobody knew where the former Iraqi president was celebrating his birthday, but that didn't stop thousands of people of Mosul from taking to the streets. Soldiers watching the skyline of Mosul from the Mosul Airfield "oooed" and "aaahed" at the sight of red and green tracer rounds flying in the sky like 4th of July fireworks. Soldiers closer to the action were not so amused.

Days later, while meeting with civilian personnel from the incoming Office of Reconstruction and Humanitarian Assistance, Petraeus termed the mayhem as "celebratory fire." While no shots were for certain fired directly at 101st soldiers with the intent to kill, some came awfully close.

The thrilling moments of Saddam's birthday highlighted an important conundrum to rebuilding Iraq. Where should the American soldiers lay down the law on Iraqi customs, like firing at will into the air to celebrate special occasions? It was a question that blurred the lines between cultural sensitivities and military necessities. What goes up must come down.

"The first thing we need to do," Col. Anderson told Maj. Gen. Petraeus after touring the city on April 22, "is establish a Civil-Military Operations Center." Petraeus was then still in Baghdad, but he understood Anderson's point. The division needed to quickly build an interface with the city leaders. "The place to do it is City Hall," Anderson said. The local government had abandoned the building during the war, but Anderson was intent on taking it back.

"If anybody was going to go anywhere for help or to give information, it was going to be at City Hall," Anderson recalled. The concept of the Civil-Military Operations Center came from Anderson's experience in the Balkans after the defeat of Slovadan Milosovich. It worked then and it was going to work in Mosul. Located at the heart of the city and just blocks from Anderson's Second Brigade riverside headquarters, City Hall provided an easily securable hub for local authorities and 101st officers to meet on neutral ground. It too had been looted, but a locally contracted construction company fixed the broken windows and painted the walls in a matter of days. Before April turned into May, the "CMOC" became operational and the temporary home to the 431st Civil Affairs Battalion, a reserve unit from Texas and Arkansas, and 101st Airborne public affairs assets. A Strike Brigade platoon secured the gates.

The CMOC's debut came on April 27, when Anderson and Maj. Susan Arnold, a lawyer with the Office of the Staff Judge Advocate, met with officials from the Office of Rehabilitation and Reconstruction. The ORHA officials were in town to do an immediate assessment of the area; Anderson was to be their guide. Colonel

(Ret.) Dick Nabb led the delegation. Nabb knew the region well; he had worked under Coalition Civilian Administrator Lt. Gen. (Ret.) Jay Garner while both were still on active duty during American-led efforts to monitor Saddam's activity in the Kurdish controlled Northern region of Iraq following the first Gulf War. At a roundtable in the Civilian Military Operations Center, in the heart of downtown Mosul, Anderson and the ORHA officials laid out what the military's role would be in rebuilding the city and where ORHA would come in. Money was at the crux. The division needed to start paying civil salaries in the area. Anderson needed Nabb's help in cracking the code of the central bank in Baghdad. They had the money and Anderson wanted a chunk of it.

ORHA had made a deal at the beginning. They had a roster of civil servants, including current and retired military, which they were going to pay an immediate twenty American dollars. It was a quick fix to a burgeoning problem. Anderson came away from the meeting without a long-term solution to the salary issue, but assured that he had a partner, not a bureaucracy, in the Office of Reconstruction and Humanitarian Assistance.

The meeting adjourned after a little more than an hour and Anderson directed the ORHA officials to the Nineveh Hotel, where he told them they had reservations. It had all been arranged, he told them. They'd be staying at the finest hotel in the city, where all of Saddam's most important visitors would stay when they came to Mosul. What he didn't give them was directions. There were two Nineveh Hotels. One was by Mosul University; the other along the Tigris River.

Blindly, the ORHA officials moved to the Nineveh Hotel, the wrong hotel, in their government-purchased SUVs. This Nineveh Hotel was easily the finest hotel in the city, an awe inspiring structure in the mold of the Egyptian Pyramids. Overlooking the Tigris, the hotel had a presence in the city almost equal to its next-door neighbor – Saddam's Mosul Palace. Its eight-story pyramid structure illuminated the Mosul skyline like the Northern Lights on a crisp January night. The Nineveh Hotel was the most "Western" building in the city. Inside, the hotel included two bars, a bowling alley and marble floors. From miles away, the hotel was as recognizable as the Empire State Building over the New York City skyline. The outdoor pool and bar cemented its status as the area's only "Five-Star" hotel. This was the kind of luxury an average citizen of Mosul could not even dream about.

This is why the average citizens of Mosul swarmed the hotel after the collapse of law and order in the city. When the ORHA delegation arrived, the hotel was hardly as regal as advertised. This hotel, supposedly fit for a king, was instead reduced to Mosul's largest playpen. The hotel's entire file database had been emptied out in front of the lobby. Every last window and mirror on the first four floors of rooms were shattered. The stench of urine was enough to turn stomachs. A band of looters had destroyed the Nineveh Hotel. This could not have been the work of a small group of outlaws. One disgusted ORHA official described the scene as "savage."

Still unaware of the Nineveh Hotel they did have reservations at, Nabb and the ORHA officials had to find accommodations at another hotel.

Colonel Joseph Anderson was supposed to be a doctor, not a soldier. Like Petraeus, he had grown up not far from West Point in the New York City suburb of White Plains, and like his future division commander, Anderson accepted admission to the United States Military Academy "for the challenge." It was a last-minute decision, he recalled, made after he rushed his application in just in the nick of time. Almost on a whim, the young Joe Anderson bagged his dreams of becoming a doctor by joining the Army – then still rebuilding from the rubble of Vietnam. The plebe year was tough. He sometimes doubted whether or not he had done the right thing. "I thought that place absolutely sucked," he recalled. "When I went there, you were treated like a kid. You had no freedoms, you made no decisions, you couldn't drink, you couldn't go off post, you were socially inept." West Point was no Animal House, but he stuck it out and in 1981, 2nd Lt. Joe Anderson was commissioned in the Infantry. He and his wife, Elizabeth, went off towards a partnership between them and the Army that would define their lives.

As a twenty-eight year old captain, he became a father. Like so many fathers in the Army, too many, Anderson missed much of his son Marc's infancy. He was deployed to Operation Just Cause in Panama while Elizabeth raised the baby. Anderson came home with a gold star on his jump wings, an award for his combat jump into battle. He had his own company, who he led into battle in the city of Rio Hato. He had his combat badge with the 75th Ranger Regiment. He came home as a guaranteed field-grade and a possible future general.

In Panama, Anderson had proved just how talented an officer he was. By 1998, he was fulfilling his limitless potential. As a lieutenant colonel, Anderson commanded a battalion with the 82nd Airborne Division, sending the last U.S. company into Haiti before the coalition left the country. Then it was off to Albania, where he led the first U.S. forces into Kosovo. As much as any field-grade officer coming to the 101st in the summer of 2002, Anderson was battle tested and ready to command soldiers in war. He also had a will to fight in the War on Terror, having lost a relative in the second tower of the World Trade Center. Anderson was a soldier, but he was also a New Yorker. In February of 2003, his sons Marc, fifteen, and Michael, eleven, would see their father off to war once again.

Marc was a football player. He was an independent young man, a trait instilled in him as a child when his father was in combat zones instead of at the dinner table. "Him and I, because of the first two years of his life, did not get to bond as much as my second child," Anderson painfully admitted later. With another deployment looming for his family, Anderson made sure to he would be the father for Marc he couldn't be in 1989. He needed his older son to take on a leadership role of his own. As a son of a colonel, classmates at Fort Campbell High School and other friends on the block would naturally turn to him to share some of the hardships. Anderson left for Kuwait feeling good about how his sons, especially Marc, would handle the coming months.

His family had been on his mind in An Najaf, Karbala, Baghdad, and now Mosul. The void in his life, like so many soldiers, was filled with faith. Anderson had been raised a Catholic. He rarely missed a Sunday mass and he wasn't going to stop because he was at war. "I think I'm going to become a priest after I'm done in the Army," he joked with one Mosul priest after Sunday mass. The city of Mosul, like Iraq, had a small but significant Catholic community. Anderson, by the time he was done, had made stops at all the Catholic churches he could find. One church Anderson frequented successfully mixed his work with his faith. The church priest was a city councilman.

"It gave me a connection," Anderson recalled of Sunday mass in Mosul. Connecting with the people, he knew from past experiences, was what was going to clean up the mess in Mosul. In Panama, he had helped heal Panama City's wounds of war. He ran weapons buy-back programs, set up checkpoints, and met and charmed locals. As any good soldier, Anderson learned from his experiences, remembered what worked and never repeated what didn't. It was a formative experience for Anderson that qualified him for Mosul duty a decade and a half later.

He followed in a lineage of Second Brigade commanders that included Col. Colin Powell, but it was Anderson who would be in command during the brigade's finest combat tour. They had fought in every city with the 101st on the way to Mosul – the only one of the three infantry brigades that could claim that distinction.

Second Brigade, simply put, was the MVP of the 101st during the push to Baghdad. Now Maj. Gen. Petraeus would call on Anderson and his Strike Brigade once again to pull his main effort in Mosul.

His company was a team of fiery, rugged infantrymen including a young Sgt. First Class Jerry Wilson. It was a friendship that began in 1986 when then Capt. Anderson was handed command of C Company, 2-187th Infantry Regiment in Panama (before Operation Just Cause). Technically a part of the Rakkassans, the company had not held up their brigade's reputation by Anderson's predecessors. It was a company that could only be described as a mess – drug problems, insubordination, and malaise. Even the company first sergeant couldn't keep up during morning runs after the first mile. Anderson was chosen because he was tough enough to clean up his company's act, but he knew he needed help. He got it from Jerry Wilson. Standing at 6'4", built like a tight end with nearly every training certification badge the Army offers its soldiers, Wilson was just the man Anderson needed. The two whipped the unit into shape. It was a special partnership. Anderson and Wilson would meet again.

As an instructor at the College of Naval Warfare in Rhode Island, Anderson was told that he was heading back to Fort Campbell in July. He was taking over Second Brigade. Colonel Anthony Tata, Anderson's predecessor, knew he was on his way out when he faced with filling his brigade sergeant major position. He had three choices, each of his battalion sergeant majors, for promotion up the brigade level. One of the choices: Command Sgt. Maj. Jerry Wilson. "I want Wilson," Anderson told Tata. "The guy I'd love to see be the brigade command sergeant major is Wilson." And Wilson it was. Just like 1986 in Panama, Anderson and Wilson were a team again.

Both were nearly two decades older. Neither had a strand of hair on the top of their heads. Anderson and Wilson at the top of Second Brigade were like brothers, in spite of their obvious genetic differences (Anderson was white, Wilson black).

During the initial weeks of 101st Airborne operations in Mosul, soldiers traveled around the city in one-vehicle convoys with their weapons on "amber" status – a magazine in the well without a round chambered. Nobody let their guards down, but everyone was aware that this city was not as dangerous as some of the spots the 101st had been before. Only a pocket of high-ranking Ba'ath Party officials hailed from the area, and Saddam's support in the area was nebulous at best. For the 101st Airborne, the first challenge would be a political. The division needed to establish a line of communication with the local populace. It would take months for the division to build a trust with the citizens; the first priority was simply to disseminate the division's message to as many Mosul locals as possible: American troops are here to help.

With next to no Arabic-speaking soldiers, the coalition needed to find some way to break the language barrier. For that, the support could only come from the local populace itself. English, as the 101st found out, was a part of the standard course of instruction in Iraq's primary and secondary schools, in spite of Saddam Hussein's distain for predominately English speaking countries. The number of people who spoke at least some English in the area pleasantly surprised the 101st field grade officers. For a country so isolated during the years of Ba'ath Party rule, the Americans did not have a great deal of trouble finding locals who spoke fluent or near fluent English. Few of the linguists that the 101st hired had actually been to the United States; most just learned by a textbook. They didn't have to know the language inside and out, but they did have to get the basic message. Before June, the 101st Airborne had hired its quota of linguists. Many qualified applicants had to be refused.

One linguist was scooped up in a hurry. He was born in Topeka, Kan., and his name was Fayz Younis Dabbagh, or just Vic, as his future 101st buddies would call him. His story started at the University of Kansas, where his mother, an American, met his Iraqi father as young civil engineering students. In 1953, when Vic was only two years old, his family left the United States to begin a new life in Iraq. Vic went on to study in England but never once made it back to the country of his birth. He had since made a life for himself in Baghdad and later Mosul, with his wife and three kids. His father died in 1977. His mother and his brothers and sisters had successfully moved back to Kansas years earlier. Dabbagh and his family were alone in Iraq – he had not seen his family in the States in more than thirteen years. With the coalition in town, this was his chance to be reunited with his stateside family. When Sgt. First Class Lonnie Harden, a 431st Civil Affairs NCO, was introduced to his linguist in April, Dabbagh had not been to the United States since his family left in 1953.

"I got a passport," Dabbagh told his new boss just after being introduced. "I'm trying to get enough money to bring my family back to the United States."

Money was not the only problem. Dabbagh's family needed their visas. Harden and his family, who also lived in Kansas, were eager to help. From Mosul, Harden called his family and asked his wife to contact Dabbagh's family just to let them know he was OK. Dabbagh had been unable to get in contact with his family since before the war. The call from Harden's wife Linda for the Dabbagh's family ended weeks of excruciating uncertainty. Linda and this family she had never met quickly became close. Vic and Sgt. First Class Harden became like "cousins." Within weeks, this became a personal matter, not just a diplomatic one. Harden and his wife worked intently on reuniting Vic Dabbagh with his family in Kansas.

Next to internal security, the core of the division's SASO effort was to solve the fuel crises. Fuel was at the genesis of nearly everything the 101st had planned to do to rebuild Mosul.

Following the defeat of Saddam, a fuel shortage crisis had reached catastrophic levels, well beyond what America experienced during the height of the OPEC embargo in the early 1970s. Fuel for electrical power, transportation and household use had gone dry. Fuel lines at private gas stations continued for miles and the black market for fuel had brought the city to its knees. The power supply in the city was running only about eight hours a day. The people of Mosul were getting restless. What the coalition and the community needed was benzene, diesel, and propane, and fast. Benzene and diesel were the building blocks of Iraqi power supply. Benzene was needed to fuel cars; diesel powered the generators that powered the Mosul homes. Neither were available anywhere. For cooking, locals used kerosene. That wasn't anywhere to be found either.

The cause of this catastrophe was a common problem for the 101st: looting. The Northern Iraq refineries had been destroyed. Truck drivers had balked at the idea of carrying fuel from Turkey and Syria into gas stations where their own security could not be guaranteed. More than $24 million in contracts, much of which to the Halliburton Corporation, were initially awarded to get fuel flowing back into the Mosul area. Fuel convoys rolling from the north were given almost presidential priority and security. In the Mosul area, fuel distribution points were established, also with heavy security, patrolled by soldiers from the 502nd Infantry Regiment and the 2-44th Air Defense Artillery Regiment.

At fuel distribution points, tickets were given to local citizens to carefully ration out the limited supply of fuel. Keeping order was sometimes a combat mission in itself, with eager locals pushing their way to the front of the line. "This is organized mayhem," Staff Sgt. James Boersma remarked at one unruly distribution site in Mosul. Propane prices at coalition distribution points were set at 250 dinar a tank, converting to less than one US dollar. Private retailers were permitted to sell their fuel at 500 dinar, still well under market value. The result of the coalition-imposed price controls was a rampant black market on fuel, particularly for wealthy businessmen who could afford to usurp the fuel from the poorer neighborhoods. The division even found a black market of fuel running through Syria.

The 101st worked to put a quick stop to the black market. "We went out and broke up a bunch of black markets and confiscated fuel," Maj. Gen. Petraeus recalled. "But the real way you break up a black market is that you have so much of a commodity that there's no reason for a black market. A black market is a secondary market in which people are paying additional money for a product so they don't have to wait in line for it. What you have to do is eliminate the line and then the black market goes away." That was the plan of attack. Internal production and additional imports would ultimately be critical. What was never an option, according to Petraeus, was raising the price of fuel.

Opening the doors of fuel trade with Syria and Turkey was crucial, but that was a short-term patchwork. The inflow of fuel from Iraq's northern neighbors needed to be supplemented by domestic production, something northern Iraqi production facilities were not capable of providing when the 101st Airborne Division arrived in the region. Iraq had an estimated potential of $25 billion in oil revenue that was going untapped because of outdated and inoperative facilities. Northwestern Iraq's two main oil refineries, the Kisik Oil Refinery and the Quyarrah Oil Refinery, were both heavily looted and in need of thorough, emergency renovations before the facilities could produce at full capacity. The Kisik refinery, which was working about seventy percent capacity before the looting, was operating at less than ten percent when the division found the broken facility.

The post-war looting had devastated the city of Mosul block by block. Local banks had been destroyed. The money vaults at many banks were broken into and cleaned. Personal finances were erased. One bank manager of the Mosul Central Bank found nothing but a dead man in his vault in the looting aftermath. Located in the heart of downtown Mosul, the Mosul Central Bank was especially hit hard by looters.

Local government and ministry offices were destroyed and would need to be rebuilt. The Nineveh Province Ministry of Education and Ministry of Water buildings, just to name two, had been ravaged. Post-war destruction continued at every target of opportunity, and no target of opportunity was hit harder than the Mosul Courthouse. The lawyers with 101st Office of the Staff Judge Advocate stopped dead in their tracks when they saw what had been done to the courthouse. It was located in the heart of the city, just blocks from the Mosul City Hall – two easy targets that were likely hit by the same band of looters on the same night. The 101st found the building so damaged that it was a wonder the courthouse was still standing. Remarkably, in rooms that were little more than four walls and a ceiling of soot, court remained in session.

The physical damage to the building, as they would learn later, was only the beginning. Nearly the entire file database had been burned to ashes. It had been standard for defendants to sit in prison for six months or longer waiting for the Iraqi court system to give them a hearing. With much of the database burned anyway, they would be forgotten. Blissfully, a clerk in the courthouse took as many important files home with him before the war.

With the Americans in charge, the burden fell on the new government to get things running again. That meant the soldiers of the 3rd Infantry Division in Baghdad, the 4th Infantry Division, then just arriving in Tikrit, and of course the 101st Airborne Division in Mosul and Northern Iraq, all had a job to do together. It was going to be up to the Army clean up the mess. That likely meant no early tickets home for anyone. For the 3rd ID, in country since September and the leading force into Baghdad, the well deserved ticket home would not be in their hands as early as expected. As for the 101st Airborne, there were simply no plans for the division to go home, it was as simple as that.

For the U.S. soldiers in Iraq and for the 101st Airborne Division, the post-war Iraq mission became a whole new ballgame on May 12. Arriving at Saddam International Airport, dressed in a blue pin-stripped Italian suit with a handkerchief in his left-breast pocket, Louis Paul Bremer III took the throne as the civilian administrator in Iraq. The king had arrived in Baghdad.

Bremer was greeted by the man he would replace, Lt. Gen. (Ret.) Jay Garner, and swarmed by a herd of bloodthirsty international media. "The coalition did not come to colonize Iraq. They came to overthrow a despotic regime. That's what we've done and now it is our turn to try and help the Iraqi people regain control of their own destiny," Bremer told the press.

Bremer had been originally earmarked to take the position later in the year from Garner, but nobody was fooled when he was abruptly sent to Iraq much earlier than planned. Rebuilding Iraq was going to be a steeper mountain than the coalition had expected to climb. The global media had sensed frustration, and Garner had to be the fall guy. Reportedly the Bush administration, in particular Secretary of Defense Donald Rumsfeld, was unhappy with Garner's early performance. It was no secret that Bremer was Rumsfeld's man. Garner had not endeared himself to the defense secretary by hiring State Department officials outside the purview of Rumsfeld. Bremer would be a loyal foot soldier. For a man who looked remarkably like a member of the Kennedy political dynasty, Bremer sure knew how to endear himself to the conservative wing of the Bush White House. With Bush's full confidence, Bremer came to Iraq with a mandate to run the country with the kind of executive authority that no American had ever had outside the United States since Douglas Macarthur in post-World War II Japan.

His qualifications were formidable, with experience in the three areas the coalition needed in the aftermath of Saddam: anti-terror strategy, economic development, and field diplomacy. Bremer had served as the Reagan Administration's ambassador to the Netherlands and was one of Washington's top anti-terrorism experts. In the private sector, he was CEO of Marsh Consulting and for eleven years, he was the managing director of Kissinger Associates, a consulting firm founded by former Nixon and Ford Secretary of State Henry Kissinger. Bremer had amassed a resume with diplomatic and corporate experience that few candidates could have matched. He was a history major at Yale and a former triathlete. At 61, Bremer looked more than a decade younger than his actual age. What Bremer lacked was experience with the military. Now he was the senior civilian in charge of more than 130,000 troops.

The handover of power was quick. There were going to be changes, for certain, starting with the new name for his office. The Office of Humanitarian Assistance, or ORHA, became the Coalition Provisional Authority, or CPA. Bremer in his first week in Iraq toured the sights, making Mosul one of his final stops. Mosul had been the talk of Iraq, in spite of the uncontrolled looting that had nearly destroyed the city, because of the May 5 elections. Bremer, with Petraeus in tow, got the chance to meet the winner of those elections, Ghanim al-Basso, at the Civilian-Military Operations Center. He also got a chance to meet a wall of protesters that awaited him outside the building perimeter. When his security helicopters started hovering overhead and the protesters started chanting, Bremer's convoy had arrived.

Bremer, Petraeus and al-Basso met for about 30 minutes behind closed doors, much to the consternation of the traveling media, who surrounded the division

Public Affairs Officer Maj. Trey Cate demanding to eavesdrop on their conversation. Afterward, Bremer met the anxiously awaiting press in front of the building, standing face-to-face with both the cameras and the protesters. He was inviting the press to notice the dissension. "We have seen the voice of freedom with these protesters." After the press conference, Petraeus and Bremer walked the streets of Mosul and met the locals. With Mosul far from coalition headquarters in Baghdad, Bremer would have to make the best out of his first opportunity to assess the situation in the North. Petraeus made sure he got the best tour he could give his new boss.

As Bremer walked towards his plane destined for Baghdad, Petraeus left him with one final message. "Money is ammunition, sir," Petraeus curtly told the new boss, "and we haven't got any." What he needed from Bremer was for him to cut through the red tape and make more money available. Petraeus' staff simply didn't have time to fill out a stack of paperwork to get their projects funded. Bremer told the 101st commander he'd "work on it," and he was true to his word. Days later, the Commanders' Emergency Relief Program was born. The CERP armed field commanders upward from the brigade level with billions in funds to rebuild Iraq – no red tape involved. It was money seized from Saddam Hussein's assets in international banks after the first Gulf War. Billions of dollars had been held in American possession and accruing interest. Now it was going to be invested back into Iraq. Petraeus was initially given no budget, no cap, on how much money to spend in the area. He was just told to spend. Petraeus was being handed a blank check.

But while Bremer and Petraeus agreed on the money, they were very much at odds over what to do with the remnants of the former regime. As Bremer and his aides landed in Baghdad from Mosul, they would begin to administer the swift de-Baathification agenda that so worried Petraeus and the other generals in Iraq at the time. It was Petraeus who understood that the Ba'ath party had worked not only as a society of the elite, but as rite of passage for decades. Uniformly removing tens of thousands of Ba'ath party members from the political process and from their jobs only served to make more enemies, he figured. But ultimately, it was Bremer calling the shots and his de-Ba'athification agenda seemed to thumb his nose at the 101st commander.

It could be said, in retrospect, that Petraeus was the first commander in Iraq to truly forge a partnership with some members of the former Ba'ath party – the "good Ba'athists," that is. In Iraq during Saddam's regime, nearly everyone of any degree of importance was a Ba'athist to some degree; survival in some areas demanded it. From the highest levels of government to the teachers in Iraq's primary schools, the Ba'ath party had enlisted a vast number of the civil servants in their ranks. And that was just the problem. Petraeus worked magic in convincing Bremer to allow the Nineveh Province schools and Mosul University to finish the school years with teachers who had been in the Ba'ath party at certain levels. All other areas of operation in Iraq cut the school year short. The 101st was happy to capture or kill the bad Ba'athists, but after a certain point, you get to a level in which folks were members of the party because they had to be. To cast all of these people off in a state-run economy, where the only jobs for those with their skills were working for the state, and to tell them that they had no future, no job, no retirement, was a way of making a whole lot of enemies.

But enemies would be made, especially after one of Bremer's first command decisions. Bremer ordered all 400,000-plus Iraqi soldiers in the military to be discharged. It was the most fateful decision in the post-war occupation. Every soldier in the military was now out of a job, and it took five long weeks before Bremer announced that they would even receive stipends. Broke, jobless, and armed – most took their weapons home with them when the military collapse – 400,000-plus newly minted enemies of the coalition were now on the streets of Iraq. The coalition had encouraged the Iraqi military to lay down their arms as American and British forces rolled into Baghdad with the implied promise that there would be a place in the new government for the old soldiers. Now the orders were to break that promise. The idea behind disbanding the Iraqi military was to rebuild the Iraqi military. That was the message delivered time and time again to the highly skeptical press and the jobless Iraqi soldiers.

The voices Bremer heard in Mosul would only grow stronger in the coming days, with several protests turning violent. On June 12 in Mosul not far from where Bremer met Petraeus days earlier, a protest of former Iraqi soldiers demanding their salaries turned unruly. Shots were fired at the City Hall building, which had been returned to the local government after the Civilian Military Operations Center relocated to the destroyed Nineveh Hotel. While nobody inside the building was hurt, two people were killed and two others were injured in the crowd of protesters. An element of Second Brigade was called into the area to corral the situation. It was a mission that would stretch for nearly two days. Thirteen protesters were arrested. Eighteen soldiers were wounded and two humvees were destroyed in the exchange. Later that week, in response to the Mosul riot and worse ones in Baghdad and Basra, L. Paul Bremer signed a temporary ban on anti-coalition protests and demonstrations calling for the return of the Ba'ath Party to power. Colonel Joseph Anderson announced the ban at the D-Main Palace, with the Mosul Television cameras rolling. "Until the 20th, we will be arresting all protesters, peaceful and violent, because of the ban."

Any gathering of fifteen people or more with obvious anti-coalition intentions was defined as a protest. After June 20, when the ban expired, all protests required advanced approval including the time and place of the demonstration. Furthermore, the protesters were required to dispatch a negotiating group to meet with the coalition to discuss their problems. The protest policy, as it turned out, was like a garden hose on a forest fire.

Anderson was the natural 101st commander to make the announcement. His forceful but uniquely charming presence was enough to charm any audience, regardless of language barriers. He was media friendly, in more ways than one. In fact, an interview with Col. Joseph Anderson for Mosul Television was tantamount to a CNN interview with Ted Turner. A smart reporter would not bite the hand that feeds him.

Fighting off some coalition officials in Baghdad, Anderson had argued for a free, independent media in Mosul with close consultation with the coalition, but no coalition executive authority. With division public affairs assets, Anderson had worked closely with Mosul television and local newspapers, including the coalition sponsored *Newsweek Mosul* (with no affiliation to the American *Newsweek*). It had become his favorite project. Anderson's expectations were simple: editorializing was fine, misleading was not. The 101st was not going to mute criticism aimed at the coalition, but it was not going to tolerate lies. At one roundtable meeting with local journalists, Anderson warned one paper, "I've been there twice already. If I come down a third time, I'm shutting you down."

His commitment to free media even became personal when he donated $3,000 of his brigade funds to start up the Mosul Television station. In return, the stationed aired 101st Airborne Division news stories, produced by division public affairs assets. The partnership produced Iraqi Freedom News, a nightly segment where 101st stories would broadcast throughout Mosul. public affairs linguist Mahir Hazem, a former Iraqi expatriate in Sweden who returned back to Mosul after Saddam's fall, became IFN's most recognizable face.

While Anderson had little formal training and less experience dealing with the media, he had no trouble stepping into the role as spokesman for the division in Mosul. His name and face quickly became as recognizable as the commanding general's. In late May, Anderson took to the radio airwaves for question-and-answer segments – unheard of for the former Iraqi government. Through Mahir Hazem's translations, Anderson adroitly fielded questions that might have knocked other 101st field grade commanders off balance. His first question came from a local who, in Arabic, asked about unpaid government salaries. It was a hot-button topic that the Strike commander had to tread lightly with. "The local government is trying to pay the salaries based on a pre-war schedule. There is a plan to resume the payments on the same schedule once again, but negotiated at a different rate among different professionals at a different pay scale." A deliberately vague promise to reestablish government payments without digging the coalition too deep a hole.

The interface between the 101st Airborne and the Mosul people had gone a long way to advertise coalition advances and break through the street fiction. "The first goal was to educate them about how this stuff was going to work," Anderson noted. "You've got to cover news, you don't censor it. What you see is what you get. That's what news is all about." The task of educating the local television station personnel fell upon the 22nd Mobile Public Affairs Detachment. Anderson, in return for the work done by the Fort Bragg public affairs unit, gave each member of the seven-soldier unit a Strike Brigade heart to sew onto their Kevlars. The move was entirely out of Army regulations, but the 22nd MPAD had become a part of the Strike Brigade family.

At the crux of Anderson's push for a free media in the region was the question of reliability. If the television and news stations had used their newfound freedoms to release misleading or categorically false stories about American soldiers, what would the division do then? What if these stories and images were being used to incite violence against the coalition? It was a question that hit Petraeus square in the face after he had toyed with the idea of placing a liaison with a local television station that was showing live feeds of Al-Jazeera television – a news source that had consistently stirred the coalition with its incendiary news stories on the war.

Concerns about provocative, fictional reporting were primarily directed at local media. Shockingly then, it was the work one of America's most respected publications that sent shockwaves through the 101st command staff. Wall Street Journal staff reporter Yochi J. Dreazen had joined the division in Mosul, shortly after the Wall Street Journal's "A-List" reporters went home. Following the division's media efforts, Dreazen went forward with an earthshaking story of a command decision made by Petraeus – without first checking with Maj. Trey Cate, the 101st public affairs officer, or Petraeus himself. "The U.S. Army issued orders to seize the city's only television station ... the directive came from the 101st Airborne Division's commander, Maj. Gen. David Petraeus."

It got worse. The article cited an ongoing tug-of-war between Col. Thomas Schoenbeck and Maj. Charmine Means, the 22nd MPAD's commander, leading to Schoenbeck's decision to relieve Means' command. Means did get sent back to Kuwait, that much was true, but for other reasons (she was later permitted to retake command of the 22nd MPAD after Petraeus learned of the action). Petraeus, facing his first cataclysmic public relations disaster of his career, went into overdrive to debunk the article. Instead of disembeding Dreazen, he immediately met with him and called a number of reporters back in the United States asking about the story. Days later, the Wall Street Journal published a story by Dreazen explaining the confusion, effectively retracting the earlier tale.

CHAPTER 6

BRIDGING THE DIVIDE

By the beginning of June, all of the moving parts of the 101st Airborne Division had come together in Northern Iraq. Colonel Ben Hodges, or Bastogne 6, and his First and Second Battalions were on their way up north. Hodges had written his wife before he went to sleep on the night of April 22nd. He had some good news. "We're getting ready to move out tomorrow to a place called Mosul. We should only be there for a couple of weeks." Thankfully, he forgot to send the letter. At Fort Campbell, Holly Hodges was spared the false hope that her husband was coming home soon. In truth, Hodges didn't even get the place right. By the time the brigade was ready to move, Petraeus redirected him south to the city of Quyarrah. The engineers had secured a Quyarrah airfield, very similar to the Mosul Airfield, days earlier. Like most of the regime's belongings, it had been looted beyond recognition. But the local populace wasn't alone in destroying the airfield. Early U.S. Air Force operations had denied enemy use of the airfield by dropping a 1,000-pound bomb every one-hundred yards along the runway. By the time the 101st engineers arrived, all that was left of the Iraqi military presence was a collection of destroyed tanks left in ruins.

Quyarrah was Hodges' new home, a city he would be in control of until it was time to go home. Local reaction to the new neighbors was muted. "I remember driving right through the heart of Quyarrah thinking it looked kind of unfriendly. It was a dirty little town. People just kind of stared at us," Hodges said. The locals warmed up to Bastogne brigade once the battalion commanders started networking with the local leaders.

Third Brigade, operating in Baghdad since early April, had arrived in remote, northwestern Iraq town of Tal Afar. Petraeus had worked hard to bring his Third Brigade to northern Iraq. He needed the soldiers along the Syrian border and he wanted his division operating together in the same region. In the middle of May, he got his wish from V Corps. The Third Brigade center of mass would be Tal Afar, but would include no less than a dozen small cities in the area. Colonel Michael Linnington would be responsible for 20,000 square kilometers of Northern Iraq. Orders in hand, they moved quickly and were in place by the end of the month.

Tal Afar welcomed the coalition with open arms. To the locals, the madness that had destroyed the city following the fall of Saddam would finally end with the Americans in town. Disputes over propane and benzene became fights, which quickly grew into full riots. Armed gangs ruled the streets. There was nobody in charge until the Rakkassans arrived. For the first time in months, Third Brigade was entering a town that mounted little resistance to their presence, but that could change. Expectations were high, Linnington knew.

Expectations had been high in Al Hillah too, where the 2-327th "No Slack" Infantry Regiment had remained since the push towards Baghdad. Lt. Col. Christopher Hughes had met those expectations quickly. After victory in An Najaf, Hughes and his soldiers had teamed up with Third Brigade to swiftly take Al Hillah. Third Brigade moved north and Hughes was tasked to run Al Hillah alone. And run Al Hillah he did. In twenty-eight days, Hughes and his battalion, following Petraeus in Mosul, established elections where they elected a town mayor, put a police force together with uniforms, turned on the power steadily throughout the city, and got the town's water running. It was perhaps the most dazzling achievement of the coalition in the first few weeks of the post-Saddam era in Iraq. Hughes had rebuilt Al Hillah to a better than pre-war standard in less than a month.

The 2-327th "No Slack" Infantry Regiment and Hughes had of course done more than just politic with the local leaders. A terrorist training camp coalescing terror groups from Yemen, Pakistan and Syria had unwisely been operating right in No Slack's back yard. Hughes' intelligence officers were aghast. The terror groups were training at a location so close to the No Slack headquarters compound that Hughes' convoys came by their location with regularity. That was until one No Slack convoy surrounded the camp. The compound held a stockpile of weapons, munitions, and hundreds of brand new, black "Darth Vader" helmets. Two more similar compounds were later found in the same area. With incredible speed, Hughes and No Slack had denied enemy elements the city as a safe haven.

By the end of May, V Corps allowed Petraeus to bring Hughes and No Slack back up north. They arrived with the rest of First Brigade at the Quyarrah Airfield by Memorial Day.

Movement of the 101st Airborne Division assets was not a one-way street. The last day of May would mark the last time the 101st saw Bravo Company, SecondBattalion of the 502nd Infantry Regiment (Second Brigade), for more than a month. The company was detached to the division to support elements of the 3rd Infantry Division patrolling the city of Fallujah, in the heart of the Sunni Triangle. Mosul had been relatively tame to that point – Fallujah was much different. For the Bravo Company soldiers, this was nothing short of a return to war.

They met an element of the 3rd Armored Cavalry Regiment at one of Saddam's vacation spots, protected by a wall covering the perimeter. The 3rd ACR soldiers had been quite envious of what they saw as a plush assignment for the 101st in Mosul – and weren't hesitant to tell the Bravo Company soldiers about it either. It didn't take long for Bravo Company to realize that they indeed weren't in Mosul anymore. By day, they pulled security around fueling stations and banks. At night, the fireworks began, literally. "They smiled at us during the day, shot at us at night," Pfc. Alexis Jacquez remarked. When the company would leave the compound for their nightly patrols, the nighttime sky would illuminate from the different colored flares flying through the air. They had even noticed the color scheme: yellow for armored elements, red for light infantry. The red flares would fly when the 3rd ACR tanks just left Bravo Company to their own devices, which was often. Nightly searches would sometimes lead to as many as a dozen arrests and scores of weapons caches.

Hostilities were not the only thing Bravo Company found heating up in Fallujah. Soldiers found the summer heat down south a good ten to fifteen degrees hotter than in Mosul. Nighttime temperatures didn't sink below ninety degrees.

If the heat wasn't testing enough nerves, the locals were. Even the local market, which looked innocuous enough, was unveiled as an enemy escarpment when Bravo Company looked a little closer. Two to three times a day, on average, the company would find weapons dealers. They even came up with a new name for the local market: "the arms market." Indeed, one could just as easily find a deadly weapon as a sandwich in Fallujah. One fruit stand, Jacquez found, had no less than a dozen AK-47s hidden underneath the apples and oranges.

On June 5, the growing instability in the Sunni Triangle hit the 101st Airborne when Spc. Brandon Oberleitner was shot and killed on a patrol. Oberleitner was the first 101st soldier to be lost during post-war hostilities. Captain William Riley, Bravo Company commander, remembered Oberleitner as "a shining example of what a soldier should be ... the kind of soldier every team leader wanted as their own." This was not just a gracious commander remembering one of his fallen soldiers; Riley revered him enough to endorse Oberleitner's application for Officer Candidate School just before his final mission.

Oberleitner's loss tainted what had been an extremely successful mission when the company returned to Mosul in late June. The city gradually calmed down in the month the company was in Fallujah, partly because the Fedayeen elements that had been orchestrating the armed resistance had largely moved up north. They would move north with them, and they would meet again.

The Turkish borders were open when the division arrived, but log jammed with vehicles. With a Turkish-speaking U.S. Army colonel operating just north of the border, goods and supplies were moving reasonably well. The Syrian crossings required a bit more effort on Maj. Gen. Petraeus' part. Responding to the need to get more goods into Mosul markets, on May 14, Petraeus and Nineveh Governor Ghanim al-Basso signed an agreement to reopen the Syrian border crossing point in the border town of Rabia. The agreement came less than a month after Petraeus arrived in Northern Iraq and signaled his sincere intention to get the wheels of trade rotating again with Iraq's northern neighbors. With Petraeus' and al-Basso's signatures, the floodgates opened for importation of consumer products and agricultural goods sorely needed in northern Iraq: food, cars, electronic items, machine parts, fuel. "If you have more money than fixed goods," Petraeus remarked about the agreement, "all you're going to get is inflation." The former economics professor at West Point didn't need to give a lecture with a slide presentation for local leaders to understand how important this transaction was. The movement towards greater market competition would swiftly drive prices down. Added revenue was going to be pumped back into the economy. This agreement was nothing short of a miracle for local businesses.

Iraqi exports also got a boost with the accord. Goods permitted under then-current U.N. sanctions began to flow, with exporting of fuel being the only exception. The accord signaled the coalition's intent for Syrain business owners to engage in trade with their Iraqi neighbors. Before the fall of Saddam, Syrian border officials had closed the crossing point to Iraqi exports as a way of thwarting the movement of Ba'ath party officials into their country.

The agreement did not come without its red tape. Petraeus had assigned Col. Richard Hatch, the 101st Airborne Division staff judge advocate, the task of writing the agreement so as not to breach the U.N. Security Council sanctions. Petraeus could not wait for the sanctions to be lifted, so he acted to do what he could within the sanctions. "Frankly, we couldn't wait for Baghdad to try and get this process started," Hatch said.

Treading lightly, Hatch researched the U.N. resolutions that governed trade with Iraq and carefully scripted the accord. In the end, nobody from Baghdad objected. Military equipment, narcotics, and anything prohibited from crossing the U.S. borders would be prohibited from entering Iraq, as would items banned by the U.N. Security Council resolutions. The Syrian border region was Third Brigade's area of operation and Lt. Col. Lee Fetterman, commander of the 3-187th Infantry Regiment, would oversee the crossing point. Security would be the key. If contraband did make its way across the newly opened crossing point, the agreement could backfire for the coalition. The economic impact on the area was immediate.

The goodwill towards Iraq's new partners in the Middle East continued. In early May, the United Arab Emirates Air Force teamed up with the 101st to deliver badly needed medical supplies to Mosul. Daily U.A.E. Air Force flights landed at the D-Rear Airfield with palates of ten to twelve tons of pediatric supplies and medications. On their way back, the flights picked up patients from the Mosul Red Crescent (the Muslim equivalent of the Red Cross) that the local area hospitals simply could not support. "It shows that this isn't just a U.S. effort, this is several countries that are working together to bring Iraq back to normalcy," said Brig. Gen. Edward Sinclair, who personally greeted the Mosul Red Crescent chapter from time to time as they picked up the medical supplies.

Another strong political message was sent to Iraq's neighbors and the people of Mosul when the 101st got to work finding and aiding the city's thousands of Internally Displaced Peoples, or IDPs, who populated the streets. Some had already found shelter, but many had not. "It was a humanitarian issue," Petraeus said. "We wanted to stop any further pushing of people out of homes and put them into homes." Various religious leaders in the area were ordered to stop forcing people out of homes. The previous victims were often Kurdish in a process called "Arabization." It was the ugliest policy of the former regime, with the Mosul area sitting on the fault line of the Kurdish-Arabic aggression. For a generation, Saddam Hussein had ordered the bloody removal of all Kurdish families south of the "Green Line." During Saddam Hussein and the Ba'ath Party's reign over Iraq, hundreds of thousands of Kurds were forced out of Arab dominated territories. With Saddam gone, the Kurds were attempting to do the same in reverse, forcing Arab families out of their homes, righting one wrong with another wrong.

Petraeus and the 101st would have none of it. It was within Iraq that the division and Petraeus flexed their strongest diplomatic muscles. Kurdish-Arab hostilities, already boiling after more than two decades of "Arabization" under Saddam, figured to be at its hottest point ever during post-war operations as Kurdish interests were finally handed the opportunity to take part in governing Iraq. Saddam's devastating 1988 chemical and biological attack on Kurdish occupied territories intensified the interethnic chasm that fifteen years later, the American-led coalition would have to bridge. It was a balancing act with the 101st Airborne Division at the fulcrum point.

It was a zero sum territory struggle. The Kurdish families needed to be able to reclaim the land that was seized from them decades ago. Conversely, the Kurdish Peshmerga forces, still patrolling areas below the Green Line, needed to move back north, leaving Kurdish families to a predominately Arab authority.

Arabic and Kurdish representatives met 101st Airborne officers in early May to discuss settling one such dispute. As 101st Airborne Apache and Blackhawk helicopters secured the area in the town of Makhmor where the meeting was to take place, a small Kurdish rally awaited them. The group rallied around a banner that read "Thank you to the coalition forces for freeing us, now keep the usurpers off our land." Few Kurds were eager to make nice with their Arab neighbors.

Inside, the meeting was not nearly as contentious as expected. Brigadier Gen. Freakley served as chief mediator with Ghanim al-Basso and Akram Mintik, mayor of the Kurdish town of Erbil, leading the dialogue. After a few brief statements from the mayors and local agricultural leaders, Freakley was asked to leave so the parties could talk without coalition mediation. "We said, 'by all means.' They had a caucus … in a small room with a small group, for forty minutes alone. They came out with a signed document," Freakley recalled. The settlement was called the Makhmor Accord, the first interethnic accord of its kind in Iraq. In the agreement, the Kurds and the Arabs had agreed to share profits from the coming year's wheat and barley harvests in the Makhmor area, a previously disputed territory in a formula agreed to by both sides.

To ensure that every local farmer was in line with the agreement, the accord stipulated that all wheat and barley farmers be registered in Makhmor for the year's harvest. Freakley was the first to congratulate the two sides on the agreement. "There will be people who will be very disappointed. I think there will also be people who understand that instead of some arbitrary whim of an oppressive dictator being carried out, that they are being governed by law, elected officials, and principled men who have agreed to have the best for all the people in that area." Later, similar agreements were reached in other portions of the province, all generally based on the Makhmor Accords.

The streams of water flowing in Mosul's downtown streets during the dry spring and summer months might have denoted that the city had just experienced some heavy rainstorms, but not one drop of rain had fallen in the city since well before the war. That's what made the splashes of water so discomforting when convoys rolled through the water streams at high speeds. The water was not rain water mixed with a little harmless Iraqi soil. Some of the streams represented Mosul's makeshift sewage treatment system. The Mosul sewage treatment facilities were only operating at twenty percent capacity. Other water streams in the streets came from broken water lines.

Access to running water and a reliable sewage system were reserved for the very privileged in Mosul. For the rest of Mosul, water pipeline breaks had rendered water faucets as dry as a stone. Much of the effective sewage treatment facilities were privately owned. Several hotels and the campus of Mosul University provided their own sewage treatment systems, most of the rest of the city was left to its own devices. Sewage in Mosul, for the most part, came straight from the homes and right out onto the streets. Fixing the sewage treatment system and getting water flowing in Mosul were part and parcel. Power again the X-factor.

"It was in pretty bad shape when we got there," said Capt. Scott McDonald, a reservist with the 926th Engineering Group. McDonald, a division manager of the Sewage and Water Authority in his hometown of Peach Street City, Ga., knew from the moment he arrived in Mosul that there was a lot of work to be done. "You couldn't drive anywhere throughout the city without seeing a major water leak."

The short-term priorities for McDonald and the 101st were to get the humans away from the untreated sewage and fix the pipeline hemorrhages, then go back develop long-term solutions. "It's like treating a gunshot victim. You don't give him a heart transplant before fixing all of his bullet holes."

Engineers at Mosul University, the Coalition Provisional Authority, United Nations Children's Fund (UNICEF), and the Department of Defense-contracted Bechtel Corporation joined with the division in the water and sewage efforts. As local labor was put to work on fixing the pipeline holes, the coalition think-tank was already drawing up plans to build on the existing water pipeline system towards citywide access to water. The issue was power. Water pressure in the system would build up to a certain level, then have the bubble burst once the power went off. Thus, with no constant pressure, water could not be pushed out to many areas. "Out of one-point-five million people in Mosul, I would say about thirty percent of them had reliable access to water," McDonald said.

"Most of these plants have to run continuously for eight hours in order to pump the water out to the outlying areas. With the power four (hours) off, four on in the national grid, they were losing the power half way through the eight-hour cycle. They weren't able to keep the pressure up in the system to get the water out to the outlying areas."

The immediate, but not permanent solution was generators. Backup generators, paid for under the Commanders' Emergency Relief Program, were brought into three major water treatment plants to stabilize the power issue. With the cycle in full swing, water began flowing in areas of Mosul that had not seen running water since before the beginning of the war. The water bonanza gripped the entire city and that provided yet another problem for McDonald: conservation. "We found that in twenty to thirty percent of the homes in the poorer parts of town, they didn't even have a faucet at the ends of their pipes. When they had water available in their neighborhood, it just ran continuously." After briefly letting the water run without rationing, the 101st was forced to rotate availability to water from neighborhood to neighborhood in what McDonald called "forced water conservation."

In Mosul, running water started to become a reality just in time for the hot summer months. In other remote areas of northern Iraq, running water was not even a fantasy. Water pipes couldn't reach into villages where no paved streets reached. For water to reach tribal villages in northern Iraq, it would have to be delivered by trucks. It was a dangerously flawed system that was started by the former regime that the new government would have to continue and augment. The existing water truck system was only good enough for each family to receive barely enough water to survive, much less bathe.

The Iraqi Ministry of Water Resources, as the coalition and the 101st Airborne found it, was a mess. After years of inadequacy, the ministry needed to be self-sufficient before the coalition could leave it to its own devices. When the 101st arrived in northern Iraq, they were a long way away from taking the steering wheel. Inadequate equipment and incompetent management plagued the ministry. Post-war looting of the Ministry of Water Resources Mosul headquarters meant the 101st Airborne had to almost start from scratch.

The 431st Civil Affairs Battalion civilian supply team and division engineers joined with ministry officials and geologists from Mosul University to start what would be a project that would continue well beyond the 101st Airborne's stay in northern Iraq. When the division arrived in the region, existing water resources were insufficient. Only half of the area's eight water drills were operational. With the drills that did work, the ministry had drilled in the wrong places. That's where the university geologists came in to identify areas where the ministry could drill with a little more success. To fix the drills that did not work, the division needed parts. Baghdad was less than expedient in getting the needed parts to northern Iraq initially, complicating early efforts to get the drills working again.

The division donated $39,000 from the CERP funds to rebuild the looted ministry office building, but that project would not be ready until September. Until the office was up and ready, the Civilian Military Operations Center would serve as the water team's center of mass. Captain John Gerald, the 431st Civilian Supply team leader, was blitzed with requests from villages for water. Many of the requests were rebuffed. "The problem is that in a lot of this area, the water is not good to drink and that's why a lot of these villages will never have a water well. A lot of times we couldn't get the water out there … the good water is not there," Gerald said.

Of the areas that could be helped, building on the existing pipe system became central. Securing the pipes was another issue. Sheep farmers were known to shoot up water pipes with an AK-47 to water their herd.

Admittedly, Gerald was a bit out of his element working with the division's water supply charge. As a registered nurse in his hometown of Amarillo, Texas, and an officer in the medic corps, Gerald was thrown to the wolves when he started working in Mosul in a field totally unrelated to what he was trained to do in the military.

Gerald's story was not uncommon with his unit, the 431st Civil Affairs Battalion or throughout the 101st Airborne Division. "Civil affairs units are not enough to rebuild Iraq," Petraeus stressed. Faced with an overwhelming civil affairs mission with scarce civil affairs soldiers, he did what he could to expand his civil affairs base. "It was clear that we needed a lot more (civil affairs) capability." Gerald was one of dozens of civil affairs officers who embedded with 101st units, just like the embedded media during the invasion of Baghdad, to tackle Nineveh's toughest issues from the front, not from a command post in Mosul. The result was a crash course not only for Gerald and his civil affairs colleagues, but for officers and NCOs who would work with the 431st soldiers. The entire 101st, in effect, would become a division-sized civil affairs unit.

When it came to working with the embryonic local governments, as much as the 101st commander could, Petraeus assigned units local ministries with a natural working relationship. The Office of the Staff Judge Advocate, for example, would work with the Nineveh Province Ministry of Justice. The division chaplain would work with the Ministry of Religious Affairs. Other assignments were less logical – the Division Support Command (DISCOM) was handed the Ministry of Youth and Sports.

Holed up in Iskandiriyah for a month and a half, Sgt. First Class Hector Jusino needed direction. "What am I doing here and when can I go home," he thought. A lot of soldiers were asking themselves that same question at that point, but Jusino genuinely wanted a purpose, not just an opportunity to go home. He had habitually volunteered for big projects in his time in the military. Now, at the end of his career in first major armed conflict of the 21st century, Jusino found himself useless. This was not the way to go out. He wanted an opportunity to do something special. He never would have thought it at the time, but that opportunity came when his company first sergeant popped his head in Jusino's tent one day with a less than electrifying assignment in Mosul.

"You're going to get mad at me," the first sergeant told him, not knowing that Jusino's assignment would leave him in Mosul for the duration of the tour. "The tasking came down and you have to rebuild this swimming pool, soccer field and basketball gym. They're going to give you a bunch of locals to work with. It's pretty much a public relations project."

Jusino was unexcited, but it was the chance to get involved, so he accepted the tasking dutifully. Besides, it's not like he had a choice. So he made the tireless convoy through Iraq with a group of his soldiers, almost falling asleep behind the wheel and crashing at one point, and swung into the Mosul Airfield where the

801st Main Support Battalion and Division Support Command (DISCOM) commanders were waiting for him. Command Sgt. Maj. Marvin Womack, 801st MSB command sergeant major, drove him down the road and introduced him to his new mission.

He was curious, but more than anything, he was just happy to see green grass after two months in the filth of Kuwait and Iskandiriyah. Jusino, an avid outdoorsman and voracious fisherman, later recalled only encountering one tree during his entire stay in the Iskandiriyah prior to moving north to Mosul. Every day, he would sit down in the shade and watch the birds fly around the tree, almost as if the tree would be the last he'd ever see. There was no need to do that in Mosul, there were trees everywhere. This may not be too bad after all, he thought as Womack's lead vehicle turned into what would become Jusino's second home for the foreseeable future.

"This is it," Womack said as he jumped out of his humvee. As it turned out, the sports complex was adjacent to the Mosul Airfield perimeter and after an opening in the airfield's fencing was cut out, Jusino would not need to go outside the secured area to go to work. From a distance, Jusino could see that he had his work cut out for him. After cutting through the perimeter fence and getting a closer view, Jusino saw a disaster zone.

"Oh my God, how am I going to get all of this done?" he asked Womack. The 801st MSB's top enlisted soldier had no response. It was Jusino's job to answer that question for himself. The pool, basketball gymnasium and small soccer stadium were collectively left as a veritable junkyard by the Iraqi military: abandoned uniforms, bayonets, weapons, ammunition. The pool was far more fit for fishing than swimming. Seaweed had accumulated so thick that it concealed the bottom of the pool. Dead frogs and trash were floating on the water's surface. The stadium and gymnasium were in ruins, totally unfit for community use. Several Mosul homeless families had used both the stadium and the gymnasium for shelter.

Still unclear on what his mission was, Jusino pressed Womack further. "What do you want me to do, sergeant major? What can I do?"

"All I want you to do is clean this place up."

"You don't want me to rebuild this place?"

"No, the engineers will do that," Womack told him. But Jusino was skeptical of that promise. He knew immediately that nobody would volunteer to help him with this duty. It would be up to Jusino to make this happen, and he immediately began thinking of what he needed to do to make the facility like new again. He also began dreaming. Why just do the bare minimum to clean up the sports complex, he thought. What could he do to make this facility worth his time? He needed help. Command Sgt. Maj. Womack was already on top of that one.

Womack a day earlier had visited the facility and found a group of Iraqi men playing a game of soccer, using trash to mark the goals at each end. Bringing along a linguist, he intrepidly stopped the game to offer the men a job. Flanked by armed guards, Womack was obviously a man of importance. The game was quickly put on time out and the players snapped to attention, almost as if they were in the American military themselves. Womack had come to explain that the American soldiers were going to rebuild the soccer stadium they were playing on, and they needed people who wanted to work. The friendly group of Iraqis could only respond with a "Oh yes mister, ha ha ha." When someone in Mosul offered a paying job, there was little room for negotiating. Womack got his message across and the soccer players were back the next day to meet their new boss. Standing proud and ready to work, the group of about a dozen locals took Jusino by surprise. They were in this for the money, he knew, but they were obviously interested in bringing their soccer field back to life.

But amongst the excited group of men stood one man who seemed quite a bit more cautious. In spite of the language barriers – Jusino did not have a linguist and wouldn't for the first week – the U.S. Army NCO could tell instantly that the quiet man was a former Iraqi soldier. "I've been in the military twenty-three years, I can smell a soldier for miles."

In a letter to the division on June 19, Maj. Gen. Petraeus laid it on the table for his soldiers: the 101st Airborne Division was going to be right where they were, northern Iraq, for the foreseeable future.

"It is clear we are going to be in Iraq for at least a few more months – but I don't know how long. I would love to be able to give each of you the date when you'll get back home; however, that is not possible as no rotation date has been set. I will share that information as soon as we get it.

"This is not an easy mission. We're still getting shot at periodically, the summer heat is becoming crushing, and tasks we have to perform are often tedious.

"It's clear that we're going to have to hang tough, take things one day at a time, give energy to our buddies, keep our heads down, and drive on. Remember, if it were easy, they wouldn't need the Screaming Eagles."

And it certainly wasn't easy – not for the 101st Airborne Division and not for the coalition soldiers in Baghdad, Tikrit, and Fallujah – when the summer heat was beating down between 120 and 140 degrees regularly starting in early June. But with the bad news came the good. Petraeus used to letter to outline initiatives he was taking to support morale, including cleaning up swimming pools conveniently located at several compounds that the division soldiers could use during days off. One initiative he considered had to be bagged. "The Division CSM and I looked briefly at wearing patrol caps and removing body armor while on missions; unfortunately, enemy activity picked up as soon as we began considering this."

Every soldier on every mission outside the confines of the installation needed to wear his or her flak vest, Kevlar helmet, and full desert uniform with the sleeves down – an unbelievably warm experience during mid-day. Water was the key to survival. Keeping the water cold was an issue in itself. Leaving a bottle of water in the Iraqi sun could heat the water to a near boiling point. Blocks of ice soon became a thriving industry in Mosul. Roadside shops, like the "Friends of America" shop set up by a group of savvy local entrepreneurs, caught business like they never imagined just from convoys stopping for a cold Pepsi. The division had Gatorade mailed by the box full and the soldiers treasured each and every package like currency.

Gatorade provided a taste of home in a literal sense. Simple things, like a music CD or a package of cookies from mom and dad, were enough to take soldiers back to the day when they didn't have to wait for two to three weeks for a letter from home on family news. Home was a long way away and the division was doing it's very best to make due with what they had: Gatorade and each other.

Expediting mail became another priority and email, once an unreachable star, started to become more commonplace. Generations of Screaming Eagles before could never imagine receiving a message the same day or even the same hour as it was written from back home. In 2003, soldiers with a quick enough Internet access were even having live conversations with friends and families back home on America Online Instant Messenger. Communications with loved ones provided the biggest morale boost that the division could reasonably provide. It was an insufficient substitute for actually being home, but email helped soldiers in Iraq send their love to their kids at home at Fort Campbell. Email helped bring together families that had been separated for months. For the soldiers, morale boosts came from the simple things, news on their sister's high school graduation, their husband or wife's job promotion or even how their favorite baseball team was faring.

For the single soldiers, morale boosts came in slightly different forms. The time held tradition of the Memorial Day barbeque was honored in style at the Mosul Airfield. Brigadier Gen. Edward Sinclair kicked the fun and excitement off, speaking during a morning ceremony in front of the airport terminal. The usually calm and collected Sinclair couldn't hold back his emotions this time around. "There's nobody in the world more proud of you than me ... there's a lot of things screwed up about America and there always will be, but America is still the best place in the world and you make it the best place."

Softball, basketball, volleyball, chess and spades tournaments were waged throughout the day underneath a steady flow of smoke coming from the grill. The highlight of the holiday came at 9 a.m., when the new Post Exchange opened across the street from the Division-Rear tactical operations center. It wasn't like the PX at Fort Campbell, but for the first time, 101st Airborne Division soldiers could walk into a store and buy their favorite cereal, a new CD, a magazine and even a new pair of socks – just like home. It was an eye-opener in so many ways. Even the hippest soldiers had no idea that Beyonce Knowles, lead singer of the popular rhythm and blues trio Destiny's Child, had released her first solo album while they were fighting a war. Or that Syracuse University, lead by star freshman Carmelo Anthony, had won the NCAA basketball championship while they were fighting their way through Iraq. The term "SARS" meant nothing to many 101st soldiers before they walked into the new PX and saw the news on the cover of magazine after magazine.

The new PX was a gateway from Iraq to the rest of the world. Imported television satellites started appearing on division compounds. At every major 101st compound, at least one television satellite was set up in the dining facility or soldier's lounge. Through the Armed Forces Network, all the popular network programming, sports events, and news were aggregated into three channels. The world was becoming smaller for the division.

Northern Iraq was becoming smaller for two soldiers on opposite ends of the 101st Airborne Division area of operation. Captain Ben Smith, at the Quyarrah Airfield, and Capt. Maggie Smith, at the Mosul Airfield, were one of the lucky married couples. They at least got to see each other once a month. They lived separate lives in separate towns, granted, but they could dial up one another on "tactical" phones for non-tactical purposes. As much as a deployment could be, the Smiths were making their time in Iraq into a fun time.

Ben particularly had a lot to talk about. The 5-101st Aviation Regiment commander, Lt. Col. Laura Richardson, had seen the regular maturation from boyish, new captain to dependable leader in Capt. Ben Smith. He had been with the battalion as a platoon leader as a lieutenant for a year before Richardson took command. But it wasn't until his promotion in October of 2002 when Richardson got to know her new operations officer. He did well with his new job, but not without his learning pains. The starting point came when Richardson first came to the unit. It was in the pilot's room at Fort Campbell, after Ben neglected to customarily call the room to attention as Richardson entered. The aftermath got ugly as his commander let him have it as Ben stood firm at the position of attention. He didn't understand it at the time, but Richardson had started to take the impressive young captain under her wings. She was happy to do it. Ben had all the makings of a great officer, Richardson thought.

The acceptance from Lt. Col. Richardson was nothing to be taken for granted. Of all the promising field grade officers in the division, Richardson was generally considered to be the star of the "Screaming Eagles," and not just because of her *Time* magazine fame. At one point, Maj. Gen. Petraeus introduced Richardson to a crowd of Quyarrah locals as "the one who gets me to spend so much money on you." Petraeus was hardly the highest ranking superior Richardson had impressed. In fact, Richardson was certainly the only soldier in the division to regularly receive Christmas cards from former Vice President Al Gore. As a major, Richardson had served as Gore's military aide. She would follow along with Gore everywhere, carrying the "football" bag with the codes ordering a nuclear attack in the event Gore needed to use them. Richardson was even with the Vice President on Election Day 2000 and thirty-nine days later when her boss found out from the United States Supreme Court that he would not receive a promotion.

Gore's loss meant a return to the "outside the beltway Army" for Richardson and her husband, Lt. Col. Jim Richardson. Both would ultimately move to Fort Campbell, she as the 5-101st commander and he as the 3-101st Aviation Regiment commander. The Richardsons in Operation Iraqi Freedom became the first husband and wife team to serve together in a war as battalion commanders in U.S. Army history. If the Richardsons were the first family in Army aviation, the Smiths were certainly the heir apparent.

The more Lt. Col. Richardson came to know Ben Smith, the more she came to appreciate his work. "He ran the TOC (tactical operations center) as well as any battle captain I've ever had," she recalled. "He knew exactly what to do in the

S-3 shop (operations). He knew what the companies were looking for, the pilots, what kind of information they wanted, what kind of information they needed, what kind of lead time they needed on missions that come down in order for them to plan accordingly. He was just awesome." Ben, his commander remembered, was a calming presence in the office, even when things got chaotic. "No matter how bad the situation, he would always find a plus side and make people laugh." Of course, there were times to make people laugh and times to get serious. Ben, her commander had witnessed, was finally finding when the right time was to do one or the other.

Much to his surprise, Ben was awarded the Bronze Star for Service in June. From his office, located at the Quyarrah Airfield, Ben emailed his wife to tell her the news. "I still honestly believe that (Col. William) Forrester saw the name 'Smith' and thought it was you, so he signed it approved! I am the only staff officer in my battalion who got one, which doesn't make any sense. Every staff officer was put in for one by the battalion commander, so it was a total brigade commander decision, and I know that Forrester didn't love me too much."

Forrester may not have loved Capt. Ben Smith too much, but everyone around the 5-101st Aviation did.

Local restaurants, just reopening after proprietors felt assured that the looting was over, reopened to a brand new clientele: U.S. soldiers. With not a McDonald's anywhere to be found, soldiers had to take a liking to local food or enjoy their favorite MREs, something that was not easy to do after eating the same twenty-four menus for nearly three months.

Only one word could describe the local food for the average American soldier's provincial taste in food: foreign. Nobody could have expected the Iraqi cuisine to mirror mom's home cooking, but few were prepared for how different Mosul's dining selection would really be. No one experience typified the local food for American soldiers more than the 101st's introduction to Mosul pizza, which scantly resembled a delivery from Dominos or Papa John's. Mozzarella cheese and tomato sauce were completely bereft from the Mosul pizzerias. In place of the golden crust Americans come to expect from their pizza was a thick pita bread. Nothing took the place of the cheese and the tomato sauce. In fact, the local pizza can simply be described as this: a thick flat bread with ground lamb meat and chopped onions. The "pizzas" were so greasy that soldiers would sprint to the nearest latrine before even finishing their meal. The locals didn't give up though and the soldiers didn't give up on them. Gradually, Mosul learned what the Americans liked and started advertising "Italian-style pizza." The new and improved pizza featured the regular crust and substituted mozzarella cheese with goat cheese. The toppings were a bit different – often the new pizzas were topped with sliced hot dogs to make up for the lack of pepperoni – but a cultural exchange between the American soldiers and the Iraqi pizzerias had been successfully forged.

The pita bread was at the base of any local meal. Almost any Mosul dinner table would have a basket of pita bread at the center. Its use was sometimes less to eat than to use as a platform to eat, like plates. Plastic silverware wasn't available in Iraq, so the pita bread was used to grab and consume. Another local favorite was chicken tika; nearly every downtown Mosul street would have at least one rotisserie with two-dozen chickens on the fire. The chickens were cut in half often with a plate of grilled vegetables. Unlike Kenny Rogers Roasters, the chickens couldn't be taken home in a plastic container, so they were placed on a paper plate and wrapped in pita bread. The idea was that the grilled vegetables would be wrapped with the chicken to form something like a fajita – something like the soldiers were used to finding at Taco Bell. Lamb meat could also be substituted for the chicken.

By June, every soldier had a favorite local treat. Some even had their favorite restaurants. One local tradition seemed to really catch on for soldiers visiting a local family or celebration. Aptly called "The Goat Grab," the ritual involved four or five people standing around a mammoth sized plate of rice, pita bread and goat meat. Vanity was left at the door as soldiers and locals alike would just grab what they could and shove it in their mouths. It was every man, or woman for him or herself. The local rice always had a certain way with soldiers. Soldiers demanded a bowl of white rice with their soup, chicken tika, anything that they found at the local market. Northern Iraq isn't exactly prime for rice fields, so the rice was naturally imported, often from the U.N. World Food Program. Rumor had it that the source of this magical rice was none other than the fields of Vietnam.

After soldiers started to notice that they were being overcharged by local food joints, the linguists were hired to do lunch and dinner runs for them. Unit meals around the table with their linguists became like the family dinnertime ritual soldiers were used to at home. Suddenly it became so apparent how truly repugnant those MREs really were.

A growing issue with the local market was the apparent lack of any sanitation standards governing Iraqi food service. American soldiers would routinely drive through downtown Mosul and quiver at the sight of a local meat market, where half-butchered carcasses would hang in the Iraqi sun covered with a cloud of flies. Street vendors earned exponentially more business when the 101st arrived in town, mostly from the sodas they offered in old-fashioned glass bottles. Convoys' regularly pulled over when they needed a soda break, slammed a cold Pepsi or Coca-Cola, and returned the bottles when they were done so they could be reused. What the soldiers didn't know initially was that the bottles they were drinking out of had not been washed before its last use – not terribly sanitary. From customer to customer, the roadside shops would sell sodas out of bottles that were just chugged and refilled.

For obvious reasons, the local food rave didn't last forever. When units started establishing Mobile Kitchen Trucks on their compounds, the local food became expendable. In a short time the MKT food, nothing more than packaged food that could travel from the U.S. to the field, ran afoul too. That's when local restaurants were invited into the division compounds to set up their own shops just for the coalition soldiers, subject to a rigorous sanitation inspection. By mid-summer, the 502nd Maintenance Company built an actual sit down and eat restaurant at the D-Rear Airfield, complete with menus and everything that was run by locals with the trademark Iraqi food.

Around Memorial Day, the American media had started to catch onto what had been a well-kept secret in the weeks following President Bush's address to the nation aboard the U.S.S. Lincoln. Americans were still dying in Iraq. The end was supposed to have been May 1, when aboard the U.S.S. Abraham Lincoln approaching the coast of San Diego, President Bush declared the end of major combat operations in Iraq. In a spectacle that wowed his political supporters and ruffled his political enemies, Bush co-piloted his S-3B Lightning, temporarily called Navy One, onto the aircraft carrier and met the sailors of the Lincoln dressed in a flight suit with his helmet under his left arm. It was excellent theatre. After changing into the standard power suit and red tie, Bush took the podium with the eyes of the world fixed squarely on him. "In the images of celebrating Iraqis, we have seen the ageless appeal of human freedom. Decades of lies and intimidation could not make the Iraqi people love their oppressors or desire their own enslavement.

"Men and women in every culture need liberty like they need food and water and air. Everywhere that freedom arrives, humanity rejoices and everywhere that freedom stirs, let tyrants fear."

With every network and cable news station in the English-speaking language broadcasting live, Bush triumphantly declared "Mission Accomplished" with a red, white and blue blazoned banner handing over his shoulders. "Because of you," Bush told the troops, "our nation is more secure. Because of you, the tyrant has fallen and Iraq is free." Saddam was gone from power. The war was won, but as the nation was finding out, the peace was not. In May alone, forty-one coalition soldiers had died, thirty-seven of them Americans. Twenty-nine American soldiers would die in June. The bloodiest months were still ahead.

The violence, for the most part, had been confined within the Baghdad-centered "Sunni Triangle." Mosul had been too remote from the problematic area to face the insurgency in the early summer months. Petraeus was not about to wait for that to change. In early July, he started requiring convoys to travel with at least two vehicles. The June 12 grenade attacks during the military protest outside City Hall had sent a clear message to the division that they better armor their paper-thin humvees as best as they could. Resourcefully, soldiers did that by filling sandbags and padding the bottoms of their vehicles. The idea was if an enemy attacker threw a grenade underneath the vehicle, the sandbags would absorb most of the blast.

In June, Lt. Col. Christopher Hughes had finished his tour with the 2-327th Infantry Regiment. He was slated to leave his battalion to Lt. Col. James Johnson. Then he would be off to his next assignment: the Pentagon. Hughes would work for a familiar boss. Lieutenant Gen. Dick Cody had left the 101st Airborne Division a year earlier, got his third star, and took over the Army's operations office. Cody instantly became the busiest man in the Army, controlling the Army's operations, laying out deployments years into the future. Now Hughes would be one of the former 101st's commander's special assistants.

He had been in Quyarrah for less than a month. The battalion was going to be there a lot longer after he left. It was like Hughes was leaving his family. With No Slack, he had accomplished more in Operation Iraqi Freedom than any other battalion in the 101st. Whatever worries he could ever have about his career, and future promotions, were taken care of with his battalion command. On June 16, it was over. Colonel Hodges took the battalion guidon and handed it to Johnson. On the seat of a C-130, Hughes was taken away from Northern Iraq to Kuwait, where he quickly outprocessed and took off for Campbell Army Airfield – a twenty-hour flight.

Having left his Army family, he rejoined the family who had been with him from the beginning less than a week after relinquishing command. To his surprise, Hughes came back to Fort Campbell as more than just a hero. His story had been played and replayed on all of the news networks. His heroics at An Najaf provided the 101st with its most lasting image of the push towards Baghdad. The kids were as proud of dad as any three kids could be of a parent.

Margerite had moved the family into a hotel for the last few weeks before Hughes' return. She had worked magic in getting the family ready to move. The furniture was already on its way to Washington – she just needed her husband before they were ready.

It wasn't the perfect welcome home for Hughes. His daughter had been off at a summer school program at Northern Kentucky University and wouldn't be able to see her father until weeks later. And he certainly would have liked more time to say goodbye to whatever neighbors he had who weren't in Iraq. But when he got off the plane, Hughes felt the kind of feelings any married deployed soldier in Iraq would have done anything to feel at that point. Clearing Fort Campbell took a few days. Taking the 101st Airborne Division "Old Abe" patch of his left arm made it official – but he would always have his combat patch on his right. Now it was off to Iowa for a couple of weeks leave. Lieutenant Col. Christopher Hughes had left one combat zone. In July, he would be introduced to another, slightly more innocuous battlefield: Washington beltway traffic.

CHAPTER 7

HVTs #2 AND #3

It was no secret. Few could hide it. Nobody denied it. As the summer months got hotter and hotter with illusions of an approaching redeployment rapidly fading away, many soldiers' spirits were deteriorating. Nobody wanted to be in Iraq.

For one aviation company, the effects of the deployment had almost become a way of life. Delta Company, 7-101st Aviation Regiment, a CH-47 Chinook helicopter company, had spent most of 2002 in Afghanistan supporting Operation Enduring Freedom. After a seven-month deployment, they redeployed at the beginning of the year and arrived back home the first week of February – only to deploy again three weeks later to Kuwait. So brief was their stay at Fort Campbell that a number of soldiers in the company did not even have time to finalize divorces before catching their flight back across the Atlantic. The separation was destroying families, and there was nothing anyone could do. Families in Fort Campbell contacted their congressmen and senators to see if there was anything they could do to redeploy the unit, to no avail. Four demoralized pilots had even requested to be taken off flight duty and reassigned to other, safer duties. Either as a show of pride or frustration, the unit erected a sign outside their sleeping tents that read "B Co. 7/101, Days Deployed … " and then the number of days they had spent in Afghanistan, Kuwait and Iraq combined. By the end of June, the sign read an even 350.

Many in the Army had expected some of the brightest young officers and most motivated young enlisted soldiers to drop plans to make the Army a career after getting back home, whenever that would be. But through all the pain and loneliness the soldiers in the 101st Airborne Division had experienced in the first four months in the Middle East, 158 soldiers in middle of a combat tour raised their right hands and reenlisted on America's 227th birthday, July 4, 2003, on the steps of Saddam's Mosul palace. Independence Day had special meaning in 2003, especially for those who had just given to the people of Iraq what the patriots of the American Revolution had given to all generation of free Americans. The fireworks were missing, but the appreciation of the holiday was very much in full splendor, and nobody missed the traditional celebrations. Major Gen. Petraeus performed the honors for the largest 101st reenlistment ceremony in memory. Thirty-six states and every major 101st Airborne Division unit were represented in the crowd of soldiers. Dozens more reenlisted simultaneously at other 101st operating bases.

What could lure a soldier to reenlist half the world away from their loved ones? The bonus, $15,000 for many military skills at the time, was certainly a factor for most of the soldiers. A number of the 158 soldiers who reenlisted knew they planned on serving the requisite twenty years to get their retirement pension. Of course, the time and place of their reenlistment ceremony was tough to pass up too. "You get to reenlist in Iraq with the general, how cool is that?" said Staff Sgt. Tim Danko, Jr., a Military Policeman with the 194th MP Company.

Petraeus was every bit as excited as the soldiers he was reenlisting. It was one of the proudest moments for the division in Iraq. "Even in our command group, everyone above us is keenly aware that we are in our fifth month of this deployment and it's getting real, real hot and that the mission remains tough ... (we) are all grateful for what you have done, for what our division has done, in liberating Iraq and now in winning the peace," he told the reenlistees.

In the 2002-2003 fiscal year, countering what many inside the division had expected, reenlistment numbers for the 101st Airborne stood at 40 percent more than the established quota. "The soldiers are proud of the 101st," said Sgt. Maj. James Plemens, a 101st Airborne Division reenlistment NCO. "A lot of units have seen a drop in reenlistment rates. We haven't seen that with the 101st." Plemens, a former recruiter, was able to convince two of his soldiers, Sgt. Claudia Tapia and Staff Sgt. David Carr, to re-up. Tapia and Carr were two of more than 500 soldiers to reenlist with the 101st and the more than 50,000 in the entire

Army – all this during a time when the rest of America was under the impression that Army morale was low.

Carr, who was in his fifth deployment during Operation Iraqi Freedom having served in Haiti, Rwanda, Saudi Arabia and Kosovo, reenlisted knowing there would almost certainly be more deployments in the near future. "I have a lot of time invested, plus I think I have a good chance in making a senior rank … I enjoy the Army and to be honest, my wife supports the Army."

Few soldiers in the Army asked to be in Iraq, not through the 125 degree heat and the constant threat of getting shot at, but a sense of pride connected all soldiers in a kindred spirit that only the soldiers could understand. The 158 soldiers who reenlisted on July 4 understood. Sergeant Tapia understood, saying she reenlisted because "it was here (in Iraq) that I decided I needed to do more."

In late July, the morale of the division would take its most crushing blow. It had been rumored that the 101st Airborne Division was going to be in Iraq for a full year, and that day those rumors were confirmed. Secretary of Defense Donald Rumsfeld signed what almost every soldier with the 101st dreaded, but knew was ultimately coming in their hearts. Both the Screaming Eagles and the 4th Infantry Division, who arrived in Iraq in April and was operating in the Tikrit area, would serve one-year tours. Every other unit who arrived in country from that point could expect the same 365 days at war.

General John Abizaid, who succeeded Gen. Tommy Franks as the commander of the U.S. Central Command in July, got what he needed. It would have been nice for the 101st Airborne Division to have redeployed in time for Christmas, but the reality was that the division was very much needed right where they were. The hopes that this would be a short war had ended. With hostilities reaching the point where one soldier or more a day was lost in the Sunni Triangle, the war, for all intents and purposes, was still being fought.

"What we have done is taken (Gen. Abizaid's) requirements and his needs, and looked at the forces in Iraq, and devised a plan to meet those needs," explained Gen. Jack Keane, then Acting Army Chief of Staff.

The 3rd Infantry Division, which had been deployed since September of 2002, would finally get relief from the bullpen, starting in September. The remaining elements of the 82nd Airborne Division not in Afghanistan or already in Iraq got the call to take over for the 3rd ID. The 1st Infantry Division out of Germany would take over for the 4th Infantry Division in April of 2004 – seemingly ages away for the soldiers who were enduring the worst of the Iraqi heat and the Iraqi violence. The 101st Airborne Division's redeployment orders were much more nebulous at that point, calling for a "multinational division" to assume control of Mosul and Northern Iraq – a multinational division which to that point had not yet been assembled.

Morale was at its most tenuous state at Tal Afar with Third Brigade. "Around the middle of summer, the troops were asking, 'When are we getting our redeployment orders?' And there were a lot of rumors on the streets, that we would be home by Labor Day, then we would be home by Halloween, then Thanksgiving, then it was Christmas," Col. Michael Linnington said. The Rakkassan chief was finding himself taking the role of both commander, and morale booster, of his brigade. "Eventually the rumors ran dry."

Petraeus confirmed the news that night at the Battle Update Brief. The division would have to make Mosul home until February and March of 2004. For the few lucky soldiers who were in their last months of their enlistment, the option of going back home was available. Officers who were scheduled to be replaced could look forward to going home also. All other soldiers just had to stick it out. Only extraordinary circumstances would allow soldiers to redeploy home.

The CG, ever prescient of the possibility that the division was destined for a one-year tour, pitched the idea of mid-tour leave in a slide-show presentation to Acting Secretary of the Army Les Brownlee during his visit to Mosul on June 25. Brownlee nodded in approval, but it was an expensive and dangerous proposition. Contracting planes and flights in and out of Kuwait would cost the Army tens, even hundreds of millions of dollars. The surface-to-air missile threat was still very high. Flying soldiers south would be risky. Force strength issues also came into play. Brownlee promised to chew over the proposal with his staff; Petraeus was the idea's number one lobbyist.

Days after learning of the one-year tour, Petraeus reached out to the families in a letter sent to every 101st Family Readiness Group. In it, he outlined his hopes for mid-tour leave, talked about their loved ones' mission and thanked his readers on the other side of the globe for their "continued support, encouragement, and understanding.

"Needless to say, none of us are jumping for joy at the prospect of staying here for a year. We all obviously would like to return home to our loved ones sooner than March of next year. Nonetheless, we are all professionals who volunteered to serve our Nation in uniform, who knew that our service might require such deployments, who recognize the importance of our mission, and who invariably are proud of what we're doing and proud to be doing it as a Screaming Eagle."

As is standard for the 101st Airborne Division, June and July was change of command season. Of course, most change of command seasons are usually conducted on the grass field of the Fort Campbell Parade Field. It was all the same for the 101st Airborne Division band, which was often given little time to catch their breaths between ceremonies. Some had wondered why the band was being deployed with the division; during the change of command season, they answered any lingering questions about their usefulness.

On June 21, Brig. Gen. Benjamin Freakley flew out of Mosul, saying goodbye to the 101st Airborne Division to take the post command at Fort Benning, Ga., and of the U.S. Army Infantry Center and School. In his honor, the soldiers of the Eagle Forward team held a reunion at the D-Main chapel to send him off, complete with a couple of locally-bought watermelons. Before letting the party begin, the "O" pinned a Bronze Star on Sgt. Maj. Hector Torres, an instrumental leader in making the Eagle Forward team work during decisive operations. "You were the first, you lived in the dirtiest conditions as anyone...I'm going to miss you." Major David Gunn, an Eagle Forward battle captain during decisive operations, presented Freakley with a poster recalling all the team's brightest moments. More than thirty soldiers who came to the reunion assembled in a single file line to shake his hand. Brigadier Gen. Frank Helmick, another product of the infantry and formerly the post commander at Fort Bliss, Texas, arrived days before Freakley left to take his post.

The 101st Airborne Division's number two, three and four rank positions changed hands just after the division began rebuilding operations in Mosul and northern Iraq. Brigadier Gen. Edward Sinclair left in June to take command of Fort Rucker, Ala., the Army's aviation's think-tank headquarters. Brigadier Gen. Jeffery Schloesser, another career aviator, became the new assistant division commander (support). Schloesser couldn't have been more perfect for that position at that time for one simple reason: the new number three was fluent in Arabic. The number four, Col. Thomas Schoenbeck, 101st chief of staff, left for Fort McNair, Fla., leaving his post for his weary replacement: Col. James Laufenberg, formerly the commander of the famed Old Guard at Fort Myer, Va.

The Laufenburg story provides a telling glimpse into the fast pace lives of the Army's senior officers. In June, Laufenburg had received some news. He would become the 101st Airborne Division's new chief of staff in Mosul. He would become the 101st's new chief of staff in less than a week. After relinquishing command of the Old Guard, he was to move immediately to northern Iraq and take over for Schoenbeck. The new job didn't come with a manual either. He knew what a chief of staff did, but the position came with entirely knew responsibilities in a combat zone. He would have to learn on the job.

Laufenburg took the orders in stride, excited for the opportunity to participate in the war. He was ready. He had been ready ever since he lost his friend, Maj. Kip Taylor, in the rubble of Pentagon on Sept. 11, 2001. Taylor had been an aide to Lt. Gen. Timothy Maude, the highest-ranking soldier to lose his life in the Pentagon attack. Laufenburg would wear the Screaming Eagle patch for the third time, serving with the 101st as a captain and a major in two different tours. His boss was not unfamiliar either. Laufenburg knew Petraeus when both were field grade officers at Fort Campbell and the Pentagon. For the next month, the new chief learned on the job with a whole lot of help from his subordinates.

Freakley, Sinclair and Schoenbeck wouldn't be the only Screaming Eagles on their way out. On May 27, the Army's "Stop Loss" program, preventing all soldiers who were participating in Operation Iraqi Freedom from getting out of the military even if they had completed their service obligations, was lifted. For 16,000 soldiers in the Iraq theatre, this was their ticket out if they wanted it. Many took it, some waited until their units came home with them. Numerous units would start to see some new faces in August as departing soldiers rotated out and soldiers straight out of Advanced Individual Training (AIT) rotated in. New commanders also started to appear with companies and battalions all over the division, although all but three brigade commanders (including all infantry brigade commanders) remained in place until the end. In the late spring and early summer, Col. William Harrison took command of Forrester's 159th Aviation Regiment, Col. David Martino took command of Division Artillery (DIVARTY), and Col. Samuel Holloway took the DISCOM guidon from Col. James Rogers.

In July, attacks on 101st troops gradually increased, and it appeared the burgeoning insurgency had trickled north. The 101st needed to respond to the increasing danger erupting in Mosul in the late summer. The onus was on Col. Joseph Anderson in particular. His Second Brigade would be tasked with patrolling the most dangerous parts of the 101st area of operation.

"The issue is not how many vehicles you have (in a convoy), the issue is what type of vehicles you have and what the people inside the vehicles are doing," Anderson said. Simply put, the protection the standard humvees provided soldiers in convoys was inadequate. Help was not on the way. The fortunate units had armored humvees, but they were usually restricted to the Military Police and a few, select infantry elements. Back in the United States, the Department of Defense was doing their best to streamline the production of armored humvees, but they wouldn't come nearly fast enough for the 101st. To protect soldiers, it was going to be up to the soldiers to fill the need. And so they did.

Using scrap sheet metal, soldiers reinforced vehicles, focusing especially on the floors to protect against Improvised Explosive Devices. Sandbags too functioned to protect against the same threat. The division looked to a factory in Dahuk for its next trick. To provide 360 degree protection for vehicles, the division contracted the factory to produce mounts for its .50 caliber and Mrk. 19 weapons. Hundreds of 101st vehicles swept through the factory and affixed their mounts. The mounts became an instant deterrent for ambushes. Convoys were taking the offensive in the face of the enemy. Ultimately though, the deciding response to the increase in ambushes was focus. "The issue was how you are going to respond to those instances. If you got hit and you ran away, you didn't fight back or fight through, you're going to keep getting hit," Anderson noticed. "And of course they were going to target easier convoys, it didn't matter how many vehicles were in them. If you looked like you were going out for a Sunday joy ride, you were going to get hit."

One summer ambush on a 501st Signal Battalion convoy provided the division with what they needed: intelligence. The convoy had been made countless times before, from the Mosul Airfield to the D-Main Palace. The 501st convoy was making the routine drive to pick up a generator. Senses were heightened because the sun had gone down, but around a dozen other 101st convoys were known to travel the route at any given time. The soldiers knew the route and the enemy knew the convoys' paths.

At 7:50 p.m., they crossed the Airfield's North Gate. The main road leading to the Mosul Bridge was just two or three miles away. They would never cross the Tigris before coming breathtakingly close to becoming another name in the news. Sitting and waiting from behind the convoy, a faceless enemy fired two Rocket Propelled Grenades (RPGs) at the fourth vehicle, a troop carrier with a gunner in the back, a driver and a commander in the right seat. One round sailed over the truck; the other hit the vehicle squarely in the back right tire. The gunner was launched into the air. If the unit had not earlier reinforced the truck with sandbags to absorb the blast, the gunner at the very least would have been killed. Remarkably, he survived with only minor injuries.

Reacting as trained, the convoy commander in the lead vehicle had his driver and the driver in the second vehicle slam their gas pedals and got out of the kill zone. They quickly returned to the airfield through the south gate, away from the ambush site. Because they were without radios, the second vehicle was oblivious to the ambush until they were away from danger. The third vehicle, also without communications, was also initially confused. Instinctively, the driver of the third vehicle turned around to support the incapacitated fourth vehicle. As the injured soldiers jumped into the vehicle, nearby locals laughed and shouted as they peeled out back towards the north gate. Only the truck commander, seated in the right seat, sustained serious injuries.

Attacks like the night ambush on the 501st Signal in Mosul were becoming more and more sophisticated as hostilities continued to intensify. The enemy, under an unknown command, had learned to fight with such precision and effectiveness that it was clear that these were not just random acts of murder. The 101st Airborne commanders needed to start learning from the enemy as the enemy was learning from the division. After Action Reviews (AARs) were being widely released to all 101st units by beginning of July. Every ambush taught the 101st something about the enemy they were up against. The lessons learned were aggregated at the brigade and division headquarters and made available on a secure Internet connection. The pre and post convoy briefs would bring the lessons full circle.

The 501st Signal too had made sure they spread what they had learned. "Sandbags work," they had stated emphatically on a slide-show After Action Review. "Convoy at night only when absolutely mission critical ... radios in each truck for intercommunication ... the camouflage net may have blocked some of the gunner's field of view – gun trucks should allow for the gunner to have maximum field of view." The last point was particularly salient. No 501st soldier ever spotted the attacker before or after the ambush.

Many division commanders quietly questioned whether or not Baghdad's weapons policy was working. In Mosul, the June 14 deadline came and went without the avalanche of weapons the 101st was looking for. With the amnesty period to turn over weapons long since over, the firearms were still at large and increasingly being used against the coalition. It's likely that few Iraqis who weren't a part of the insurgency objected to the all-out ban on RPGs, mortars, and heavy machine guns, but private citizens had complained that they couldn't protect themselves without their AK-47s. Mosul's remaining wealth of firearms was never more apparent than the structured Thursday afternoon gunfire. Most local weddings, the division soldiers quickly figured out, took place on Thursdays. Whereas any other day of the week the sound of nearby gunfire might lead a soldier to stop in their tracks, Thursdays were different. The so-called celebratory fire remained a problem for months, so much so that the division hired a local TV producer to make a public service announcement to highlight the harm that could be caused by rounds that were shot into the air inevitably coming back down.

Of course, the locals didn't limit themselves to firing aimlessly into the air. As the weapons program went dryer and dryer into the summer, the division increasingly noticed an explosion in ragtag vigilantes. With only one infantry brigade and an additional battalion patrolling one of Iraq's largest cities, the solution to the vigilante problem wasn't going to come easy. The 101st's relatively small element in the sprawling, populous city was supplemented only by the largely underdeveloped police force. They could not be everywhere, every time, and some trigger happy locals took notice. The enemies of the enemies, in Mosul, were not the 101st's friends.

The weapons policy was strong for certain, but remaining questions about whether it was strong enough lingered. Some even thought the policy was perpetuating the gun culture in a country with more than one firearm for every man, woman and child. The weapons policy had failed to stop fathers from celebrating their daughter's wedding by firing AK-47s into the sky and it had failed to stop terrorists from shooting at convoys. "It just didn't ban weapons," Col. Joseph Anderson remarked. "What would have worked best was a weapons buy-back program. Of course, a weapons buy-back program would have taken a lot of money." A lot of money indeed. The population of Iraq is twenty-five million people.

Availability of weapons hadn't sparked the insurgency, but it certainly fueled it. In June, the division started going door-to-door with a clear focus on the banned weapons. The policy mandated that all households give up their weapons above 7.62 mm, and hold no more than one weapon under that line. When the targets in question were mosques, the newly trained police took over. At every door step, the soldier knocked, waited for an answer, and politely explained to the families why they needed to inspect their homes.

Four days in July, the 14th to the 17th, had provided a good indicator for how far the 101st Airborne had come in improving security in the streets and defeating the Saddam and Ba'ath party loyalists who the coalition had believed were behind the attacks. July 14 marked the 45th anniversary of the overthrow of the British supported King Faisal in 1958. July 17 was an especially incendiary day for coalition forces. On that day in 1968, the Ba'ath party assumed control over Baghdad in a coup – ultimately leading to the rise of Saddam Hussein to power in 1979. These four days were primed for increased attacks on coalition soldiers, for obvious reasons. In response, the coalition launched Operation Soda Mountain, an operation designed to increase readiness and force protection measures against any anti-coalition assailants.

The onus was on Second Brigade, whose troops were sure to draw fire during patrols in Mosul. On the streets, dismounted patrols would almost invite fire so the enemy was identified, and then shoot or arrest an enemy for information. "Cordon and Knock" operations aimed to surround the targeted area, often a house or an apartment, and knock on the door looking for answers. Never would they treat anyone like a criminal or an enemy unless they knew that they were indeed a criminal or an enemy.

Convoys were reinforced and soldiers were more vigilant than ever. Major Gen. Petraeus ordered that all convoys include at least three vehicles (he later added a requirement for a fourth vehicle during night hours). The division and the coalition had learned a lot about how the enemy was conducting ambushes, and how to defend against them. Soldiers were trained on how to react to an ambush, sometimes using Matchbox cars for clarification. Non-commissioned officers became tougher and tougher on their soldiers, making certain their soldiers cleaned their weapons everyday.

July 17 came and went without a deadly attack in northern Iraq, to the relief of the division. Operation Soda Mountain ended with sweeping successes and surprisingly no coalition fatalities. In Mosul and throughout the 101st area of operation, 141 raids were conducted leading to 611 arrests, including sixty-two former Ba'ath party leaders believed to be coordinating the insurgency in Mosul. Of greater importance were the vast sums of weapons seized during Soda Mountain. More than 4,000 mortar rounds, 1,300 rocket propelled grenades, and 635 small arms were taken into coalition hands and away from insurgent forces.

Eager to showcase the progress the division had made since arriving in Mosul, Maj. Gen. Petraeus made certain everyone was ready for the July 21 visit from Deputy Secretary of Defense Paul Wolfowitz, Secretary Rumsfeld's number two. Visits from congressional delegations were becoming such a weekly rigmarole at the division headquarters that nobody really noticed when another one came walking through the front door. Dignitaries like Wolfowitz were different. Time stopped at the D-Main Palace when arguably one of the ten most powerful people in Washington walked by with Petraeus in tow. This was truly a momentous occasion for the 101st and the deputy secretary of defense. Wolfowitz was the most vociferous Bush administration insider from the immediate aftermath of Sept. 11, 2001, on the need for regime change in Iraq. In a cabinet meeting at Camp David on Sept. 15, 2001, Wolfowitz had pushed for a possible invasion of Baghdad as the fires at the World Trade Center were still burning. This was the first chance for the man called by *Time* magazine as "the father of the Iraq war" to see what was going right in Operation Iraqi Freedom, as well as speak to the soldiers fighting for Wolfowitz's agenda. Petraeus was his tour guide.

Wolfowitz pinned twenty-three Purple Hearts on soldiers to begin his day. He ate breakfast with a group of soldiers, met with Governor al-Basso, and received the obligatory briefing from the 101st CG on what was going on in the division area of operation. Culminating the day's events was a press conference with the parade of media that followed along all day. Wolfowitz's visit was uneventful as VIP visits went and he flew back to Baghdad before the sun went down, as his itinerary dictated. Had he known what was going to happen the next day in Mosul, he may have ripped his itinerary in half.

In the beginning, when asked "why are we going to war with Iraq?" soldiers would reply with answers as diverse as the Army itself, but invariably two subjects would be in focus: to get Saddam's weapons of mass destruction and to get Saddam. As of July, neither had happened. The former was an issue the 101st was working on. The division chemical assets examined several sites of possible chemical and biological weapons; none turned out to be anything more than a pesticide.

Coalition forces were relatively certain Saddam Hussein had moved into his hometown of Tikrit, where he had his strongest support among the local populace. There the 4th Infantry Division, whose headquarters were located in Tikrit at another palace once owned by Saddam, established check points around the city in hopes of strangling him and his supporters.

Saddam Hussein sightings in Tikrit and even in Mosul were as common in Iraq as Elvis Presley sightings are in Las Vegas. The average soldier in Iraq on more than one occasion saw an innocuous pedestrian walking down the street that looked eerily similar to the former dictator. Locals made a habit of reporting Saddam sightings to coalition forces too – few of which turned up anything. It was in Mosul and northern Iraq though that leads started to go somewhere regarding Saddam's most powerful and ruthless sons, Uday and Qusay Hussein. On May 11, a shepherd in the town of Sufuyah reported that Uday had been under the protection of a local family, staying in a bunker for the past forty-eight hours. A Peshmerga general reported the lead to Col. Michael Linnington, Third Brigade commander, and after investigation, Linnington had adjudged the tip to be credible. He requested immediate Unmanned Arial Vehicle (UAV) surveillance of the area while his brigade intelligence battle staff, attempted to contact the original source. The shepherd could not be found and attempts to get UAV coverage of the area were unsuccessful. Uday must have moved out of the area before the 101st could get a beat on the number three High Value Target (HVT).

The two sons were the source of the most horrifying stories of the former regime, with one son, Uday, arguably the most evil administrator of his father's reign over Iraq. Uday was Saddam's first son. His trophies included his own private zoo and zoo-like parties, where Uday's presence could suck the oxygen out of the room. He had reportedly made a habit of raping the girlfriends of other Ba'ath party officials and branding them with the letter "U" on their foreheads before releasing them back to their mates. Uday also controlled the Iraqi Olympic team, running that institution with unconscionable barbarity. The winners were given medals, the losers were tortured. Uday even had his own torture device in his office. He was the playboy; Qusay was the more disciplined, stable brother who had been anointed the heir apparent to Saddam.

He was the more cerebral of the brothers. Qusay had endeared himself to his father as the more viable alternative after his sibling's wicked antics had alarmed even Saddam Hussein. The younger brother, of course, was only marginally less sadistic than Uday. Qusay had been known to find entertainment in watching political enemies get fed, head first, into a wood chipper.

As the war began, the coalition knew that the two sons were more than figureheads. After Baghdad was taken and as the insurgency enflamed, the coalition suspected the two sons were again at the top of whatever command authority existed between the former regime and the disjointed irregular forces. Uday had commanded the Fedayeen forces that fought the invading forces in April along the Tigris River. Qusay ran Saddam's security forces. Neither had likely ceded authority after the regime lost control of Baghdad. Indeed, one former Iraqi intelligence official told *Newsweek* magazine that the two sons had command authority over 35,000 insurgent troops, loosely organized.

They were HVT #2 and #3, the top two targets below the ace of spades, Saddam Hussein. When locals came to the 101st compounds purporting to know their whereabouts, the division was compelled to listen. "We had a lot of folks, be it sheiks or folks off the street, that would come in and tell us that 'they knew where Saddam was, etcetera.'" said Lt. Col. D.J. Reyes, the division's top intelligence officer. "You can imagine after a while that it just got to be a tedious drill, trying to determine their credibility."

Information continued to flow into the 101st Airborne Division commanders and a number of tips, considered by Reyes and his subordinates as credible, were followed with combat operations, all unsuccessful. The repeated false leads had made the division intelligence staff more than just a bit skeptical of tips like the one they received on July 21 at 10 a.m. A local citizen approached the D-Rear command point asking to see an American soldier who could help him: he had information on Uday and Qusay Hussein. An NCO with a human intelligence team attached to the division (for just this purpose), met and interviewed the informant.

The source had no prior rapport with the division, but the intelligence team NCO assessed the lead was credible – the man had been a well-known Hussein family loyalist. He pointed to his home, located just miles down the road from the D-Main Palace, where he claimed he was harboring both sons. "His motivation was to get them out of his house because he was starting to feel uncomfortable, knowing that coalition forces were looking for them," Reyes recalled. The owner of the home had received millions in contracts under the U.N. Oil for Food program, endearing himself to the Ba'ath party regime by kicking back money from the contracts towards the Hussein family. His Saddam loyalties had wavered when the regime fell – he even flew a Kurdish Peshmerga flag outside his home. Then his neighbors noticed some odd changes. The man took his Peshmerga flag down and instead of his smoking his standard cigarettes, he started smoking some very expensive cigars. Neighbors were no longer invited inside his home. Then he started driving a brand new black BMW. The human intelligence team NCO immediately pushed the information up to the D-Main. Major Eric Suam, one of

Lt. Col. Reyes' deputies, moved quickly to pass the information to an element of Task Force 20, a secret special operations unit that was operating in coordination with the 101st in northern Iraq. Task Force 20 immediately began planning operations to capture or kill the two brothers as the division readied for a follow-up interview. The source was going to be put through a polygraph test.

Sweating under the weight of what would become the most important moment of Operation Iraqi Freedom to date, the source struggled to even remember his own name. The test came back a failure. The chief of staff and the D-Main Palace responded with a yawn. "When I first heard about it, I thought, 'Yeah, this could be something.' When they put the guy under the lie detector test, and he flunked it, then I didn't think anything about it," Col. James Laufenberg recalled. The intelligence NCO, whose name has never been publicly released, refused to question his own instinct. He continued to follow up the lead and insisted to his superiors that the source was indeed credible. The lie detector failure could have been the end of the lead, but the he had a hunch the polygraph system was the one that was lying.

"We were a little skeptical," Petraeus recalled. "We had so many of these people walk in everyday and ask for 30 million dollars. But there was enough to it that we thought it definitely had to be pursued."

The informant had told the division that Uday and Qusay Hussein were both staying in the home. Five other men, the source's wife and two kids were staying at the house. Task Force 20 presented overhead and frontal shots to Maj. Gen. Petraeus at a 10 p.m briefing. Petraeus immediately approved the raid, to begin the next morning. Few in the tactical operations center went to bed that night thinking July 22 would bring the division Saddam's two most valued lieutenants. With Petraeus' approval, Task Force 20 spent the night moving forces from Baghdad into position. Company B, 3-327th Infantry Regiment, was set to reinforce the Task Force 20 team. MEDEVAC units would be on alert. The next morning, the division interviewed the source at every angle. This time, he passed every test. He went back home and, unbeknownst to the two high value targets he was returning to, Amercian soldiers were right behind him.

The battle staff assembled in the morning, with Col. Laufenberg listening to the radio like a boy listening to his favorite baseball team in action. Petraeus and Brig. Gen. Frank Helmick had both left the D-Main Palace on separate engagements, keeping abreast of the operation on the radio net. The raid began with a simple knock on the door. The homeowner answered with his son at his side – both, along with other family members in the city, were quickly taken out of harms way. First reports started coming in at 10:15 a.m. Cordially, the coalition forces had invited the targets to surrender. The building was surrounded, although Uday and Qusay were apparently not convinced. Final warnings went unheeded before TF-20 entered the building. Without firing their weapons, TF-20 swarmed into the first floor. The brothers had slipped into a second floor room and started to return fire at TF-20 as they attempted to move up the stairs. Two Task Force 20 personnel were wounded, and after the brothers and whoever else was in the building started shooting at the surrounding forces outside, another 3-327th Infantry soldier was shot. Somewhat incredibly, none were seriously hurt. The TF-20 element pulled back to reassess with the division commanders how they were going to continue the assault.

The shots effectively tipped off to the division that they had indeed found Saddam's sons. Now the D-Main sprung into action as the first reports came in over the radio. "Shots fired!" Laufenberg felt a jolt of energy go through him. He turned to Reyes, who was just as shocked. "Well, there's somebody in there." He had only been on the job for three weeks, but it was the first time Laufenberg could remember a "cordon and knock" search being instantly met at the front door with gunfire. Helmick, after getting word of the resistance, changed his morning plans. He was on his way to the scene. Petraeus, out in the western part of the province, ordered his pilots to divert his Blackhawk back to Mosul as well. He wasn't going to sit on the sideline for this.

The brothers were not going to be taken out of the target building alive. Colonel Anderson too had been somewhat surprised by the resistance. He had just got out of a school opening ceremony and was on his way to a police station when he got word of the resistance. The police station engagement would have to be cancelled. When Anderson got to the scene, he would be in command. With two of the three most valuable targets in Iraq right in front of him, collateral damage was a second concern. A U.S. Air Force aircraft could drop a Joint Direct Attack Munition (JDAM) on the target within 10 minutes if such a move was called for by Anderson. He balked at the suggestion. There were too many friendly forces close to the target, and more were on the way.

Helmick had earlier notified Second Brigade to have a reaction force in place to cordon off the area. The reinforcements would come from Anderson's Delta Company, Third Battalion, and they would be led to the area by his chief operations officer, Maj. Brian Pearl. Anderson needed Delta Company in case he needed to "prep" the building further before the second try at entering the building. From the air, a squad of UH-58 Kiowa helicopters was on its way towards the building with the same mission. At 11:22, Helmick arrived. So too did a large crowd of locals who started to amass far too close to the action. Anderson dispatched an element to keep the spectators away from the firefight.

The shootout continued. The 3-327th element arrived and began prepping the building with their own .50 calibers, shoulder fired missiles, and Mk.19 grenade launchers. Kiowas began swarming the building, but their pre-assault fires misfired. The pilots couldn't get in close range of the building, and the Kiowas were turned off but instructed to circle around the target. Anderson also dispatched three AH-64 Apaches, but the firepower would have to come from the ground. Final assault preparations were given at 11:53 a.m. At Helmick's instructions, TF-20 made a second attempt to reenter the building.

Once again, they were fired at, this time with nobody hit, and they again pulled back out.

The issue of ending the assault with a devastating JDAM bomb again faced Anderson and Helmick, who were commanding the operation side by side. TF-20 personnel were insistent on the air raid, but Helmick was too concerned about collateral damage. "We're not going to do that, God dammit!" With a Mosque across the street and a crowd assembling across the street, Helmick feared a Mogadishu-like scenario if the building were destroyed in an air raid.

Instead, just before noon, Pearl and the Second Brigade reinforcements arrived. With Kiowa rockets having done little damage and having received Petraeus' approval over the radio, Helmick called on the Second Brigade anti-tank company. For more than thirty minutes, the target was hit with TOW missile after TOW missile. Eighteen missiles in total were fired at the building in the one-sided engagement. All hit their targets with precision. The missiles devastated the target. Each of the eighteen TOWs exploded in a brilliant cloud of fire and nobody outside of the building, neither a soldier nor an Iraqi spectator, was hurt in the blasts.

As the final rocket was fired into the building, an uneasy calm settled over the target and the soldiers who destroyed it. The firefight was over. The silence could only be broken by sound of the division commander's helicopter as it approached from the Mosul horizon.

Landing about twenty yards from Uday and Qusay's front door, with Anderson and Helmick speechless, Petraeus dismounted his helicopter and casually walked towards his ground commanders on site. "Frank, Joe – what's the situation here?"

TF-20 moved into the first floor, passing by a parked black BMW. This time, there was no AK-47 fire to greet them at the doorway. Only one person remained alive in the building. A boy later identified as Qusay Hussein's teenage son was hiding under a bed on the top floor. When he saw the TF-20 personnel enter, he fired his last shots and missed. TF-20 returned fire and didn't miss.

At 1:20, Task Force-20 entered the upstairs room. There Uday and Qusay Hussein lay in the adjacent bathroom, bearded, fat, and clearly dead. The two sons, the boy, and their lone body guard were killed in the raid. No coalition troop was lost. Moments after the raid was completed, a small element from the 431st Civil Affairs Detachment arrived to calm the crowd, but the word had already leaked. Instantly, the buzz in Mosul spread from street to street.

Some would later complain that TF-20 and the 101st should have found a way to take the two sons alive, so they could provide information about their father. That was unlikely on both accounts. The two sons were determined not to be taken from the firefight alive – even stuffing mattresses in the window in a pathetic attempt fortify the building from the shower of TOW missiles. Any expectation that the two sons would have ceded the location of the ace of spades was widely doubted by most American commanders.

Lieutenant Gen. Ricardo Sanchez, who replaced Lt. Gen. William Wallace as CFLCC commander shortly after the overthrow of Saddam, announced what had been leaked to the press hours earlier: Uday and Qusay Hussein had met their maker. "Saddam Hussein's sons were responsible for the torture, maiming and murder of countless Iraqis. Now more than ever, all Iraqis can know that the former regime is gone and will not be coming back."

From the Fort Campbell Public Affairs Office, just back from a deployment to Afghanistan, Master Sgt. Kelly Tyler answered the avalanche of media inquiries with her trademark sincerity. "The 101st kicks ass!"

Naturally, there was rampant skepticism in the streets of Iraq of the coalition's claim that Uday and Qusay were indeed dead. The images released of the two sons, with beards and clearly dead, did little to answer the Iraqi public's cynicism. Many Iraqi's were even offended that the American's did not follow strict Islamic custom, dictating that Uday and Qusay's bodies be masked, refrigerated and held until a family member came to claim them. That was unlikely to happen, though the coalition did extend the invitation for any Hussein family member to come to the Baghdad International Airport and carry out Uday and Qusay.

As the coalition, and more importantly the American media, revisited the

Uday and Qusay saga, the stranger the tale became. The two sons had carried a suitcase packed with some essential, and certainly non-essential, items to help them survive their escape from the coalition. Among the items found in their packages were several packages of men's underwear, dress shirts, cologne, a silk tie, a supply of Viagra and a single condom – along with 1.2 million dollars in cash.

And many questions arose from the realization that only one body guard surrounded two of the three most important members of the former regime. Several body guards, according to published reports in *Newsweek* magazine, had abandoned the two sons. After firing several members of his security personnel on a whim, Uday pleaded with the men to come back. They never did and the sons were practically on their own for the duration of the war.

Specialist Robert Woodward, an Army photographer with no relation to the man who took down Richard Nixon, earned a two-page spread in *Newsweek* Magazine for his picture of a TOW missile exploding on the target. After months of battling the civilian media from America's top news sources, the Army journalist finally had his moment to show his own talents. Woodward made the best of the opportunity. The picture would instantly become among the most recognizable images from the Iraq war.

Petraeus, realizing the potential pitfalls of making the sight into a Mosul tourist attraction, wisely had Uday and Qusay's former safe haven destroyed and completely cleared within a week of their deaths. Chunks of the building instantly became a favorite "war trophy" for division soldiers. They weren't the only ones coming out of the raid with a valuable war trophy, as it turned out.

On a map of the neighborhood, the division Staff Judge Advocate's office drew a circle around the Uday and Qusay house where nearby homes claimed to have been damaged by the concussion blasts in the raid. The radius, Capt. Jon Boyer was told, was over a mile. In what was one of the odder sights of the 101st tour in Iraq, Boyer, escorted by an infantry squad, carried nearly $200,000 in cash from a Special Operations fund in a backpack, to be doled out to the crowd of homeowners filing claims in the immediate aftermath of the raid.

Uday and Qusay had picked the wealthiest neighborhood in Mosul to hide. The neighborhood not-so-coincidentally was home to a number of formerly very high ranking Ba'ath party officials, people the division had been keeping a close eye on for months. They had been quiet during the 101st Airborne occupation of Mosul, causing little trouble but capable of financing all kinds of trouble for the coalition. Now, after Saddam's sons' deaths in their own back yards, the sleeping giants awoke. Their homes had been damaged, most with just broken windows, and they wanted to be paid.

CHAPTER 8

TURNING THE CORNER

Armed with a clipboard, a fresh face and a degree, a young man with a Coalition Provisional Authority badge brazenly approached Maj. Susan Arnold, a CPA military liaison. "Who's in charge here?"

"Who's in charge of what?"

"This entire operation. I want to know who's in charge." Arnold couldn't suppress a grin, but he wasn't joking around. He was angry, he wanted answers – he looked like he barely legally able to drink. Arnold, a Staff Judge Advocate officer, had become accustomed to this kind of behavior from her civilian counterparts at the CPA. It was as if the top of the military chain of command in Iraq stood only where the lowest end of the CPA began. At Fort Campbell, she was a field grade officer. In Iraq, she found herself taking heat from a prim fraternity brother. She assumed the man was looking for Dick Nabb, a retired colonel and the Northern Region chief for the CPA. But she was more amused than angry, so Arnold tried to do her best to assist him on her own.

Such exchanges were not uncommon between 101st soldiers and American civilians in the area. When Lt. Gen. (Ret.) Jay Garner left the country, the Coalition Provisional Authority took on much more of a State Department flavor as retired military officers went home with their departed boss. Nabb stayed, and Arnold was thankful he did. He was one of the good guys. It was Nabb who had lobbied for the 101st's move up to Mosul to establish a presence in the area. He didn't need to be in the country, but Nabb had fallen in love with the Kurdish people during his stint under Garner during Operation Provide Comfort. He wasn't young, but he was sure energetic. Nabb made certain to stretch himself every which direction, accepting every invitation to meet with every local official whenever asked. Arnold fed off of Nabb's drive.

In Sinjar, Arnold's husband, Lt. Col. Hank Arnold, was settling into his command with the 2-187th Infantry Regiment. The two had scant contact with one another, only seeing each other for four days when Lt. Col. Arnold was with the Eagle Forward staff. The two were so remote that, with her husband left without internet connection, Maj. Arnold would pass hand written letters through Col. Michael Linnington. She stopped mailing letters to her husband when she learned her mail was being circled in and out of theatre, taking weeks for the letter to go less than a hundred miles.

In July, Arnold moved out of the CPA office. She wasn't sorry, although she would miss the food, which was unquestionably better at the CPA headquarters. Her new job was at the D-Rear Airfield where she would go back to being a prosecutor for the SJA Office, sans any CPA prima donnas. Her new work would be no vacation. The courts martial from actions in Iraq had begun. Once at her new post, Arnold was almost immediately handed paperwork on a senior non-commissioned officer (NCO) who was accused of carjacking a Sheik's sports utility vehicle. The law of the Uniform Code of Military Justice was not going to be suspended because the 101st was at war.

In addition to her role as a prosecutor, Arnold would also have time for other SJA projects. Indeed, she was the first person Capt. Jerry Teresinski sought for help on his pet project. Teresinski was a reservist brought into the area when the SJA office realized they didn't have nearly enough lawyers to complete their mission in Mosul. In the spring, he had been one of Philadelphia's top DAs. Like many reservists, Teresinski had dropped a successful civilian career to join the force in Iraq.

Teresinski started working as soon as he arrived in June on the bar association and a court appointed attorney program in the new Mosul judicial system. Both were groundbreaking projects in a city and country where the right to councel was nothing more than a fantasy. Teresinski, with Capt. Jamie Phillips and Sgt. First Class Kevin Strakal, worked daily on meeting local lawyers and judges and setting up early elections for bar association leadership positions. More than 3,000 lawyers showed up to the elections. Teresinski was overwhelmed, but the elections went off without a major hitch. The process of building the court appointed attorney program was not as seamless. Convincing defendants that they had a right to a lawyer was tantamount to teaching calculus to a dog. The idea was necessary, but Teresinski was careful not to impose American jurisprudence in Iraq, rather bring them into compliance with international laws on human rights. They were a long way from that point. There was never an Iraqi equivalent to America's Miranda rights. The rights of the accused were to shut up and hope for the best.

Teresinski and Arnold went to work, training the Mosul attorneys on what would be a vastly new Iraqi jurisprudence. Both were aghast when they learned that Mosul, a city about the size of Teresinski's City of Brotherly Love, had only six public prosecutors. The horror continued when they learned what was done to defendants who stood before a Saddam appointed judge – or "Saddam's henchmen," as Teresinski referred to them. One of Ambassador L. Paul Bremer's first acts as coalition administrator in May was to write the basic rights of the accused into law. It was like going back to law school for a lot of Mosul attorneys, and Teresinski and Arnold were their professors. For three weeks – not a lot of time to learn all the new subject matter – the Iraqi attorneys learned all the new Iraqi statutes on slide show presentation after slide show presentation.

Each attorney would be paid about $100 a month until the Ministry of Justice could pay them a stable salary. The goal was to train about 400 attorneys before the end of the year. The importance of the court appointed attorney program was apparent. It was at the heart of Maj. Gen. Petraeus' efforts to establish rule of law in northern Iraq – a point not lost by Petraeus himself during one of the first graduation ceremonies. "Before this program, if you didn't have any money, you didn't get an attorney, and those in jail didn't get any representation. Sometimes the only way to get a court date would be to confess after you were tortured."

As the court appointed attorney program blossomed, so did the Mosul court itself. After months of renovations, aided by local volunteer work, the court had started to resemble its former self. Colonel Joseph Anderson donated $15,000 of his CERP funds to rebuild the lawyers lounge. The perimeter of the court house was also refortified to guard against a similar disaster like the one that destroyed the building in April.

"They weren't a helpless people," Teresinski said. "They just needed to be empowered."

Before long, the word of Teresinski's project got back to his hometown. His colleagues were impressed, so much so that before he would set sail on his way back to Philadelphia, his friends at the District Attorney's office were already pushing him to run for the top District Attorney position. The humble Teresinski balked at the idea. "I'm not a politician. I just try to do good things."

After the decision to disband the Iraqi army, the 101st needed to rush to put them back to work. Petraeus knew keeping the violence down in Mosul depended on finding ways to get the Iraqi vets to work and getting the weapons out of their hands. In Mosul, the interface for that process was the Veterans Employment Office (VEO), located just a block from the Tigris River in a building that was riddled during decisive operations. Petraeus donated $100,000 directly out of his Commanders' Emergency Relief Program fund to get the VEO standing as soon as possible; Col. David Martino, the new Division Artillery commander, kicked in with an additional $50,000. By July, out of the rubble bloomed an air-conditioned, fully furnished facility where soldiers from one military could reach a helping hand to soldiers in another. Captain Rick Schega ran the program along with seven subordinate soldiers and seventy-two locally employed workers. Former military personnel could simply walk into the office and register, and it was the VEO's job to find them employment from there. "When these soldiers find out that we're giving them ninety American dollars a month to guard a building, they can't believe it because just two or three months ago, they were only getting three dollars a month," Schega said as the VEO began operations. Two thousand former soldiers gained employment through the VEO in the first month, gaining the coalition two thousand more friends.

Veteran pension and government salary payments were also in full swing by July. Twenty-four million in U.S. currency and 1.2 billion Iraqi dinar arrived at the D-Rear Airfield on July 10, one of the largest money deliveries into Mosul. Heavily fortified convoys moved the money to two local banks secured by coalition soldiers – local banks that were not nearly ready at that point to safeguard their own reserves.

The money drops helped stabilize pension and salary payments to military and government employees – something the coalition had been severely behind on. By July, the coalition was even beginning to pay civil servants bonuses. "Because we are the government now, we are responsible for paying our employees," said Maj. Nathanial Balentine, a 431st Civil Affairs Battalion CPA liaison, as the money arrived. "This will help them feed their families." Incredibly, government and military salary and pension payments were back on track just months after the former government was defeated and the new government took over.

A payment center just four miles down the river from the D-Main Palace was established specifically for veterans' pensions. Retired military, partitioned by rank, were eligible to pick up a $120 monthly stipend on their designated day. The 2-502nd Infantry Regiment took the responsibility of patrolling the location, where in June a suicide car bomber succeeded in blowing himself up down the road at the pay site blockade but failed to take anybody with him.

Concerns about Arab-Kurdish hostilities were starting to be alleviated too. It would have been incomprehensible in May for the division to expect so little trouble in bringing the two formerly warring factions together without widespread violence. Coming into the region, Maj. Gen. Petraeus knew the chasm between the Kurds and the Arabs was going to have to be bridged by the division.

For several reasons, the Kurds sought their own interests in Mosul – interests they refused to be denied. The area had once been their land too. Saddam's Arabization had forcefully removed the Kurds from the land they built and owned. Decades later, the Kurds stood in Mosul again as the Kurdish Peshmerga forces joined with U.S. Special Forces to take the city without the help of any other coalition force of division strength. They were owed their city back.

The difficult balance for the 101st stood with the Peshmerga presence in Mosul. Kurds patrolling the predominately Arabic city was tantamount to lighting a match in a pool of gasoline. This could not last if any kind of stability in Mosul was going to endure. The "negotiations" began when Col. Joseph Anderson allowed the Peshmerga elements operating in his city to secure their compounds without U.S. encroachment. It was a give and take. The Peshmerga couldn't go outside their compounds in uniform and with weapons, but as long as they stayed within their fences, they presented no problems. In the beginning, the agreement didn't sit well with a number of rogue company level Peshmerga commanders. No less than a half a dozen times, Anderson's patrols arrested Peshmerga soldiers for doing exactly what they shouldn't have been doing.

Arrests turned into diplomatic squabbling. When they inevitably lost their weapons, the Peshmerga would ask for them back and Anderson would have to deny that request. It was nothing short of a juggling act with the forces that were as responsible for taking Mosul from Saddam as anyone.

Anderson later authorized ten places where the Peshmerga could establish compounds. All were within his area of operation, but safely out of the way of his brigade. Many of the Peshmerga forces, Anderson found out later, rotated in and out of the Mosul compounds from bases in the Kurdish town of Dahuk. For the most part, the Peshmerga didn't bother Anderson's Second Brigade and, in turn, Anderson didn't pay too much attention to the Peshmerga. Everything for Anderson was smooth sailing with his Kurdish friends until one late summer incident forced him to rethink the agreement.

Anderson and the commanders of the 3-327th Infantry Regiment had discussed running boat patrols up and down the Tigris River. Because of the problematic logistics and Anderson's belief that the patrols would not have been fruitful, the Second Brigade commander decided against the idea. The 3-327th commanders weren't listening and on July 2, their clandestine boat patrols were unmasked after one of the ugliest incidents in Mosul during the 101st's tour.

It could have been the first or the last in a long line of boat patrols that Anderson never authorized, but regardless, the July 2nd patrol was not properly coordinated with the Second Brigade operations office or more importantly, with the Peshmerga. The boat, they thought, was an insurgent boat, not a coalition patrol. From their building, the Peshmerga element staged at their compound opened fire at the 3-327th boat, and the boat fired back. Four OH-58 Kiowa helicopters were called in to reinforce the boat patrol, still oblivious to the fact that the compound was housing a friendly element. In the exchange, a local reporter who had stayed at the compound and a Peshmerga soldier were killed.

Anderson learned about the incident at a ceremony in Irbil. Suddenly, Mosul wasn't big enough for both Anderson's brigade and the Peshmerga. "Then we started going in their compounds. We gave them autonomy, but then we started going in and doing inspections, and then we started finding mortars and RPGs, and they weren't allowed to have those kinds of weapons."

By August, the Peshmerga forces weren't causing any more problems for Anderson and his brigade. In fact, by late summer, it was the Peshmerga, or at least soldiers formerly of the Peshmerga, who had forged its own partnership with the 101st Airborne Division.

The U.S. Army and the U.S. Military are often credited for being a catalyst for radical social change during the civil rights era after President Harry S. Truman ordered the desegregation of the United States Armed Forces in 1948. In Iraq, the military would take the lead again in changing the social climate – with the help of the most diverse Army the world has ever seen.

The 2-44th Air Defense Artillery, with no enemy threat to combat from the air, was tasked to train, equip, and mold the Joint Iraqi Security Company. It was an experiment and the ambitions were modest. The new company was earmarked to be used to man security points around ammunition supply points in Mosul. Eventually, as the thinking went, they would grow into a Homeland Security fighting force in Iraq. Other coalition units in other regions of Iraq received similar orders, but the 2-44th ADA's mission would be much different. The Joint Iraqi Security Company trained by the 101st Airborne would combine soldiers from the Kurdish Peshmerga forces and the former Iraqi Army, predominantly Arabic, as well as new volunteers from both sects. Nowhere else was a unit tasked to combine two warring adversaries into one coherent fighting force.

Captain Brian DeLeon, a former Eagle Forward battle captain, commanded the company of 2-44th ADA soldiers who played the role of drill sergeants for the JISC. The training predominately took place in Deleon's back yard, at the 2-44th ADA's main compound in Mosul, starting in late May. It was clear from the first day that the Peshmerga soldiers were light years ahead of the former Iraqi soldiers. The Peshmerga came to train dressed in their green battle-dress uniforms and red berets, not one soldier minutely different from another. They marched perfectly in sequence and gave proper military courtesies not only to their own superiors, but their superiors wearing the American flag on their right shoulders.

Simply put, the soldiers formerly employed by Saddam looked like a defeated bunch. They marched out of sequence, they knew nothing about showing military customs to their superiors, and they exhibited little interest in learning how to be productive soldiers. DeLeon had an uphill battle ahead of him.

Language barriers between the Kurds, the Arabs and the American instructors had to be bridged. Several linguists were employed to explain tasks and skills from DeLeon and his instructors, once in Arabic and over again in Kurdish. The JISC was trained in firing an AK-47, run through exhaustive physical training and certified in military common tasks that every U.S. soldier is tested on during Basic Training – first aid, drill and ceremony and weapons handling. Most of the time, the 2-44th company just taught by example and eventually their pupils started to respond.

The instructors were hardly trained for this, with a few exceptions. Sergeant First Class Daniel Foley had been an instructor for young non-commissioned officers in the Army's Primary Leadership Development Course (PLDC). He knew all about training soldiers. A good number of his subordinates though were as wet behind the ears as the recruits. They got a crash course on training soldiers, courtesy of Foley and courtesy of the U.S. Army Sergeants Major Academy, which provided a rigid program of instruction for the 2-44th ADA team.

The training was not easy, not for the recruits or the instructors. The mercury on the thermometer regularly rose above 110 degrees. The workday often began at four in the morning and ended after midnight. It was a taxing regimen on the recruits but an even more exhausting workload for the instructors. In less than a month, the recruits were expected to be schooled in basic rifle marksmanship, first aid, hand-to-hand combat, and lots and lots of drill and ceremony. Foley sometimes found himself getting as much sleep in a week as he was used to getting in one night at Fort Campbell. "Your heart really had to be in it," Foley said later. In just three weeks, it was like sticking a funnel down their recruits' throats and pouring. "We needed more time, I would have wanted more like eight weeks to do what we did." The division didn't have that kind of time.

As the first training cycle reached the last week, it was apparent that the Peshmerga soldiers were so far ahead of their Iraqi counterparts that several of their most outstanding soldiers would be retained to work with the 2-44th ADA as instructors for future cycles. Thus, in an ultimate test of the new Arab-Kurd goodwill, the Kurdish Peshmerga soldiers would be in charge of their former enemies of the former Iraqi army. If the Arabic soldiers of the Iraqi army failed to leave their distain for Kurds at the door, life in the JISC would be unbearably difficult.

Not everyone made it to the end, but in July, the Joint Iraqi Security Company had completed their training and graduated as a team. Their company guidon, with two hands clasped together in the center, provided a stark illustration of what the new company had accomplished. (The guidon had in fact been designed by the students without any influence from their American trainers.) They had cooperated and graduated and in doing so, they had formed a cohesive fighting unit of two sworn enemies. The new company used Iraqi rank, but used much of the customs developed by the Kurds. It took some work, but the company looked like a team, with both sects of Iraq indistinguishable from one another in the formation. Dressed in their newly provided uniforms and black berets, the Joint Iraqi Security Company joined the coalition and went to work at the Mosul ammunition supply point, across the street from the D-Rear Airfield. It was no small task either. Foley was later told the supply point was the third largest in the world.

They were just the first. There would be more companies to follow in their footsteps. After the first company graduation, the JISC took on a new name: The Iraqi Civil Defense Corps. The new name aimed to draw focus away from the political significance of the unit. They were more than just a statement; the ICDC was going to be an active member of the coalition.

Vetting for the ICDC was done at the Civilian Military Operations Center. Recruiting would not be easy. There was, naturally, initial apprehension from some locals to join a military that fought with former enemies, not against them. Locals were also uneasy about supporting the coalition forces. "I'm not sure a lot of folks were convinced we were the winning team," said Lt. Col. Donald Fryc, 2-44th ADA commander. "It was a recruiting challenge." Either for pride or for a paycheck, unemployed Iraqi men came for the opportunity to join. A vast majority of the recruits were from the former Iraqi army, but former Fedayeen soldiers were automatically expelled once their former allegiances were uncovered. The pay was good. Privates received a $60 paycheck each month. Senior enlisted received upwards of $120 a month. Officers got around $150 to $200 a month. Actually getting them the money was not always easy. Bogged down in the coalition bureaucracy, the 2-44th was not always able to squeeze out their payroll from Baghdad. DeLeon often had to tell soldiers that their pay was late in coming. Before they could deliver their late paychecks, a number of soldiers walked out on the ICDC.

In the coming months, Deleon, Foley, and the 2-44th Air Defense Artillery instructors would train company after company, ten in total, with two brigades manning security points across all three infantry brigades area of operation. Colonel Ben Hodges rushed to one graduation in August in Mosul to welcome one company. The graduation was on Saturday; the company was patrolling a pipeline for Hodges by mid-week.

The plan to have the ICDC pull security on fixed points was just one of four measures the 101st had identified to eventually hand over their responsibilities to Iraqi forces. The Syrian, Turkish, and Iranian borders were being patrolled by overstretched American troops. They needed to be immediately reinforced. Iraqi police needed to begin participating in patrols in their own streets – not simply the American Army. Lastly, the Iraqi army, after being disbanded in May, needed to be rebuilt. In Mosul, the birth of the new Iraqi army came on July 19 with the opening of a new army recruiting center in a formerly abandoned building. The building was renovated and equipped with new computers, desks and a photo identification system – just like a standard military entrance processing station for the American military. Twenty applicants began processing on the first day, exceeding all expectations. Business immediately started to boom in the following days, much to the excitement of the 101st Airborne command staff. Not everyone was welcome. Five non-waiverable disqualifiers were established for anyone walking through the recruiting center doors. Former members of the Iraqi Republican Guard, level four or higher Ba'ath Party members, former Iraqi intelligence officers, former Iraqi soldiers who held the rank of colonel or higher and anyone who had "violated any human rights at any time," according to the code, were automatically screened out of the new army. Physical requirements would also be rigidly enforced.

After applicants were given the go, they were given a specified date to report when they would load onto a bus and ship to Kirkuk for basic training. The coalition had planned on training 1,000 soldiers by the end of summer and 9,000 soldiers by the end of 2003.

The anarchy ruling the streets of Mosul in the months following the fall of Saddam stemmed from one main source. The police force was incompetent, corrupt and respected by few in the community. The association with the police and the Ba'ath Party regime was imbued in the Iraqi culture. The former Iraqi dictator had tactically dressed his police in green fatigues that resembled his military's uniforms as a way to assert his dominance over the Iraqi people. Little was done to coral corruption within the force. Literally, the only way for a local to report a crime effectively would be to bribe the police. Nearly all other reported crimes were ignored.

The level of violent crime, drugs and utter disregard for the rule of law in Mosul reflected incompetence of the police force under Saddam. Soldiers manning check points around Mosul uncovered at least one stolen car a day. The sound and even the sight of gunfire from short distances were routinely ignored by Mosul police. There was absolutely no rule of law governing the local traffic. It was not uncommon for a convoy to weave around a man riding a donkey, herding his sheep. Soldiers often had to dismount their vehicles in order to direct traffic at congested intersections. There was just nobody to patrol the streets except the soldiers.

Employing soldiers to run the police force was not a long-term option, but the police forces around northern Iraq, especially Mosul, were too ineffective to leave to their own devices. In Mosul, the division needed 6,500 policemen on the streets. The total was based on Houston, a city larger than Mosul but a city that faced nowhere near the level of crime. "Our job," Col. Joseph Anderson noted, "was to co-work with the police. We were not filling any holes." The "million-dollar question" facing Anderson, Petraeus, and every field grade commander in the Nineveh Province was who was going to fight what crime? There was a fine line. Was it up to American soldiers to stop a crazy driver, or to arrest a man from shooting into the sky after his daughter's wedding? Could the division, in turn, expect the police to take part in raids on suspected enemy homes?

The goal was Iraqification. When the police were ready to deal with crime, they would and they did. And when the police were ready, criminals arrested by the police went to prison, not a coalition compound detention facility. Professionalism was the key to building a reliable police force. The 503rd Military Police Battalion, an attached unit from Fort Bragg, N.C., developed the standard program of instruction for the police in Mosul. In fact, officials from Baghdad had come to Mosul ready to give point-by-point instructions on how to train police. The delegation was led by Bernard Kerik, the former New York Police Department chief of police. Kerik knew something about training police, but knew even more after being told what the 503rd had been doing. He and the delegation from Baghdad left with a new program courtesy of the 503rd to take back to Baghdad. The programs focused on cleaning out corruption and changing the basic mindset that had tarnished the force for so long. Cadets were also trained in hand-to-hand combat, filing reports, investigative techniques and weapons training. The new force needed to learn to communicate with the locals. Five levels of force, in sequence, were drilled into the new policemens' head – verbal persuasion, unarmed self-defense, use of riot batons, threat of deadly force and, lastly, use of deadly force. At the end of many training days, the 101st MP assets would help put the teachings into practice, including the police cadets on night patrols.

All three infantry brigades had developed their own, separate police academies for their areas of operation. Anderson's area of operation was vastly different than the normally quiet Tal Afar and Quyarrah. Colonels Linnington and Hodges had developed three-week programs; Anderson needed his cadets for eight weeks with returning police getting by with a three week program. Again, the reserves would pull their weight for the 101st Airborne Division. The 1156th Law and Order Detachment, a reserve unit from West Virginia, was tasked with training the academy cadets. Many of the 1156th soldiers were themselves state police.

Once the cadets became policemen, they looked vastly different than the police that patrolled the streets of Mosul months earlier. The new police walked the streets, armed with 9 mm pistols, in their new blue uniforms. Anderson started refurbishing fourteen police stations to supplement the thirteen existing, stable police stations in the city by the time the first academy graduates started on the job. The Mosul police headquarters, destroyed during the post-war April riots, was earmarked for an $118,000 CERP fund rebuilding project. "The Warriors Club," an Iraqi veterans club for former generals in Mosul, was quickly turned over to an information center for the police. Another military intelligence center in the city became a 911 quick reaction center.

Most important to the new force was to earn back the trust of the people they were paid to protect. That was slow to come around. Colonel Hodges, speaking to his first academy graduating class in Quyarrah, gave a stern directive to the new police officers. "For this town to prosper, for this town to prosper, you must respect the people you protect ... do not take money or favors, protect all people equally. The better you treat the people, the more help they will give you."

Training the new fire department required the division to make firemen out of rank amateurs. Soldiers with the 938th Engineering Detachment, a reserve element out of Idaho, could only chuckle when they learned that the fire department had routinely flooded burning buildings – a futile and potentially explosive method for fighting a fire. It was amusing but troubling for the Idaho reservists. They would be the ones to train the new Mosul Fire Department.

Reservists from the 482nd Firefighting Engineers, a Kansas reserve element, would help. Specialist Eric Voss, a part-time soldier, full-time firefighter from Halstead, Kan., would anchor the academy. Voss would comment after his first academy graduation cycle that he'd "hire these guys in my civilian department. They're 100 percent ready to go." There were truly no compromises afforded to the cadets. In the past, the local firefighters had never walked into burning buildings, choosing only to fight the fire from a safe distance. Under Voss, as a part of their training, they learned to walk into a burning building, fight the fire and save anybody who was caught inside. The training was as real as could be offered. Every cadet received more than a thousand hours of training, including a special day at the Mosul Airfield when they were expected to walk into a burning bunker and extinguish a fire. "It was melting the fire shields," 938th Engineering Detachment instructor Capt. Mark Pruett remarked. "That's how hot it was."

After the final day of the eight-week academy in October, the first thirty certified graduates of the post-Saddam era graduated. The money came through for the new department. Before they were ready to take to the streets, the 101st Airborne Division would spend more than $300,000 to equip and train the firefighters.

In the spring, a group of soldiers from the 431st Civil Affairs Detachment made a bit of history while on a mission about forty miles north of Mosul, just by finding something fun to do while their officers and senior NCOs were at a briefing. They were at the Mosul Dam, formerly named the Saddam Dam, and by jumping in a lake located down the street from the dam, they likely became the first people ever to swim in what was Saddam Hussein's personal vacation home during his reign. The area surrounding the dam was arguably the most breathtakingly beautiful area in Iraq any soldier with the 101st would have the pleasure of witnessing. The area's vast rolling hills and radiant blue lake provided a veritable fisherman's paradise for the Arkansas and Texas-based reserve unit. It quickly became a popular destination.

The unit's public works and utilities team convoyed to the area several times a week in their first two months in Mosul – never with their fishing rods. Aside from its spectacular beauty, the dam and the lake were critical to the local infrastructure in providing electricity and water to the local area, particularly farmers. The dam had the capacity to provide more than 750 megawatts of electricity to the northern Iraq power grid. A nearby water pumping station was also a sensitive target for infrastructure rebuilding efforts. If the water pumps could successfully irrigate water to farmers in the area, local tomato and potato harvests would see production rates unseen before. Neither operations were functioning at full capacity at the time the 101st arrived; fixing the Dam and the water pumping station became an early top priority of the division.

Mismanagement of the dam was beginning to debilitate the facility, particularly the water pumping station. Coalition inspectors found the dam's foundation alarmingly deteriorated and tenuously holding on. It had originally been built and run by a South Korean company. When Gulf War I was launched, their engineers were evacuated and the facility was left for the inexperienced Iraqis. Sergeant Sean Driscoll, a 326th Engineering Group squad leader who had no prior experience with hydraulic plumbing outside of his own bathroom, was tasked to rebuild what the last twelve years had destroyed. It was a formidable task.

Driscoll got to the facility and immediately ran an assessment with some help from a group of specialists from the Army Corps of Engineers. The results were jaw dropping. Two of the main water pumps that the facility ran on needed to be replaced if the facility was going continue to be operational. Ten more pumps at three of the auxiliary pumping stations also needed to be replaced. The issue was power. Three to four times an hour, the power would go out at the facility. The result was the rapid attrition of the pumps when the water, flowing upward through the pipes, would lose its water pressure and come crashing down with prodigious weight. One small auxiliary pumping station, Driscoll found, had been flooded from the same process.

The water pumps were just the beginning. Several stop valves, which plug the water flow when needed, were destroyed. The computer system was archaic, likely left by the South Koreans in 1991. Now they needed parts, fast. It was worth the effort and the money, everyone involved agreed. Each water pump held the capability to pump 3.5 cubic meters of water, or 300 gallons, a second. The result of getting the water flow stabilized for the northern Iraqi farmers could not have been overstated.

At the time the division arrived, the water pumping station was only irrigating water at a thirty percent capacity for the land that depended on the facility. That would not be good enough for the 2003 harvest. The facility was at the heart of efforts to irrigate water to remote farmers who were thirsty for water for vegetable and wheat harvests. "That irrigates about 280,000 acres in western Nineveh. That's their main source of irrigation," said Capt. Wade Reeves, 431st Civil Affairs Food and Agriculture team. Reeves, a veterinarian with the U.S. Department of Agriculture, oversaw operations to get the facility operating at around a fifty to sixty percent level in the short term, one-hundred percent in the very long-term future. At a $20,000 price tag, two new hydro-pumps were installed in the main facility – but that was not a long-term fix. The problem was power and the water irrigation system could only power itself for thirteen hours a day.

For the water thirsty farmers of northern Iraq, their futures hung in the balance. The coalition needed to stand up the water irrigation system enough for the local farmers to have a bumper crop in the fall and into next year. Power was the key.

The dam was in equally dire straights. The turbines were lacking the necessary oil lubricant and could not operate at full capacity without an emergency delivery of a specific brand of oil compatible with the facility. If the coalition had been able to assist with the operations of the facility, the dam would likely have imploded by the end of the year, causing a catastrophic loss of energy to the northern Iraq power grid.

The efforts to regenerate the 750 megawatts of power hinged on getting the four turbines working again – that would be fixed with the turbine oil. Workers who lived in government-subsidized housing needed to be paid. Three to four thousand workers and dependents lived in the area; they needed food and medical supplies. The foundation needed direct and immediate attention. Coalition engineers and the 431st Civil Affairs Detachment initially oversaw operations that essentially injected cement into the dam's base, like a tooth filling. The 926th Engineering Group did initial geological assessments of the dam and later took over the ongoing project from civil affairs.

The city of Mosul took an immediate liking to their newfound freedom of speech, something that was not afforded to the Iraqi people before defeat of Saddam's regime. Citizens had the right to participate in their government like they never had before, and their new government would never have the right to impede on that freedom. A group calling themselves "The Voice of the Youth of Mosul" was among the very first and most vociferous organizations to exercise their freedom of speech in May outside the Civilian-Military Operations Center, then located in downtown Mosul. They were there to challenge the coalition and they held a banner demanding a list of needs from the new government. Brigadier Gen. Freakley took notice and met with the group personally. His message for the group: work with us, not against us, and put your words in to actions. The division needed help cleaning the Mosul court house after the April riots. Freakley asked the organization for help and immediately got fifty volunteers to go to work. The 101st quickly found out it had an able ally in The Voice of the Youth of Mosul and wanted to continue working with the group as a way to support volunteerism in the community. Membership boomed once the word got out, and by the end of June, the organization grew to more than 400 volunteers. As "The Voice" participated in more and more coalition projects in Mosul, the division was able to use their new friends for more than labor. Through the volunteers, the 101st kept the pulse of the Mosul people and established two-way communications with the community through the organization. The Voice had become exactly what their name stated: they were representing the people of Mosul and were able to successfully bring any requests and complaints to the 101st Airborne Division command staff.

The division needed a reliable partner in the city, and they found it with The Voice of the Youth of Mosul. In addition to providing a liaison with the community, they also helped with coalition initiatives in city employment and healthcare, including rebuilding a Mosul nursing home. Their volunteerism was rewarded when Maj. Gen. David Petraeus began supporting their efforts through his CERP fund. Their skilled and unskilled labor helped the division with rebuilding projects in ways that normal contractors couldn't. They were dependable and they worked harder for less. Working directly for the CG with The Voice was Capt. Julie Simoni, who had been tasked to watch over division's CERP projects. "They have all nationalities, all religions and some women that help ... originally this organization was opposed to U.S. occupation."

The 101st Airborne Division had done more than win over the hearts and minds of The Voice of the Youth of Mosul, the division forged a partnership in the efforts to rebuild Mosul. More such friendships were needed.

In that mission, the Commander's Emergency Relief Project fund was the ultimate weapon. CERP funds were instrumental in funding nearly every 101st Airborne Division rebuilding project. Schools, hospitals, roads, municipal buildings, even a summer camp for Mosul kids were supported by the CERP funds. The division commanders had deep pockets and were eager to spend. "There was no budget for CERP," Petraeus said later. "We were never told the amount we had allocated to us. We were just told to spend money, which we did very aggressively."

But nobody thought the money would last forever. The expenses were mounting. The division was responsible for paying civil salaries much longer than Baghdad had told Petraeus to expect. The salaries weren't the only unexpected expense. Equipment needed for water irrigation and power was still AWOL. The division, not Baghdad, would need to foot the bill. Nobody was sweating the phantom budget more than Simoni, a former military police officer before law school turned her into an Army attorney. As the division CERP officer, Simoni had watched a $10,000 spending limit for each brigade commander on one project explode into a $50,000 cap by July. The division was drawing money at $500,000 increments.

Nobody had to worry about the fog of uncertainty surrounding the Commander's Emergency Relief Project funds, not short-term at least. More money was trickling into the CERP fund as high-level Ba'ath party officials, with cash on them, were arrested trying to leave the country. Money not found by looters in Saddam's palaces was also being poured into the pot. So as long as the money existed, not one American tax-payer dollar was going to be spent on an Iraqi school, health clinic, or road. But like all good things, the CERP funds were bound to come to an end.

Hundreds of locals waited in line daily outside of the Civilian Military Operations Center to file claims against the coalition, and the Office of the Staff Judge Advocate initially was anything but parsimonious in awarding those claims. Vehicle accidents, property damage and just about anything that locals could claim the coalition was culpable for was brought before the 101st SJA claims office. While obviously bogus claims were rejected, many indemnity seekers in the beginning did not find too much trouble in getting money shortly after the division arrived in Mosul, provided their charges were verifiable. Claims were never slighted for families of lost policemen and firemen, who were given a standard $1,000 in American currency for their loss – a tremendous sum in the Iraqi marketplace. "It generates good will and we're putting money back into the economy," said Lt. Col. Richard Whitaker, 101st Airborne Division Staff Judge Advocate. "Now, after we got taken advantage of for two or three weeks, we started tightening things up a bit."

The SJA's approach to claims changed in the summer months. For better or worse, the CMOC was the interface between the people of Mosul and the 101st Airborne – a natural place for the SJA claims office to operate from. The first claims were awarded on June 25 when around sixty locals were paid anywhere from sixty to seven-hundred dollars. They would hardly be the last. Captain Jon Boyer had seen about everything from the division claims office at the CMOC. After a disastrous ammunition supply point fire in June, Boyer had followed over a thousand claim reports for families claiming to have suffered structural damage to their homes in the incident. In the first three months on the job, Boyer had handed out more than $600,000 in claims – two-thirds of that total came directly from the ammo supply point calamity. Most of those claims were legitimate, Boyer conceded. Others were laughable.

Boyer, a remarkably humble Harvard Law graduate, could not help but laugh at the shameless stupidity of what he called, "The Gator attack" claim. The story began when a group of American soldiers, outside the wire, ambushed a man's car on four-wheel carts (called "Gators") with screwdrivers as their weapons. The man brought his car to stop. The soldiers then surrounded his car and smashed in the windows with their flatheads. Defenseless, the man just shielded himself as the assailants ransacked his car. The claim was swiftly rejected, as were more than half of the attempts by locals to get a quick buck courtesy of the coalition. One man even had the audacity to make separate bogus claims in the same day to the same paralegal, Pfc. Ryan Deckard. Deckard the second time around instructed the man to wait by as he summoned a Mosul police officer.

Specialist Evelyn Soto got the hang of dealing with the parade of claimants that awaited her each morning. Like a drill sergeant, she aligned them in a single file line. Anybody who thought they were deserving of a claim had to first get through the stalwart Soto. Deckard and Soto had been dealing with their usual routines when perhaps the most asinine claim the office ever took came right up to their desk. A fifteen-year old kid, walking with a dramatic limp, claimed he had been hit directly by a division cargo truck while riding his bicycle. Knowing that local cars had been reduced to tin foil after colliding with the division's vehicles, Deckard and Soto were immediately skeptical. Through his interpreter, Deckard asked what time he had been hit. "10:15, today." Deckard looked at his watch. The accident happened forty-five minutes ago. The minimum wait in line to get to the claims desk was more than five hours. The boy, having instantly recovered from his limp, walked out penniless.

Legitimate traffic accidents, not uncommon in the chaotic Mosul streets, were the cause of a many of claims brought to the SJA lawyers. Soldiers who couldn't adapt to the rules of the road in Iraq, where the other guy has the right-of-way in any given situation at any given time, often traded some paint with local commuters and gave the claims office some more paperwork. "Some people (gave) us a hard time, but they're orderly in a sense that when we can't help them, they get very emotional and they don't want to hear 'no,' but they don't make threats or swear at us," said Spc. Spencer Beatty of the SJA claims office. "Americans would probably do worse in the same situation." Many soldiers would have been shocked to have learned that indeed Iraq did have traffic laws, most of which mirrored the American laws.

With Petraeus' mid-tour leave proposal at a standstill in Washington, the division headquarters began offering four-day Rest and Recuperation (R&R) in a selected site in the Kurdish region. Soldiers selected by their chain of command could go to rock climbing up in the hills of northeastern Iraq, they could opt for a contracted hotel in the Kurdish controlled city of Dahuk, or they could wait for a trip to Qatar – the R & R site established for the entire coalition by U.S. Central Command. The favorite spot was Qatar: Soldiers could drink there without repercussions under General Order Number 1, prohibiting the possession or consumption of alcoholic beverages.

Officers were unlikely to go anywhere. The lower enlisted had top priority on R&R. That's why Capt. Maggie Smith laughed when her husband emailed her with the idea of skipping to Dahuk for their first wedding anniversary, September 14. "We've had the most fabulous first year of marriage of any newlyweds ever had fighting a war," he told her. Maggie told him that there were too many enlisted soldiers in the battalion that had not gone yet for her to go, but Ben was persistent. A week before their anniversary, Maggie's office phone rang with a call from none other than her husband. "This is Captain Smith."

"Honey, it's me. I got my battalion to donate a couple of slots for R&R. Just ask if you could have a couple of days off to go to Dahuk." The R&R slots were for one week after their anniversary, but it was better than nothing. She got the two days off without much resistance from her superiors. Maggie did, however, get some resistance from her back just before her anniversary and a little more than a week before she was scheduled to go on R&R. It was nothing serious, she just injured it at work and was prescribed some "strictly business" pain killers from the battalion flight surgeon. She had never been one to take prescription drugs, not even aspirin, but she wasn't one to ignore the doctor either. So with some water out of her canteen, she downed two and went to sleep in her cot. They knocked her out like a prizefighter.

She was abruptly awoken in the middle of the night in a daze. It was her first anniversary with Ben, who strangely was looking down at her, carrying a rucksack on his shoulder. "Happy Anniversary, muffin." It must be a dream, she thought. "I have some presents for you." He had managed to fly over the Mosul Airfield and visit his wife, who was still unsure if she was awake. Maggie was awake, she soon realized, and they both started unwrapping Ben's gifts. She was a history major in college so Ben got her some good historical fiction novels. The dust had destroyed one of her alarm clocks so Ben got her not one, but two replacements. Then he pulled out a small box. "Wow. How did you get these in Iraq?" Ben had somehow got his wife a pair of diamond earrings. How he got them would remain a secret. Maggie had the most wonderful husband in the world, she knew when she woke up the next morning.

The diamond earrings had made the two days at Dahuk all the more romantic for the war-tested newlyweds. It was the first time in eight months either had seen a bathroom with plumbing and a room with air conditioning.

Ben and Maggie Smith's storybook marriage was one of the fortunate ones. Others were not so lucky. For soldiers half the world away from their husbands and wives, staying together until death do us part was easier said than done. It seems incomprehensible that a husband or a wife could abandon their spouse while he or she is fighting a war, but that was the reality for too many soldiers in Iraq, half the world away from home. Infidelity happened at Fort Campbell and infidelity happened in Iraq. Twenty-year-old privates who married their high school sweethearts before going to basic training found out their sweethearts loved someone else now. The "Dear John" letters of this war came by email.

With the end of the road already set at February and March of next year, the onus to watch over demoralized soldiers landed on the platoon leaders and first-line supervisors. If ever a problem arose, they would report to their commanders. Ultimately, the most effective councelors for soldiers would be their chaplain. NCOs invited, asked, begged, pleaded their most at-risk soldiers to talk to their chaplain when things at home got rough. It's tough to keep secrets when you've been with the same people for six months in war. There's no reason to try.

Specialist David Goldberg, an engineer with the 52nd Engineering Battalion, was one who slipped though the cracks. For reasons only known to Goldberg, he took his own life in Quyarrah. The death was officially listed as caused by "non-combat gunfire." Goldberg had enlisted in the Army Reserves in February, just a month before the beginning of the war, in hopes of fighting in the war before it ended. "He told me that he wanted this experience to help him become a better person," Staff Sgt. Fernando Torrez remembered in his memorial service. "In the short time we knew him, we saw a young man with terrific potential." Goldberg was twenty-years old.

His labor force assembled and his mission defined, Sgt. First Class Hector Jusino next turned to the engineers in his mission to rebuild the Mosul sports complex. Taking a couple of engineering officers around the complex, Jusino explained in detail why he needed their support to make his project work. The pipes that pumped water into the pool were destroyed and needed replaced. The stadium's stands needed extensive structural repair. This was the kind of stuff he couldn't do with determination and hard work alone. When he finished, the officers could only promise that they would get back to him.

In the end, much to Jusino's disappointment but not to his surprise, the answer was no. The resource-strapped engineers responded to Jusino's request days later with a sheaf of paper explaining why they could not take on the project. Lack of supplies and specialized training were the main reasons given. Undaunted, Jusino went back to Command Sgt. Maj. Womack. "They said they couldn't do it, sergeant major. But you know what, I bet that I can." It was a promise to do what the engineers couldn't. It was promise that he knew he couldn't keep without some serious good fortune.

Jusino could have easily given up on the project in the face of his superiors, doing only what he needed to do to get the place cleaned up before moving on. That would have meant leaving these nineteen men jobless before they could even get started working for the coalition, something they were so excited about doing. So with only $5,000 to work with, he drove on. Every day, with his work crew and three to four roving guards patrolling the soccer field and gymnasium, he went to work with only the promise of keeping these motivated locals employed. It wasn't even until more than a week into the project that Jusino got a linguist after his battalion commander, Lt. Col. Jerry Chastain, offered him one after spying on his resolute NCO at work one day.

Mohammad Bashir, a local Imam who spoke as fluent English as any linguist the division had found up to that point, became Jusino's new right hand man. He was a poor man in a monetary sense but rich in any other standard. Jusino, a Catholic, and Mohammad would find time each day to discuss, but not debate, religion. It was the kind of dialogue about Islam and Christianity that Jusino looked forward to every day he was with Mohammad. He had a son, Jusino found out, that he could not afford to send to college. That tortured Mohammad.

With his translator to help him, Jusino was eager to get to know his workers. He found out that one man, an engineer, had lost his job when his office building was bombed after coalition forces suspected the building was being used to store weapons caches. Then he turned to the man who he suspected was a former Iraqi soldier. To that point, he had no problems with the man, but he was certain to keep an eye on him at all times. Located so close to the Mosul Airfield and with tenuous security around the complex, Jusino could be a soft target.

It was only when he got to know the man did he let his guard down. His name was Salim Sultan and yes, he was former non-commissioned officer in the Iraqi army. In fact, he had served in the first Gulf War in Basra and recalled horrific attacks against his position in Basra by American attack helicopters. That was where his deep seeded fear of Jusino and the American soldiers was sewn. It is entirely possible that Salim was working for the very Army and the very division that he had fought on the battlefield in 1991.

After the war, he left the Iraqi army, going AWOL until Saddam's forces tracked him down and threw him in jail. After his release, Salim lived on the streets without hope. He had no money, no car, and no education. That was how Sgt. First Class Jusino found him when he reported for work each day.

Each man had an interesting story to tell. Many of the men had reasons not to trust Jusino. But in time, Jusino earned their trust. One day Jusino gathered up a stockpile of toothbrushes, toilet paper, deodorant and candy that had been mailed to his unit chaplain and calibrated the goodies into bags for his workers. It was a sign of appreciation and it worked to perfection. As they were rummaging through their new toys, Jusino knew through that simple gesture, he had made nineteen new friends. "I'm here to help you, I'm not here to hurt you," he told them before Mohammed gave the group the translation. Jusino locked eyes with Salim. The two soldiers reached an understanding.

Salim became Jusino's go-getter. If ever he needed lunch, a tool or even an engineer, Salim could make it happen within an hour without fail. His dependability set him apart. Soon, the two soldiers' kindred spirit blossomed. Jusino's realized how much of a difference this sports complex had made in the lives of these men. For Salim, this was his life. This pool, basketball gym and soccer stadium had given him what he never found after he left the military. He had something to wake up for in the morning. So did Jusino. When the cash started going dry before the job was done, he knew he couldn't just give up on the project and on his workers. So he went back to the well, and the well was Command Sgt. Maj. Womack and his commanders at the Mosul Airfield.

Womack was in his corner, he had no doubt about that. But Sgt. First Class Hector Jusino needed the support of more 101st Airborne treasurers than just his sergeant major. Jusino was a political science major in college, but lobbying for money was not something he was trained to do. "They wanted to do the project, but they did not see the impact the project would have in the community," Jusino recalled months later. "I could see the political impact we were having in the area and I was trying to tell these people, these high ranking people in the D-Rear, the importance of the project.

"I was saying it wasn't a matter of just cleaning that place. If you want to have a positive impact on the community, you better build it and give it back to them." The sports complex, as he had learned through his local friends, was not for the people of Mosul before the coalition occupied the city. The Iraqi military had built the complex and allowed civilians to use only the soccer field for tournaments. Otherwise, locals could only watch from a distance as the Iraqi soldiers enjoyed summer dips in the pool. To hand over the sports complex in better condition that what even the Iraqi soldiers saw it in, Jusino thought, would present the people of Mosul with a tremendous gift from the coalition that would be sure to resonate throughout the city. It was an opportunity for the 101st to make a powerful statement just as the division was starting to get settled into the city.

Jusino, of course, had his skeptics. He eventually did get what he needed, money. And when he got money, he asked for more. The cycle wouldn't and couldn't stop until the job was done. Several officers in the D-Rear saw the project as a waste, and they weren't shy about sharing their views to Jusino. Jusino, who nearing retirement had little to lose, wasn't shy about sharing his own views to his superiors either. "Why would you give them something clean and unserviceable? They only thing they know about America is that America has money, that America has democracy and that America has freedom. And you want to give them a half-finished job?" Once the project was done, he figured, the 101st could start organizing sporting events with local and American teams. Leaving the rest of the job up to the Iraqis was no good, Jusino argued. He took the heat, but he successfully kept his skeptics at bay long enough to continue with the project.

The money and resource eater was the pool initially. It was so dirty that to clean the pool, Jusino and his staff needed to drain it dry and scrub the bottom with mops and brushes. More than 12,000 gallons of water was needed just to flush out the filth and garbage from the pool. This was a bigger deal than just cleaning the bathroom tub. "It took four days just to get the trash out of the pool," Jusino recalled. For the basketball gymnasium, he wanted a professional level court. So at each end he had glass backboards installed, just like the ones the National Basketball Association uses. Maybe, he thought, the next great NBA import would come from this very gym. The soccer stadium would take considerably more work than the other two parts of the complex. First, the grass needed to be green again instead of its then straw-yellow hue. The stands looked like it had been a target of a B-1 Air Force Bomber. Spectators once could have taken a seat and watched a game in any one of about 1,000 seats that covered about half the field. But post-war looting had made a number of sections to crumble like a stale cookie. Then there was the paint. Jusino wanted to touch up the work done around the soccer stadium before reopening the facility. Apparently done after the invasion of Kuwait, the previous owners had decorated the entrance of the soccer stadium with the Iraqi and Kuwaiti flags romantically juxtaposed with one another.

Jusino and his nineteen men were not going to be able to man this project by themselves, not in any reasonable length of time. He needed more men and he needed local engineers who could help him with more than just hard work and dedication. For that, he tapped into the money well again, and again he encountered stiff resistance from a number of his superiors. Given his mission and the realities his chain of command gave him, Jusino concentrated on just making the facility clean enough for the community to enjoy, then prepared to hand over the facility to the people of Mosul, prematurely or not. It was something Jusino was not happy with; he knew there would still be work to be done. There was no way he could fix the water pipes running in and out of the pool with the resources and time he had on hand. The stadium would just be a lost cause, he thought. It left a foul taste in his mouth.

CHAPTER 9

BACK TO SCHOOL

President Kennedy gave his 1962 speech with a prescient concern of not only the Cold War military missions, but the post-Cold War operations as well, according to speech writer Ted Sorensen. The United States military, if it was going to defeat communism, was going to need to put its own blood, sweat and tears into building democracies, sometimes from the ground up. "It's been even more true in the last few years," said Sorensen. "Dozens of border disputes, ethnic disputes, religious disputes, when they rise to the point of threat to international peace and security, sometimes it means that the United States needs to intervene." And those kind of disputes have come often after Nov. 9, 1989. As the heavy hand of communism fell with the Berlin Wall, and various multi-nation states escaped its grasp, Kennedy's concerns of growing instability were realized. Afghanistan provided an unmistakable case in point. In 1979, the Red Army swept though the country, forcefully removing the despotic Afghan President Hafizullah Amin and installing its own communist regime. The next ten years under communist rule for Afghanistan would destroy the country. Led with support from the U.S. Central Intelligence Agency, a group of paramilitary fighters calling themselves the Mujahideen doggedly resisted the Soviet-led occupation. In 1989, they succeeded, but only after a struggle that left about a million Afghanis dead.

The effect of self determination, without Soviet influence, was a double-edge sword for the new Afghan government. After a failed attempt by the United Nations to peacefully transfer power away from the lame duck regime in 1992, the Mujahideen swiftly took control of Kabul and spread control outward, establishing an Islamic Republic throughout the country. They wouldn't last long. Plagued by years of internecine warfare, the Mujahideen government lost control of the city of Kandahar in 1994 to a band of Islamic militants. The Taliban government was never recognized by the United Nations, but that didn't stop their militants from quickly gaining control of the Pashtun controlled areas and, in 1996, taking over the Mujahideen stronghold of Kabul.

After the Soviet despotism was removed from the equation, a new tyranny took its stead. What was once an isolated interethnic dispute over the tyrannical rule of the Taliban regime became an international threat to global security on Sept. 11, 2001. The solution to the unbalanced equation in Afghanistan would ultimately come with the American military.

A remarkable turnaround from tyranny to democracy had begun in December of 2001, when Pashtun tribal leader Hamid Karzai took control of an Afghan government. In the first year alone of coalition operations in Afghanistan, 588 million dollars was spent on rebuilding the country. The result: 1.7 million refugees returned to their homes. Young girls, who had been prevented from attending school under the Taliban regime, were now in classes.

The skill in diplomacy that the American military brought to Operation Enduring Freedom was working. It was working in Afghanistan and, after six months, it was working in northern Iraq. Effective field diplomacy was becoming the 101st Airborne Division's most lethal weapon.

Captain Mathew Konz had proved himself in An Najaf and Al Hillah. His Charlie Company had fought in and won both battles without losing a soldier. Now he was wowing his commanders with his adroit skill in dealing with potential armed enemies without firing a shot. His transition from war fighter to peacemaker was seamless. Konz, or "King Konz," as he would soon be known as, would carry the soldier-statesman label better than anyone in the town of Hamman al Alil, just south of Mosul.

Konz, age thirty-one, took control of the town of 30,000 and the surrounding twenty-five villages with the mission of building some kind of legal authority where none existed. In Hamman al Alil, that task could have been Mission Impossible. He was told by his then battalion commander, Lt. Col. Christopher Hughes, not to wait for guidance. He was being handed the city *carte blanche*. Hamman al Alil was no ordinary town either. No less than half a dozen Arabic tribes and even a pocket of Kurds made the area among the most incendiary of the entire 101st Airborne Division area of operation. Mosul University's forestry college was located in the town, adding a group of European-educated professors to the mix. When Konz and his company found the town, the Mosul police had been taking trips to Hamman al Alil twice a month to stop interethnic violence. Locals would fire their AK-47s "to celebrate because they were happy the war was over or because their favorite soccer team just scored a goal," Konz recalled. And the situation only got worse when the freed prisoners, released by Saddam as the coalition crossed into Iraq, found their way to Hamman al Alil to settle some old scores. Konz had only 350 soldiers to stabilize the area.

This was before the Commanders' Emergency Relief Program had armed Konz with money, so he put the local police back to work by paying them with military food rations – completely illegal under military code. Nobody noticed. All anybody over his head cared about was getting the town's police and governing authority stood up and running. The first institution, the police, was a progress that threw the Konz into the fire on rebuilding Iraq. Initially, when Konz ordered the police back on the job on his MRE for work program, the policemen asked who's authority they would be under? Konz smiled and told them firmly, "I'm the authority." They were back to work the next day. They, by in large, were also no older than eighteen and prone to taking bribes.

Seventeen policemen showed up the first day, twenty-six would come the next day. Then Konz laid down the law on those who laid down the law. "We hired more, we fired more," he later recalled. After just a few weeks, locals started to feel safe again. People even started to sleep on their roofs to beat the heat, something they would did not feel safe doing before Konz was in charge.

But Konz wasn't in charge for long. He was only in charge when he found out that the local mayor was in fact not even a resident of Hamman al Alil. He had lived in Mosul and commuted to his town. That wouldn't last. Konz met with the local muktars, or local community leaders, to begin the process of assembling the local government. Rising up was Naji Hassan Rajeb, a young law student, no older than Konz, who was anointed mayor by both the muktars and the Charlie Company commander. Konz also put together a local council, "selected, not elected," as he admitted, but soon complaints lodged at the town mayor would force an election to build a true local council. That would come in September and from the election would come a legitimate six-member council with Rajeb still at the top. By September, Konz's initiatives were thriving. Job markets had put angry, poor locals to work. Local markets were booming.

Security was an issue, as anywhere else in northern Iraq, but Konz had a solution for that too. In what could have saved lives in his own unit in the later months, Konz offered incentives for his employees in the local government in exchange for weapons. He was looking for grenade launchers and anti-aircraft weapons. What he got was a lot of small arms, but it had made a difference. Whether with the local governing council or his employees, many of who did no more than pick up trash, Konz had developed a trust with the people of Hamman al Alil. Intelligence started to come in to his soldiers on known terrorists and potential ambushes.

Konz had built such a rapport with the local community and the governing council that he became a permanent fixture in the town when their constitution needed one final signature. The document, which stayed well within the lines of the coalition's democratic initiatives, was signed by all of the council members, muktars, and the mayor but not Konz. He didn't see a need for him to put his signature on the document, but the locals insisted. They had even put his own dotted line at the bottom with the caption, "Captain," which was really all the governing council knew him as. Konz still resisted, thinking that, in time, he would be gone. The local leaders needed to run their government without American supervision. He was especially frustrated when Hamman al Alil leaders brainstormed titles for Konz, who eventually relented to the idea of his signing on the constitution.

"King" Mathew Konz would mark a significant promotion for the Auburn University graduate. "Listen, I'm just an infantry company commander," he tried to explain. It would have been amusing, but he would have had a lot of explaining to do when he met his battalion and brigade commander as newly crowned royalty. In the end, they just agreed to call him the "Commander of U.S. forces in Hamman al Alil," and Konz willfully signed.

"In reality, I was king, but that that wasn't the impression I wanted them to have," Konz recalled.

In brokering the pay-for-weapons agreement with the locals, Konz had taken the 101st one step closer to the Kennedy vision that seemed to unwittingly guide the division from the beginning of Operation Iraqi Freedom. "Above all," Kennedy had told the West Point Class of 1962, "you will have a responsibility to deter war as well as fight it. For the basic problems facing the world today are not susceptible of a final military solution.

"Our forces, therefore, must fulfill a broader role as a complement to our diplomacy, as an arm of our diplomacy, as a deterrent to our adversaries, and as a symbol to our allies of our determination to support them."

Konz must have also understood this point, made by Ted Sorensen, one of Kennedy's closest confidant: "A military victory endures only if the military victor achieves the moral high ground. Winning the hearts and minds of the people through nation building and expenditures and civil works and so on is one way of doing that."

Nobody had it worse than Delta Company, 2-187th Infantry Regiment. They were the most mobile infantry company Col. Michael Linnington had – which is exactly why he put them on the most remote, the most dirty, and the most lonely mission the division had. Delta Company began manning the Syrian border entry points in the early summer, well outside of Sinjar and without much interaction with anybody outside their own company.

With their supply of fast moving humvees with mounted .50 caliber machine guns and Mk.19 grenade launchers, they could quickly respond to any actionable intelligence of enemy crossings from Syria. It was a zero sum game. The more weapons they collected, the more weapons they took out of the hands of people who wanted to fire them at coalition soldiers. It wouldn't be an overstatement to say that their performance translated directly to the developments in Mosul, Quyarrah, and even further south into Baghdad.

First Sgt. Patrick Keough was in charge of keeping his soldiers' heads in the game. None of his soldiers had any way of contacting family back home – no Internet, no satellite phones. Patrols along the border would often lead to nothing. Their meals were still the same MREs they had been eating for six months. But every once in a while, they would find a vehicle at a traffic control point with a weapon or two – one or two lives saved down south. "When things came screaming across the border, they came fast," Keough remarked. When brigade intelligence officers saw a heavier flow of traffic coming across the border, that usually meant a movement of enemy personnel and weapons. It was at those points that Delta Company would be called up on a moment's notice to set up interdiction points.

They needed to stay unpredictable. If the enemy knew they were always going to be at one point, the natural counter was to go the other way. Keough and Delta Company began hiding behind bends in the roads. If vehicles packed with weapons came down the road, Delta Company would get a clear view of their target before the vehicle could maneuver out of the line of fire. Then the company began air assaulting into areas around the border, literally landing on a suspected enemy convoy. Before the enemy could get a beat on that tactic, the company started meeting weapon convoys behind Sinjar at a choke point along the way to Mosul. The only thing that stayed consistent about the Delta Company tactics was its element of surprise.

In the summer, the company took part in training for their eventual replacements – the Iraqi Border Guards. Like the other nascent Iraqi security forces, the IBG was not self-reliant, at least not like the coalition wanted them to be. They were dependable for manning fixed check points. That was their mission until they were trained well enough to go out on patrols with Delta Company, which eventually they would. The goal was to train a battalion of IBG, or about a thousand troops.

When they weren't training the border guards, or thwarting a convoy of weapons moving into northern Iraq, Delta Company had little to do but think – think about their loved ones back home, their drinking buddies, or even about their favorite football team. It was hard for anyone in Mosul and Tal Afar who knew what they were doing to not feel sorry for them. With Labor Day just a couple of weeks away, most of the division had steady access to Internet, phones, and television. Not Delta Company. At least not until division and Third Brigade communications officers decided they needed to bend over backwards to tie up that loose end. Football season was just around the corner.

The satellite phones and Internet connection made their way towards the lonely company, but that wasn't enough. If northern Iraq was going to be home until February of 2004, and that much had been decided, then the Delta Company football fans needed a new mission: to secure as many satellites as possible so nobody would miss their Saturday and Sunday gridiron fixes. Their brigade commander, Col. Michael Linnington, (an Philadelphia Eagles fan) was particularly sympathetic towards the company's needs.

The Armed Forces Network (AFN) was the only way the soldiers in Iraq were going to be able to watch their football action. Mosul television was just not likely to broadcast any American football game. AFN was not ideal, but it would keep the soldiers from being totally remote from their hometown team, as they had been for much of the baseball season. On three to twelve stations, depending on the satellite, AFN would pool together the top sitcoms and television dramas, the major news stations, sporting events, and anything else of interest from the average cable system back home. AFN Sports, for example, could jump from the Notre Dame-USC game on NBC directly to Game 1 of the World Series on FOX. While AFN cut through the fat, it could not please everyone. With soldiers hailing from all over the country rooting for 31 different NFL teams and any number of college teams, the game on TV might not always be the game everyone wanted to see. Agreeing to a particular station on a communal TV was sometimes a contentious process.

Some compounds did miss a few early weekends, but by mid-September, nearly every soldier in the division had access to a TV where they could catch their teams in action – Delta Company, 2-187th Infantry Regiment included. Keeping awake was another issue – the Sunday NFL slate did not start until 9 p.m. Iraq time. By the time the Monday workday began, the weekly Sunday night game was entering the fourth quarter. Monday Night Football, for the soldiers in Iraq, was more like Tuesday Morning Football. Few Third Brigade soldiers stuck in the remote locations along the Syrian border were complaining. "It didn't matter what time it was," First Sgt. Keough remembered. "It never interfered with missions, but if there were no missions, the whole company was stacked in that room watching football."

Football on the small screen was not the only thing that made life in Mosul more palatable as the summer months passed. The summer heat fell off a cliff after Labor Day. By the end of September, the D-Main Palace and Nineveh Hotel swimming pools had closed for the year. Army-issued black fleece jackets and gloves that were totally useless during the summer started to become handier, especially in the early mornings. Food after September no longer came in a cardboard box for most 101st soldiers. Kellog, Brown & Root (KBR) in August had started to build dining facilities at the D-Main Palace, the D-Rear Airfield, the Q-West Airfield, Third Brigade's Tal Afar compound, and Camp Claiborne in Mosul. All of the facilities were open by mid-September. The smaller compounds would get one or two meals a day delivered to them from the nearest major dining facility.

After Labor Day, movie stars started flocking to Mosul like Hollywood and Broadway, or at least Baghdad. Actresses Britney Murphy and Alyssa Milano and musician Kid Rock breezed through Baghdad in the summer, skipping Mosul. Similar United Service Organizations (USO) shows never made it up to the 101st Airborne until September 25, when superstar Bruce Willis stopped by with his blues band, "Bruce Willis and the Heartbreakers." Unlike the Washington dignitaries who visited the 101st, Willis came to Mosul to entertain the troops. Posing with several hundred Second Brigade soldiers, Willis substituted the standard "Cheese!" with his patented "Ippie Ky-yah, Mother Fucker" when the flash bulbs went off.

Later, he jumped into a CH-47 Chinook and landed with his band in Tal Afar to entertain a crowd of Third Brigade soldiers. "I wanted to sign up and fight with you guys, but they told me I was too old," Willis told the Rakkassan crowd. Colonel Michael Linnington donated his uniform top to Willis midway through his show, after Linnington's name and rank were appropriately removed. Never had someone outside the 101st wore the Screaming Eagle prouder than Willis that night. Afterwards, Linnington presented Willis with a Third Brigade coin and flag.

General Richard Myers, chairman of the Joint Chiefs of Staff, led a Christmas delegation that included comedian Robin Williams, pro-wrestler Kurt Angle and the voluptuously dressed sports reporter Leeann Tweeden (a crowd favorite, especially with the male soldiers). Myers was in town primarily just for support – he did not talk much business with Petraeus while in Mosul – but earlier visits from the Army and Washington's elite were much more substantive. In a three-day span in August, seven stars visited Petraeus and the 101st. General Peter Schoomaker, who had been sworn in as the first Army chief of staff to come back from retirement weeks earlier, toured Mosul and met with Ghanim al-Basso in his downtown office. Lieutenant Gen. Ricardo Sanchez, usually confined to his Baghdad post as V Corps commander, met with a contingent of Albanian troops that had landed in Mosul, as well as the Mosul sheiks.

Representative Ike Skelton, the leading Democrat on the House Armed Services Committee, came with a delegation of a half-dozen members of congress. Petreaus eagerly whisked the delegation to Kisik in Third Brigade's area of operation to show off the newly rebuilt Kisik Oil Refinery. It was one of the division's jewels. The facility had been destroyed after Saddam's fall and after five months, Col. Michael Linnington and a crew of contracted workers rebuild the refinery to beyond pre-war standards. It took $78,000 in CERP funds, but beginning day one, the facility produced at a rate of 732,000 liters of fuel a day – vital to heating homes, fueling automobiles, and keeping the electricity running throughout northern Iraq. In addition to the fuel, more than a hundred permanent jobs were created in the area just by reopening the refinery. A similar refinery would open in Quyarrah in the fall, to the delight of Brig. Gen. Frank Helmick, who was swiftly told "you have thrity days" to get it running after he reported its existence to Petraeus.

One former soldier, Sen. Jeff Sessions (R-Ala.) also managed to make the trip in August. Sessions had been a thirteen-year veteran in the Army Reserves before launching his career in public service. In his second term in the Senate, Sessions had earned a seat among the most dependable conservative voters in the chamber. As a member of the Senate Armed Services committee, Petraeus knew Session's visit especially was a golden opportunity to do more than just play host.

With every dignitary visit, Petraeus would give a standard slide-show briefing on what the division had done and was doing. By the time Sessions landed, Petraeus was beginning to feel a bit like a museum curator. This briefing though would have a bit more of a tactical edge than the usual routine. The end was in sight for the Commanders Emergency Relief Fund. The funds were not expected to last into the winter months. What Petraeus needed from the senator was a voice. He needed money, repeating to Sessions what he told L. Paul Bremer months earlier: "Money is ammunition."

Petraeus flooded Sessions with chart after chart and more facts and figures than he could ever handle. The numbers of the first three months in Mosul were staggering. By August 1, only five months into the occupation, the division had spent nearly eight million dollars of Commanders' Emergency Relief Program funds. First, Second, and Third Brigade had each spent over a million by themselves, but all three infantry brigades couldn't keep up the pace. Colonel Michael Linnington in Tal Afar was in the most trouble. He had just $3,000 on hand, patiently waiting for his CERP reload from Baghdad, when Sessions came to town.

The CG found an ally that day in Sessions, an ally he would need in the coming months. The CERP funds were about to run dry. Petraeus and the 101st needed more ammunition. After Baghdad ran out, the money could only come from inside the Washington beltway.

Sixteen years earlier, Petraeus had foretold this kind of exchange in his Princeton dissertation. "Counterinsurgency operations, in particular, require close political-military integration," he wrote as a field-grade officer momentarily turned civilian-grad student. "Unfortunately, this requirement runs counter to the traditional military desire, reaffirmed in the lessons of Vietnam, to operate autonomously and resist political 'meddling' and 'micromanagement' in operational concerns.

"This tendency can result in problems, for while military resistance to political 'micromanagement' may often be well founded, it can be counterproductive if carried to excess." Indeed, Petraeus seemed quite amenable to the idea of Washington meddling in his affairs. The money, or ammunition, the 101st desperately needed would start to come later in November thanks to a man who had saved Petraeus, quite literally, a decade earlier. Senator Bill Frist, the Republican majority leader in the U.S. Senate, would lead the charge in forwarding millions in government appropriated funds towards Iraq. The infusion of money was a shot in the arm, but not a cure-all for the division. There would be far more guidelines on how to spend the money. It would take time, and there would be a costly period of time in October and November where the 101st would have to run on empty, but crucial 101st projects that needed funding to finish would get their money.

For Col. James Laufenburg, division chief of staff, and Capt. Julie Simoni, the CERP treasurer, there would be a whole world of paperwork to fill out for the funds that never existed before. And when the seized Saddam CERP money went dry, it was Laufenberg who was tasked with combing through the paper work that follows any appropriated funds from Washington. "From the unit perspective, I don't think they noticed any difference, but there was a whole lot more accountability," he recalled. Washington money, as the 101st chief was about to find out, doesn't come nearly as cheap as money seized from Saddam Hussein after the first Gulf War. The red tape that Petraeus lobbied to avoid when he met with Bremer in June had reappeared.

Using Vietnam, Korea, and smaller conflicts in recent American history as a guide, Petraeus, in his 1987 dissertation found, what would become the foundation for his work as a division commander in northern Iraq. "Particularly in 'small wars,' military leaders should not allow the experience of Vietnam to reinforce the traditional military desire for autonomy in a way that impedes the crucial integration of political and military strategies … for while military force may be necessary in a counterinsurgency, it is seldom sufficient."

He may not have realized it at the time, but inside the sometimes mind-numbing slide show presentation, Senator Sessions had just received a textbook instruction on how to occupy a country, the 101st Airborne Division way. Some in Washington and in Baghdad had proposed fighting the insurgency with "Israeli tactics," using the same brute shows of force the Israeli military had used to combat Hamas and Islamic Jihad terrorist cells. While Petraeus never aimed to coddle the enemy, he saw the insurgency differently. The intent of the 101st was to first win the hearts and minds before crushing the enemy and losing local political support.

From the top to the bottom, the 101st soldiers had begun to understand that winning the peace didn't just mean killing the enemy. In Mosul, soldiers wearing the Screaming Eagle patch were showing a new kind of gallantry on a new battlefield. While the bravery that made heroes out of ordinary men in past wars was being put to the test everyday, it was the compassion of the soldiers wearing the 101st Screaming Eagle patch that was the talk of the Army. Through the frustration of nearly everyday attacks, the soldiers kept reaching out. Soldiers like Sgt. First Class Hector Jusino had become the modern day Audie Murphys.

Hector Jusino's time in the military came to a crescendo once he arrived in Mosul. All he wanted to do before he left the military was to make the best of his final tour of duty. In the backyard of the Mosul Airfield, Jusino got the opportunity to do just that. His project with the Mosul sports complex, contiguous to the D-Rear Airfield, had become his to make or break. It was his reason for being in Mosul, he figured, and he sprung out of his cot every morning to go to work on the sports complex. But with his unit, the 801st Main Support Battalion, ready to pull the plug on Jusino's funding, the determined NCO was close to giving up. His passion for the project, through the constant bureaucratic hassle at his unit, had ebbed.

Ready to move on to something else, Jusino got a show of support just when he needed it. His three-vehicle convoy arrived at work as usual on one June morning, with his linguist Muhammad in tow. "Muhammad, what do those signs say?" Inside the basketball gymnasium, Salim Sultan and the other workers had decorated the facility with banners, not made by them, but made by other locals who had supported Jusino and his men in rebuilding the facility. "They say, 'Thank You.'" Jusino just chuckled and for a moment, everything seemed all right.

Everything was not all right, he found out later. The division was given a choice, either support Jusino until the project was finished and the facility is operational, or cut and run after the facility was only aesthetically fixed. To choose to cut and run would have meant savings of tens of thousands of dollars, and that's what the Division Support Command decided in June. While the facility would be usable again, Jusino knew the decision would mean his ambitions for the sports complex would have to be modified. Defects in the facility – like the cracks in the soccer stadium's stands – would have to be overlooked. His project had become one of the first casualties of the new limitations on the CERP funds.

He had regularly briefed his commanders and Command Sgt. Maj. Marvin Womack on the numbers and the progress of the project, but only Jusino knew the kind of impact the project had on the community. The "political" impact that the project had in Mosul just wasn't something that could be illustrated in a slideshow presentation. Then he had to tell his workers that the project would be put to a premature end. They too took the news hard. For now, the downtrodden Jusino and his men would just have to drive on with what they had. Whatever visions they had of the new facility were going to have to lowered, and in the end, the local workers would have to find new jobs.

For Salim Sultan, there was no other job to find. He hadn't started planning on what he would do once his work was finished, he was enjoying himself too much. Jusino and the workers had become like family. Salim had been the one that got the word out about the facility. The word spread quickly. By the time the division decided to cut funding for the project, soccer teams from throughout Iraq had scheduled trips to play teams from Mosul at the stadium. A bit of a friendly rivalry had emerged with a team from Baghdad.

Jusino was not ready to give up, not on Salim and his workers. He sent an email to the 801st MSB executive officer, asking for reconsideration. "I was fearing unrest," Jusino recalled. "It had come to me that the Iraqis were going to get angry if we didn't finish it … they felt that if I hadn't finished that project, I was betraying them."

The goal was to return the entire facility to the people of Mosul by the end of the summer. It had been an ambitious timetable, but Jusino was determined to make it work. The project started with the pool. Several exasperating days and 12,000 gallons of water later, the pool was cleaned. Working for just five dollars a day, Salim Sultan and the local workers picked up trash, mopped the gymnasium floor and took pride in just doing what they could do to help reopen the facility. Then, through the heat of the brutal summer months, Jusino's team painted walls, watered and mowed the soccer field, and rebuilt destroyed sections of the stadium.

Now, the job was done, or as done as the job could have been without more money. In the end, nearly $100,000 of CERP funds had been donated to the project. Colonel Samuel Halloway opened the reborn facility with the obligatory cutting of the ribbon and presented Jusino and his team with his challenge coin. "This should stand as a testament to our shared love of athletics and sport," Halloway said during his brief speech. "We turn this stadium over to you, the people of Mosul, and share hope that its use will continue to stir memories of what we have accomplished together."

Halloway may have gotten the spotlight during the opening ceremony, but it was Jusino who was the man of the hour. "The Army had decided to give something back to the people of Iraq," he said, standing as proud as a man possibly could. "I leave something for the Iraqi people that they can use and they can cherish in the future."

A local soccer team and a team assembled of the division's best soccer players opened the new stadium. In a bit of an upset, the American soldiers beat the locals in their own favorite sport. The complex was in a high traffic area, especially for coalition soldiers. For as long as the 101st Airborne Division operated in Mosul, few soldiers passing through the Mosul Airfield could overlook Jusino's accomplishment. Convoys entering the compound through the terminal entrance invariably passed by the complex. It was hard to miss the evolution of the soccer stadium. Was this new sports complex the most crucial of advances the 101st Airborne had made in its first five months in Mosul? Maybe not. But what was certain was that 101st had given the people of Mosul something that the soldiers, one in particular, had taken pride in. That was important, to the soldiers and the people of Mosul. Jusino and his team had done more to beautify the complex, they had helped beautify a city.

"I feel like I've come to Iraq and come to war and instead of destroying, I had a chance to build. I hope that in the long run, the Iraqi people get to the position where they can use this facility to the max and try to put somebody through the Olympics through training at this complex."

For months afterwards, Jusino would drive by the complex and see exactly what he had dreamed he would see all summer. Kids, adults, fathers and sons were playing soccer, shooting hoops, and taking a dip in the pool.

Summer vacation for the children of Mosul had been like no other. One hundred and twenty one soccer teams, ages eight to eighteen, participated in a 103-game youth league season. One August morning, Brig. Gen. Frank Helmick showed up with jerseys and soccer balls for the division's adopted team in the predominately Catholic village of Al Qosh. The team came from the Virgin Lady Orphanage and, for the rest of the season, would be called the "Screaming Eagles," complete with the Old Abe patch on their left sleeves. In September, they won the league championship.

The entire 101st command staff really took it upon themselves to support the local orphanages, making it a favorite humanitarian project of everyone at the D-

Main Palace. In September, just before the temperatures started to go south, the CMOC pool welcomed dozens of local orphans to swim with soldiers from the 431st Civil Affairs Detachment. Helmick, who had come up with the idea, broke his own heart when a prior engagement ran overtime and prevented him from crashing the party.

The fun in the sun was fun while it lasted, but what was summer vacation for the students of Northern Iraq was anything but for the field grade commanders tasked with rebuilding more than 800 dilapidated schools in time for the first day of class. Some schools did not make the deadline; most projects were completed just as the students were released back to school. At the nexus of the division's massive school rebuilding initiative was the Nineveh Province Education Headquarters, which opened in Mosul in August. At the headquarters, education supplies were collected and distributed to local schools and it was certainly the supplies that the schools would need the most. Nearly all of the schools at all levels in the region lacked even the most basic language and mathematics books.

By late summer, the school initiatives had infected the local populace. Aware that the new Iraqi government would prioritize education ahead of military, and that schools would never again be used as ammunition dumps, locals started taking pride in their schoolhouses. Baghdad coalition headquarters had set October 1 as opening day for all primary and secondary schools, and for four months the coalition had worked towards a new "shock and awe" for the Iraqi children on the first day of school.

Neglect under the Ba'ath Party regime had destroyed the Iraqi education system and the coalition was intent on a new beginning for the Iraqi children. The 2002-2003 school year ended in late June and early July after missed days during the war were made up. The 101st Airborne command staff knew they were short of time to rebuild the more than 800 schools in the Nineveh Province before the students came back in September. The bulk of the efforts would come during the summer break, but many rebuilding and construction initiatives had to start immediately. The northern Iraq schools were in a state of emergency.

One soldier, Chap. (Maj.) Carlos Huerta, the 1-320th Field Artillery chaplain, was especially appalled by the schools and took it on himself to do something about it. Huerta, the only Jewish Rabbi in the division with perhaps the strongest Brooklyn accent of any soldier in the Army, first saw the school conditions in a West Mosul primary school in the 1-320th area of operation. The school was left in ruins. The ceilings were so corroded with water leaks that it was a wonder the building was still standing. Outside, the playground was nothing more than a junkyard. The school's bathroom was even less inviting than a simple hole in the ground.

In his green notebook, the rarely vulgar Huerta described the school with one, succinct word: "Shit."

Drawing $10,000 from the CERP funds, the division employed a local contractor to give the school a quick fix. The plumbing was rebuilt, leaks in the ceilings were fixed, walls were repainted and new supplies, including chalkboards, were provided. In just three weeks, the school was reborn. Huerta and the 1-320th Field Artillery command staff had a cause to celebrate. On July 22, the school reopened with the kind of party the students and teachers could have only dreamt of before the coalition arrived. The 2-320th Field Artillery commanders, including Battalion Commander Lt. Col. Mark Murray, converged to see what they had accomplished. "To see what it looked like before ... filthy latrines, no running water, no safe place for the kids to play. Now it's a tremendous source of pride for me and our soldiers to see it through," Murray remarked after the ceremony. Colonel Joseph Anderson joined in the festivities too and Governor Ghanim al-Basso cut the ribbon, opening one of the finest gifts the 101st Airborne Division had given the city of Mosul to that point. Huerta spoke to the students and teachers during the ceremony and did so without a linguist. Huerta had made a point to learn the language when he arrived in theater and remarkably learned enough to carry on a conversation in just months.

This was one school; the 101st Airborne had identified more than a thousand more that needed extensive renovation and rebuilding. In tandem with the Bechtel Corporation and U.S. State Department's USAID, the division mobilized soldiers and civilian contractors in every sector of the Nineveh province to get to work on the schools. Some needed simple repairs, like broken windows and new supplies; other schools needed a much larger effort. Division field grade and general officers made a daily hobby of cutting ribbons and welcoming students and teachers to their new schools. Rebuilding the schools of northern Iraq became a relief project that inspired the entire division, from the brigade commanders to their lower enlisted drivers. Soldiers who just wanted to get involved would volunteer to help deliver school supplies with their commanders. Those who didn't have a choice helped out magnanimously.

The 1-377th Field Artillery Regiment, an attached unit from Fort Bragg, had made a group of empty electrical warehouses outside Mosul their home when they arrived in the city in May. Like several other warehouse complexes the 101st had found along the way to Mosul, this compound was easily securable with a twenty-foot tall wall surrounding the 360-degree perimeter. Once the battalion started settling into the facility, locals who had worked at the warehouse before it shut down flocked to the gate looking for employment. Lieutenant Col. Tracy Lear, the battalion commander, quickly found his gate guards getting a crash course in diplomacy.

Lear and the 1-377th Field Artillery were virtually alone in the outskirts of Mosul. The division had no other compounds for miles, and locals in that area of the city never hestitated to bring whatever issues they had right to Lear's doorstep. He didn't mind – that was what he was there for.

So when one man, a school superintendent of a primary school just down the road, approached Lear's soldiers for help on a school, the 1-377th "Gunslingers" were eager to help. Just a few weeks after the unit secured the area as the 1-377th FA tactical operations center, the man who was unable to speak English, approached a gate guard and handed him a note. The note was written by a man named Walid. He needed help in rebuilding his dilapidated school. The 1-377th Field Artillery Regiment took the notice and went to work.

After an $8,000 contribution from the Division Artillery commander's CERP fund, the 1-377th FA employed a civilian contractor to make Walid's wishes come true. Electrical wiring and plumbing, constant problems with nearly every Iraqi school the division encountered, were fixed. The school was given seven new air conditioners for the hot months and new heaters for when the thermometer goes south. What the unit couldn't immediately provide were new school supplies. That was where a small town with one big heart took the baton.

Word from Capt. Mark Hayry, a favorite son of Spencer, Wis., (pop. 2,000) spread quickly when he was deployed with the 1-377th Field Artillery and the 101st Airborne Division. His mother Pam, a schoolteacher, and father Bruce, the town's postmaster, were well known around the small community. So when Capt. Hayry emailed home looking for help in gathering school supplies, his mom and dad canvassed the community like seasoned politicians.

It started when Pam Hayry mentioned the school and the project to her church group mid-week before heading out of town for the weekend. When she came back on Monday, the Hayry's received a phone call from the local newspaper. In a town like Spencer, all news is local. All local news, the Hayry's quickly saw, was focused on them after the newspaper interviewed them about the school project and after the story was published. The Hayrys had two sons at war, with Sgt. Jeff Hayry, a mechanic serving north of Baghdad, also deployed at the same time as his brother. The story of the Hayry's fight to not only support their sons, but to support their sons' missions, became the talk of Wisconsin.

Soon surrounding towns of Marshfield, Colby, Abbotsford and Unity got involved. The women of the Hayry's church, the United Methodist Church in Spencer, went to work sewing 130 tote bags for the students to carry their new supplies to school. Children in school were put to work packaging the goodies. Local businesses became involved too. Wiskerchen Cheese, a local Wisconsin cheese producer, donated $1,000 for shipping costs. A nearby Land O' Lakes production facility pitched in with boxes and material to package and ship supplies. Captain Hayry was inundated with boxes of supplies for the school. Crayons, coloring books, pens, pencils, playground balls, and "anything else you can think of that belongs in a school" were packaged to Hayry in Mosul and personally delivered to the school and the kids.

One man sent a check for $200 with a brief enclosed message, "From one Christian to another." When the Hayrys stopped by the local video store, the store clerk recognized them and introduced them to their plan to send a collection of spare movies to the troops. "The generosity was overwhelming," Pam Hayry remembered.

The first packages made their way to Mosul in the fall. Twenty-six boxes with 988 pounds of goods were poured into the 1-377th Field Artillery Mosul compound to an overwhelmed battalion. Captain Hayry and a group of 1-377th FA soldiers made numerous visits to the schools to make sure the goodies were getting to the students. Not once did they get out of the school without utter pandemonium breaking loose. In most American communities, basic school supplies are expected in public schools. Not in Mosul. In the Iraqi schools the 101st dealt directly with, any school supplies were gifts. Kids celebrated a convoy pulling into their school like American teenagers at a pop concert.

With the power of instant communications and digital imagery, the pictures of Hayry and the kids were forwarded back to Wisconsin within days. The students Pam Hayry taught, who were involved with the project, had seen the images. Many of them had relatives in Iraq. "I talk very openly about my feelings," Pam Hayry said. "I showed it to my students and there were tears, a lot of tears, a lot of happiness. People were just amazed."

As the northern Iraq students went to school on October 1, the 101st Airborne Division had finished 330 rebuilding projects, spending $2,040,513. An additional 382 schools had not yet been completed. From August and through the fall, the division field grade commanders made a daily hobby out of cutting ribbons and, for the first time in recent memory, the students made a daily hobby out of going to school. It had been three months of summer vacation for the kids, anything but for the 101st Airborne Division.

More than 300 school renovations had been completed by the first day of school – totaling more than $2 million from the Commanders Emergency Relief Fund. An additional 382 schools were earmarked for more construction. "In the past, they had mud houses for schools," Lt. Col. Kevin Felix, 2-320th Field Artillery commander, noted before opening up one school in the village of Tall Abtah. "Now they have brick buildings."

It was a swift turnaround from ground zero in April, when few schools in the Nineveh province had enough desks, chalkboards, paper, pens and books to conduct class. Many students didn't even attend school. Running water was a luxury that many schools didn't enjoy. Those schools that did enjoy running water were left with decayed plumbing that rendered the bathrooms inoperable. The smell of sewage in many schools filled the classrooms. The student-to-teacher ratio was astronomical. More than a thousand primary and secondary students were often stuffed into schools with fewer than twenty classrooms. All of that changed over three summer months. The immediate focus on education provided the people of northern Iraq with the most noticeable change under the American-led occupation.

As rebuilding operations continued around the First Brigade area of operations, the 101st Aviation Regiment, who shared the Quyarrah Airfield with Bastogne Brigade, took over projects in the immediate area around the compound. That meant twenty-three schools in and around Quyarrah now belonged to Col. Gregory Gass. Providing water towards remote villages in the area was up to the 101st Aviation Regiment. Over one-hundred kilometers of roads in the area, most of which led from the area north towards Mosul, would need to be reestablished with Gass' CERP money. The last responsibility was especially important. Colonel Hodges was having trouble getting vital aid to a number of blightened villages in the region, simply because there were no two-lane roads from Mosul to the areas.

Some projects did not progress nearly as swiftly as the division would have liked. Captain Kellie Rourke, an Eagle Forward intelligence officer who moved back to the 101st Aviation Regiment after the transition to rebuilding operations, found out how difficult babysitting local contractors could be in one hair-raising experience in September. In a routine convoy in Quyarrah from school to school, checking the progress of First Brigade's investments, Rourke had found one school almost untouched since the division wrote a $2,500 check to a local contractor. With the classrooms unfit for class, all desks were empty – no teachers, no students. Windows were still shattered and the school was filthy. "When we asked (the school faculty) about it, they said it was the guards' duty to clean the school."

Rourke was incensed by the company's lack of initiative. "We have a school like this, the Ministry of Education is providing them teachers and yet they have taken so poor care of their school. We want them to demonstrate that the village cares about their school."

The school would eventually get cleaned and the windows would be replaced, but not before the students were taught at a nearby school while the contractors finished the job they were paid to do weeks earlier. Local volunteers had become indispensable in saving the school, filling in wherever they could for paid construction companies that simply did not want to show up for work. "Every village has an educated local. Those people are helping us." Rourke said. "Many of the villagers are chipping in money and paying teachers themselves."

And that's what it took sometimes. The frustration of the 101st with the contracting companies seemed to reach its peak in the weeks before the October 15 transition date, when the coalition was going to remove Saddam Hussein's face from all Iraqi currency. Every Iraqi national bank was to be renovated to a set standard of security before the exchange. Contracts were awarded in late August and early September, leaving only six weeks for the work to get done. For that to happen, people would need to show up to work. Few did without American browbeating.

As the October 15 deadline approached, Second Lt. Paul Kreger, a Second Brigade civil affairs liaison, and Sgt. Toby Tucker, a 431st Civil Affairs NCO specializing in bank renovations, convoyed out of the CMOC on a mission to check on the progress of four construction companies who were set to begin work on six banks. The Mosul state banks, the Rasheed and Rafidan banks, had all been left in shambles by looters after the fall of Saddam and had been operating in temporary locations ever since.

Kreger and Tucker started their convoy at a bank located on a street corner just a couple of miles from the Nineveh Hotel. A crowd had surrounded the bank, a confused group of people expecting their salaries to be paid that day at an empty bank, the two thought. Once the two dismounted their vehicles and finagled their way through the onlookers, it became apparent that nobody had come to the bank that day expecting money. The bank had burned to the ground. In a promising note for coalition forces, the embryonic Mosul Fire Department had acted swiftly to control the blaze.

They later found out that the contractor had not provided a security guard, like they were paid to have done, and some lucky looter took advantage. Kreger and Tucker were incredulous. Unfortunately, it would be only the beginning of a very long day. From bank to bank they went, and from bank to bank they found not one worker. At the last bank of their tour, Kreger exploded. "We're 0 for six today. The deadline is tomorrow morning."

The demand was met and the contractors got to keep their jobs. For the bank that had been destroyed by the late night fire, nothing had changed. The division still expected to see an operational bank sprout from that a pile of smoldering rubble – no extensions and no extra pay.

Kreger's frustration was shared by some at the D-Main Palace, but Col. James Laufenberg, the division chief of staff, was a bit more understanding. "We had a very small team (of contractors) in Mosul, and they were overwhelmed. I called it the Titanic. They were getting, on average, about two hundred requests for contracts a week. They only had the ability to work off about 40, and that was in a good week. It was sinking really fast." That's where the Iraqi contractors filled in. They were less than dependable. "Their standard is not the U.S. standard," Laufenberg added. "If you were expecting a U.S. standard product at the end of the day, I think your standards were a little high."

"Like any venture you go into as a businessman," said Col. Gregory Gass, 101st Aviation Regiment commander, "you've got to figure out who you want to contract with and who you don't. We made a couple mistakes, but then we figured out who we could trust and who we couldn't. The one's we worked with the most were very dependable. We wouldn't give them the money until they finished the project."

The division's troubles with contractors were not limited to those they hired from the local economy. Tensions between the division commanders and contracted workers operating in northern Iraq seemed to reach new heights as the division's CERP pocketbook got lighter and lighter.

The original division of responsibilities was vastly different than what emerged in the summer. The civilian contracted companies were to take on the school projects and the 101st would tackle the more pressing infrastructure issues, like water and fuel supply. That changed when division realized the volume of the load the schools presented.

School rebuilding chores were shared among units in all areas of northern Iraq, with the assistance of the Bechtel Corporation. With inevitable scarcity of funding on both sides, a tug of war had emerged between Bechtel and the 101st commanding general. The squabbling reached a head in the summer when Petraeus asked, politely pleaded, then demanded a progress report on several schools in Mosul from several Bechtel officials. He needed them for a visit from Secretary of Defense Donald Rumsfeld, who was due by the end of the week when the CG really turned up the heat. At a Battle Update Brief, in front of his entire staff, he turned to a Bechtel representative and let him have it. "Listen, I'm meeting with Rumsfeld in two days and Bechtel hasn't even given me an assessment. You've got forty-eight hours or I'm going to tell him that you're unsatisfactory."

The officials quickly responded, but Petraeus and the 101st command staff didn't cool off in the face of their contracted colleagues. Bechtel, based out of San Francisco, had been sent to Iraq with a cool $680 million to go to work rebuilding Iraq just after the fall of Saddam. In the beginning, only $20 million was cut for northern Iraq, making battles over money between the commanders and the contractors nearly a daily event.

Even when they could agree on who did what, the coordination between the 101st and the civilian contracted companies was less than seemless. "I became frustrated at the continuous assessing going on," Col. Laufenberg recalled of his experiences with the U.S. contractors. "And then they go back, and nothing happened. They go back again, and assess some more. It was assessment and assessment, and no action." By the fall, Laufenberg, Petraeus, and all of the 101st field grade commanders had grown increasingly disenchanted with the contractors from the States. They simply refused to get down to work without swift impetus from the commanding general. When they did get down to work, their standards often exceeded what the division and the local government needed. Petraeus and his chief of staff especially lost sleep over the October 1 school deadline. What the division needed to get the schools up and operational by the time the children went back to school. Instead, the contractors aimed to build a school that resembled a school in the United States. It was ambitious, but their renovations often took far too long.

CHAPTER 10

THE LONGEST AUTUMN

From Second Brigade came one of the most interesting stories of a soldier in combat in the 101st's tour. The American infantry is as diverse as America itself. Infantrymen come from the plains of Nebraska to the city streets of New York. They just don't often come from the Ivy League.

But the perception from people outside the Army of infantrymen as hardheaded grunts was beginning to change. Major Gen. Petraeus, an infantryman and a graduate of the Woodrow Wilson School of Public and International Affairs at Princeton, was right at home his entire career with "The Queen of Battle." If Petraeus had help break the infantry stereotype within the 101st, it was one Second Brigade enlisted soldier, a specialist, who rewrote the character altogether.

In civilian clothes, usually a pair of khaki pants and a polo t-shirt, Stephen Carley struck more soldiers in his unit as better suited for the Fort Campbell Post Library than Strike Brigade. Carley came to Fort Campbell in December of 2002, having graduated the previous spring from Columbia University with his Master's in International Relations. With few soldiers in his unit with any kind of post-secondary education, Carley came to his unit a bit more ballyhoo than the usual import from the Fort Campbell Replacement Detachment, and with infinitely more to prove. But Carley proved more wise than smart. He took his civilian education for what it was worth in the enlisted corps: nothing. Instead, Carley approached the Army as his first day at Columbia and his NCOs as his professors. He knew little about the infantry and there was no reason to pretend like he did just because he had his Master's.

While he clearly had settled for a job after grad school that paled in comparison to what he was qualified for and certainly would have received had he chose not to enlist, Carley found the Army challenging. He was never a natural athlete – a very slender six feet when he arrived with the 101st – but he always approached morning physical training like a mid-term exam. He always stood at parade rest for an NCO, wore the heart on his helmet with pride, and never had a regret. In short, in his very brief time at Fort Campbell, Carley had learned the basics of 101st Airborne soldiering.

In only two months though, Carley would have to learn the advanced curriculum of 101st soldiering by fire. A long way from the comfort of graduate school, war would made Carley forget about what he did before the Army as soon as the first bullet whizzed past his head. He had only his M-4 Carbine and his brothers during the push to Baghdad, and it was his M-4 and his brothers for certain that got him through.

On the other end was Mosul, where Carley proceeded with his post-Army plans. He wanted to go to law school as soon as he was discharged and he wasn't going to let the fact that he was in a war zone derail his schedule. This was not going to be a logistically easy feat. Carley had not yet taken the Law School Admission Test (LSAT), the entry exam for law school, and was obligated to the Army only until August 2004. With the Carley stuck in Mosul until February, he had a problem. With a little help from Capt. Jamie Phillips, the Second Brigade Staff Judge Advocate, and no exceptions to policy from his chain of command, Carley became the first person to ever take the LSAT exam in a war zone.

"There was a lot of red tape," Carley said, in a blatant understatement. "The only other places around here I could have done this were Tel Aviv and Cairo." Carley suggested to his commander that he could take a couple of days leave to take the exam. "That was out of the question."

Left with few options, Carley asked what it would take to legally administer the exam from Mosul. That's where Phillips came in. The Second Brigade JAG officer called friends back home and asked them to help. After a few phone calls and some determined lobbying, the exam was set. From the Second Brigade command center, at a designated time with Phillips proctoring, Carley took the exam. Phillips watched Carley take the exam in utter amazement. Never once did he lose his focus, even as the sound of gunfire literally surrounded him. This was certainly not how Phillips remembered taking his LSAT.

On his application's personnel statements, Carley wrote about what he knew. "The Army teaches you to function with a level head when the stakes could be no higher. It puts you in a situation where you have to work with and fight beside individuals from every socioeconomic and educational background.

"It has the effect of opening ones eyes."

And for Carley, the Army had the effect of opening doors. In the end, Carley decided to delay entry into law school to volunteer for the Bush-Cheney reelection campaign.

October 15 was another day Maj. Gen. David Petraeus had circled on his calendar. Saddam Hussein's face would be removed from any and all Iraqi currencies once and for all. In his stead would be images of monuments of Iraq. The changes were sweeping. The currency exchange was estimated by coalition authorities as the largest in world history. In the first day alone, twenty billion Iraqi dinars would be exchanged. No Saddam currencies would be legally accepted anywhere in Iraq starting October 15. They would be worth only the paper they were printed on.

The comprehensive plan to unite Iraq under one currency had been laid out beyond October 15. By January 15, Kurdish controlled areas were to recognize the new dinar, instead of using the Swiss dinar, as their economy had used before. To meet the challenge, the coalition and the division had to make sure the banks had adequate security and legitimacy to support the exchange.

The Iraqi dinar would now be printed on a stronger, insoluble paper which, in contrast to the Saddam dinar, would not wilt if it ever got wet. There were also new markers to combat fraud. The new currency would have a certain foundation of legitimacy that the former currency, which had almost been uniformly erased anyway by the American currency since April, did not have. Petraeus and the 101st had spent $90,000 in preparing the Iraqi banks for the currency exchange, an investment that was not certain to give the division the return it wanted until a last minute rush to prepare the banks. Second Lt. Paul Kreger and Sgt. Toby Tucker had specialized for two months in making sure the contractors were on track to make the deadline. Until the last week, they weren't. More than just a few officers in the D-Main Palace were sweating. It was a part of a gamble – the 101st, in contrast to other division areas of operation, had entrusted the Iraqi Ministry of Finance to take the lead in the operation. Kreger and Tucker were hands-off advisors, until the contractors neglected to come to work in the first scheduled days of renovation.

Right: Command Sgt. Maj. Marvin Hill (with one of his enlisted aids), the division's top enlisted soldier, collects only a few of the crates full of Christmas cards that arrived in time for the holidays for the division soldiers. (Photo by 101st Airborne Division Public Affairs)

Below: A group of UH-60 Blackhawks, wrapped in plastic to protect the aircrafts from corrosion during the trip back to the United States, wait to get loaded onto the U.S.N.S. Benavidez at a Kuwait City harbor. (Photo by Sgt. Thomas Day, 40th Public Affairs Detachment)

Right: Colonel Michael Linnington and Command Sgt. Maj. Jaoquin Diaz fold up the Third Brigade colors. (Photo by Spc. Joshua Hutcheson)

Below: Like their American counterparts, an Iraqi Civil Defense Corps soldier salutes one of his fallen brothers. As the division left, the Iraqi security forces increasingly took control of the Nineveh province, for better or worse. (Photo by 101st Airborne Division Public Affairs)

Above: Coalition troops patrol the an Iraqi waterway by boat. (U.S. Army) Below: A young officer briefs Maj. Gen. David Petraeus and Brig. Gen. Ben Freakley. Petraeus demanded that officers keep their briefings short and exclude any superfluous information. (U.S. Army)

Above: The intense Iraqi heat and punishing sand took its toll on the 101st equipment early in the Iraq tour – leaving lower enlisted soldiers to work magic just to keep their vehicles running. (U.S. Army) Below: A 101st patrol takes the hill with no opposition. (U.S. Army)

Above: Two Second Brigade soldiers establish a mortar point. Their regiment is marked on their Kevlar helmets with the Second Brigade heart, a trademark dating back to Normandy. (U.S. Army) Below: Two soldiers flying in the passengers seats of a UH-60 Blackhawk helicopter fly over Northern Iraq. (U.S. Army)

Above: From the top: Col. Michael Linnington gives a briefing to his Third Brigade staff in a forward operating base south of Baghdad. (U.S. Army) Below: This photo, staged by the 101st Public Affairs Office, was used in a historical video and morphed into a similar photo of American soldiers, holding a Nazi flag, taken after the German surrender. (U.S. Army)

Above: Dust storms paralyzed the 101st's initial push into Iraq, disabling air operations for days at a time. (U.S. Army) Below: The 101st air assault capabilities allowed for helicopters to drop soldiers into fire fights with unequaled speed and agility. (U.S. Army)

Above: A Squad Automatic Weapon gunner takes a knee during short halt while on patrol. (U.S. Army) Below: A 101st squad on a dismounted patrol. (U.S. Army)

Above: A Third Brigade "Rakkassan" convoy leader readies his team to move out. The Rakkassans are identified by their trademark Torie logo, sewn to their Kevlar helmets. (U.S. Army) Below: Dark smoke welcomes one 101st patrol home for the evening. (U.S. Army)

Above: A First Brigade squad sweeps through a suspected insurgent home. The "Bastogne Brigade" wore its trademark Club on their Kevlars, a marking – like Second Brigade's heart – that traced its roots back to Normandy. (U.S. Army) Below: Digital battlefield: Inside Kuwait, American staff officers prepare their movement forward. (U.S. Army)

Above: An American combat unit, with their chemical uniforms on and masks strapped to their hips, moves into Iraq. (U.S. Army) Below: A Second Brigade Infantry Squad Automatic Weapon gunner ready for the enemy. The SAW fires a 5.56mm round, is fully automatic, and is light enough to be carried and fired from the standing position. (U.S. Army)

Above: Dust storms paralyze this young soldier like they paralyzed 101st air operations in the opening two weeks of the Iraq war. This particular soldier protects himself with a neck gator and protective eyewear – both mandated parts of the uniform for soldiers caught in the stiff desert winds. (U.S. Army) Below: American soldiers, with their chemical uniforms on and masks strapped to their hips, mount a CH-47 Chinook helicopter and move forward. The Chinook is a troop/cargo-carrying helicopter crewed by a pilot, co-pilot, and crewchief. (U.S. Army)

A 101st Soldier takes his weapon of choice, an AT4 shoulder-fired missile device, before moving out on patrol. The AT4 is a shoulder-fired anti-tank weapon that is preloaded and can fire only one round. (U.S. Army)

A 101st unit arrives in Kuwait with their equipment stuffed in their rucksack and their chemical masks strapped to their hips. (U.S. Army)

Above: A 101st patrol during the initial push into Iraq. (U.S. Army) Below: A 101st patrol looks into a targeted home of a suspected insurgent. (U.S. Army)

Above: Guns and Roses: A First Brigade soldier charms a young Iraqi girl and her family. (U.S. Army) Below: Three 101st soldiers approach a CH-47 Chinook helicopter to take them over the Iraqi desert. (U.S. Army)

Above: A 101st element watch a battle from a distance. (U.S. Army) Below: A 101st element sets up security during a long halt. (U.S. Army)

Above: A group of First Brigade commanders discuss upcoming movements inside Iraq. (U.S. Army) Below: Little kids and grass, the allure of the 101st's 2003 home base, Northern Iraq. (U.S. Army)

Like a group of unleashed hounds, a 101st patrol rushes over a hill. (U.S. Army)

Above: A towed Howitzer artillery piece fires as one 101st soldier protects his hearing from the blast. The M119 Howitzer, a weapon dating back to the 19th century, was used sparingly in urban areas. (U.S. Army) Below: A towed Howitzer blasts a round into the Iraqi sky. (U.S. Army)

A Rakkassan patrol with an Iraqi linguist in tow. The 101st recognized the need for linguists early and immediately began hiring locals who spoke fluent or near fluent English. (U.S. Army)

Above: A presence patrol marches up a Northern Iraq street. (U.S. Army) Below: A unit, decorated for the occasion, readies for an assault. (U.S. Army)

Above: A 101st support unit on a short halt as they move through Northern Iraq. (U.S. Army) Below: Guard duty in Iraq, a lonesome shift. (U.S. Army)

Above: A communication specialist calls up a report inside Iraq during the initial push toward Baghdad. (U.S. Army) Below: An Iraqi woman approaches a 101st vehicle. Iraqi kids often approached American soldiers to make friendly; Iraqi adult women more often than not, wanted only American pocket change. (U.S. Army)

One 101st soldier comes home to his forward operating base as an exhausted waits by the door. (U.S. Army)

A 101st soldier in repose. The M4 carbine is a 1994 update of the M16 used in Vietnam, providing infantrymen with a lighter weapon on patrols. (U.S. Army)

Above: A 101st helicopter convoy over the Iraqi sunset. (U.S. Army) Below: A 101st helicopter lands. (U.S. Army)

A 101st unit arrives on the battlefield. (U.S. Army)

Above: A 101st UH-60 Blackhawk lands in Northern Iraq. The power of a Blackhawk in takeoff and landing can be felt from a radius as large as a football field. (U.S. Army) Below: An American tank – rendered inoperative by the Iraqi dust and heat – is carried off the field by an American cargo truck. (U.S. Army)

Above: A UH-60 Blackhawk convoy lands at a Northern Iraq LZ. (U.S. Army) Below: The UH (Utility Helicopter)-60 Blackhawk has been in the Army's air fleet since 1979. It provides commanders with maneuverability around the battlefield, able to carry two pilots, two crew chiefs and 11 combat equipped soldiers. (U.S. Army)

Above: The AH (Attack Helicopter)-64D Apache Longbow Helicopter is an armored helicopter equipped with targeting acquisition features that allow pilots to fire at a target and move onto the next target before the rocket they just fired hits its target. It has been used extensively in Iraq and Afghanistan. (U.S. Army) Below: When a helicopter convoy the size of the one pictured comes across the horizon, it can only be the 101st Airborne Division arriving in the neighborhood. (U.S. Army)

With a nudge here and there and daily check ups on the construction workers, Kreger and Tucker were able to beat the deadline – barely. Once the banks were on their way, then there was the issue of who would control the banks.

The already difficult maneuver of rebuilding the Iraqi banks was made worse by corruption. The heads of both the Rasheed and Rafidan banks were removed after their own high-level Ba'ath Party connections were exposed. For months, the division had to deal with bank managers they knew to be thieves. Kreger and Tucker's boss, Lt. Col. Curtis Craft, equated the experience to "dancing with the devil."

The end of the Saddam currency would be marked in the morning, when the banks opened up at 8 a.m. to get an early start. Bundles of dinar would be dipped in maroon dye and destroyed. The banks, which would be a certain target for anti-coalition forces, would be secured by the Iraqi police. Iraqi money and the Iraqi economy, more than at any other point in the coalition occupation, would be in Iraqi hands.

"We got tired on the old regime and all the times our currency value would change," said Qutyba Saleh, a downtown Mosul Rafidain bank manager. "We hope this exchange will leave our old problems behind." Some of the old problems were certain to be left behind. For the first time in nearly a generation, every acre of Iraq would be under one, unified currency. Other problems were not so easily fixed. The Iraqi currency would still be very weak, exponentially weaker than any currency in the European Union and certainly the American dollar.

On October 1, CBS' *60 Minutes II* aired a report they titled, "War and Peace." It amounted to what many soldiers returning from Iraq had been begging for since the late spring and early summer upswing in violence – a positive, 360-degree report from the American media about the Iraq post-war reconstruction effort. Correspondent Scott Pelley had followed down a Florida reserve unit in Baghdad for the story, then caught a ride up to Mosul to interview the coalition's newest, biggest star.

"The paratrooper with a Princeton PhD.," as Pelley labeled Petraeus, was put right under the spotlight on one of American televisions' biggest stages. "Northern Iraq," the CG told Pelley, "is really seen as what the rest of the country could be." Pelley was quickly impressed by Petraeus when he pressed the scholar-soldier on the issue of opening up the Syrian border. "We were about to dump huge amounts of dollars on the market in Mosul by paying of salaries that had not been paid for some government officials and government workers. And with this great increase in the amount of dollars chasing those goods, the logical result would be inflation."

"Wait a minute, you're the commanding general of the 101st Airborne Division?" Pelley asked Petraeus. He couldn't believe he was hearing these economic theories from a general.

"Well, I admit, I once taught economics at West Point in a previous life."

Also in focus was Lt. Col. Joe Buche, who took over the 3-187th Infantry Regiment in June from Lt. Col. Patrick Fetterman. Buche had been running a remote area around the Syrian border, so remote that the battalion had not fired a shot in a three consecutive months in the summer, as noted in the report. "There's a whole potpourri of folks that live there. I've got a bunch of Kurdish people. I've also got some Arabs, mostly the Shamer and Jehesh tribes. Further south, there is a Yessiddi population. I've also got a few folks who are of Turkomen heritage," Buche told *60 Minutes II*. "The security in my AO is pretty stable. A lot of it has to do with working hand in hand with the people that are here."

Buche took Pelley on a Blackhawk helicopter, doors open, to show off his territory, including the breathtaking Mosul dam. The aircraft landed right on the spot and Buche took the cameras right into the main pumping station. "After the war, the pumps were down and the harvest was on its way to disaster," Pelley told the American public. "That's when the 101st switched from swords to plowshares."

One of the stars of the *60 Minutes II* report, Sgt. Sean Driscoll, only got to watch a video recording of the report from home months later. It was an image of himself in better days. After arriving back in Mosul from two-weeks of mid-tour leave, Driscoll put the body armor back on and mounted a cargo truck due for Tal Afar. He would be back at the water pumping station the next morning, he figured. Those plans changed when the truck was hit with an Improvised Explosive Device (IED), a weapon insurgent forces had just then started use with regularity. Three others were injured in the blast but Driscoll was the most serious.

He had taken shrapnel in his arm, so much so that it nearly blew his arm off. Driscoll would regain some use of his arm, months later, but he would never see the water pumping station again. It was a shame. In just months, Driscoll had seen the facility regain its self-sufficiency – its Iraqi engineering staff included. Several German engineers from the water pump manufacturers had taught the staff how and how not to operate the facility.

More than $250,000 of CERP funds had been spent on the project. Eighty megawatts of power drawn from the Syrian power grid had fixed the power fluctuation issue. Now the facility was drawing a continuous, twenty-four hour a day, power feed. By the time Driscoll was evacuated back to Fort Campbell, the water pumping station rebuilding project had soared above any reasonable expectations.

Maybe it was a blessing that Driscoll got to see his family before war would permanently scar his body. Indeed, it was a blessing that Driscoll got to see his family at all during mid-tour leave. What had started as a seemingly routine briefing to Acting Secretary of the Army Les Brownlee in June had become a reality for Maj. Gen. David Petraeus' soldiers and soldiers throughout the theater. It wasn't much, only fifteen days, but the opportunity to go home for any amount of time before February of 2004 had seemed like a distant fantasy for the 101st soldiers. Now soldiers, most of whom were lower enlisted, were on planes starting in early September destined for Baltimore, Atlanta, or Dallas. In the beginning, soldiers would have to find their own transportation home beyond that point, but the Army would later pay for any link-up flights home.

The importance of mid-tour leave on soldier morale could not be overstated. Soldiers who had left pregnant wives at home got to see their kids for the first time. Marriages that had been strained by the seven months apart were resuscitated, or sometimes culminated. Questions were answered. Every once in a while, a soldier got the OK to go home at just the moment he or she could only dream of.

Corporal Nick Degreek had seen war, his own promotion, and more twelve-hour days working to repair power generators during his first eight months in Iraq. The heat had made his job indispensable to the division headquarters. For the division command points to operate, they needed power and they couldn't count on the local supply. That meant that Degreek, who specialized in repairing generators, would have to work magic. Generator after generator came in towards his motorpool, having wilted in the summer heat. Degreek too would feel the heat of a different kind. With commander and senior NCOs hovering over his shoulder, Degreek found himself paralyzed when requests for missing parts from the United States fell on deaf ears. All he could do was to work undercover deals with other unit motorpools around the 101st to find what he needed. That was a frustrating process.

In Clarksville, Tenn., just outside of Fort Campbell, Degreek's wife Jessica had gone through an equally frustrating eight months. She told her husband she "had some news" when the two talked for the last time in Kuwait. Now she was as pregnant, alone and raising their daughter McKenzie without any support mechanism. Her husband wrote everyday, sometimes with the most trifling reports, for the first two months of the war. She had tried to keep up the best that she can with her husband's letters. Nick, on the other hand, had feared getting a "Dear John" letter that never came. When he got access to email, almost every action was reported back home. He would have more than three hundred emails saved in his email account by the time he redeployed. But as much as he wrote, and as much as he thought about Jessica, Nick Degreek couldn't help his wife out of bed in the morning. It was an awful way to go through a pregnancy.

The pain of being apart had taken its emotional and physical toll on Jessica. The two had been inseparable since high school, and she needed her husband now more than ever. In Iraq, Nick had heard talk that soldiers were going home on mid-tour leave, but he knew better than to get his hopes up. He didn't think he would be a priority; his commander, Capt. Tito Villanueva, thought otherwise. Villanueva put Degreek on one of the first flights out, leaving Nov. 6. Jessica was due before the end of the month.

He landed in Baltimore after two days of travel, jumped on a flight to Nashville and was reunited with his wife and daughter. Thankfully, Jessica had not given birth yet as Degreek kissed his wife for the first time since February. Her last doctor's appointment was in two days, but she wouldn't make it. Jessica, just as she walked out the front door one morning, looked at her husband with a look in her eyes that could knock her husband of his feet.

"Ok, it's game time." Nick, the two remembered later, remained remarkably calm in this the second time around. The two jumped in the car as Jessica's mother stayed back with McKenzie. She had time. It would be another twenty-four hours before she would actually give birth. Nalani Degreek was born on Nov. 12. The couple would have the next ten days to enjoy the newest edition to their family. Nobody could have scripted Cpl. Nick Degreek's mid-tour leave tale better.

Nick had wanted to share Nalani's birth with his friends at the motorpool. He had almost nobody to smoke cigars with. That all changed when he returned to Mosul. Degreek came back armed with a handful of pictures, a book of stories, and recharged to finish the stretch run of his deployment.

Before Sgt. First Class Hector Jusino said goodbye – he was slated to join the division's G-5 (Civil Affairs) office – he wanted to make sure his new friends were set. "When we left Kuwait and got into Iraq, I started seeing the poverty that was in Iraq and it really hit me hard. I started thinking, how unlucky could you be to be born in a country like Iraq, in the desert, and have a government like the government Saddam had and be in the lowest level of humanity. From Kuwait to Mosul, I didn't see anything but poverty." The parallels he saw between his Iraqi friends' lives and his own upbringing in Puerto Rico were striking. Jusino had been raised on the dole. Now, in his fifties, Jusino took it on himself to make sure his friends wouldn't have to live like they had and like he had as a young man.

Some of the images he saw when he arrived in Mosul were enough to give anyone the chills. "There was a guy who had a hernia the size of my arm. Some of the workers I had, I had to pick worms off some of their faces," Jusino recalled. "They lived like animals. They lived like a cow that wasn't taken care of. This was the way that these people were. Malnutrition, some of them were going blind, and some of them had been beaten by (Saddam's) authorities." Jusino's linguist, Muhammad, an English teacher for thirty-five years, was jobless after it was discovered that he was not a member of the Ba'ath Party. He was forced to retire on a one dollar a month pension.

It was the drive to make the lives of his workers better that made Jusino's tour such a success. "Maybe it was my background. My father died when I was three years old and my mother didn't work … we were very poor. We lived off Social Security benefits. I saw poverty in Iraq and I remembered growing up. When I went to Iraq, it was similar.

"I'm a one hundred percent believer that poverty has a solution: education, training, and money. Not just giving money to people. The solution to poverty is teaching skills to people for them to learn how to make a living. One of the problems that group had over there, I would say the main problem, was that they had no skills.

"You take any human being anywhere, you give him a chance, and you teach him how to make a living, and he will never be poor. That was something that attracted me to the military. When I joined the military, many people I met could barely write or read. And the military would take that guy and shape him up to a productive man."

It was in his nature to help people, and starting with nineteen men who needed a chance to make a decent living, Jusino focused himself on giving at least one of them that chance. "I told myself, I wouldn't leave Iraq without getting one of them out of poverty." He wanted to teach them how to be a contractor and get them a contract with the coalition in Mosul on post. "And that's what I did with Salim."

It seemed unimaginable in May, when Jusino first met the former Iraqi soldier, that Salim Sultan would be able to make the kind of strides that he had made in such a short time. Just months earlier, Sultan was unable to even speak to Jusino, still shaken from the first time he had made contact with the American Army in 1991 in the first Gulf War. Through the blood and sweat the two had put into cleaning up the sports complex, Jusino and Salim had forged a genuine friendship that bridged the chasm that existed between the two of them when they first met. Jusino trusted Salim, and Salim began to take on a managerial role in the sports complex project. He never let Jusino down, not even once. Now, with the project nearly complete, Jusino choose Salim as his next project. He would not be the easiest worker to mold into a contractor – he had a fifth grade level education – but Jusino felt the strongest bond towards him. "He was a very smart guy with no education and he had no skills. He used to sell fruits on a stand in Mosul."

Salim was a bit confused and even afraid. He did not want to let his boss down, but he didn't think he was capable of meeting Jusino's expectations. "Look," Jusino acutely told Salim, "I have chosen you because you have shown leadership and you have what it takes." Salim didn't fully appreciate Jusino's point until after he started taking his friend's lessons in business out into the city. Jusino knew it would not be an easy project, but he didn't choose Salim because he wanted it to be painless. He wanted to teach Salim to be an active participant in the local economy because it was going to be people like Salim, with no education but a fierce desire, who were going to spark the rebirth of Mosul. If he could make a productive man out of Salim, it would be infectious, he figured.

On this project, Jusino never asked for help or money. Maybe he wanted to keep it an enlisted thing, but Jusino told nobody but Command Sgt. Maj. Marvin Womack about his plans. Womack himself didn't find out about Jusino's new mission until he "smelled it," after noticing that his NCO seemed to have other priorities during the workday. He wasn't upset, not at all in fact. Womack just told him to march on, gave him a pat on the shoulder and told him, "You're a good man, Sergeant Jusino."

Having already taught Salim's new trade at the sports complex, mainly construction and "area beautification," Jusino went to work on teaching his friend the basics of business financing and management. Everyday for a month, Jusino and Salim had a one-on-one class. Salim already knew how to be a leader. The challenge was getting him to put what he already knew into practice without a net to catch him when he falls. Jusino was not going to be there for his friend when he went back to the United States.

Salim also needed to know how to network. He needed connections with the coalition. So Jusino brought him on post at the Mosul Airfield to meet who he needed to know, like Command Sgt. Maj. Marvin Womack. He would start with the little projects around post, cleaning up trash, etc., and the quality wasn't the best at first. But he learned and he got better. Soon, he would have people working for him. And finally, before Sgt. First Class Jusino left, he would have his own contracting company with a downtown Mosul office. He even bought a house with a brand new BMW in the driveway. Jusino had accomplished his mission. He had got his friend Salim out of poverty.

Salim's education was not free however. "The other thing that I told him," Jusino recalled, "the way that you're going to pay me back is that you're going to take these guys that are working for you, and one way or another you're going to get them employed. You're going to set up a way of teaching them a skill." This was not a request. Salim took a solemn vow to make sure the opportunities that he got from Jusino were spread to the other workers with the sports complex project. "Little by little, each one of them got employed. One of them opened an electronics store with TVs and radios. A bunch of them went to the Veterans Employment Office in Mosul (then opened for civilians). I sent them there with letters of recommendation and they got jobs working for a construction company building a housing area sponsored by the military."

And then there was Muhammad, his linguist. He used to live in a mud house, but that mud house wouldn't be home for long. He started working with Salim after Jusino left, making good money too. In Clarksville, Jusino received a letter. It was from Muhammad. He had bought a new house. His gifted son who he was previously unable to pay for school for was now covered. "The goal that I put on myself was to get one of them out of poverty. I think that I got more than one. That wasn't what the Army told me to do, but I took a chance that the Army gave me."

The story of Sgt. First Class Hector Jusino in Iraq would have a less than triumphant ending. He came down with a hernia in October and was promptly redeployed to Fort Campbell. The early redeployment came as a crushing ending for Jusino, who claimed he was "blessed by God" to come to Iraq. He wanted to finish the deployment, but nobody, not even Jusino himself, could claim that he left Iraq before his job was done. Saying goodbye to Salim and Muhammad proved more difficult than he had ever imagined, but he had exchanged addresses so they could keep in touch. While he will likely never see the two again, their long distance friendship promises to stay strong for a lifetime.

Jusino's marriage had been less bullish after their painful separation. Hector had left his wife Christine in February in an aloof daze. Admittedly, he was focused so much on doing his job in Iraq that he had forgot how much he would miss his wife and two daughters. He would be reminded as soon as he got to Kuwait and realized that he was half the world away from his home. Annika's tenth birthday and Melissa's seventh would both come while Jusino was deployed.

He made sure to make the best of opportunities to call home after he and the division stabilized in Mosul. Both of his daughters were doing well in school and Christine, left alone to support Annika and Melissa, was doing so without any problems. Hector had been away from home before; she knew what she was doing with the kids. It was the emotional separation more than the geographical separation that had frustrated Christine. There were just so many emotions that Hector could share from Southeast Asia on satellite phone. For a marriage that had survived everything for eleven years, the deployment had created a chasm that the Jusinos struggled to bridge up to the moment Hector walked off the plane and saw his wife and kids.

Hector's chest was pumping like an engine when he walked off the plane at Campbell Army Airfield. He was still unsure about where his marriage was going, and he knew Christine felt the same way. Neither one could imagine fracturing the family with a divorce, but Christine needed her husband to open up again. She needed to feel like she did when they first fell in love in Germany.

Christine had been waiting several hours at an airfield hanger with other families waiting for soldiers to return. There weren't many soldiers coming back on this flight, but the hanger was still decorated with "Welcome Home" signs, many of which were probably left over from Fort Campbell units returning from Afghanistan. She didn't bring a sign; she just brought the two kids. That was all Hector needed. Through the brisk October breeze, dressed in his khaki Desert Camouflage Uniforms and carrying his M-4 over his shoulder, Sgt. First Class Hector Jusino emerged from the pack of soldiers as a broken man who just wanted to see his family. His confusion was painted on his face, but everything started to make sense once he saw his family. There his wife stood with Annika and Melissa like a beacon of light at the end of an eight-month tunnel. "I'm home."

For Christine, the moment felt like the night she learned how to dance to Hispanic music from a soldier named Hector. It was time to start over, she thought, and that's exactly what they did. At the kitchen table, with their daughters, they talked about anything and everything that Christine wanted to talk about. For the first time, Hector told his wife about all about the sports complex and his new friends, Salim and Muhammad. The spirit of their marriage, dormant since Hector left in February, started to reemerge.

For the duration of the division's operations in northern Iraq, the 101st had operated as one cohesive unit. With the exception of the small units in the three stable Kurdish provinces, no one division soldier was more than a few hours' drive away from another. With one exception. The 716th Military Police Battalion, a so-called non-divisional unit based at Fort Campbell, had operated in Karbala since April. Their commander, Lt. Col. Kim Orlando, had led his unit in one of Iraq's more dangerous cities for several months. During the daylight hours, Orlando and the 716th trained local police forces, protected coalition convoys, and patrolled the city with the First Marine Expeditionary Force. His unit's mission after the lights went out, primarily, was just to enforce curfew. But it was far more than just a babysitting job. The enemy came out at night, and the 716th was always there to meet them.

Orlando was well known by his soldiers as a fearless commander who would never shy away from confronting the enemy. Never was that more apparent than when Orlando began pushing his battalion's patrols throughout their area of operations to meet a group of forces led by a young outlaw cleric. At the age of thirty, Muqtada al-Sadr was gradually amassing the support of thousands of radical Muslims. He was afanatical leader who had been able to cash in on the family name as the son of Grand Ayatollah Allah Muhammad Sadiq al-Sadr. The al-Sadr family – tatamount to the Kennedy family in Shi'ia Islam – had campaigned during Saddam's regime to change Iraq's schools, government and society to strictly conform to Islamic law. In 1999, al-Sadr's father had been killed along with two of his brothers in what many of his supporters saw as a murder mission orchestrated by Saddam Hussein.

Now, with Saddam no longer in power and his father dead, young Muqtada al-Sadr's rise had taken the coalition by surprise. In An Najaf, he and a band of his followers surrounded the Golden Mosque of Ali, where Lt. Col. Christopher Hughes had won over the support of Grand Ayatollah Sistani, to demand that Sistani leave the country. Publically, al-Sadr denounced violence. But his newspaper and his rhetoric made a clear call to violent opposition of the coalition and whomever else opposed al-Sadr. Earlier, al-Sadr had ordered the murder of a rival Shia cleric shortly after the cleric returned to Iraq after years of exile.

Orlando saw al-Sadr for what the coalition would see him months down the road. Muqtada al-Sadr would grow in stature and in popular support to become one of the most dangerous anti-coalition forces in Iraq.

And so it was on October 16, long after the coalition established curfew in the area had expired, when Orlando and several of his men found a gang of armed militants walking the streets of Karbala. Orlando, a field grade officer among a pack of enlisted subordinates, approached the men. The gang was a part of a band of anti-coalition insurgents in the area loyal to al-Sadr. The exchange between Orlando and the men heated up. One of the men brandished a pistol; Orlando reached for his nine millimeter. Then, shots rang out from Al-Sadr's militia on roof tops who clearly had been waiting to ambush a coalition patrol.

Orlando, Staff Sgt. Joseph Bellavia, twenty-eight, and Cpl. Sean Grilley, twenty-four, were killed in the firefight. Orlando was the most senior officer to that point to be lost in the Iraq theatre. The ensuing firefight claimed the lives of ten Iraqis.

In Mosul, Petraeus was awoken by his chief of staff after midnight. "Sir, Colonel Orlando was just killed down in Karbala." Petraeus popped up with a charge and rushed downstairs. He knew and liked Orlando a great deal. Orlando's wife, Sherry, at work at the Fort Campbell Public Affairs Office, was going through her usual day after sending her two sons off to school when her husband had been shot. She had been alone for eight months, but she too had been in the military. The two had met when both were junior enlisted soldiers. Sherri, like every faithful military wife, had trucked along without her husband before. Now she was going to get a visit from a division chaplain. Petraeus felt his heart sink.

Days later, Petraeus made the trip to Karbala to remember the three soldiers. The service took place in an amphitheatre, adjacent to the battalion headquarters. Losing a battalion commander was unprecedented – unprecented for the 101st Airborne Division and unprecedented for the entire coalition in Afghanistan and Iraq. Petraeus' ability to connect with soldiers was never stronger than during the memorial service in Karbala. "How we deal with adversity defines who we are and what we're made of. Times such as these call for the best in all of us. There is nothing tougher than a loss of a brother in arms. But great soldiers and great units – and you are good soldiers and this is a great unit – pull together in times like these.

"The loss of these soldiers has saddened all of us, all of us who knew them and who served with them. We want to find meaning in such a loss. Above all, we want an answer to the question, 'What good could come of this?' The answer to that question is not easy. And so perhaps we can determine what good can come from this by further asking how we should live our lives in view of our limited days and limited opportunities to make a difference. And may God bless our division and our wonderful United States of America."

Two weeks later, Petraeus was back in Karbala to hand the 716th Military Police Battalion command guidon to Lt. Col. Ashton Hayes. "As many of you know, there is a formula for change of command ceremonies," Petraeus told the MPs. "Today's ceremony, however, is not a normal change of command. If it were, we would be standing on the freshly-cut grass of the division parade field. Our families would be in the bleachers and, of course, the outgoing commander would be sitting next to the incoming commander." At Fort Bragg, with no premonition that he would be on his way to Iraq by weeks end, Hayes got the word that he would be assuming command of the 716th MPs.

Standing in front of his still weary soldiers, Command Sgt. Maj. Michael Hayes (no relation to his new commander), the 716th senior non-commissioned officer, rallied his troops like a championship football coach. "Two weeks ago, this battalion took a hit, but it did not falter and it did not stumble."

The battalion called themselves "The Peacekeepers," but nobody could keep the peace in the coming months and years in Karbala. The firefight that killed Bellavia, Grilley, and Orlando would be the first of a bloody battle between insurgents and the coalition that would continue long after the 716th MPs redeployed home.

On October 25, what the division commanders had feared for months finally happened. The Commanders' Emergency Relief Program funds evaporated to zero. The waiting game began. Promises that the division had made for months were put on ice, at least until Senator Bill Frist helped the CERP funds reappear. It had been expected that the free spending of the division was not going to last. During one interview, to illustrate his own willingness to bend over backward for the Iraqi people, Petraeus was quoted as saying, "We don't know the meaning of the word 'No.'" With the division next to penniless, sacrifices were going to have to be made, and Iraqis were going hear 'no' to their pleas for funding. Soon, it wouldn't take long for the division to notice a direct correlation between the dollars spent on Iraqis and the bullets fired towards coalition soldiers in Mosul.

"The turning point began around late summer, early fall. Probably in the August, September timeframe," Col. Joseph Anderson said. "But the hard-core attacks didn't really begin until the late fall."

Sergeant Michael Hancock, an artilleryman, had reported to his unit on Oct. 5 to begin his second tour of duty with the 101st Airborne Division. Less than three weeks later, he would be dead. His squad leader, Sgt. Joshua Forbess, had gotten to know Hancock pretty well in the short time he had with him. They had become instant friends. Hancock had also made an impression with his first sergeant, First Sgt. Mathew Nagel. Nagel had seen Hancock's gutty determination years earlier, when both were at Fort Stewart, Ga. It was time for a Physical Training (or "PT") test. They had divided up his unit into halves, with one half going on the first day and the other half on the second. Hancock went on the first day, scoring a 299 out of 300. "But being the caliber of soldier he was, he decided he hadn't done his best. So the very next day, Michael retook that PT test," Nagel remembered. "This time, he scored a three-hundred."

Hancock had been in the Army for eleven years. He had four kids and a wife, Jeannie, waiting for him at home. Hancock's final mission was guarding a grain silo. The guard element was ambushed, leaving Michael Hancock dead in the firefight. "Your family loves you, your battery loves you, your section loves you," Forbess told his friend during Hancock's memorial service. "And I love you. I'll see you on the high ground."

Sadly, Hancock's death was just one of many as the insurgency in the Nineveh Province came together like a worsening storm. Enemy elements from every direction had coalesced in Northern Iraq at exactly the wrong time for the 101st Airborne Division. It was really quite surprising that the insurgency did not reach Mosul earlier. The first corner of the resistance triangle came from new enemies under a familiar tent. "We had our own Fedayeen, we didn't need any migratory Fedayeen," Anderson remarked in response to the suggestion that the armed resistance came from the same enemies causing trouble in Baghdad. "The Army is what made that country run." Hundreds of the general officers in the Iraqi military had been natives of Mosul. Finding soldiers to fight in the coalition was hardly a problem for leaders of the insurgency. They just needed a trigger mechanism. They found it when the Commanders' Emergency Relief Program funds went dry and expectations of programs of reconciliation – to complement the de-Bathification program – did not materialize in the Sunni areas.

The Ba'ath party militia had been quiet, likely because the 101st Airborne's successful efforts to reach out to the former moderate Ba'ath officials. With the money gone, the agreement had broken down. In the months they had been placated by the Commanders' Emergency Relief Program funds, the former Ba'ath party leaders loyal to Saddam had organized, gained resources and recruited. At some point in the early fall, the Ba'ath party militia joined with the Fedayeen in Mosul and were poised to strike.

And then there was the final element, the key ingredient that found a way into Mosul through the hills of northern Iraq. They called themselves Ansar al-Islam. Their reign in northern Iraq came to an ignominious end during the initial weeks of Operation Iraqi Freedom, when the U.S. air and Special Forces operations decimated their terrorist organization, forcing whomever was left up north into Iran. The remaining elements of Ansar al-Islam didn't sit quietly in Iran. It was likely that many in the senior leadership knew the American forces from Afghanistan. In fact, many in the division suspected the organization knew its terror tactics from Al Qaeda. They were showing all the fingerprints.

They had used the summer in Iran to recruit and reconstitute. In September and October, they moved. To meet them at the points of entry along the Iranian border was a sixty-one member Long Range Surveillance (LRS) company. Of all 20,000 soldiers serving in Iraq with or attached to the 101st Airborne, there were none more important than those sixty-one soldiers when the insurgency started to heat up.

There was no place in Iraq like the mountains along the Iranian border. One mountainous area was so heavily mined from the Iran-Iraq war that skulls and bones from soldiers killed in action remained nearly fifteen years later. "In that portion of the Iranian border, because of the extreme terrain, a relatively small number, about eight-hundred or so, could actually control the avenues of approach into Iraq," Maj. Gen. Petraeus theorized. "That was a doable mission. What we were trying to do initially was just prevent vehicles full of explosives, weapons, bad guys and money from coming through. If you could control the valleys, you could in fact do that. It was so very mountainous – six, seven thousand foot mountains." The question was, were there in fact terrorists capable and motivated enough to climb the mountains?

Teaming up with the LRS company was the Iraqi Border Patrol, 600 strong, who had been trained by the company during the lonely summer months in the mountains. They were a work in progress, to put it lightly. They needed specified knowledge of how to follow confidential informants and investigate leads. "I can tell you right now, if I dropped 20,000 troops here right now, it wouldn't help you," U.S. Customs Special Agent Larry O'Donnell told Capt. Thomas Hough, the LRS company commander. Quality mattered more than quantity. The Fort Bragg-based unit, with a little help from O'Donnell, were still teaching the basics at the time the division really needed them. By Labor Day, snow started to accumulate on the mountain tops as terrorists started moving across the Iraq-Iran border.

It was never more apparent that Ansar al-Islam was effectively crossing the border and linking up with their leadership than after one three-day operation that nabbed 519 illegal border crossers. Chief Warrant Officer 2 Kevin Turner, after watching a parade of nomads cross a main entry point without so much as a holler from Iraqi customs, lost his cool with the entry point chief. "How can you sleep with yourself, knowing our soldiers are getting killed in Mosul?"

The triangle had come together, along with the evaporation of the CERP funds, at the moment in the calendar that was already circled by division commanders. The last week in October marked the beginning of the holy month of Ramadan for the Islamic faith. During the month of Ramadan, practicing Muslims fast from daybreak until sunset, abstaining from consuming tea, tobacco and even water. It was a prime season for shooting at Americans. "You're always going to be a martyr if you kill an American, today, tomorrow, or the next day, but if you kill one during Ramadan, you're going to be a martyr of martyrs," said Anderson.

Aware of the security concerns the coalition would face during the period, Coalition Administrator L. Paul Bremer wrote a letter to all elements of personnel in the country urging extreme caution and sensitivity towards the Iraqi people. "Ramadan is one of the most holy of Muslim holidays, focusing on sacrifice and prayer. This sacrifice is manifested in almost daily visits to the mosque and an increase in charitable giving to the poor. I ask all of you to show the Iraqi people an extra degree of respect and support during the month of Ramadan."

Bremer's pleas did not fall on deaf ears, but the division commanders knew being overly sensitive in this time period could be potentially deadly. In the summer, as the insurgency was started to take shape, Petraeus had ordered all of his commanders to answer one question before launching a combat operation: Will this operation take more bad guys off the streets than it creates?

The question forced the 101st commanders to think outside the box to put all the pieces together. What was only a game of cat and mouse with black market arms dealers in the spring and summer had become something far more serious. The insurgents had organized and provided a unified front in Mosul. The Ba'ath Party militia had appeared to focus its efforts on undermining the progress in the city by aiming attacks not as much on the coalition soldiers as the Iraqi police. Those same police officers found themselves in the crossfire in one of the most touchy conundrums the division faced in Mosul. Mosques, it became obvious, were actively supporting and participating in the insurgency, distributing leaflets and broadcasting anti-coalition messages on the streets. The police, predominately if not entirely Muslim, would search the Mosques as a proxy force for the division.

With the increased enemy presence came a marked increase in Second Brigade patrols. No longer did the brigade sit back and wait for intelligence to be corroborated and corroborated again. Once they got the intelligence, they moved.

Division intelligence had plotted on a map of Mosul where and when attacks against coalition forces had taken place, and who was suspected of organizing them. A purple marking meant Ansar al-Islam was suspected, red corresponded to the Ba'ath Party militia. The pattern was fairly clear by mid-October. Ansar al-Islam had established the Southeast quadrant of the city as their home base and the Ba'ath Party insurgents had focused on the other side of the Tigris. Petraeus adjusted accordingly.

From October 12 to 18 the 101st rounded up eight Ansar al-Islam operatives, killing scores more. One operation, in the Rakkassan area of operation, netted the number two leader of the organization. Several different "safehouses" for Ansar al-Islam were shut down. And then, they ran. For the domestic insurgents, life would get no easier. In the five months from June to October of 2003, Second Brigade arrested about 400 suspected insurgents. In November things had heated up to the point that 400 additional suspected insurgents were arrested in just one month.

In the United States in the fall of 2003, baseball was the talk of every street corner in every town. The Chicago Cubs and Boston Red Sox were hot prospects to meet in the World Series. Both had gone nearly a century without winning a title. In their way stood the Florida Marlins and the mighty New York Yankees. People from the streets of Manhattan to the fields of Nebraska were glued to their TV sets, watching perhaps the most dramatic playoffs in baseball history. Soldiers in

Iraq, however, were less in the loop. Most soldiers who could stay up to 4 a.m. to watch the games live often did so alone. When Aaron Boone sunk the Red Sox World Series hopes with his eleventh inning home run in Game 7, the D-Main Dining Facility was open with the TVs on, but only about a dozen determined fans took advantage of the opportunity. Even fewer were watching the dramatic ending of the Marlins seven game victory over the Cubs.

"America's Pastime" was not the game of choice for America's deployed soldiers. That distinction went to football, which would back crowds into whatever room held a TV – college or pro. Some commanders even let soldiers sleep in a bit on Monday mornings. The first NFL games started at 8:30 p.m. Mosul time.

Lieutenant Col. Richard Whittaker, a University of Tennessee alum, made certain he found some way to watch or even listen his Volunteers live from half the world away. If the Internet connection was quick enough, Whittaker could even get the play-by-play online. "It was the highlight of our week," he later recalled. The highlight of the year for Whittaker likely came when UT upset the highly favored Miami (FL) Hurricanes, 10-7. Whittaker, of course, was not the only Tennessee die-hard. A group of soldiers who shared the 101st Staff Judge Advocate's UT allegiances took over a northern Iraq water tower, painted it orange with a white "T" and sent the image straight to Volunteer football coach Philip Fulmer. The support energized the entire athletic program, Fulmer recalled in a later visit to Fort Campbell. The women's basketball team even used the photo for recruiting.

The flavors of fall had indeed made their way from home to Iraq, but one fall tradition was simply never recognized. Halloween was not to be celebrated in Iraq – few non-commissioned officers were allowing the uniform standards to be modified. No costumes, no trick or treating, no apple bobbing. The dining facilities didn't even have candy corn. Anybody who did want to celebrate the holiday had the option of dressing up like a soldier and trading candy they received from care packages. Ben and Maggie Smith just opted for a night of waiting in line for the Internet café. The Mosul Airfield had been alive with anticipation for the opening of the new facility, which opened across the street from the terminal.

Ben Smith had again managed to find his way over from Quyarrah to see his wife. Maggie had already made plans to check out the Mosul Airfield compound's hottest new spot, so Ben just kind of tagged along. She had not emailed home in three weeks. After about a half an hour of waiting in line and ten minutes ferociously typing an update home, she hit "send" one second too late. Her connection shut off and the email was deleted before it could make its way to Colorado. "Honey, look at it this way," Ben told his cursing, frustrated wife, "just a few months ago, we were burning our own poop." Maggie's husband always had a way of putting life in Iraq into some kind of perspective.

"We sure have come a long way," he continued. "Don't worry, we'll be home in a few weeks."

"That's what you said last week," Maggie responded.

"Well then, we only have a week to go … yeah."

In August, Maggie Smith handed over her platoon and took her new position with the 9-101st Aviation S-3 (Operations) office. Her move made the Smith's the 101st Airborne Division's first family of Aviation Operations. Both Maggie and Ben were now running their respective battalions' operations offices. The two would have to work together planning missions. It was the first time in their marriage they would have to work together. The two would still work at opposite ends of the 101st Airborne Division area of operations, but their commanders no longer frowned upon their daily conversations on the tactical phones.

1-800-FLOWERS couldn't deliver in Mosul, understandably, and Ben was having nightmares trying to figure out how to get Maggie her Tuesday flowers. What he could do instead was send his wife a hand-written letter to fill the flower void, a concept that seemed unnecessary with email and their almost daily phone conversations. In his atrocious penmanship, addressing his wife as "Muffin," Ben wrote a letter dated August 19 that Maggie saved throughout the rest of the deployment to read whenever she missed her husband:

I am back. It is 2 nights later. We gave gone two more days through this deployment, and we are two more days close to being together.

I have been lying her tonight thinking of you. I have been also thinking of other girls (NO! Not that way silly). But I have been thinking about what was so different, so much more right, so much better, so much of a fit, that you are than any other girl I have dated.

I'm sure you don't want to know the details of my past relationships, but they are important because each one taught me something about you. Each one prepared me to know what you would be like.

Ben had been in love before, but never like this. With marriages crumbling like an avalanche around them, the two had maintained a loving relationship from afar.

On November 6, Ben Smith was handed his next mission. Ben, Chief Warrant Officer 3 Kyran Kennedy, Staff Sgt. Paul Neff and Staff Sgt. Scott Rose would fly Aircraft 26431, affectionately known as "The Goat." It was Ben's favorite aircraft, mostly because of the catchy name. They would be the lead of a two-helicopter escort for Maj. Gen. Thomas J. Roming, the Staff Judge Advocate of the Army, to the Fourth Infantry Division headquarters in Tikrit. It was a VIP mission, generally one of the most despised duties for any Blackhawk pilot and crew chief. Yet Kennedy, Neff and Rose volunteered for the mission. Why? Because Smith, one of the most adored officers in the 9-101st staff, was being looked at for the coveted Pilot in Command status.

Ben was excited about the opportunity; Maggie was not. Weeks earlier, one Maggie's friends from flight school had been shot down near Tikrit, with everyone in the aircraft walking away from the landing. Days earlier in the same city of Tikrit, a CH-47 Chinook helicopter carrying thirty-six soldiers on their way to their two weeks mid-tour leave was shot down further south in Karbala. This time, fifteen soldiers never walked away in what was the most deadly single attack on the coalition since the end of major combat operations. The enemy had plenty of anti-aircraft surface-to-air missiles, and they were using them to shoot down coalition helicopters exactly where Ben was heading.

Both Smiths had seen the news. "Ben, just be careful out there," Maggie told her husband over the phone the night before the mission.

"Geez, can't a guy go to war without his wife nagging him all the time?" Ben, as usual, was being facetious, but he had made a point. Maggie couldn't leave her role as Ben's wife behind just because they were fighting a war together, both as United States soldiers. It was a conundrum that every married couple faced in Iraq. The Smiths too had bent some rules to maintain some kind of proximity. Kissing, after all, was prohibited under U.S. Central Command orders. So when could soldiers let their guards down and just be who they were outside of uniform – especially when their husband or wife is in their platoon formation?

For Maggie Smith, the opportunities to even try to be a normal wife for her husband were infrequent while the two were in Iraq. Outside of An Najaf, just as Maggie had found a shady spot to sleep for a couple of hours, her husband popped up from behind her. "How was your day, honey?" Too tired to show any kind of excitement, Maggie just responded with a grin and a "Fine, and you … ?" For eight months, the too had lived an on-the-go marriage. The weekend R & R in Dahuk had given the two a moment of normalcy in what had been a tour of bedlam.

They were as married to the Army as they were to each other. Maggie was no more nostalgic for the morning cups of coffee with her husband than on the night of November 6.

"I love you, honey," she told her husband before she hung up the phone. There were no four more prudent words to say that evening. This would be Ben's most dangerous mission, she knew as she went to bed that night. Ben was heading right into one of the most dangerous cities in Iraq.

She also later found out that the Pilot in Command evaluator would not be able to fly with him for the mission. In spite of the setback, Ben stuck with the mission and insisted on flying lead. The crew, Kennedy, Neff and Rose, also willfully accepted the mission. As the sun rose on the morning of November 7, Ben Smith, his crew, two of Roming's subordinate officers and "The Goat" took off from Quyarrah Airfield for Tikrit. Flying in the rear with the general was Chief Warrant Officer John Nicholao, Ben's friend and mentor.

Ben Smith and his Blackhawk convoy was approaching the 4th Infantry Division headquarters in Tikrit, where they would stay most of the day. It was the end of a mind-numbing two-hour flight over the northern Iraq countryside – flat and dry. The terrain underneath his aircraft changed little from Quyarrah to Tikrit, but the monotony ended when their destination was near. The ridgeline surrounding the city had allowed for insurgent air defenses to attack, a terrain feature the faceless enemy exploited again. Concealed behind a hill around the northern approaches into Tikrit, the enemy had positioned a shoulder-fired surface-to-air missile to aim toward the approaching aircraft. The same type of weapon had been used to shoot down the 82nd Airborne CH-47 Chinook weeks earlier. It was a deadly and accurate weapon the 101st Airborne Division aviation assets knew the enemy had. The coalition had frantically searched the Sunni Triangle in an effort to collect every such missile they could find after the end of major combat operations – met with only a fair amount of success. For six American soldiers, the efforts weren't successful enough. As two coalition helicopters approached, the artillery piece waiting behind the hill fired towards the lead helicopter.

There is no way to record the thoughts of the dead before their last moment. Indeed, the attack on "The Goat" may have never been noticed or seen by its passengers. In the flash on an instant, Aircraft 26431 exploded in a brilliant cloud of fire. Chief Warrant Officer Kyran Kennedy, Staff Sgt. Paul Neff, Staff Sgt. Scott Rose and Capt. Ben Smith were dead. The two Staff Judge Advocate soldiers from Washington in the aircraft were also killed.

The attack had happened so quickly that Smith and Kennedy could not even warn one another of the artillery piece on the ground, if they ever saw it at all. Nicholoa and his copilot, carrying Roming and the rest of his staff, quickly maneuvered out of the kill zone, knowing that there were no survivors.

The morning of November 7th was supposed to be the day Capt. Mike Troxill took command of the 159th Aviation Regiment's Headquarters and Headquarters Company. Maggie Smith, who knew the outgoing commander Capt. Chuck Rambo, woke up early that morning to fill up her coffee cup to send her friend off. It had started just as another morning closer towards going back home to Fort Campbell. She woke up without the slightest premonition that she was now a widow.

Maggie would find out the bad news in the worst possible way, just two hours after Ben was shot down. In her office, next to the coffee maker was a list of Significant Activities, or SIGACTS. The usually trite list of events often included things like, "B COMP DELIVERS BOOKS TO SCHOOLS." This day was different.

"5-101 ACFT SHOT DOWN OVER TIKRIT," the morning SIGACTS read at the top. "Oh my God." Frozen, she just stared at the board for several moments thinking there must be some kind of mistake. When Maggie realized there was no mistake, she grabbed the nearest phone and started to call over to the 5-101st. "Ben's flying, he wouldn't be there," Maggie thought to herself. She hung up with false comfort before the other end could pick up the phone.

For the next several hours, Maggie Smith and Capt. Mollie Sabo, a bridesmaid at the Smiths wedding, sat outside, chain smoking, doing their best to convince themselves that Ben wasn't piloting the moribund helicopter. Meanwhile, Lt. Col. Timothy Jones, the 9-101st Aviation Regiment commander, worked the phones to get some kind of a confirmation. Ben was always lucky, Maggie rationalized. He had always won at board games, bingo, he could even guess the correct card out of a shuffled deck. Everything is going to be OK, she told herself. But everything wasn't OK, Lt. Col. Jones knew after he spoke with Lt. Col. Laura Richardson, the 5-101st commander.

Smith heard the door open and close behind her and instinctively knew who had just walked out. She turned her head towards Sabo, one of her bridesmaids, as if to seek support for what she knew was coming. Sabo locked eyes with Jones and grabbed her friends' hand. Jones would have given anything at that moment to give his soldier a bit of good news, but nothing could bring Ben Smith back. "Maggie, Ben's was in the helicopter. He didn't make it."

CHAPTER 11

THE STREAM OF TEARS

Lt. Col. Timothy Jones told Maggie Smith to pack her bags. She was going back to Kuwait that night. Mollie Sabo, who was with Maggie on the best day of her life, would be with her on the worst. She received an instant OK from Jones to go back to Kuwait and to the United States with Maggie. First, Maggie had some decisions to make. On DD Form 93, Maggie was listed as Ben's next of kin, meaning that only she would be notified by the Army. It was up to her now to either send a uniformed soldier to Ben's parents' doorstep or call herself. Her voice, she knew, would automatically signal to Mr. and Mrs. Smith that something was grievously wrong. She had already lost Ben, she didn't want to lose them too. So it was, the next day, an officer in his dress green Class A uniform knocked on the Smith's doorstep with an American flag in hand. Maggie's own parents could only find out direct from their daughter. It was late at night in Iraq and early in the morning in Colorado when Maggie's mother received only her third phone call from Iraq. She had a morning business meeting, on her way out the door when the phone rang. The phone call paralyzed Maggie's family, as if they had lost their own son.

Midnight, that same evening, Maggie and Mollie sat outside the Mosul Airfield terminal waiting for an Air Force C-130 cargo plane to land from Kuwait. It was a routine flight over the world's most dangerous air space that the flight crew made, often at the highest altitude they were capable of flying. Landing at the Mosul airport meant dropping onto the runway like a stone, preventing the possibility of an attacker outside the compound getting the C-130 in mortar range. But on this flight, they would take the risk. In spite of numerous intelligence warnings of planned attacks on coalition aircraft, the Air Force crew insisted on taking the risks to bring the wife of Capt. Ben Smith south to Kuwait. It was a gesture Maggie greatly appreciated. Maggie Smith, with Mollie Sabo in tow, left Mosul for the last time a little after midnight. Just like Ben predicted a week earlier, Maggie was on her way home.

In Kuwait, Maggie was told about a 4th Infantry Division air strike against a suspected enemy enclave responsible for the attack on Ben's helicopter. It was the only news that could make her smile at that point. Nobody was going to take the loss of Ben and his flight crew laying down. It was a brief moment of respite from the pain that Maggie would carry for a long time. For the first time since March, Maggie could walk around the compound without her M9 Carbine and her body armor. Having been away from civilization for ten months, she felt out of her skin.

Getting out of Kuwait was expedited for Maggie and Mollie Sabo. They were on their way back to Fort Campbell after only a day of red tape – unheard of for other outprocessing soldiers. The flight would last more than twenty hours with a stop in Europe to refuel. On November 9, they were home. Then came the voluminous and painful paperwork. The Army is as bureaucratic as any institution in America, and even as one of the newest widows in the war in Iraq, Maggie Smith still had to fill out form after form, just like any returning soldier.

Back in Quyarrah, on Veterans' Day, the fallen four soldiers were remembered in the most emotional memorial ceremony the division had experienced to that point. For the first time, Maj. Gen. David Petraeus, a man who had been to every memorial ceremony of his division, couldn't hold back the tears. Like the previous soldiers who had lost their lives, the loss of the Smith and his crew hit Petraeus like he had just lost four of his own children. Smith, Kennedy, Rose and Neff were the first soldiers in the 101st to lose their lives in a division helicopter to enemy fire in Iraq. "They were a very tight knit unit. All of those four had their own stories." Petraeus found Rose's death especially personal: he had known his father from his days with the 82nd Airborne Division.

Sitting several chairs down from the commanding general was Lt. Col. Laura Richardson, a commander who had seen Ben Smith become the most reliable officer under her command. All four 101st soldiers lost in the attack were under her command. Smith was remembered by his friend, Capt. Patrick Petrino. Petrino introduced Smith to those who didn't know him already with the kind of sense of humor that would only be appropriate. Smith's desk was constantly a mess, but as Petrino remembered, "you could ask him for a specific memo or paper and he would only have to move two or three sheets to come up with it."

Petrino really got to know Ben Smith when both were in a mess hall line, waiting for breakfast. After Petrino passed on bacon with his eggs, without missing a beat, Smith told the server, "I'll have the bacon he didn't get."

Chief Warrant Officer 2 Jimmy McElhaney, an ardent Republican, remembered his friend and favorite political sparing partner Chief Kyran Kennedy (a Democrat) as a meticulous leader who "was never there to say, 'no we can't do it.' He just came up with other, safer ways to do it." Staff Sgt. Paul Neff had asked his girlfriend, Sabrina, to marry him just before he left home for war. She said yes. It was yet another love story with a heartbreaking ending. Neff was survived by his seven-year old son Christopher. The story of Staff Sgt. Scott Rose was narrated last by Sgt. Bradley Green. Rose was the son of a retired colonel. He and his wife Michelle were expecting when he left for war. They had hoped the deployment orders would wait until she gave birth, but when his daughter Megan was born in April, Rose could only celebrate with Green and his unit. It was his first child, a daughter he would never meet. "He came to me and asked me if I was nervous when my daughter was born," Green recalled. "Of course I said yes and we talked for hours about being a dad and how wonderful it would be when we went home."

Maggie Smith too had daydreamed about going home. Less than a week after she lost her husband, Maggie walked to her front door under vastly different circumstances than she had envisioned. Waiting for her was her dog, Ellie. She hadn't seen her dog in eight months. For several minutes, she sat at her front porch, hugging her dog. She thought it was her only companion left, but she was wrong. Maggie had been totally oblivious to the crowd that waited for her inside her house. Her mom, dad, brother Mike, and all of Ben's brothers and sisters were waiting for her. Ben's mother and father had wanted to come too, but somebody had to take care of the pigs. "I knew I would forever be a part of the Smiths and that somehow we would get through the next months together," Maggie Smith recalled. "It meant so much to me that they rallied up and hit the road to comfort me upon my arrival."

She has never considered reverting back to her maiden name. She drove back to Swinky, Mo., several times before Christmas, once to plant a tree on the Smith family farm at the spot where Maggie and Ben had been married. "I feel like family there. I feel like I'm home." Maggie couldn't have felt more at home when the entire town of Swinky came out to honor their fallen hero during Ben's funeral. Buses full of children from communities outside the small town even came in to join in the ceremony. The streets of Swinky were lined with the Red, White, and Blue, and seemingly nobody in the entire town went anywhere that day without an American flag in hand. The local Knights of Columbus chapter engraved a chalice with Ben's name, with which communion at Ben's church would be given every Sunday. Swinky would never forget Ben Smith.

And then there was her second family – her friends and comrades in Iraq, who had rallied around Maggie. "As I left Iraq, many members of my battalion collected 'bus money' to aid me in my immediate travels home," she remembered. "Occasionally on Wednesdays, it's not uncommon for me to receive an anonymous batch of flowers resting on my front porch."

In a combat setting where commanders like Col. Gregory Gass balanced the mission of winning the peace with destroying the enemy, tools like the Apache helicopter served more as an image of overwhelming force than an actual deliverer of the coalition's deadly firepower. "A lot of times, when a brigade commander was talking to a non-compliant local or group, we would have an Apache fly by or land nearby. It basically scared them quite a bit. We used that a lot," Gass remarked.

Convoys, especially ones carrying a high-ranking military or local officer, often received an Apache and Kiowa escort from Gass' regiment. So too did the fuel convoys. "Any convoy that had an Apache or Kiowa flying with it was not hit. Of course, we didn't have enough aircraft to fly with every convoy." When the Apache did have to be used for more than just a show of force, it had to be precise. All targets had to be positively identified. The Apaches had the capability, and the radar, to be both accurate and use its force against the people it needed to be used against effectively. "Before you shot anything, you had to make sure it was a bad guy you were shooting at," Gass said.

One early fall operation put Gass' precision and positive identification demands to the test. A long-range surveillance company had identified and was watching a terrorist camp in a small village on the western outreaches of Mosul. The night began for one Apache Longbow team after they arrived at the Mosul Airfield after a daylight mission. There they met their brigade commander, Gass, who had some bonus work for them. Gass had temporarily been operating out of the Mosul Airfield and had kept a keen eye on the developing situation.

The long-range surveillance company had been spotted and advanced upon by the enemy. Gass knew they needed help if they were going to avoid potentially casualties. The two Apaches refueled and took off in a hurry.

At the target area, the Apache pilots immediately saw that the LRSC team was in trouble. The enemy forces had two vehicles near the tower the 101st LRSC team had used as a small compound. Dressed in robes concealing their weapons, they were poised to strike the tower. What had constrained the pilots was the need to ensure they were indeed enemy targets. They wouldn't have to wait long. In plain view of the Apache team, a man took out his AK-47 and pointed it at the tower.

Now it was time engage. The two Longbows hovering above the compound descended towards the enemy position and fired rocket after rocket, destroying the two vehicles and the forces who occupied them. After the dust cleared, the other aircraft landed and quickly got the LRSC team out. Only one division soldier suffered a serious wound in the incident.

At that point, Gass and his pilots were becoming quite familiar with rapidly responding to what the division called, "time sensitive intelligence." If the division headquarters got a lead on an enemy position, it was up to the infantry and aviation to move quickly before the lead disappeared. In September, the D-Main palace got word of a terrorist facility far in northwestern Iraq, south of the Euphrates River, remote from any coalition presence. It was a long way to go, more than 400 kilometers, but they needed to move before the enemy slipped away. With such a short notice, the division was able to package all of its Aviation assets together for the raid. CH-47 Chinook helicopters from the 7-101st, under the command of 159th Aviation commander Col. William T. Harrison, joined with Gass' Apaches and Blackhawks from the 6-101st Aviation to form a complete force of 101st Airborne Division air power. The Chinooks and Blackhawks would deliver the infantry to the fight and, if needed, the Apaches from the outside ring of support would join in. They wouldn't be needed.

Inside the enemy compound, the division found an enormous cache of weapons, around $50,000 of Iraqi dinar (millions in Iraqi currency), and 71 enemy combatants that were apprehended. It was a scenario that was played and replayed by the division numerous times. It was almost like a game of cat and mouse. Seldom, when the enemy compounds were spotted, did Gass' Apaches have to actually fire upon the overwhelmed enemy.

Governor Ghanim al-Basso had established himself as the head of state in Mosul almost as much as Petraeus did as leader for the 101st. His credibility, reliability and legitimacy had been established – and he owed much of it to his mentor. "They had a personal relationship as well as a professional. They worked closely together. Where General Petraeus needed to establish the rule of law, he would do that if need be. If the governor was getting off track with something, General Petraeus would gently bring him in line and tell him where his right limit and left limit were," Laufenberg observed. "What General Petraeus was trying to do was mentor the governor, teach him how the system was supposed to work knowing you can't mirror the Iraqi government after the U.S. democracy."

For the most part, that meant leaving al-Basso to his own devices, except when his errors were so grievous that the safety of his soldiers were at risk. There were perceptions of nepotism in al-Basso's administration – a practice Petraeus cautioned the governor against – but nobody in the division was about the force the hand of the coalition's number one ally in Nineveh.

Petraeus' chief of staff too didn't give al-Basso's practices a second thought. "Was I concerned that he hired his sons as aides and all that kind of thing? Yes, but you know what, everybody did that. It was part of their culture." Nepotism was tolerated, at least at a low level, but corruption was another issue entirely. It went on, certainly, but when corruption was found it was dealt with and heads inevitably rolled. The 101st had set a moral code and encouraged their contractors, local liaisons, and government officials to follow it strictly. Some didn't.

Enter "The Untouchables," as Lt. Col. John Bell called his anti-corruption crew. Bell, a civilian judge in Cock County, Tenn., was tasked in the fall with assembling a sixteen-member oversight committee to find and fire dirty officials from top to bottom. The commission's Elliot Ness would be Saad-Mohammed Mekhler, a local attorney, who led fifteen other local attorneys, organized in five-member teams. Stopping corruption was an ambitious idea, so the commission set up a hotline for leads to be followed. False leads would be followed too – with swift prosecution. The idea first came from Lt. Col. Richard Whittaker, the division Staff Judge Advocate, and blueprinted by Capt. Rick Taylor, another SJA attorney. They later received help from the U.S. Federal Bureau of Investigations. The commission's success was immediate and officials in Baghdad scrambled to build similar anti-corruption commissions.

The Untouchables first Rendezvous with Destiny came in October when two mid-level officials were caught taking bribes. They followed with several more major investigations and before the end of the year, the commission would be a permanent fixture in the Mosul local government.

By the beginning of November, the division was losing an average of one soldier a day to the upswing in violence, and the bloodshed would only continue for the 101st in Mosul. One early November attack would claim another soldier from a division husband and wife team. First Lt. Joshua Hurley, a platoon leader with the 326th Engineering Battalion, was killed with another soldier in an Improvised Explosive Device attack en route to the Mosul City Hall Building. Hurley was a Virginia Military Institute graduate, a Ranger, and was remembered as being a tough, reliable and approachable young officer. "Josh always had the ability not to let anything bother him," remembered First Lt. David Wilson, his friend and fellow Alpha Company, 326th Engineering Battalion platoon leader. "He always had a kind word. Whenever he was given a task, he completed it, and there was never any doubt that Josh would be there in a pinch.

"He should know that my last push up of the day will be for that Airborne Ranger in the sky." First Lt. Teresa Vaught, Hurley's wife, was quickly redeployed with her deceased husband, but she would return less than a month later to finish out her tour.

Hurley's death would only add to the stream of tears that was already flowing throughout the 101st – then came what Petraeus would later call, "the worst day of the whole thing." It was the bloodiest attack on the division during the tour, and it came on November 15. No 101st Airborne soldier who served in Iraq will ever forget that day.

The deadliest day for the coalition to date began with a routine patrol. A Second Brigade infantry platoon, looking for trouble, found it at a bank. They started taking fire and called for help. In the skies was the aerial Quick Reaction Force (QRF), a Blackhawk helicopter with two pilots and 10 soldiers on board, ready to air assault anywhere in Mosul they might be needed. When they got word they were needed around the bank, they moved.

From the north, from Tal Afar on its way to the Mosul Airfield, was another Blackhawk with two pilots and eight soldiers on board, supposed to be transiting the Mosul airspace several hundred feet above the Quick Reaction Force aircraft. For the soldiers in the back, they were going home for two weeks of mid-tour leave. What happened next is unclear. The two aircraft, conducting totally unrelated missions, collided. What is clear is that for the soldiers coming from Tal Afar, they were simply at the wrong place at the wrong time.

"By many eye-witness accounts, something was fired at from somewhere," said Col. Joseph Anderson. What is generally accepted by the 101st Airborne Division commanders is the theory that Blackhawk #531, the aircraft entering the city from Tal Afar, descended and turned away from the ground fire toward Blackhawk #548. One ran into the other, both lost control and both aircraft crashed.

The aftermath the next morning painted a clear bottom line. Seventeen soldiers were lost, the single highest death toll of any one attack of the war in Iraq to that point. Blackhawk #531 had hit a building and split in half. The rubble of one half of the helicopter burned above the other half, sitting three stories below on the sidewalk. There were no survivors aboard. In a telling sign that the insurgency had hit families well beyond the scope of the Infantry, soldiers from the reserve component and the Third Brigade Quartermaster Company were killed in the attack.

In the Second Brigade helicopter, only the pilots' quick thinking in aiming the aircraft towards the roof of another building saved his own and several other lives. The co-pilot, Warrant Officer Erik Kesterson, was not saved; he died in the impact.

Anderson met the local fire department at the scene at around 7:30. He had got word of the accident after his daily evening update. "Anytime you have the loss of life, it sheds a whole new light on everything." First reports are often wrong, Anderson figured, but when he got to the scene, he knew there was no mistaking what had happened. Petraeus too had hoped maybe there was some kind of confusion in the reports back to the D-Main. Lieutenant Gen. Ricardo Sanchez had just left the D-Main Palace after receiving a face-to-face update on the area, when the word started to come in on the radio. The initial reports indicated that just one helicopter went down. Minutes later, he received word that a second helicopter had crashed.

The next day by noon, the wreckage was cleaned up and the area was cleared. All that was left was the investigations and the memorial ceremonies, a total of six during a two-day period. "The losses we suffered are almost beyond comprehension," Petraeus remarked in a letter to the Fort Campbell community, printed in the base newspaper. "Our fallen comrades were friends and fellow soldiers with whom we served and sacrificed, fought a tough enemy, and helped a nation rebuild. The losses will not, however, cause us to falter or fail. To the contrary, these losses will lead us to redouble our efforts and drive on."

Like every memorial ceremony the 101st held to that point, no ceremony would begin until the CG's Blackhawk landed on the scene. Six of the fallen were remembered in a 4-101st Aviation Regiment ceremony in Tal Afar. Second Lt. Jeremy Wolfe was not a fresh faced lieutenant who found a lot of resentment among his soldiers. He was a former enlisted man with the 25th Infantry Division in Hawaii. After his enlistment, he went to college at the local Hawaii Pacific University and earned a commission under the Army's Green-to-Gold program. He was just two months out of flight school when he flew his final mission. A native of Wisconsin, Wolfe was survived by his wife Christine and his family in the Badger state.

Wolfe's copilot was Chief Warrant Officer 2 Scott Soboe. He had fourteen years in the Army at the time he received the deployment orders in February. Soboe had first enlisted as a mechanic. He and his wife Franseska had one son, Dustin. Sergeant John Russell was first an Infantryman before moving over to Aviation. He was remembered as a tough NCO but not one without a sense of humor. Specialist Ryan Baker too knew how to smile when things got tough. He had a son, Tristan. Specialist Jeremiah DiGiovanni and Specialist William Dusenbury only knew Fort Campbell and the 101st Airborne Division. They were on their first, and last, duty assignments.

Warrant Officer 1 Erik Kesterson had been in theatre only eight days before he lost his life in the helicopter accident. His story began after Sept. 11, 2001, when he rejoined the military after a brief foray in the civilian world. Two years later, he left for war as a warrant officer and in love. Kesterson was engaged to Catherine Hogan.

Kesterson was memorialized at the D-Rear Airfield with Staff Sgt. Warren Hansen, his crew chief. Hansen had been enlisted in the Army in 1986, serving in the first Gulf War and losing his life in the second. Captain Pierre Piche, Sgt. First Class Kelly Martin Balor, and Spc. John Sullivan were on their way home for leave. Their unit, the 626th Forward Support Battalion, remembered their fallen soldiers during their separate ceremony. Piche had planned on resigning his commission after he got home for good to become a teacher. His friends spoke of his undying love for his wife Cherish during their eulogies. Balor's loss meant the loss of a friend and an office keystone for the 626th FSB. He had been filling a first sergeant's role for much of the deployment. At Fort Campbell, his wife Kelly Jean and son Kyle would face a very somber Thanksgiving indeed. And Spc. John Sullivan, known as just "Sully" to everyone who knew him, would never get to see his newborn twin sons. His wife Katrina had given birth to Aiden and Gavin in September, their second and third child. Older daughter Jade was also too young to really understand why daddy wasn't going to be coming home.

Specialist Damien Heidelberg had also planned on going home for two weeks. He had a helluva lot of stories to tell. A mail clerk assigned to Third Brigade, his convoy had been ambushed just weeks earlier. His friends remembered his courage under fire during their eulogies. Heidelberg refused to leave the area as the rounds came flying his direction, calmly tending to several wounded soldiers. He too was a father. Heidelberg only saw his one-year old daughter Staceyera for about six months before deploying in February.

"These soldiers and their distinct personalities can never be replaced," Capt. Vincent Generoso said during his remarks at the 1-320th Field Artillery memorial ceremony. Generoso lost five soldiers from his Charlie Battery. Sergeant Michael Acklin, Sgt. Eugene Uhl, Pfc. Richard Hafer, Pfc. Sheldon Hawkeagle, and Pfc. Joey Whitener were all lost on the patrol helicopter.

Command Sgt. Maj. Jerry Wilson, in contrast to his commander Col. Joseph Anderson, played the same role he always played at Fort Campbell. His job was not to meet with Sheiks or distribute pencils to schools, his concern was only with taking care of soldiers. Like every sergeant major, he was tough. He had wowed Anderson more than a decade earlier in whipping a company of bottom feeders into well-disciplined company of soldiers. In Iraq, from Karbala to Uday and Qusay's doorstep, the two were running a brigade-wide success story that was making news all over the globe. Anderson got the limelight, but it was Wilson who was making sure the soldiers maintained focus.

Wilson was Anderson's right hand man. Whenever the commander had a question about his brigade, the sergeant major had an answer. Anderson had a lot of questions. No matter how busy his schedule was, Anderson hustled at least once a week to every element of his brigade to get an assessment on his soldiers. Nobody needed to remind him that his soldiers missed their families too. Wilson, in turn, kept the heat on his NCOs to make certain the enlisted workforce wasn't being overstretched. He too would make a daily sweep through the brigade compounds, making certain his soldiers weren't forgotten. "His whole focus was soldiers," Anderson said plainly.

The commander had set out in the morning on Nov. 23 towards a meeting to screen fourteen women applicants to join the Mosul local governing council. The sergeant major also took off before lunch to do a run through of some of his brigade's compounds. Anderson would be back for dinner chow; Wilson would not.

The SUVs that were used in convoys had worried a number of division commanders. They were called NTVs, for Non-Tactical Vehicles, for an apparent reason. They left little room for maneuvering weapons in the event of an ambush and provided thin protection from an IED. In the lawless traffic of Mosul, the possibility of a horrific accident with the NTVs were far from remote.

Anderson left for his council meeting in his humvee. Wilson took off from the Second Brigade command compound in a NTV. Anderson left with his usual security element. Wilson, frustrated that his humvee was inoperable, moved out against all of his senior commanders' instructions and went outside the wire without another vehicle in tow. He would travel through the city of Mosul with only his weapon and his driver – a decision that would later flummox the division and Second Brigade staff. As his convoy pulled towards a Second Brigade compound at the Mosul train station, the enemy came at him with small arms fire from both directions. In a horrific ambush, both Wilson and his driver, Spc. Rel Revago, were riddled with enemy fire. When the NTV crashed into a brick wall, both were dead.

The commander was alerted about his top enlisted soldier just as he got finished with the local council. The local firefighters had been the first responders to the attack. Anderson's operations officer gave him the word, and he scrambled out immediately. Only after the mob dissipated did the commander reach the scene. "Personally, he was a friend of mine. Professionally, he was a partner," Anderson recalled. "It did upset a lot of people because it showed that nobody was immune from that kind of stuff, but it also undercut the brigade because of who he was."

Who he was, as it turned out, was one of the most popular soldiers in the division, as evidenced by the turnout at the memorial ceremony honoring Wilson and Revago. "I had never thought that I would be giving a eulogy to my air assault buddy," Anderson said during the service. "His only aspiration was to be with and lead soldiers."

Sitting in the front row was Command Sgt. Maj. Marvin Hill, the division command sergeant major. Hill was Wilson's predecessor as the Second Brigade top enlisted soldier, and also counted him among his closest friends. In his eulogy, he recalled a conversation they had days earlier, during a visit from Sgt. Maj. of the Army Kenneth Preston. "Sergeants major tend not to tell each other how proud we are and how we feel about each other. But I did that day, and I'm glad I did. So often there are things we wish to say to one another, but never do. Well, I'm glad I told Sergeant Major Wilson that day."

Thirty-eight days, from October 16 to November 23, had claimed thirty-three lives from the 101st Airborne Division. After the division laid to rest the seventeen victims of the Blackhawk disaster, the 101st had passed the 3rd Infantry Division as the division with the most combat fatalities in the Iraq war to that point. "This was a culmination, in some degree, of some of these policies where some of the former military were frustrated that they weren't part of the future of Iraq," Petraeus remembered. "Certainly for some of the former Ba'ath party and Fedayeen, there was no way they were going to be a part of the future of Iraq.

"The criminals that were let out of jail by Saddam were a big factor in this, because they'd been out of jail by then for six to eight months, didn't have any jobs or salaries, no way to feed their families, were not a part of regular society, and had demonstrated a willingness to kill in the past. They were very available guns for hire for these former regime elements who had a lot of money." Indeed, the money trail often led Petraeus and the division directly to the leaders of the insurgency. Uday and Qusay Hussein, when they were killed, had the equivalent of $1.3 million in Iraqi currency in cash. A Fedayeen colonel, found just days after Saddam's sons, had just under a half a million.

To fight the insurgency, Petraeus balked at the idea of fighting a delicate war. "I don't want a fair fight. We set conditions before every single fight that we had, so that the moment our soldiers got shot at, we were immediately able to respond with overwhelming force." Reserve forces, a key component of any air assault, were ready to move on order from any division compound in Mosul. The 101st, the quickest reaction force at a division level that the United States Army had in its arsenal, fought the insurgency in the tough fall months with all of its firepower with unparalleled agility.

There was no point in Mosul where the fighting stopped, but it ebbed as the Commanders Emergency Relief Fund reemerged and, more importantly, as operations aimed at insurgent forces began to take their toll on the enemy. On November 10, Col. Michael Linnington's Third Brigade uncovered three large weapons caches, one of which was found a foot underground. That same day, a man approached the D-Main Palace with a delivery. More than 300 grenades, two grenade launchers, and ninety-two rocket propelled grenade rounds were now safely in the division's hands and not being fired at division soldiers. The next day, November 11, would be another fruitful day for theInfantry. Second Brigade nabbed eight targeted individuals by cordoning off their homes and knocking on the door. Nine separate engagements were also reported to the division that night, but not one wounded soldier. More individuals believed to be participating in and leading the insurgency were apprehended in the days and weeks that followed, including during one particularly active night when Second Brigade conducted raids at thirty-five separate sites simultaneously, getting twenty-three of those they were after – all with only one shot fired.

The increased influx of prisoners for the 101st meant an increased importance on properly holding the prisoners. "That didn't mean Ritz-Carlton," said Brig. Gen. Frank Helmick who was tasked with overseeing the treatment of 101st prisoners. "More like a Motel 6." Each of the brigades had a holding facility, where prisoners were held anywhere from seven to twenty-one days. The division level holding facility, just 200 yards from the landing strip at the Mosul Airfield, was often just a final step before the most dangerous insurgents were moved south to the coalition's mainframe prison: Abu Ghraib. Seemingly prescient of the front-page issues the American commanders would face have with prisoner treatment, Helmick would make regular, unannounced visits to the holding facilities, examining every final detail. Heating in the winter and air conditioning in the summer, water, medical care, and a clean latrine were all guaranteed. "We didn't even have that stuff," Helmick remarked.

The process was transparent. Helmick routinely toured the prisons with local city council members. For family members of locals who had been taken prisoner, a hotline was established to keep their families updated on their status. If the prisoners couldn't offer any intelligence, or if it was later determined that they posed no threat to coalition soldiers, they were released. If they were a threat or otherwise a source of intelligence – like a former Iraqi general who turned himself in before the October spike in attacks – Helmick sent them to Abu Ghraib. "We didn't have anything to hide."

The news was not all bad for the 101st in November. The Northern Iraq planting season had successfully been stabilized. Brigadier Gen. Helmick had earlier hosted a conference at Mosul University with hundreds of farmers and Ministry of Agriculture officials from Baghdad. "I anticipate a bumper crop for 2004 – we have no other option," Helmick flatly told the farmers. More than 260,000 metric tons of wheat and 200,000 metric tons of barely had been paid for by the ministry to local farmers – a part of which was worthless. It was life support for the Iraqi agricultural economy. Neglect and disease had rendered some of the crops inedible.

Additionally, officers from the 431st Civil Affairs Battalion had been working with the farmers to teach proper planting techniques. The division supplied modern equipment, at no cost, to bring the farmers up to date with what was commonplace in the United States. The Ministry of Agriculture, with strong division encouragement, set prices at $140 a ton for wheat, a more than thirty percent increase than what the previous year's crop went for, which did not undercut prices from neighboring Syria and Turkey. The idea was to provide a long-term solution to the agricultural crisis without upsetting Iraq's trade partners. Without the coalition aid to the Northern Iraq farmers, there was no telling what kind of economic catastrophe could have ensued.

Up north in Tal Afar, Lt. Col. Christopher Pease, the 1-187th commander, was enjoying his most successful month in Iraq. Pease's Second Battalion in November also opened up the first children's clinic north of Mosul in the town of Sinjar. More than one-hundred local parents and children waited at the door for urgent care. In Badush, a $50,000 investment into another heath clinic was finally completed. Brigadier Gen. Jeffery Schloesser had thrown his CERP weight into the project, spending $38,000 just on rebuilding the structure. The remaining $12,000 stocked the health clinic with vital supplies, and it would need every medicine and hospital bed it could handle. The Badush clinic served the entire 8,000 population of the town and the neighboring twenty-five villages. When it opened, the health clinic had thirty-five employees on the payroll with three dentists.

On November 3, he graduated 171 new policemen from his academy. The oldest graduate was fifty-three. The theme of timelessness was nothing new for Pease and the 2-187th Infantry. Two days earlier, Pease's battalion celebrated the first graduating class of an adult education center in the town of Zumar. The idea behind the course was to teach illiterate citizens, many of whom had absolutely no education, how to read. The first initiative, training the police, had fueled the second project. Pease and Sgt. Gary Phillips, his top training NCO at the Tal Afar Police Academy, had scripted a tough physical and written examination for the new cadets. More than 600 policemen had patrolled the streets of Tal Afar when Pease's battalion took control of the majority of the city. All of them would go through the Academy if they wanted to keep their jobs.

Phillips, himself a former Nashville police officer, made certain the cadets were physically ready. They were trained on weapons, a code of conduct, and hand-to-hand conduct. Phillips and Pease even took the division requirements for the police academies and made them tougher. Three weeks of hell couldn't stop most cadets. It was the written examination that pulled cadet after cadet from graduation. "There were guys who would run barefoot just to get a job, then they would take the written exam, and we would lose half the guys," Pease recalled.

Illiteracy stopped hundreds of otherwise qualified policemen from taking to the streets. Pease couldn't let them slide through – if they couldn't read, they couldn't file a police report. So he spent $30,000 of Col. Linnington's CERP funds to build and launch the Adult Learning School, and it was hardly an empty investment. He contacted the local superintendents and called several teachers in the area from retirement. They were happy to help. Seventy-five students enrolled in the first class. Cadets joined with primary school-age children and senior citizens in the area in the class.

Shortly after the first graduation of the literacy course, Pease started to see policemen in uniform he recognized from the school. It was only a handful of motivated cadets, but the opportunity for cadets to learn to read and earn their uniform had at least been exercised.

The response to the literacy school and the new police force was immediate. The school was a program that would continue after the Rakkassans left Tal Afar, supported only by the local superintendents. The response to the police was less than idyllic. Local citizens still saw them as undependable. When bright new policemen joined the force they were excluded by their senior superiors from important jobs, often because the leaders were taking bribes from the people they were after. There were issues with equipping the force also. "They got the training and they did the best they could when we were there to enforce it," Pease said. "But they didn't have the comms (communications equipment), they didn't have the weapons, and they didn't have the vehicles and you can't be a cop without comms, weapons, and vehicles."

Requests for equipment were often filtered through Mosul, with much of the equipment going directly to other areas. With other priorities taking precedence, Col. Michael Linnington simply could not afford to give the Tal Afar police what they needed. Again, the penny-pinching environment was felt by 101st commanders. It was not how Pease wanted the story to end, but the underequipped force would show its might early. "They arrested rapists, murderers, theifs – they definitely kept their prisons full."

In the fall, a familiar taste of Fort Campbell was delivered to the deployed 101st. The division began rotating soldiers through Air Assault School, which picked up their equipment and set up at the Quyarrah Airfield. The school and its instructors were deployed from Fort Campbell in October. By November, the school was in full swing. It is widely known as the most challenging badge to earn in the entire Army, with the coveted and rival Airborne badge alongside the Air Assault badge in stature. The deployed edition of Air Assault School would be comprised. The instructors were still the same, and none of them took it easy on any student. But instead of the scheduled two weeks of instruction, there would only be one. The required twelve-mile road march, the most physical demanding examination of the school, was scratched. Bringing the Air Assault School to Iraq was a way to get soldiers trained for combat while in combat. Both the obstacle course and the repel tower were a part of the deployed Air Assault School. They were not there long. By late December they would be gone.

When the redeployment plans were confirmed in July, soldiers knew that the holiday season this year would not be spent with family. It was reality, so when the holiday season began on the last Thursday in November, most soldiers just sought to make the best of their combat Thanksgiving. This would not be the usual Thanksgiving for any 101st Airborne Division soldier, but nobody would go without the usual Turkey and mashed potatoes. At the all of the major division compounds in Mosul, Quyarrah, and Tal Afar hosted their own Thanksgiving dinners, and no division soldier would be forced to settle for the turkey and mash potatoes MRE. The D-Main dining facility spared no expense – shrimp cocktail, an eight-foot long birthday cake and several dozen turkeys. If the soldiers couldn't go home, this had to be a close consolation prize. Sergeant 1st Class Richard Griffith, an NCO with the 3-327th Infantry Regiment, shared Thanksgiving with a framed picture of his wife and kids in front of his plate. Regrettably, with General Order Number 1 still in effect, only non-alcoholic sparkling cider could be served with dinner.

To ring in the holiday, in another open letter to the division and the families at home, Petraeus did his best to put a positive spin on a difficult holiday for his troops. "Some 6,000 miles from here, our families will gather today with loved ones, giving them thanks for all the blessings of life in our great nation. In some 19,000 homes, however, there will be an empty place – a seat that should be filled by you. While we may not be where most of us would like to be today, we still have much for which to be thankful. Although we are not with our families, we are surrounded by friends and comrades-in-arms – fellow soldiers with whom we have shared the 'brotherhood in a close fight.'"

After Thanksgiving, commanders started thinking about a subject that had seemed like a distant thought in July, when the division was told officially that the combat tour would last into 2004. Redeployment was finally on the horizon. The soldiers started making their plans for when they went home. Visions of Caribbean vacations that had danced in their heads for almost a year started becoming plans in December. Of course, before anybody started reaching for the suntan lotion, there was work to do. Moving a division from Northern Iraq to Kuwait takes time, resources, and plenty of planning. Redeploying south to Kuwait, some operations officers would come to know in the month of December, would take as much energy and hassle as the pilgrimage north in March and April. It was a good problem to have.

There was another problem for soldiers who left their field jackets at home, thinking that they would never get cold in the Middle East. By December, the daily temperatures were hardly what a soldier would expect coming into Iraq. In July, the division was dying for air conditioners. Five months later, soldiers were sleeping in fetal positions, nostalgic for the days when they went to bed in ninety degree heat. The division scrambled for heaters, and before the winter cold really hit, most compounds were set. Indeed, as the division started on their way out the door, the luxuries really started moving in.

The engineers had built a small strip mall at the Mosul Airfield that had opened early in the fall. You could find a new watch, eat lunch, check your email and even dip your feet in the fountain they had built in front. Soldiers were wowed. Then in December, just across the street from the humble strip mall, ground was broke on a new Post Exchange and even a new Burger King. Suddenly the strip mall didn't look so hot. The new PX would be just a construction site until long after the 101st Airborne was scheduled to leave town. Then the ultimate carrot. Soldiers, even in the cold, continued to sleep in tents. In December, new trailers with air conditioners and heaters for the volatile Mosul weather, started getting set up on the division compounds. They were almost as good as some of the barracks the enlisted soldiers would return to in three months at Fort Campbell. The trailers would stay for the new tenants, but the 101st sure would have liked to have them in the summer.

Indeed, as life was getting better for the 101st soldiers, the perspective of what the division had gone through for the last eight months became clearer and clearer. They had survived on nothing but MREs for the first three months in Mosul. They had slept on sand and rocks on the drive up to Nineveh. They had nothing but a hole in the ground for a makeshift toilet.

December was not without attacks on division soldiers. In back-to-back days, Second Brigade lost two soldiers, both barely old enough to enlist in the military when they paid the ultimate sacrifice. Specialist Ray Hutchinson was killed in an IED attack on his convoy on December 6. A day later, Pfc. Jason Wright was lost in an attack as he guarded a gas station in Mosul. Days later, both were remembered in separate ceremonies.

Hutchinson was a native of Texas. He wrote for the school newspaper and played for the band. He also was a state champion rock climber. Hutchinson had wavered between staying in the Army and becoming a warrant officer or leaving it all behind. He was only 20. His company commander, Capt. Michael Wiser, remembered Hutchinson as someone who "always held his chin up."

"You are my hero, and I salute you."

Private First Class Jason Wright was nineteen years old when his battalion, the 1-502nd Infantry Regiment, memorialized him at a ceremony. Wright had been shipped off to Iraq just four months after arriving with the 101st and less than a year after attending his senior prom. The Michigan native was remembered as one of the most likable soldiers in his company, "an ideal liaison to the Iraqi people," his commander, Capt. Erik Hartel remarked during his memorial ceremony.

Wright had been picked to drive Sgt. First Class Michael Davis' vehicle. Davis was known as the toughest noncommissioned officer in the company, but even he found few complaints with Wright. "He always had the correct response when you asked him anything. He was my driver, my friend, and my son."

For one day in December, the reason behind all the pain and sacrifice became as clear as water. In the famous deck of cards with the Ba'ath Party Regime's fifty-five Most Wanted officials, one man at the top had continued to elude the coalition. High Value Targets Numbers two and three, Uday and Qusay Hussein were both crossed out, but the top target remained at large. On the second Sunday of the month, his game of cat and mouse ended.

"Ladies and Gentlemen, we got him!"

And with that, Civilian Administrator L. Paul Bremer in a press conference from Coalition Headquarters in Baghdad, confirmed the reports buzzing from one media outlet to another. Saddam Hussein was under coalition custody. December 13, in a certain sense, would be Iraq's Independence Day. Once and for all, the man who had ruled Iraq at nearly every street corner with an iron fist was now nothing more than a prisoner.

The reports trickled in on the Armed Forces Network just before lunchtime. Nobody could contain their jubilation. The linguists, most of whom had lived most of their lives under the watchful eye of Saddam, were in shock. At the Nineveh Hotel, a crowd of thirty Iraqi linguists crowded two feet away from the television to see if the reports were true. Then the images were released. Bearded, broken, and shamed, Saddam Hussein was never again going to terrorize the people of Iraq. At 66-years old, Saddam looked like a common hobo in New York City's Central Park. He had been pulled out of a hole in the ground, termed a "spider hole," in a home outside of Tikrit. The soldiers of the 4th Infantry Division were the heroes. It was a most abject defeat for Saddam.

According to reports, the drama unfolded much like the July 22 raid that claimed Uday and Qusay Hussein. Just after eight o'clock at night, over 600 4th Infantry Division soldiers, supplemented by an element of Special Forces, raided his lightly fortified compound fifteen miles outside Tikrit in the village of Ad Dawr. It was called Operation Red Dawn. The home Saddam was found in was owned by Qais al-Nameq, one of Saddam's personnel assistants. Al-Nameq's two sons were taken away along with Hussein.

Unlike the raid that took the lives of Saddam's two sons, this operation did not end in a firefight. Although the former Iraqi dictator had hidden in his hole with a firearm at his hip, he did not fire back at the soldiers, and he did not resist as he was taken away. Saddam, like his two sons, was found with weapons and lots of money, reminiscent of his former authority. About $750,000 was found in the home, all in $100 U.S. bills. Finding the money, nevermind the man behind the money, was likely enough to thwart hundreds of ambushes against coalition soldiers.

His escape route was two boats, just a stones throw away from his spider hole, which would have evacuated him down the Tigris River. A cheap orange and white taxi was also found in the home. The spider hole had apparently been a prepared hiding spot for Saddam, equipped with a ventilation system. In fact, the spot was so well hidden that the 600 soldiers foraging the home could not find the target until shortly before they were ready to give up.

When he was found, Saddam introduced himself as "the President of Iraq." 4th Infantry soldiers treated the former dictator more like a zoo animal – smoking cigars, stroking his beard, and taking pictures that would soon make the rounds across the World Wide Web.

America woke up on Sunday morning to the earth-shattering news. President Bush rushed to the White House to beat a snowstorm headed directly for Washington. On his way, he got a phone call from Secretary of Defense Donald Rumsfeld. "We think we may have him," Rumsfeld told the President. It was speculation then; several hours later it was fact. Bush, knowing full well the political benefits as he entered the beginning of his reelection campaign, addressed the subject from a live address from the Cabinet Room of the White House shortly after noon Eastern Standard Time. "This afternoon, I have a message for the Iraqi people: You will not have to fear the rule of Saddam Hussein ever again. All Iraqis who take the side of freedom have taken the winning side. The goals of the coalition are the same as your goals – sovereignty for your country, dignity for your great culture, and for every Iraqi citizen, the opportunity for a better life.

"Now, the former dictator of Iraq will face the justice he denied to millions."

From London, America's most unconditional ally Tony Blair celebrated his own moment in the sun. Blair was facing fanatical opposition within his own Labor Party for his support of the invasion of Iraq, and had earlier survived a no-confidence vote from parliament by the narrowest of margins. "It removes the shadow that has been hanging over them for too long of the nightmare of the return of the Saddam regime. This fear is now removed."

Rumsfeld later that night, in his first interview since the raid, told CBS' *60 Minutes*, "Here was a man who was photographed hundreds of times shooting off rifles and showing how tough he was, and in fact, he wasn't very tough. He was cowering in a hole in the ground, and he had a pistol and didn't use it and certainly did not put up any fight at all. In the last analysis, he seemed not terribly brave."

In Tikrit, Maj. Gen. Raymond Odierno, the 4th Infantry Division commander, was more succinct. "He was caught like a rat."

General John Abizaid, U.S. Central Command commander, was quick to parry any speculation that Saddam's capture would mark the end of the armed insurgency. "We've got a lot of fighting ahead of us," Abizaid told the press after meeting with Gen. Richard Myers, Chairman of the Joint Chiefs of Staff. "There are people who don't want the new government to come forward. There are people who want to fight to the death to prevent (the new government) from happening."

The coalition would find out in the coming months whether Saddam's capture would demoralize or emboldened his loyalists. For certain, not all of the insurgents were firing at coalition soldiers for a return to power for Saddam. At the time Saddam was apprehended, the Pentagon estimated that 9 of 10 insurgents were self-identified loyalists to Saddam. But in spite of that, few thought Saddam Hussein could have been at the fulcrum of the insurgency. It was a point not lost to President Bush, even during his address from the White House Cabinet Room. "The capture of Saddam Hussein does not mean the end of violence in Iraq. We still face terrorists who would rather go on killing the innocent than accept the rise of liberty in the heart of the Middle East."

CHAPTER 12

CHRISTMAS IN IRAQ

Major Gen. David Petraeus, speaking to the Tigris River Valley Commission at the D-Main Palace, took the opportunity just two days after Saddam's capture to make an emphatic point in front of most of the local government's key players. "We need to make sure they," referring to those remaining low-to-mid-level Ba'ath party officials who weren't participating in the armed insurgency, "are a part of the solution and no longer a part of the problem."

He continued. "I hope that Saddam's capture will convince them that there will be no return of the former regime. It's up to us to convince them to become a part of shaping the future of Iraq." Governor Ghanim al-Basso sat to his right; Col. Ben Hodges, the First Brigade commander, sat to his left. Government officials from throughout the Nineveh Province sat in a horseshoe around the three leaders. It was perhaps Petraeus' boldest step of his eight-month administration over Nineveh. Few within the coalition had thought much of the idea of using Saddam's capture to reach out towards the Ba'ath party rank-and-file – only to crush the remaining party officials. The old perceptions had remained. Few "De-Ba'athification" policies had been modified to include reconciliation since May. The coalition was still excluding lower-level members of the Ba'ath party, despite Petreaus' best efforts to change the policies.

It was an issue that galvanized the 101st commanding general. "The numbers involved were staggering," he later argued. "This (the Ba'ath party) was not just a handful of people, this was tens of thousands of individuals who were affected.

And when you have ten family members relying on that individual for food, shelter and clothing, you've created a heck of a lot of enemies."

Shortly after Petraeus' edict, a number of former Ba'ath party officials in Nineveh expressed firm commitments to take part in the new post-Saddam Iraq. Hodges got pledges from a group of former party members to jump on board shortly after the Tigris River Valley Commission meeting. Another official, knowing he was on the division's most wanted list, turned himself into Hodges less than a week after Saddam's apprehension. Several more officials showed up on the D-Main Palace gates with weapons to turn in – one with 41 AK-47s and a promise to bring more later in the week. The cooperation given to Petraeus and the 101st after Saddam's ignominious end was unprecedented, by known and even unknown Ba'ath party officials. And in the weeks that followed, over 7,000 former low-to-mid-level Ba'ath Party members participated in ceremonies held throughout Nineveh Province to denounce their former Party affiliation, renounce the use of violence, and pledge support for the new Iraq.

Coinciding with Saddam's capture, the 101st launched "The Charm Offensive" – a reenergized push to win over the people of Northern Iraq. The gameplan never changed. Petraeus' instructions were the same as they had always been. But with redeployment on the horizon, the division couldn't lose its focus. The Commanders' Emergency Relief Program was gaining strength and the last two months were crucial to laying the foundation for Petraeus' successors in Northern Iraq.

In December, the 926th Engineering Group, a reserve unit out of Alabama, began repairing a ruptured oil pipe line that had been leaking into the Tigris River. Millions of gallons of drinking water had been lost due to the pipe line break. The problem had been identified in October, but the engineers thought they had the problem isolated. That changed when several rainfalls flooded the oil from a dry creek into the Tigris. Nearly $100,000 was spent to get the project going.

Brigadier Gen. Frank Helmick and Col. Joe Anderson were on hand to open up the new rebuilding project of the downtown Mosul police station in mid-December. The new station would serve as the command and control point for all the police forces throughout the city. The division invested $118,000 towards the project, pocket change in comparison to what the division had spent on the police force since April. The ceremony was a passing of the torch of sorts. Anderson would not be in Mosul for too much longer. He would not be there to walk the police force along, something he had been doing since he arrived in Mosul. His subordinate officers had routinely identified incompetent and ineffective police patrolling the streets. In the first five months alone, Anderson had fired two police chiefs. The third, Mohammed Barhowie, would finally earn Anderson's respect. Now, in Mosul, nobody could complain that the force was not getting what they needed to do their jobs. They had been issued AK-47s and 9mm handguns. Every police officer had new blue uniforms with internationally recognized rank. The sounds of police sirens were unrecognizable to many Mosul locals. The police, thanks to some heavy CERP spending by Anderson, now had police cars.

The thousands of projects that the division was about to leave behind was a marvel of management by the field grade and general officers. Anderson oversaw almost a thousand CERP projects alone in Mosul. "You had to figure out which projects contributed. We had a campaign plan – a matrix that tracked all the different projects and how we contributed to the overall well being of this province by all the different categories and all the different functional areas. There were really essentials – water, electricity, medical. Then there were the 'good-to-haves' – schools – and then there were the 'nice-to-haves.'"

What Anderson's chart failed to account for was the X-factors like one forty-six year old reserve specialist who took the division's efforts to new levels. Specialist David McCorkle could have just served out his tour in Iraq with the 318th Tactical Psychological Operations Battalion one day at a time. He could have stayed with his job in sales at IBM instead of joining the Army reserves two months after Sept. 11, 2001 (losing more than 100 pounds in just three months in order to get in). Nobody in his unit was oblivious to the fact that he was making a fraction of what his work in St. Louis was paying him before he landed in Iraq. There were reservists that took a moderate pay cut to serve for certain, but McCorkle was making more than $200,000.

McCorkle's remarkable story isn't just about duty, honor, and country – it's about his boyish passion to make the best of his time in war. He certainly did. It began in Mosul after McCorkle struck up a friendship with a nine-year-old boy who had become his family's primary breadwinner selling Pepsi to soldiers. His name was Yahya. McCorkle, through an interpreter, came to learn that Yahya's father had recently died and he, left with no other way to survive, had not been to school since.

"When he smiled, he reminded me of my two sons. I thought about how I would feel if my sons were in Yahya's situation. He always wore the exact same clothes everyday, and when I would speak to my wife about him I would call him, 'the boy in the purple shirt.' Somehow my heart went out to this boy and I knew I had to help him."

McCorkle later met Yahya's mother and offered her a deal. "I'll help you financially if he returns to school." With that, the boy was off the Pepsi pushing business and on his way back to school.

The boy in the purple shirt had sparked something inside McCorkle that would become the foundation of American Aid for Children of Nineveh Iraq, or AA-CNI. He launched the idea in August, after his unit was relocated with Lt. Col. Hank Arnold's 2-187th Infantry Regiment in Sinjar. From his non-secure internet connection, McCorkle started emailing his business contacts in St. Louis, New York, Washington – anywhere he could raise money to get the Iraqi kids off the streets and into classrooms. He wasn't asking for much, only fifty dollars a month, to sponsor an Iraqi child. The money would go directly towards school supplies and clothing with no overhead costs.

McCorkle spent the fall building AA-CNI into a non-profit corporation that would remain long after he left Northern Iraq. He hired representatives in Sinjar, Tal Afar and Mosul to serve as overseas delegates after he was gone. Several more teachers and bankers in the region were hired to oversee the trust. He established his own website, www.iraqkids.org.

In his last several months in Iraq, McCorkle didn't let up a bit. "Maybe I'm just like Rhett Butler in *Gone with the Wind* – a sucker for a lost cause. I've had my share of naysayers. They're everywhere. You never get away from them, no matter how hard you try. But I know what I'm doing and I know it won't be easy. I just might be that sucker for a lost cause, but I'm not about to stop trying."

The tears flowed again on December 2 at the D-Main Palace. There, four days earlier, Sgt. Ariel Rico was killed in a mortar attack on the compound. He was an artilleryman with the 3-320th Field Artillery Regiment. The attack came mid-day on a lazy Friday – the Muslim holy day and the one day of the week usually reserved for most of the division as a day off. Rico was near the dining facility when he was hit. Major Trey Cate, the 101st Public Affairs Officer, mournfully huffed, "I'm sick and tired of typing up press releases on dead soldiers."

More heartbreaking than the nature of Rico's death was the circumstance. Nobody needed any kind of reminder that the division was nearing the end of the road in Iraq. "All my guys were going to walk off the plane together, hugging our children and kissing our wives," said Staff Sgt. Scott Benge, Rico's platoon leader, at his memorial ceremony in the shadow of the palace. "We were going to have a barbeque and talk about everything that happened to us – funny, sad, even the things that don't sit well with us. Today I realize there'll be one empty chair. Conversations will go on, the times we shared together will be talked about, but that chair will remain empty, and no one will ever fill it."

Rico's wife Jessica and seven-year old daughter Jadelyn also had to deal with that empty seat. He and his wife had been through Rico's five-year military career that included a tour in Korea.

The D-Main was home to the commanding general, the assistant division commander of operations (Brig. Gen. Frank Helmick) and countless field grade officers. It regularly hosted V.I.P.s for lunch and dinner not even fifty meters from where Rico was killed. None of this appeared to be unknown to the enemy. If it wasn't clear before, it certainly was after the mortar attack: the Mosul Palace was High Value Target #1 for the insurgents in Mosul.

And if the insurgents were going to go after their targets, the 101st was going to go after its targets as well. Operations continued to become more large scale and frequent, especially with Anderson's Second Brigade. "We had some pretty good raids going on almost every night," Anderson said. "We really cranked it up."

The relentless attacks kept the insurgent forces off balance and likely prevented any localized command structure from one ragtag bunch to another. What the commanders didn't see was any kind of movement outside of the city, either to Baghdad or further south. It was a frustrating nut to crack.

Iraq knew about the Internet, by in large, only in tales about the West before the West rolled through their capital. The introduction of the World Wide Web was perhaps the most noticeable change in the Iraqi society less than a year after the war began. It was also at the core of rehabilitating Iraq's primary, secondary, and certainly its post-secondary educational system, after the physical renovations had been completed. The free flow of information into the Iraqi schools, some figured, could help protect schools from anti-western Muslim doctrine – a plague with Iraq's Saudi Arabian neighbors. Others figured it could also spark the entrepreneurial spirit in the country's younger generation. No matter what the rational, it was an instant priority of the coalition and the 101st Airborne Division. Not surprisingly, the 101st commanding general made sure the more than fifty telecommunication projects in his area of operation were in sure hands when he met with local and coalition officials in the field in a December meeting.

"Our vision for Northern Iraq is a very modern region in which people from many different ethnicities, tribes, and religions work together, do business with each other, and they are all supported and enabled by a first-rate telecommunications system," Petraeus told a group of local businessmen and Col. Tom Catudal, L. Paul Bremer's chief telecommunication's advisor. "I think you all know that telecommunication in Northern Iraq had really led the way for the rest of Iraq. The accomplishments have really been extraordinary."

Few could argue. Eleven new Internet cafes had opened, courtesy of the 101st, in Northern Iraq. More than 200 computers had been delivered to Mosul University. Inoperative and utterly destroyed telephone lines were fixed, in part, by crucial donations of optic fiber by American telecommunications corporations AT&T and Bell South. Iraqi linguists were introduced to email for the simple purpose of keeping up with friends once the 101st soldiers went home. Nearly $4 million was donated to the cause by Petraeus, putting telecommunications near the top of his project list. "What has made all our success here isn't just the dollars, it's not even the donations, it's really the initiative that we together have demonstrated," Petraeus said.

The initiative didn't end with that December summit, of course. Days later, the division's communications office delivered and installed the last of 233 computers for the Mosul City Hall, network the local government with Baghdad. All the computers had the ability to translate English to Arabic. More than $150,000 was spent in connecting City Hall online.

Across the street from City Hall, on December 22, Petraeus culminated his banking initiatives by opening the reconstruction of the Mosul Central Bank. The bank had been looted clean and destroyed in April, so much so that the cement walls and ceilings had begun to melt in the inferno. All that remained was a burned out cavern, unrecognizable from its former self. It was the most heartbreaking target of the post-war looting. The bank was one of the most modern structures in the city, designed, according to locals, by one of Iraq's most revered architects.

The Mosul Central Bank was being rebuilt to serve as a keystone for all the banks in the city. Iraq's central bank acts similarly to America's Federal Reserve, with three branches serving the southern region, Baghdad, and Northern Iraq (The U.S. Federal Reserve is broken down into twelve branches). The Mosul Central Bank was to be the headquarters of the Northern Iraq reserve. That meant a new target for thieves, looters and terrorists – a fact not lost from the minds of the coalition engineers who designed the new bank. A new perimeter fence was to be installed with thicker walls and security system that would never let anyone out of sight. The initiative would cost more than a million dollars, but the division this time wouldn't have to foot a dime. All the funding came from the Iraqi Finance ministry. When the blueprint was laid out, the project was scheduled to be completed in early 2005.

Petraeus had more Christmas gifts underneath his tree that week. During the bank opening ceremony, he used the moment to announce that a private company had spent seven million dollars to renovate and own the Mosul Hotel, a landmark that had once housed 101st soldiers and had been mortared several times. He continued. Another private company had spent seventeen million dollars to build a new supermarket in Mosul. Two investments in one week that nobody thought were imaginable in Mosul just months ago.

It would not be the first time the 101st Airborne Division would spend Christmas at war. In 1944, the division spent December 24 entrenched in the snowy hills of Bastogne, continuing their fight to hold off Nazi forces surrounding the town. Santa never made a stop in a 101st foxhole during that pivotal battle. But fifty-nine years later, the yuletide spirit had caught the division, and more surprisingly, even the linguists, most of whom were local citizens who did not celebrate the holiday.

Inside the Civilian-Military Operations Center in Mosul, a group of linguists erected and decorated a Christmas tree so large it was a wonder how they fit it through the doors and into the Nineveh Hotel lobby. At the doorway of the D-Main Palace, a savvy soldier with a keen sense of humor thought to stand up a blow-up snowman. As Christmas approached, the snowman earned several new decorations, including his own Screaming Eagle combat patch and toy rifle slung over his shoulder. He was a combat soldier too, everyone figured. Soldiers at the D-Rear Airfield put on a live nativity scene. And on Christmas Eve, there was no more touching show of Christmas spirit than the carolers of the 431st Civil Affairs Detachment, who went around the CMOC singing every holiday tune in the book.

Christmas Eve services were heavily attended. Division chaplains had been orchestrating field services for ten months, even during the push to Baghdad. For Christmas, Chaplain (Lt. Col.) Chester Egert held midnight services to a packed crowd of Christians from all denominations. "It's different in Iraq," Chaplain John Stutz remarked. "You're not with your family, but in a way, it's the same, because you're with your Army family." Stutz had been attached to the division from his home base in Fort Sam Houston, Texas. He was put in charge of organizing the Christmas events for soldiers in Mosul. "A lot of the stuff we treasure in America, we don't have here. But what we're learning is that the stuff isn't what makes the joy, it just makes big piles of material possessions. The true joy comes from inside."

That didn't mean the soldiers didn't enjoy unwrapping a present or two on Christmas morning, Stutz knew. Operation Shoebox was a trust established in the United States where donated boxes of goodies were shipped to Iraq in time for the holidays. Stutz was involved in coordinating the delivery. "These aren't cheap things that are being sent to us. Some of these boxes are filled with fifty dollars worth of gifts," Stutz explained. Citing the Dr. Seuss classic, "How the Grinch Stole Christmas," Stutz sought out the "Grinchiest" soldiers for Operation Shoebox deliveries. "They're the ones who usually need the gifts, not because they can't get what's in the gifts elsewhere, but because they're usually the ones who need to be handed a gift to let them know that there's always someone out there looking out for them.

"We want to make their heart increase three sizes."

Lieutenant Col. Donald Fryc, aided by one of Stutz's chaplain corps comrades, took his Christmas Eve to "strike" a homeless shelter just outside his Mosul compound. "We had a cold spell of about two or three days and it really struck me that there was a great need out there in the winter months for the kids." For every coat his unit, the 2-44th Air Defense Artillery Regiment, could deliver to the children of the area, that many children would be spared from freezing. Fryc sat in front of his computer emailing friends and family night after night, gathering up whatever support he could for "Operation Santa Strike."

The response was overwhelming. "I asked them to carry the message to their churches," Fryc recalled. "They all replied back and said, 'The boxes are on the way.'" Chaplain (Capt.) Jay West had worked with the homeless shelter for months, never giving an indication that his unit would soon be delivering a truck load of presents to the children.

On December 24, the secret was over. Without warning, Fryc, West, and about two dozen volunteers from within the 2-44th ADA swarmed the shelter. The children flocked towards the vehicles in uncontrolled mayhem. Their parents were right behind. Fryc's timing could not have been more perfect. The temperature when the convoy rolled into the shelter was in the forties with punishing winds and rain. It was a Christmas gift to the broken families of the shelter but even more of a gift to the parents of the unit, most of whom hadn't seen a smiling face of a child like the ones they saw that day in almost a year.

About 200 overcoats were handed out that day. Fryc also received about 500 pounds of clothes, shoes, and toys from friends in the United States that made their way to the orphanage. "From a chaplain's perspective, I would hope those folks learned today that the American soldiers have the biggest heart in the world," West remarked after handing out the last overcoat. Of course, no amount of overcoats and clothes would have been sufficient. When the boxes were empty, mothers and fathers came face to face with the soldiers and asked why there wasn't another coat for their child. Lieutenant Col. Fryc heard their complaints, but knew he and his battalion had done a good thing that Christmas Eve.

For the battalion commander, one final gift to a young boy was the most lasting memory of the day. He had been a moment away from abandoning the scene when the five-year old climbed on top of his humvee, barefoot. Fryc rummaged through several empty boxes at his feet, finding the last pair of shoes. "I tell you," he recalled, "he smiled a smile that I'll remember for a long time."

"It's amazing what these folks don't have," Fryc continued. "These people, day in and day out, they're fighting for their survival."

When anti-coalition sentiments had undoubtedly reached a height, the 101st Airborne Division's answer was to destroy the enemies and win over as many friends who weren't involved in the insurgency. That meant lots of missions like "Operation Overcoat." And on they came. Egert and Stutz, amongst their busy holiday season schedules, found time to deliver 200 heaters to the local mosques and churches, a nearly $30,000 project. Stutz, in his rough Texas accent, remarked after one delivery, "We're both the guns and the roses."

The supplies would continue to flow into local schools. More computers would be delivered into government buildings. Everywhere a 101st soldier went, the image of readiness and compassion had to be presented. Smiles for the kids, overwhelming raids for the insurgents.

Christmas morning was not as most 101st soldiers had imagined a year before, but it was certainly special if nothing else. Units had their own Christmas trees – most artificial – with gifts from soldier to soldier that sometimes tested the bounds of appropriateness.

Acting Secretary of the Army Les Brownlee made his third visit to the 101st area of operation for Christmas Day, putting the holiday in perspective during a quick pep-talk at the D-Main Palace. "When you get to my age, there are a lot of Christmases that you forget. Let me tell you something, you will never forget this Christmas." He would have known. This was not Brownlee's first combat Christmas with the 101st Airborne Division, having celebrated Christmas as a junior officer in Vietnam.

Major Alfred Rascon, a Medal of Honor recipient from Vietnam, also joined the 101st in Mosul for the holidays. Like Thanksgiving, the dining facilities would pull out every resource to make the holiday special. They even imported eggnog for the event. Command Sgt. Maj. Marvin Hill, a man who had kept rigid standards on maintaining perfect soldierly bearings within his division, dressed up as Santa Claus. Few soldiers could have hoped for anything more than a phone call home, and most got just that from their units' satellite phones.

Some Christmas traditions remained. The recreation centers at all of the compounds showed classic Christmas movies. Other traditions just weren't quite the same. Christmas shopping was predominately restricted to the small shopping centers located in the compounds, supplied with items from the local economy. Wrapping paper was non-existent.

Time magazine, in contrast with other publications, has always prided itself on honoring their Person of the Year based on who has most strongly influenced the year's headlines, irregardless of whether or not that person has influenced the world for good or bad. Adolf Hitler and Ayatollah Khomeini sit alongside Franklin Delano Roosevelt and Pope John Paul II as past honorees. But 2003 was a year in which no one leader, politician, religious figure, or celebrity had influenced the globe more than one single institution. That single institution was the U.S. Armed Forces. In a year when they defeated and began occupying a country as big as California in just a month, plucked the world's bloodiest dictator from a spider hole, and suffered more than 500 combat deaths, who else but the American Soldier (with the other service members of the other military branches implied) could be *Time* magazine's as the 2003 Person of the Year?

"To have pulled Saddam Hussein from his hole in the ground brings the possibility of pulling an entire country out of the dark. In an exhausting year when we've been witness to battles well beyond the battlefields – in the streets, in our homes, with our allies – to share good news felt like breaking a long fast, all the better since it came by surprise. And who delivered this gift, against all odds and risks? The same citizens who share the duty of living with, and dying for, a country's most fateful decisions.

"For uncommon skills and service, for the choices each one of them has made and the ones still ahead, for the challenge of defending not only our freedoms but those barely stirring half a world away, the American soldier is *Time*'s Person of the Year."

Indeed, the soldiers of the United States had held the balance of a presidency on their shoulders. Heading into 2004, an election year, no issue mattered more than the fight for Iraq. President Bush's post-September 11 popularity had sunk to ominously low levels for a man looking for reelection, even as Saddam Hussein remained in coalition custody. His prospective democratic rivals, including then-frontrunner Howard Dean, Gen. (Ret.) Wesley Clark, and Massachusetts Sen. John Kerry, had mocked his May 1 "Mission Accomplished" speech aboard the U.S.S. Abraham Lincoln. Iraq, had become what Sen. Edward Kennedy derisively called, "George Bush's Vietnam."

But unlike the Vietnam generation, the popularity of the soldiers of 2003 never correlated to the war they fought in. They were not spit at when they returned home, as noted in the *Time* article. They never embarrassed their families by their profession. Even the protestors who had charged through the streets of Manhattan and Washington, D.C., almost weekly in 2003 had never blamed the soldiers for following their orders. Simply put, the men and women of the U.S. Armed Forces, unlike any time since World War II, were heroes again. Few soldiers could illustrate that point better than the platoon profiled.

The Survey Platoon, Headquarters Battery, 2-3rd Field Artillery Regiment could tell the world all about the war in Iraq. They called themselves, "The Tomb Raiders," and they had been in theatre since the beginning of the war. In October, they lost their platoon leader 2nd Lt. Ben Corgan after his vehicle drove into an IED.

Specialist Billie Grimes, a white female, Sgt. Marquette Whiteside, an African-American male, and Sgt. Ronald Buxton, a white male, graced the cover of the December 29 issue. Aside from their diversity, the three soldiers provided the perfect image of the twenty-first century U.S. Army. Grimes was the only female in her unit. Her brother, at the time of the article, was himself on his way to Iraq. He had already been to Afghanistan for six months. Grimes had enlisted in the reserves in college, against the wishes of her family. Whiteside was another deployed father, half the world away from his six-year old daughter Brashawn, who stayed with her grandmother in Pine Bluff, Ark. He had held his platoon leader, Corgan, as he died in the October IED attack. Whiteside did not have a whole lot to like about the Army, but against all expectations of his family, he reenlisted for three years while in Iraq. Buxton, age thirty-two, had left a pregnant wife when he went to war. On August 18, his wife Audrey gave birth to his second child, Jared, while Buxton continued with his one-year deployment. Buxton got a synopsis of the event though a static filled phone conversation with Audrey from her hospital bed.

Together, the three represented the face of the Army that hardly resembled its World War II predecessors. Even the most farsighted of commanders in 1944 could never have seen a woman like Grimes serving on the front lines, which she very much was in Baghdad. And how the veterans of World War II would smile at the sight of Whiteside, serving in a military that was only desegregated sixty years ago, fighting in a platoon comprised of whites, blacks, Latinos and even a soldier from Micronesia. Perhaps no soldier was as well rounded as Buxton, who had served in the first Gulf War. Buxton taught himself Arabic during the deployment. The days of the stereotype enlisted grunt had indeed come to a close. The *Time* magazine profile on Buxton noted that when Buxton's oldest son, Brenden, asked his mother where daddy went, Audrey would reply, "He's helping the other kids in Iraq because they don't have all the things we have."

Then there were the men who told their stories. In a column entitled, "What Happened That Day on Patrol," *Time* Managing Editor James Kelly told the story of three of his writers, Romesh Ratnesar, Michael Weisskopf, and James Nachtwey – the team that was sent to write about the 2-3rd Field Artillery platoon. The three embedded in Baghdad for the story. "For three weeks," Kelly wrote, "the team ate, slept, and went on patrol with the 'Tomb Raiders."

What they saw was what soldiers in Iraq's hottest hot spots had seen everyday. They heard nearly hourly explosions – so commonplace in Baghdad that few soldiers even stirred in their beds when mortars and small arms fire rocked compounds just blocks away. They marched with the soldiers and received no luxuries that the soldiers themselves didn't get. They were not VIPs; they were simply soldiers.

Never was that so apparent than on their night patrol on December 10. Weisskopf, a *Time* correspondent who had embedded in Baghdad for four weeks earlier in the war, was riding in a Tomb Raider humvee when a grenade landed in the back of the vehicle. In a knee jerk reaction, he grabbed the grenade in an attempt to throw it out of harm's way. It exploded in his palm before he was able to toss it away. Nachtwey, the photographer sitting to his right, saw Weisskopf's arm maimed to a handless, bloody stub. Everyone in the humvee, including two soldiers in the driver's and passenger's seats, were hit with shrapnel. Specialist Grimes, the platoon medic, applied a tourniquet to Weisskopf's arm and prevented any further bleeding.

As was explained to him later, by wrapping his hand around the grenade and absorbing most of the blast, Weisskopf likely saved his own life and certainly one or two other lives in vehicle.

Weisskopf's injury had brought the violence in Iraq onto a non-combatant – hardly the first and certainly not the last civilian to come under attack by insurgents. Convoys of fuel and supplies, manned by civilian contracted truck drivers, had become a soft target for ambush. The truck drivers were paid well, armed and sometimes given a military escort, but starting in winter of 2004, they came to Iraq with the clear understanding that they too would face the fear of combat. Daily images flooded the American airwaves of not only American contractors being held hostage and often murdered on camera, but also workers from overseas contracted companies meeting the same fate.

The images of Americans in captivity – held under the whim of murderous madmen – galvanized support for the war for some and reinforced skepticism for others. All had strong responses. One image, taken in April (more than a month after the last 101st soldier left Iraq), has remained indelible. Private First Class Keith Maupin, a reservist with the 724th Transportation Company, came to Iraq at the age of 20. On April 9, his convoy was ambushed with RPG's and small arms; he and Sgt. Elmer Krause were unaccounted for in the aftermath.

A week later the Arab television equivalent of CNN, Al Jazeera, aired footage of Maupin sitting on a floor, flanked by two masked, armed insurgents, with his bonnie cap flipped upward to identify his face. He was declared captured by the Pentagon on April 16. On April 23, Krause's remains were found and identified.

Two years after Maupin was declared captured, he has still not been released from captivity, if he indeed is still alive.

New Years Eve was just another dry holiday for the division soldiers. Once again, General Order Number 1 still didn't budge. The party was at the Mosul Airfield's recreation center, put on by the Division Support Command. It was in a building that had rung in 2003 as an Iraqi Officers Club. In 2004, the division did their best to celebrate the New Year like they were already back in America. One division soldier, who had organized the New Year's party, explained, "Since we can't bring the people to the club, we're going to bring the club to the people."

The year 2003, save two months, had been spent entirely in Iraq for the majority of 101st Airborne Division soldiers. There were very few memories in 2003 of loved ones at back home, but a wealth of memories made of loved ones in Iraq. It was a year when the bonds of families were tested while at the same time, the bonds of brothers and sisters in arms were strengthened. It was a year that claimed the lives of over fifty division soldiers. There was a great deal of painful memories for the division soldiers. The amount of personal damage that a year apart from loved ones could not be tabulated, but as the end of the deployment approached, it could be said that very few soldiers regretted their experiences from the past year.

The year 2004 would be different. Nobody knew if they would be back where the year started by the time they ringed in 2005, but there was a sense of optimism with the Screaming Eagles. The realization that they had reached the end of the road was settling in. Most of the division would be on their way home by the end of the month.

Mission Redeployment officially began on January 1, when the Headquarters and Headquarters Company of the 159th Aviation Brigade lined up and prepared to move on their way to Kuwait. Captain Michael Troxell, who had flown supply armadas during decisive operations with the 159th, was now in command of its headquarters company (a company he took command of the day after Capt. Ben Smith's death). He would be the first commander to hit Kuwait before the floodgates opened.

There would be two ways to Fort Campbell for the 101st Airborne Division. Twenty-two percent of the division, many of whom combat support elements, would fly from Mosul to Fort Campbell via Incirlik, Turkey, starting around the second week of January. Those fortunate soldiers did not have to carry heavy equipment into Kuwait on a three-day convoy. The unfortunate ones would. And when they reached their destination, Kuwait, the fun would really begin. Nobody would be on their way home until their equipment passed stringent U.S. Customs inspections. That meant hours, even days, at the wash racks making certain every particle of Iraqi dirt was washed off. It was, after all, a good problem to have after a year-long tour of duty.

After nearly a week of delays and countless man hours on repairing vehicles, the company set off on January 5 out of the Mosul Airfield. The way to Kuwait took them along virtually an identical path than the one the company had took ten months earlier, along Highway 1, the road that connected Baghdad to Mosul. It took civilian contractors and journalists about four hours to go from one city to another; for the 101st convoys, it would take a day and a half. Their three-day movement from Northern Iraq to Kuwait would take them through Quyarrah, where they would stay the night at the airfield. They would move through Tikrit, where they would refuel at a 4th Infantry Division compound just weeks after they made a name for themselves by apprehending Saddam Hussein. And they would go right through Baghdad, still very much a hotbed of enemy activity. Throughout, they were an easy target for an ambush. It would be no victory tour. It was little secret that the forces in the North, and soon the 4th Infantry Division, would be rolling south in mass. Highway 1 was a choke point, especially for the 101st. Once they exited off Highway 1, it got no easier. Troxell had circled an area of Baghdad that division intelligence had instructed him to avoid. He wisely heeded their admonition.

The danger of attack was never far from anybody's mind, but if anybody in the company had noticed, what they saw along the way to Kuwait was a vastly different Iraq from the one they had toured ten-months earlier. Several new shopping centers had emerged outside of Tikrit. Police managed busy intersections where only anarchy had reigned. It was hard not to notice the beginnings of a new highway system connecting the southern region of Iraq to the highways that just ended around An Nasariyah. It was equally more difficult not to smile at the sight of their replacements rolling north as the 101st rolled south.

Troxell and his company were not ambushed along the way to Kuwait, allowing Col. William Harrison to breathe a sigh of relief. He and the rest of his brigade were on their way. From January 5 to February 10, the division was scheduled to send between 100 and 250 vehicles a day from Northern Iraq to Kuwait.

Anderson had also got a leg up for the 101st's successors in Mosul on what was certain to be a keystone project for the coalition in 2004. Putting the pieces back together of what was the Iraqi army was going to be a prodigious mountain to climb. But of all the Iraqification forces, the new Iraqi army was of the least concern to the 101st. Most of the recruitment and training was controlled and orchestrated by Coalition Provisional Authority officials in Baghdad. That didn't mean the 101st stayed out of the process.

It started in the spring when Anderson turned what was a Mosul school into a recruiting station. He later built another school for the neighborhood. Then he used his radio station for advertisements. Whenever he met local unemployed capable young men, he was sure to plug the army as an option. Once the civilians turned into recruits, Anderson's brigade escorted bus convoys with future Iraqi soldiers down south for basic training. In December, Anderson found a prime spot for the Iraqi army to build a headquarters between Mosul and Tal Afar. "We helped with the moving pieces and the infrastructure to recruit," Anderson said, "but we were not physically involved with the training." The 101st had trained internal security forces in every major town in the area of operation, but no division soldier had been directly involved in training Iraqi soldiers for the new army. That would change.

"Our first and foremost task was the police, the ICDC and the (Fire Department). That was what we did from Ground Zero," Anderson said. "Training programs, academies, uniforms, weapons, vehicles, radios – that was all done by our guys with help from nobody."

With coalition-supported media in Mosul taking off, Anderson wanted to keep the ball rolling on this his favorite project. Where he had once done his weekly call in show from a trailer, now his Saturday morning convoys were pulling into a professional studio with professional equipment. "The feedback was continuously thumbs-up," Anderson recalled. "We just continued to try to do more things." To a fault, Anderson thought, when the CG came to him with an idea. In December, Petraeus had his most off-the-wall plan, not only for the TV station, but for all of Mosul. It was an idea that made even his most loyal subordinates chuckle. Petraeus wanted the 101st to produce a talent show for local television much in the mold of "American Idol." "No way in hell this will this work," Anderson told his division commander.

But it did. Mosul locals ate the show up. Anderson had been right about everything pertaining to his media efforts, but he was wrong on the talent show idea. In just weeks, the show was the talk of Mosul. Petraeus perhaps became too enamored with the Mosul TV business, however. A later idea of his to launch a television show in the mold of "Cops" tanked.

The talent show fiasco aside, Anderson had flawlessly orchestrated one of the 101st's most successful projects in Nineveh. In a country where free media was an oxymoron a year before, Anderson and the 22nd Mobile Public Affairs Detachment had launched a phenomenon that gripped the province at every street corner. "At our count at one point, there were forty-two newspapers," Anderson said. Some weren't telling the truth and Anderson threatened to shut them down if they didn't start. Most got the message and started doing just what they should be doing, even if they were publishing opinions that weren't favorable to the coalition. At City Hall, Thursday morning press conferences with Brig. Gen. Frank Helmick were so successful that the assistant division commander likened one local reporter to Helen Thomas of the White House Press Corps.

There was room for self-congratulations, but the focus of the last few weeks in Mosul turned towards laying down the foundations for the replacements to take over. The front end of the incoming Stryker Brigade elements had begun to arrive for duty in late December. "You just could not do these projects haphazardly," Anderson remembered telling the Stryker Brigade officers. "When we first got there, we tried to do things independently because we didn't know who the key players were in the government to make all of those decisions. As time went on, it became a process involving many more locals and much less military."

The Iraqification process continued moving forward as the turnover neared. At the crux of the Stryker Brigade mission was the handoff of power. The civil institutions that the 101st had built for almost a year would get their moment to fall or shine once the division left. They would not just be observers, but the Stryker Brigade patrols would certainly never get in the way.

The Stryker Brigade and ultimately the people of Northern Iraq would now be the custodians of the CERP projects that the division had worked to bring to life. "What we laid out for them," Anderson recalled, "was where we had been and where we thought we needed to go." Stryker Brigade commanders immediately began accompanying Petraeus and Anderson to Mosul City Council meetings with a pen and notepad. The Strykers got a crash course in diplomacy with the local officials.

CHAPTER 13

THE LONG ROAD BACK TO CAMPBELL

Major Gen. David Petraeus was still in command in Mosul, but for the soldiers who had arrived in Kuwait, Brig. Gen. Jeffery Schloesser was at the top. He was sent there with one mission: to get the division back to Fort Campbell safely and effectively. It would be a massive effort. For two months, the division would pick up most of its personnel and all of its heavy equipment for a 10,500 mile movement back home. It was all a part of the single largest movement of American troops since World War II.

Third Brigade would be the first of the three infantry brigades to move. They had been in Afghanistan for much of 2002, Iraq for nearly all of 2003, and it seemed only fitting that the division give Col. Michael Linnington and his troops as much of 2004 to spend with their families as possible. They would be in Kuwait by mid-January, gone by the first week of February. Following the Rakkassans would be Col. Ben Hodges and First Brigade from Quyarrah, minus their Third Battalion who would remain in Mosul for until the beginning of February. The aviation and artillery assets would move with the two infantry brigades, bringing their massive equipment along with them.

On February 1 and 2, the remaining elements in Mosul, along with Petraeus and Col. Joseph Anderson were scheduled to depart for Kuwait. February 2 would mark the division's transfer of authority – they would be gone from Mosul and northern Iraq for good.

Home for the 101st would be Camps Doha, Arifjan and Udairi, with Doha serving as the command and control point. Camp Udairi became an unfamiliar place for the division. At some point after the division left for war in March, Camps Pennsylvania, New Jersey and Udairi had been morphed into just one large compound of sand and dust. Something else was unfamiliar about the Kuwaiti camps. It was quite cold and rainy. In fact, for most of the month of January – Kuwait's rainy season apparently – it rained everyday. It was ironic really. The division's enlisted soldiers in Kuwait, after nearly a year of taking every drop of water supply with extreme thrift, saw rain pour from the sky and shoot out of a hose for the first time in a year.

The term "washrack" would instantly become a part of every soldier's everyday vernacular as soon as the convoys hit Kuwait. It was priority Number One. The day convoys rolled into Kuwait, they would move towards the washracks, wait in line for a minimum of four to six hours, and mount an incline with an opening underneath. For the rest of the day and into the night, a group of two to three soldiers for every one vehicle would grab a hose and spray every last square inch of their humvee. Once they were done, or they thought they were done, an inspector (often an MP) would come through with a rubber glove. Inevitably, a missed spot would be found and the soldiers would have to go back at it. Once the washrack process was over, the vehicles would be moved into a sterile yard to be loaded up on a U.S. Navy ship docked in Kuwait City. It was all a painless process in comparison to what had to be done with the division's helicopters.

In addition to washing out all foreign soil in a similar washrack process, helicopters had to undergo a special "shrink-wrap" process to protect their sensitive equipment from the ocean environment. They too would be loaded up on a ship and moved across the Atlantic, exposing the helicopters to saltwater corrosion. "If it's going home via the ship – and a large number of our aircraft are, some two hundred – they're going to be shrink-wrapped," Schloesser said in Kuwait. The division's aviation units had to wrap their aircraft in the cocoon-like plastic wrap and suck the air out from below. The end result was a protective plastic covering sealed so tight that the aircraft's contours were plainly visible from outside the wrap.

The redeployment of the 101st followed by the 4th Infantry Division would put a strain on the Kuwaiti bases. The line at the dining facility during the 101st's redeployment would take upwards of thirty minutes to get through. Around 6,000 vehicles and 1,600 containers would pass through the bases from the 101st alone

– stretching the facilities and the permanent personnel in Kuwait to the absolute limit.

The lead elements of the 159th Aviation Regiment, a 101st Airborne unit, were the first to finish processing through Kuwait on their way home. It would not be a painless flight, but their chartered flights were due to arrive home late-afternoon the day after their flights left Kuwait.

After a year, the long flight home was a like a victory lap for soldiers like Sgt. Ruy Diaz, who like so many soldiers arriving home after their lengthy combat tours came home to his spouse and kids. His wife Frances and daughters Coraliz, seven years old, Anbrea, five, and Alejandra, three, waited for his return since March 1, 2003. "It's awesome," Diaz remarked before jumping on his plane. "It's the break I've been waiting for."

The pre-departure rigmaroles were tedious for certain. Soldiers received briefing after briefing before finally swiping their ID cards and boarding the planes around 1:30 a.m. local time. Colonel William T. Harrison, 159th Aviation Regiment commander, made the forty-five minute drive from Camp Doha, Kuwait, to the local airport just to send the soldiers off.

"It's been a great honor to serve with you," Harrison said. "Thanks again for everything you've done over here."

For a number of soldiers with Bravo Company of the 7-101st Aviation Regiment, the redeployment culminated their double-duty service in both Iraq and in Afghanistan. Chief Warrant Officer 3 Rob Devlin returned home in late January of 2003 after an eight-month tour in Afghanistan – only to be whisked away to Kuwait two weeks later to begin what would be a year long combat tour.

His wife Gaylynn and son Brandon, ten, and daughter Vanessa, six, endured nearly two years of Devlin deployments. "Being deployed has made the family stronger and made the time that we spend together that much more important. You kind of take that for granted when you're home all the time."

The trip back would span nearly an entire day in the air, with a stop in Europe to refuel. Everyone was patient. Bravo had spent eighteen months in Afghanistan, Kuwait and Iraq. What could one more day away from home amount to?

Back in Northern Iraq, the 101st continued to teach their successors as the Stryker brigade wowed the battle toughened division with their new toys. The Strykers were the Army's newest force. They came to Mosul with their new vehicles – an armored vehicle on four wheels. It combined the protection against IED attacks and small arms fire, in theory. The vehicles were also maneuverable enough to attack objectives quickly. Northern Iraq would be the Stryker Brigade's debut.

The division at every level made certain that their successors were not going to be unprepared going into their tour of duty. The program was called "right-seat-ride." A 101st company commander patrolling an area of Mosul, for example, would take the new company commander earmarked for that same area to show who was who and what was what. The idea was to make a seamless transition. The reality was more complex. By the beginning of February, the people who had earned the trust of the local leaders were going to be gone. The diplomacy that had been gradually built by Maj. Gen. Petraeus and the 101st was going to have to be rebuilt, almost from the foundation up, by the Stryker Brigade.

It would have been easy to simply bypass the right-seat-ride program in favor of a simple slide show presentation for each company and field grade commander. It certainly would have been less dangerous. No convoy was given immunity from ambush and as the staff of the 2-17th Cavalry learned, the dangers in the skies remained until the moment they reached Kuwait. While showing a 3-17th Cavalry Regiment (Stryker Brigade asset) pilot the route from the Quyarrah airfield to Mosul, Chief Warrant Officer 2 Michael Blaze became the final causality of war for the 101st Airborne Division in Iraq on January 23.

The day was a foggy one and several battle staff officers had cautioned against flying into the rough sky. Major Jimmy Blackmon, an experienced Kiowa pilot, went ahead of Blaze and his Stryker pupil along the same route. The fog was dense indeed, but Blackmon made it back without too much of a problem. Then Blaze went up. "This weather looks bad, I'm ready to turn back," he told the battle staff at Quyarrah in what would be the last words anyone ever heard from Blaze. The staff gave him the OK and the aircraft started its retreat just ten minutes after takeoff.

It's unclear what exactly happened to Blaze and his copilot, although nobody has ever suggested that the aircraft was shot down by enemy fire. What is apparent is that Blaze lost control of the aircraft. The Kiowa crashed in a field miles from the Quyarrah airfield. It was a heartbreaking ending of an outstanding tour for Blaze. He had fought in Karbala, An Najaf, and in the skies of Northern Iraq for seven months.

His wife, Capt. Kate Blaze, had recently received a transfer from the 426th Forward Support Battalion to redeploy with her husband. She was waiting at Q-West when she found out her husband's flight would never land at the helipad.

The Blaze tragedy would not alter or slow the right-seat-ride program. The 2-17th Cavalry was due to begin movement south in two days, but their battle staff would still find themselves again in the middle of a bloody catastrophe as they lined up their convoys.

While the most of the division was on their way out, one catastrophic incident on January 25th provided another tragic reminder that the dangers of war need not come from the enemy. A patrol boat manned by four newly arrived Stryker Brigade soldiers, four Iraqi police officers and a linguist inexplicably capsized moving up the Tigris River in Mosul. The soldiers had earlier met the Iraqis on the riverbank to do a joint patrol only minutes before the boat overturned. Two Iraqi policemen and the linguist drowned. Three of the soldiers and two of the Iraqis found their ways to the riverbank. One soldier, a staff sergeant with the Stryker Brigade, was missing.

Colonel Joe Anderson and his Stryker Brigade successor in Mosul immediately dispatched teams to look for the missing soldier. A Stryker Brigade OH-58 Kiowa was inbound to circle the immediate area from overhead. By 6:30 P.M., well after dark, the search crew had come up with nothing.

From the ground, the 2-17th Cavalry staff made contact with the Kiowa crew to warn them of the nearby power lines. Piloting the Kiowa was First Lt. Adam Mooney and Chief Warrant Officer Patrick Dorff – both in their first few weeks in theatre. Nestled just behind the bridge in the area was one particular power line "as thin as a pinky" as one battle staff officer remembered that was virtually invisible after dark. 101st aircraft had nearly struck that same wire several times trying to maneuver around the bridge. The 2-17th Cavalry admonition was heard loud and clear, but the crew was looking to fly low, which the Kiowa's capabilities allowed them to do. With limited visibility and no experience in the area, just minutes after the warning from the ground, the Kiowa's tail made contact with the wire with their tail rotors while hovering over the site. The aircraft crashed nose down into the river.

It was bedlam at the division headquarters. An Iraqi emergency rescue team arrived on the scene with limited equipment but limitless bravery. With most of the aircraft underwater, the team was able to dive in close enough to the fuselage to see that the two-member crew was gone.

U.S. Navy Divers arrived the next day from Baghdad to find the pilots. With the frigid cold temperature of the water and the likelihood that the pilots had been dragged down to the bottom of the river, there was little hope that either survived.

It was later determined, weeks after the helicopter crash, that the pilots had indeed escaped the aircraft alive after they hit the river, but later drowned in the current as the aircraft sunk to the river bed. The Stryker Brigade NCO, Staff Sgt. Christopher Bunda, was also later found, dead. He had apparently drowned after the boat capsized. One of the Iraqi policemen also drowned in the disaster.

In Iraq, the fight for the hearts and minds of the Iraqi people was at a violent standstill. In Washington, the equally tempestuous fight for support of the Iraq war from the American people took a serious blow.

"Let me begin by saying, we were almost all wrong and I certainly include myself." David Kay had been tapped by CIA Chief George Tenet and President George W. Bush to lead a 1,400-person search team to find the weapons of mass destruction that the administration had promised in the months leading to war. On January 28, Kay testified in front of the Senate Armed Services committee and told America that the weapons were gone and it was "highly unlikely" that they would be found. His testimony directly undercut intelligence reports that had been postulated as fact by the United Nations, President Bill Clinton, and by Secretary of State Colin Powell during his January 2003 speech before the U.N. Security Council.

Kay's findings were not disputed by the Administration or the Coalition Headquarters in Baghdad. He had spent seven months in the country, seeing several hundred sites and interviewing thousands of Iraqi officials. He simply uncovered no smoking gun. In one embarrassing disclosure, Kay suggested that a suspected mobile chemical weapons lab was instead a manufacturing facility for weather balloons. A number of 101st Chemical Corps officers could have told Kay, if he asked, all about several missions that led to relatively harmless pesticides.

Tenet, in the end, would be at the crossfire of the Kay report. According to *The Washington Post*'s Bob Woodward – who followed the administration in during the lead-up to war in his 2004 book *Plan of Attack* – Tenet had told Bush with his arms raised to the sky that the case against Saddam was a "slam dunk." In the immediate aftermath of Kay's testimony, calls for Tenet's resignation came from both sides of the isle. Bush remained loyal to Tenet through the heat, but in the Spring of 2003, Tenet's resignation came.

The differences between Camp Doha and Mosul were as stark as black and white. When a soldier got hungry, there was no waiting for the dining facility to open or worse yet, turning to the nearest box of MREs. There was a mall complete with its own food court with Subway, Burger King, and even its own Starbucks. The Post Exchange was the kind of shopping center a soldier could only dream of in Mosul. For the first time, soldiers could buy and wear civilian clothes after they were finished with their day's work.

Wednesdays were surf and turf night for dinner at the Camp Doha dining facility – crab legs, lobster tail, and steak. The other six days of the week weren't too bad either. The post had its own movie rental store, with no charge for soldiers to take out a movie for a night. Camp Doha had its own library and education center. Permanent party personnel were taking college courses at the compound. It wasn't quite home yet, but Camp Doha was about as close as anyone could have imagined.

Super Sunday was no disappointment. The New England Patriots lined up against the underdog, and favorite among the Dixie-heavy crowd of soldiers amassed at Camp Doha, Carolina Panthers. Everyone was invited to the Camp Doha nightclub to watch the game on a movie screen with catered food but still no alcoholic beverages. The game would last until seven in the morning Kuwait time, but few would go to bed before the gut-wrenching finish. For the second time in three years, quarterback Tom Brady led the Patriots up the field in the last minute to set up the game winning field goal attempt for the Super Bowl Championship. For the second time in three years, kicker Adam Venitieri converted and New England won the game 32-29.

The Super Bowl was dramatic. The race for the Democratic Presidential nomination was not. Former Vermont Gov. Howard Dean's political flame quickly extinguished after a disappointing third place finish in the Iowa Caucuses. Later losses in New Hampshire and South Carolina would seal his fate. Massachusetts Sen. John Kerry, a candidate most pundits had given up for dead just a week before Iowa, roared back to almost unanimously win the nomination. In the end, he would lose only three states – Vermont, to the hometown hero Dean, Oklahoma, to Gen. (Ret.) Wesley Clark, and South Carolina, to his eventual running mate North Carolina Sen. John Edwards. The stage was set for the 2004 campaign in which the Iraq war was certain to be the central issue.

As soldiers packed up their storage containers for U.S. Customs inspections, the issue of what could and could not be taken home finally reached a head. If it was in the container, more than likely the Customs agents would find it. Some inspectors were more understanding than others on certain grey area items, but with the guidance from the Staff Judge Advocate given to all units, the general rules of thumb were completely understood. "If it is a necessary component of a weapon to operate, it is illegal. If it is or was alive, it is illegal. NO BAYONETS!!!"

V Corps Fragmented Order (FRAGO) 160M went into more detail. Authorized, according to the regulations, were "helmets and head coverings; uniforms and uniform items such as insignia and patches; canteens, compasses, rucksacks, pouches, and load bearing equipment; flags, military training manuals, books, and pamphlets; posters, placards, and photographs." Essentially anything innocuous taken from an Iraqi compound was permitted. Items that could be used as a weapon in the United States and items that delved too much into cultural and societal sensitivities were strictly prohibited. If any soldier took a personnel item from a Ba'ath party official's home, those items too were prohibited from leaving the Middle East.

"Former Iraqi regime or Iraqi privately owned articles of a household nature, including but not limited to, silverware, goldware, chinaware, linens, furniture, rugs, fixtures, and electrical appliances," according to FRAGO 160M, were not coming home. Also of note was the regulations surrounding the posters of Saddam Hussein found at every block when the division first arrived in Mosul. Some of the posters were going for a lot of money on various Internet auctioning websites. They were the ultimate "war trophy" and, under the FRAGO, were permitted to be taken back to the U.S.

In his closing hour in Mosul, Petraeus never looked ahead. No "short-timers" syndrome. In his final weeks, he and the 101st staff worked feverishly to help "Task Force Olympia," as the headquarters replacing them was called. In the second week of February, Task Force Olympia would show 101st the door. "King" Petraeus would have to abnegate his crown in Mosul.

"We felt committed to do everything thing that we could to make the handoff as good a situation as possible and to do everything we could for the Iraqi people, Brig Gen Ham, and Task Force Olympia. We worked extremely hard," he recalled. "We did obviously try to cram as much as we could in the last few weeks, but we always felt we were in a race."

On January 6th, complete with a five-tiered cake, Petraeus and Governor Ghanim al-Basso had celebrated the Iraqi Army's eight-third birthday. Petraeus used the celebration to activate two new battalions of the Iraqi Civil Defense Corps and another battalion of the Iraqi Border Police – the last of the Iraqi internal security forces trained by the 101st Airborne Division. "Iraqi soldiers are reestablishing traditions of selfless service to the nation and to all Iraqis, helping to secure Iraq's borders and sovereignty, and helping defend against terrorists trying to disrupt the great progress achieved in the new Iraq since liberation," Petraeus told his coalition partners, speaking to the ICDC and the police for the final time.

The next day, Petraeus opened a school that had particular interest to him. The story of the school, in the Mosul suburban village of Kanash, began in a dawn raid in November which Petraeus had joined. No terrorists were found, but after tea with the local sheik, who had earned a college degree in England, a ravaged school was uncovered, in desperate need of support. Somehow, the millions in Commanders' Emergency Relief Program funds that had been spent in the summer had missed the school. Petraeus went to work in fixing that. The school project began less than a week later, and after two months and $10,000 the work was done. It would be the last ribbon Petraeus would cut to open a new school.

For the 101st and Petraeus, who had been so good at being the first at so many things in Iraq, the last two weeks in January would mark their lasts. Mosul and Northern Iraq weren't perfect, but the 101st had done a lot of good indeed in the region. "There is a race in this kind of operation … a race against a point at which you become an army of occupation instead of an army of liberation," Petraeus later observed. "We were very conscious of that. I, personally, was extraordinarily conscious of it. You can extend the amount of time that someone might regard you as liberators as opposed to occupiers by good conduct, good deeds, good, effective communication. And we tried to do all that stuff.

"But over time, inevitably, even the most wonderful liberators will come to be viewed as occupiers, and that is particularly true in a country where nationalism is as big a sentiment as it is in Iraq. We knew that over time we were going to fly too low over people's houses, we were going to cause traffic jams at traffic control points, cause collateral damage, and injure innocent people who got caught in the cross fire. Over time, that kind of stuff accumulates.

"I made speeches on television, did call-in shows, cut dozens of ribbons, did newspaper interviews, and did everything else imaginable to try to extend that perception of liberation instead of occupation. So did all our brigade commanders and many of the other leaders. But inevitably, at some point, you will eventually be seen as occupiers. With that in mind, we tried to accomplish as much as we

could before that point arrived. We took it real personally, we took it real seriously.
"We wanted to win."

It wasn't just about winning for the division during the one-year tour in Iraq, it was about winning with the highest degree of legitimacy and popular consent. At the heart of Petraeus' command philosophy was the objective of thoroughly defeating an enemy by all means necessary, then bringing every ally possible into the fold. Petraeus must have been aware of the actions of Gen. Ulysses Grant at Vicksburg. At the moment when some lesser generals would have seized the moment to pummel the enemy, Grant instructed one of his Quartermaster companies to hand out food rations to the defeated Confederate soldiers instead of rounding them up for trial. The goal then, as it was for Petraeus in 2003, was to heal a broken country. Both generals took the same logical but extraordinary means to the same ends.

The morning of February 2 would bring a smile on the faces of just about every Screaming Eagle. It was the transfer of authority. The division guidon would be cased and sent on its way home to Fort Campbell. The Stryker brigade-led follow-on force that would take the 101st's stead would do so with a force just a third of the size of the Screaming Eagles. The First and Third Infantry Brigades had already packed up and left. Much of Third Brigade had already landed in Kentucky. Now Second Brigade, with Col. Joseph Anderson still in command to the end, would lead the last of the division on their way home. The remaining elements of the division headquarters would redeploy directly out of Mosul. Major Gen. Petraeus would fly out by helicopter, greet the final 101st soldier crossing back into Kuwait, and arrive back home on February 14th – Valentine's Day.

Colonel Ben Hodges had loaded up his First Brigade on one large convoy down to Kuwait – avoiding any major attacks. Anderson wanted to take a different approach. He instead snuck small convoys around the hot spots in the Sunni Triangle, not through them, and came home with only one minor and ineffective IED attack on his brigade. In the end, the 101st did not lose a single soldier in any redeployment convoy.

The division had left Mosul a much better community than the one the chaotic, looted city it had entered in April, but it was still very much a war zone.

Homecoming for the division was stretched over nearly two months, but on March 5, Brig. Gen. Schloesser arrived with the last flight of 101st Airborne Division troops. There they met Petraeus and a crowd of family members who had woke up in the wee hours in the morning to catch the plane landing. The cheering crowds, American flags, and flashing cameras – it was as if every soldier walking of the plane was the president of the United States.

It was indeed a much different reception for soldiers than the Vietnam generation. No soldier was instructed to change into civilian clothes before they left the airport. No faithful spouse skipped out on the homecoming in embarrassment. No matter what the American people thought of the war, the warriors were heroes.

Petraeus, ever aware that the soldiers in the formation in front of him were not eager to hear him speak for too long, released the last remaining 101st troops to meet their loved ones after a cogent congratulations.

Colonel Anderson had been back at Fort Campbell for three weeks when the last of the division had returned, but he had next to no time to enjoy his homecoming. He had only spent one day in Kuwait, then flew back on a commercial airliner with his new brigade sergeant major, Command Sgt. Maj. Brian Stahl. The rush was to get back and begin the process of retraining and reequipping the brigade. After uncasing his brigade's guidon in a ceremony on April 2, Anderson congratulated his soldiers making it home but cautioned, "we don't know how long" the brigade would stay at Fort Campbell. It was a not so thinly veiled signal that his brigade would be going back to war before too long.

Anderson the commander never superceded his responsibilities of Anderson the family man. Waiting for him in Nashville were the same three people who had been waiting for him after Kosovo: his wife Elizabeth and his two sons Marc and Michael. He had missed Marc's football season, but he had all the time in the world to hear about what he missed as he sat in a civilian vehicle for the first time in a year. "It was odd getting in a car and driving home on an American highway and being with my family like you never left." It was almost like he never left – almost. Anderson did not sleep one minute that night.

Two weeks after the final 101st troops arrived, the President of the United States himself welcomed the division home. It was President Bush's second visit to the post in just three years; he visited Fort Campbell in the fall of 2002 to welcome home the troops who had served in Afghanistan. By comparison, neither President Clinton or President George H.W. Bush had spoken at Fort Campbell in their combined twelve years in office.

Bush brought a star-studded show with him to post. Country singer Daryl Worley opened for the President, singing his Sept. 11 inspired "Have You Forgotten." Command Sgt. Maj. Marvin Hill was the emcee of the event – doing quite admirably in entertaining the soldiers who were forced to wait for several hours in the sun while the U.S. Secret Service swept through the area.

Just before lunch, the President and First Lady Laura Bush arrived at the Post Airfield. It was the Laura Bush's second visit to post in less than a year, having visited the post in June to speak at the Fort Campbell High School graduation. Petraeus met the commander-in-chief with a firm salute and a handshake. The two were going to get better acquainted over the next few months. From the airfield, the President had a lobster tail lunch with a group of selected soldiers at the Second Brigade dining facility.

The 101st engineers had worked for a week setting up the stage for the President. All of the symbols of the division – the helicopters, the vehicles and a Screaming Eagle flag large enough to see from the sky – were on display for the commander-in-chief. At just after eleven o'clock, the motorcade arrived at the Post Parade Field. "I'm glad to be back."

Bush was wearing a flight jacket with a 101st patch on both shoulders. "Since we last met, you deployed over 5,000 vehicles, 254 aircraft, and 18,000 soldiers in Kuwait in the fastest deployment in the history of the 101st. Since we last met, the 101st liberated the cities of Najaf, Karbala and (Al) Hillah. You secured southern Baghdad, and sent 1,600 soldiers by helicopter to Mosul in the largest air assault in military history. Since we last met, the sons of the dictator went into hiding until they were found and dealt with by the 101st and Special Operations.

"Since we last met, soldiers from Fort Campbell have helped to organize the first truly free local election in Iraq in 30 years. Since we last met, you helped to build medical clinics and rebuild schools. By your decency and compassion, you are helping the Iraqi people to reclaim their country."

Bush's speech was a hybrid of a genuine thank you and a stump speech in what was the infancy of his reelection campaign. A speech in Wisconsin days later, called the official beginning of the Bush-Cheney '04 campaign, combined several soundbites Bush used at Fort Campbell. With an avalanche of criticism aimed at the President over the David Kay report, Bush sought to answer the lingering "WMD" questions with a soundbite he would use repeatedly over the course of the 2004 campaign. "September the 11th, 2001, taught a lesson I will never forget. America must confront threats before they fully materialize. In Iraq, my administration looked at the intelligence information and we saw a threat. The members of Congress looked at the intelligence and they saw a threat. The United Nations Security Council looked at the intelligence and it saw a threat. I had a choice to make – either take the word of a madman or take such threats seriously and defend America. Faced with that choice, I will defend America every time."

Bush finished his speech by recalling the division's history, both in World War II and in the previous twelve months. "Like your fathers and grandfathers before you, you have liberated millions from oppression. You have made us all proud to be Americans, and you have made me proud to be your commander-in-chief." Then the presidential convoy moved to the 101st Airborne Division's Pratt Museum. There he met family members of the soldiers who were lost in Iraq. No division-sized element hitherto had lost more in Iraq than the 101st Airborne. No media credentials were given out to see Bush and the families.

Captain Maggie Smith was waiting in uniform. She was one of only a handful of soldiers/widows in the 101st. It had been five months since she had lost her husband in the helicopter attack outside Tikrit. In her grief, she had not kept up to date with the day-to-day events in Iraq. She was too busy putting the pieces of her life back together.

Ben's family, or "Mom and Dad Smith" as his Maggie Smith knew them as, had become closer than ever with their daughter-in-law since Ben's death. They made the trip up from Swinky to meet the President. In three months, Maggie would be off to Fort Rucker, Ala., where she had met her husband in flight school. She would also be further away from the Smith family geographically. In a lot of ways, it would be the beginning of her new life. "I will not be the same, and I understand that we lost four dedicated aviators that horrible day in Iraq," she recalled. In Alabama, Capt. Maggie Smith would continue on with her military career, seemingly undaunted that her husband lost his life while serving in uniform. "If I didn't put my boots on each day, my life would have completely changed. Life was so very difficult at home. I needed the normalcy of work." As for what the future holds for her career, Smith is unambiguous. "I intend to lead, train, and serve our great Army for many years to come. When my time comes to turn in my gear, I may very well settle on a quiet farm, but you can rest assured that I will never regret, question, or forget the sacrifices made to secure our way of life."

It was with that conviction that Maggie Smith met the President. Each family had been assigned a portion of the room so Bush could speak to all the families individually. A bit nervous, Smith and Ben's parents, Bill and Kathy waited in chairs as the President quietly moved from family to family. When the President finished with the family before them, the Smith's stood up. Bush seemed to know exactly who they were before they introduced themselves. "Mr. President, I'm Captain Maggie Smith. My husband Ben was lost in a helicopter attack near Tikrit on the seventh of November."

"I remember that day," the President quickly replied, and there was little reason to doubt that President Bush was being sincere. The air strike that was launched in response to the attack was ordered directly from the Oval Office. Smith pointed to her right, where the families of Chief Warrant Officer Kyran Kennedy, Staff Sgt. Scott Rose and Staff Sgt. Paul Neff were waiting.

"Those are the families of the other crewmembers who were lost that day." Bush gestured to each but made certain he would not be hurried with the Smiths. The Smith's never felt hurried with the President either. For several minutes, the President and the family talked about everything from the war to fishing to the Smith family farm in Swinky, Mo. Maggie Smith was so at ease with the commander-in-chief, she completely forgot to ask him about Saddam's secret location.

Before the President moved on to the next family, the Smith's made one point clear: Ben was proud to serve. Maggie Smith was and remained a supporter of the President and did not question his decision to invade Iraq, a decision that would lead to Ben's fatal mission. "I am certain that we took out three enormous WMDs – Saddam, Uday and Qusay. There is no looking back. Yes, I want nothing more than Ben at my side, but this cannot be fixed and I will not perceive our actions as pointless or avoidable. We serve with faith in our leadership, pride in our country, and hope for enduring freedom. Ben died with faith in God, love of us all and freedom of choice. This I am sure of."

Maggie Smith was a sure vote for the President in 2004, Jack Jenkins was not. It had been eleven months since he lost his son, Sgt. Troy Jenkins, in the streets of Baghdad. He was invited, along with his live-in partner and Troy's surrogate mother Fran, to meet President Bush, but declined. They called Becky Weiss – the woman they had come to know as the daughter they likely would have had if Troy had lived to return to the United States – but she too had no interest in meeting President Bush. "Are you going to bail me out of jail if I do go?" Weiss asked the Jenkins.

Neither the Jenkins nor Becky Weiss could understand why Troy went to Iraq, or why America waged a war that would eventually claim his life. "We didn't agree with the war before Troy went, we didn't agree with the war when he died and we still don't agree with it now," Fran said. "We try to be impartial, but when you lose a child, the objectivity goes out the window."

Jack Jenkins, himself a veteran, is not as vocal as Fran, but no less skeptical of the war his son died in. "Every time you see the news, you wonder how many are going to get killed over there." They are not political people and have never taken part in an anti-war demonstration, but when asked, the Jenkins will share their feelings with anyone. Nearly a year after Sgt. Jenkins' death, his family had never been told any specifics on how he died. They knew only that their son had died in an unexploded ordnance disaster. They had no idea that Jenkins died in an attempt to save a group of young Iraqi girls. That changed when they sat down for dinner with Sgt. First Class Pete Johanningsmeier. "Sergeant Jo" came with a band around his wrist in remembrance of his friend's life – a band he vowed to wear with him the rest of his life – and an American flag folded under his arm. He handed the Colors to Jack and tucked inside the Flag were Troy Jenkins' dog tags.

In June, Troy's unit, the 3-187th Infantry Regiment, held a ceremony at Fort Campbell to give thanks. A news crew from NBC *Nightly News* was there to profile the camera shy Jenkins family. Someone with an organization called "Scroll Saw Portraits" saw the news report, painted a portrait of Sgt. Jenkins in his Marine uniform and mailed it to the Jenkins' doorstep in Louisiana – no cost, no need for a thank you. Gradually the reserved Jack Jenkins was opening up to Fran. Finally, one day didn't always seem worse than the previous day! Part of the reason was Becky Weiss.

The three had become a family since Troy Jenkins came home with and American flag over his casket. They talked almost weekly following Jenkins' death. Becky filled the void for the Jenkins family not only left by their son, but by their former daughter-in-law. Amanda Jenkins had never found a home in the Jenkins family, especially after Troy came home from Afghanistan to the news that she had been unfaithful. They had married young, too young maybe, and Amanda Jenkins saw an opportunity when her husband went to war to live the life she never had as a young mother. Still she went to the funeral in California, dressed in a pair of jeans and a voluptuous "Britney Spears shirt," as Fran remembered. When Fran asked her why she was dressed so casually at her husband's funeral, she responded, "because that's what Troy would have wanted me to wear." The next day, according to the Jenkins family, Amanda was seen on a date with her new boyfriend.

It was the last time Fran or Jack has seen or spoken to Amanda. The funeral was also one of the last times they have seen or spoken to their grandchildren. Shortly after seeing the kids in June for the memorial ceremony at Fort Campbell (which Amanda did not attend), Amanda changed all of her phone numbers, closed all contact with the Jenkins family, and forbade her children from ever speaking or seeing Troy Jenkins parents. Jack and Fran have made several trips to California to try to see the boys since, all with no success.

Major Gen. David Petraeus was told in April that his tour with the 101st Airborne was coming to an end. His successor would be Maj. Gen. Thomas R. Turner, the commander of the U.S. Southern European Command and a West Point classmate of Petraeus. It did not take an insider to predict a promotion for the 101st commander, and it was only logical that his next job would not be at a desk somewhere in the Pentagon.

He had orchestrated what every observer saw as the most successful effort to win the hearts and minds of the Iraqi people. He was perhaps one of the coalition's most valuable resources – a general with proven success in combat and with the inherent instincts to strike an appropriate balance between the force and a firm handshake. He had obviously done his homework coming into Iraq. Petraeus didn't gloat when Bremer reworked the de-Ba'athification policy in April to fit what he had been recommending from the beginning, but it did provide him with some vindication. To fire everyone from level four and above gave them no incentive to help the new Iraq succeed – Bremer, as Petraeus exited Stage Left, finally acknowledged.

Arguably no other division level commander in Iraq handled the sensitivities of the Iraq mission and use of force to suppress the insurgency better than Petraeus. U.S. Central Command commander Gen. John Abizaid thought so. When, in mid-April, after the situation throughout Iraq had boiled over and Iraqi Security Forces began to crumble in much of the country, Abizaid asked Petraeus to bring a team back to Iraq and to see what lessons could be learned from what had transpired. Petraeus, who at the time had just arrived in Washington for a required general officer seminar, headed back to Fort Campbell immediately, gathered a team of ten 101st members and headed back to Iraq for three weeks of traveling around the country to review the situation. In early May, they briefed General Abizaid in Baghdad and headed back to Fort Campbell.

Abizaid was impressed, so much so that he requested Petraeus by name to lead the training of the new Iraqi security forces. Major Gen. Petraeus was to become Lt. Gen. Petraeus and report to Baghdad shortly after he turned over command of the 101st to Turner.

Petraeus was called to Washington in April to meet with Bush, Secretary of Defense Donald Rumsfeld, and Abizaid, with the cameras focused right at the commander-in-chief. The meeting was focused primarily on the ongoing prisoner abuse scandal that had owned the headlines for much of the spring. It also served as mechanism for Bush to show his support for Rumsfeld, who was facing calls for his resignation from the left and some on the right. Images of Iraqi prisoners being sexually abused and humiliated had been revealed by journalist Seymour Hirsch of the *New Yorker* magazine and aired on CBS's *60 Minutes II*. In a war that was being waged politically as much as it was militarily, the images of abuse at the Abu Ghraib prison were as damaging to the coalition's cause as any insurgent attack to date. Petraeus, appearing on CNN's *Wolf Blitzer Reports*, compared the images to a "punch in the gut."

But Petraeus was not in Washington to talk about the ongoing scandal. He was there to get his instructions and head on back to Iraq. When he and his wife Holly had speculated where their family would go after the end of their tour at Fort Campbell, Petraeus had quipped, "What's the worst they could do, send me back to Iraq?" Sure enough, Holly would have to soldier on without her husband once again; the Petraeus family was provided a home at Fort Belvoir, Va., during the former Eagle 6's second Iraq tour.

To that point, more than 800 U.S. troops had been lost in Iraq since May 1, 2003 (more than 4,600 had been wounded). "Iraqification" was limping along at a pace that left little hope for an early exit out for the Americans. Throughout Iraq, recruiting goals were not being met and training those who did enlist was insufficient. During one ignominious episode, the country's single Iraqi regular army battalion ordered into combat in Fallujah refused to even get on the helicopter. The end result was an Iraqi fighting force that could not stand up to the insurgents. Until they did, it would be the American-led coalition fighting the enemy for them.

The enemy was a loose coalition of Jihadists and Ba'ath Party loyalists, sworn rivals during the Saddam era, together with thousands of criminals released from jail by Saddam in the months before liberation. The Jihadists were likely a rag-tag bunch, united only by a common hatred of the American-led coalition. Muqtada al-Sadr, the young cleric who had been rising to power when Lt. Col. Kim Orlando and his 716th Military Police Battalion met his militia in Karbala, had become one of Iraq's most vocal anti-coalition leaders. Al-Sadr's movement and his ability to hold thousands of armed insurgents at his command had quickly become the coalition's fiercest threat around the Sunni Triangle. He had become so powerful that the coalition authorities sometimes appeared more concerned with appeasing al-Sadr than destroying his militia.

Nobody dared to suggest that the coalition should take a similar approach to Abu Massab al-Zarqawi. If an attack against the coalition had all the terror fingerprints of Osama bin Laden and Al-Qaeda – like the bombing of the U.N. Headquarters in Baghdad in August of 2003 – common thinking led all focus on al-Zarqawi and his coalition of terrorist groups: Unity and Holy War Movement and Ansar al-Islam. Al-Zarqawi was the most dangerous and most wanted man in Iraq – perhaps the most powerful Al-Qaeda operative in both the Afghanistan and Iraq wars. It was clear as the war in Iraq entered its second year that he, and nobody else, was at the top of the Al-Qaeda chain of command in the Iraq theater.

The division's change of command ceremony was May 14. Lt. Gen. John Vines, the 18th Airborne Corps commanding general, stood facing the parade field with Petraeus to his right and Turner to his left. Command Sgt. Maj. Marvin Hill stood in front of a formation of the entire division – as well as elements of the 5th Special Forces Group and the 160th Special Operations Aviation Regiment – a formation of roughly 15,000 soldiers, with division helicopters behind them. In the sergeant major's hands were the 101st Airborne Division colors with a large number of streamers hanging from the top, symbolizing the many battles in which the division had fought since its activation. By custom, Hill was the custodian of the division colors.

With the cameras trained on those four, Hill passed the colors to Petraeus, who in turn passed them to Vines, who then handed them – and command of the 101st Airborne Division – to Maj. Gen. Thomas Turner. After returning to the reviewing stand and listening to remarks by Lt. Gen. Vines, Petraeus took the podium. "The soldiers of the 101st and the other units on this field have done a lot over the past two years," he observed. "Proud new chapters have been added to the histories of the Screaming Eagles.

"It has been the privilege of a lifetime to have soldiered with the great troopers on the field before us. They have been extraordinary."

Petraeus, the 40th commander in the Division's history – and the 8th to command the division in combat – was handing off the division command to a man with whom he seemed to share little in common, although they were West Point classmates and had been good friends for years. Turner was a child of the 82nd Airborne Division and had never before served in the 101st before commanding it. He was not as academically accomplished as his predecessor. Turner did not care about public relations – in fact, he seemed to loathe the idea of standing in front of the media. Simply put, for a division that was defined by Petraeus and he by the division, Maj. Gen. Turner was every bit the anomaly that Petraeus was when he took command two years earlier.

"General Turner," Petraeus told the division, "is a great leader, a great trainer, and a great soldier. He'll be an awesome 'Eagle 6,' and I have absolute confidence that the Screaming Eagles will soar to even higher levels during his time at the helm."

Turner's orders on taking the podium were very clear: get the division trained and ready for deployment. It was no secret that his tour with the 101st would not end before most, if not all, of the division deployed back right to Iraq.

On May 17, the U.S. Senate approved President Bush's nomination of Petraeus to lead the security transition effort in Iraq and his promotion. Command Sgt. Maj. Hill and Mrs. Petraeus had the honor of pinning the three-star rank on his shoulders. In June, with a new U.S. Central Command unit patch on his left arm but the same "Screaming Eagle" combat patch on his right, Petraeus arrived for duty. His name became instantly synonymous with "exit strategy." Indeed, it was Petraeus' mission to recruit and train the Iraqi Army, Special Forces, National Guard (formerly called the Iraqi Civil Defense Corps), and the Iraqi police so that they, not the Americans, could eventually fight the insurgency in the streets of Iraq's hottest hot spots. If Petraeus wasn't already a household name by July of 2004, Newsweek magazine fixed that.

The former 101st commander, standing with his hands clasped together at his waist, grazed the cover of one of America's most popular weekly newsmagazine. "Can This Man Save Iraq?: Warrior-Scholar Lt. Gen. David Petraeus is Training Iraqis to Fight for Themselves. Inside Mission Impossible." It was an in-depth introduction for Petraeus, fulsome with observations from admirers, but also reporting comments from some detractors. Writer Rob Nordland had uncovered an apparently envious colleague who anonymously called him a "perfumed prince" and others who criticized his affinity for anyone carrying a notepad and a camera.

But through the envy, there was no denying his skill as a soldier and a statesman. Newsweek certainly didn't. Of his actions with the 101st during his tour as a two-star, Norland wrote, "virtually everyone agrees his command there (in Mosul) was a textbook case of doing counterinsurgency the right way."

In his new mission, Petraeus' aim was to build the new Iraqi Army with dependable officers first, then work his way down. He wanted quality soldiers, not just a large quantity, and he wanted them equipped. He was told that he could get whatever he wanted from the Pentagon, no questions asked.

The former division commander did not leave a finished project, that was certain. Mosul went from perhaps the safest major city in Iraq for coalition troops in May of 2003 to one of Iraq's most violent areas in little over a year. Few could argue that point after just a week before the article on Petraeus was published, sixty-two Mosul citizens were killed by suicide bombers and small arms fire in a coordinated attempt to kill as many people in the city as possible. Up to the point the division redeployed, the 101st had lost more soldiers than any other combat division in the Iraq theater. As with the rest of the country, Mosul was a more dangerous city in March of 2004 than it was in March of 2003, when the Iraq war began. The Commanders' Emergency Relief Program spent a great deal of money only to see many of its projects come under constant attack by terrorists and armed insurgents.

But what Petraeus and the 101st left was a base of support for the coalition. Just weeks after the final 101st troops left Mosul, the city and Governor Ghanim al-Basso made certain the legacy of the Screaming Eagles remained. If the rebuilt schools and health clinics, the new police force and firefighters, the new standards of law and justice, the general increase in the standard of living among the people of Mosul – if all of the symbols of the 101st's work in the area did not leave a defining stamp on the city, a final gift from the city to the division certainly would. The street that passed right in front of the D-Main Palace, one of Mosul's busiest highways, was renamed "101st Airborne Division Highway" – complete with several misspellings.

"What have you done to win the hearts and minds of the Iraqi people today?" That was the question Petraeus asked of his soldiers every day in Iraq and, presumably, of himself every night before he went to sleep. And what had Dave Petraeus done to win the hearts and minds of the Iraq people? It's a question that he answered everyday for a year in Iraq. He woke up for twenty-one days in March and April commanding one of the three U.S. divisions that overthrew a dictator of twenty-five million people. For ten months, he woke up with the mission of spending 56 million American dollars to rebuild a Northern Iraq infrastructure that scantly resembled a civilized society while simultaneously leading a war against an armed insurgency. His tour in combat was more than just a rendezvous with destiny. It was a constant test of his command philosophy, one which history will grade when the outcome of the war is decided.

EPILOGUE

In August of 2005, the first soldiers from the 101st Airborne Division landed in Iraq for the division's second year-long tour in three years. Under the Army's new "modular" formations, the 101st would be scattered around the entire country, from Mosul to the Al Anbar Province, with elements from the 4th Infantry Division supplementing the 101st. With the new formations, commanders would get the best of both worlds, with the ability to strike an enemy position with both the 101st's helicopters and the 4th Infantry's tanks at a moment's notice. Some 4th Infantry units would answer to the 101st division commander, Maj. Gen. Thomas Turner, as some 101st units would answer to the 4th Infantry commander. The idea was championed by Army Chief of Staff Gen. Peter Schoomaker, and it would change the face of the American military on the Iraq battlefield. The enemy too had evolved as the 101st returned to Iraq.

The weapon of choice had become the Improvised Explosive Device, or IED. In 2003, the division lost five soldiers to IED attacks. In the first five months of the division's second tour, thirty soldiers had lost their lives to roadside bombs. The militants fighting the insurgency have also changed in two years. In 2003, the enemy was predominately a ragtag bunch of Ba'ath Party militia loyal to Saddam Hussein. With Hussein in prison standing trial for crimes against humanity, the former Iraqi dictator is no longer a rallying point for the insurgent campaign. In his place is the Jordanian-born Abu Masab al-Zarqawi, a close ally of Osama bin Laden and leader of Al Qaeda's network in Iraq. While questions of Zarqawi's credibility among the insurgents have been raised, his campaign unquestionably has found increasing support among Iraqis frustrated with the U.S.-led occupation.

Zarqawi's war has not just limited itself to American targets, but against the Iraqi government and against Shia Muslims as well, sparking a civil war that threatens to turn Iraqis cities into battlefields long after the last American troops has left the country. Every Iraqi acting in support of the new Iraqi government has become a target. Police officers take to the streets with masks to hide their identity in fear that their families could be slaughtered when they return home from work.

In the beginning, it was a war to disarm Saddam Hussein of WMD, deny the Al Qaeda of its sponsors within the Iraqi regime, and spread democracy across the Muslim-dominated Middle East. Now, with theories of WMD and high-level Iraqi sponsorship of the Al Qaeda and the September 11 terror attacks long since disproved, the fate of the final argument in favor of war – to build a durable democracy in the Muslim world – lies with the American military and their successors in Iraq. As the war enters its fourth year, the battle has become an exercise of tactical patience for American commanders and their battle-hardened troops.

Sometime in 2004, the Pentagon was forced to deal with the reality that the insurgency's foundation reached far beyond a small band of outlaws and terrorists. Enter Gen. George W. Casey – the former Army vice chief of staff who was succeeded in that position by former 101st commander Gen. Dick Cody – who took command in Iraq in the summer of 2004 from Lt. Gen. Ricardo Sanchez and refocused the anti-insurgent campaign. The goal of winning Iraqi hearts and minds became secondary to establishing Iraqi enfranchisement. Casey instructed his commanders to begin operations aimed at defeating the threat aimed at Iraqi voters, who were to take to the polls on January 30, 2005, to elect a 275-member assembly who would write Iraq's post-Saddam constitution. The election was widely expected to be a bloodbath, with soldiers and voters alike coming under a barrage of attacks at the polls. But under the threat of execution, Iraqis went to the polls well beyond the rate of America's 2004 presidential election. Casey's plan had worked. While the Sunni-dominated territory largely boycotted the election, the overwhelming turnout in the Kurdish and Shi'ia territories forced the hand of Sunni leaders against the American occupation. They too needed to participate in the Iraqi democracy and would in the next round of elections.

Election Day was a success, but hardly the V-I Day the American public had clamored for since the insurgency launched in May of 2003. It is hard to predict a moment where an American convoy can traverse through Iraq's Al Anbar province without the threat of ambush, but the war has nonetheless entered its final stage. As the Iraqi government takes shape and the Iraqi internal security forces – the police, Army, and National Guard – begin assuming control from the American forces, the fuel that flames the insurgency will begin to run dry, American commanders hope. Now the Iraqi security forces must wrestle the country from insurgents or three-year democratization effort will fail.

To prepare for the handover and for the possible fight ahead, Major Gen. Turner's Task Force Band of Brothers – a name harkening on the HBO mini-series on the 101st Airborne Division in World War II – has embedded Military Transition Teams, or MITTs, with the mission of training Iraqi units in the field until they are ready for battle. It's a gradual process – no Iraqi element is thrown into a firefight alone until they have first fought under the supervision of their American trainers.

After returning home from his second Iraq tour, Lt. Gen. David Petraeus was assigned to command the Command and General Staff College at Fort Leavenworth, Kan. He would go from being the Iraq war's "out strategy guy" to being the "lessons learned guy." It was an obvious assignment for the battle tested general and as of June, 2006, he remains at the college and, much to his wife's approval, has no current orders to move to back to Iraq for a third tour.

Petraeus' focus now is to retrain an Army to meet the challenges it has faced for the last three years. On Petraeus' command, the National Training Center at Fort Irwin, Calif., has refocused field-training exercises on the complexities of the Iraq battlefield. He is rewriting training doctrine to focus more on intelligence, urban warfare, roadside IEDs and the battle to gain community support within an area of operation. In short, he is training the Army to perform as his division did in Mosul.

"This is politically driven," Petraeus said of the insurgency and the approach to defeating it. "That's what people just don't understand."

American withdrawal – the unquestioned aim of the American public and both the Bush Pentagon and their political adversaries – will come only when the Iraqi civil authorities are ready to fight. Victory will come not by the barrel of an M16, but with the establishment of a stable Iraqi government, even as the insurgency continues to rage.

In April of 2005, Becky Weiss earned her Master's degree in Social Work and continued with her life's work: helping kids like a teenage boy who was referred to Weiss after he lost a brother in a car accident. She had treated some tough clients before, but this young man was especially obstinate. Several sessions with the boy failed to get him to share his feelings with Weiss. Then he said something that would change not only him, but her, "You don't know what it's like to lose someone close to you."

In the two years since Sgt. Troy Jenkins was killed in Baghdad, a lot had changed. The man Becky Weiss had dated for five years, Curtis White, was back in her life. They were to be married in September. It took a lot of work, but Becky needed to move on from Troy, and Curtis was willing to look past the period of time when his fiancé loved another man. For Jack Jenkins and his partner Fran, Becky's engagement was difficult to accept. It could have been her and Troy, after all. That day in Iraq took a son and maybe a future daughter-in-law out of their lives. But while she would never be family, Becky would always be a Jenkins family friend. Jack and Fran speak with her several times a month. When Becky called to tell Jack and Fran that she was engaged, Fran responded like a concerned mother. "Is he the one? Do you love him?"

He was and she did. Fran and Jack gave the couple their blessing.

To Becky, Troy Jenkins was a blessing, giving her perspective. "People just pop into your life for a reason. I don't know why he died, but I'm a much stronger person because of him … I just think God works in those ways."

With that newfound strength, she swiftly retorted the young man's accusation. "Yes, I do know what it's like to lose someone close." And then, she told him about Sgt. Troy Jenkins, the man who died because he considered the lives of several small children more important than his own. It was the first time she talked openly about Jenkins. "Trauma will change a person one way or another," she told the boy. For Becky, the experience of losing a loved one was enabling. "I've grown so much because of Troy." Now Mrs. Rebecca White, she continues her career on the weekdays, "does yard work and lives a pretty boring life" on the weekends, but remains close with Jack and Fran.

After his return from Iraq, Sgt. First Class Hector Jusino followed through with his plan. In 2004, he officially received his retirement papers. His career changed; home did not. Every Sunday, he can be seen at Catholic Mass at Fort Campbell's Soldiers Chapel watching his wife sing in the choir. The Jusino family remains in Clarksville and doesn't plan to move.

Colonel Joe Anderson will not be Colonel Joe Anderson for long. When the April 2006 list of promotable colonels was released, his name was on it. So too was Col. Michael Linnington. Both will become brigadier generals sometime later in 2006 or early in 2007. For Anderson, a return to Iraq is likely. After a tour as an aide to Secretary of the Army Francis Harvey, he is now off to Fort Hood, Texas.

Captain Maggie Smith remains at Fort Rucker, where she met her future husband, commanding the Thaddeus S.C. Lowe Army Heliport. Three years after her husband's death over Tikrit, she continues to retain her married name and remains in close contact with Ben Smith's family. "Recently Ben's sister had a baby boy she named Ben. I'm proud to say that I am his Godmother," she reports.

Lieutenant Col. Christopher Hughes completed his work at the U.S. Army War College in Carlisle, Pa., and returned to Washington, working for the Army's operations office. He has a new title as well: Col. Christopher Hughes. This summer he took command of Joint Task Force-Bravo, a U.S. Southern Command operation based in Honduras. In the event of a natural disaster in Central America, Hughes' JTF-Bravo will likely be the first to be called into action. His wife Marguerite and youngest son will stay in Washington while Hughes is deployed – likely for a year – as his daughter returns to Boston University for her junior year and his oldest son starts at Northwest Missouri State University ("My old school," Hughes said with pride).

For many 101st soldiers, the return to Iraq also meant a return to Mosul. What they saw was much different city than the one they left in the winter of 2004, no doubt. The bond that was formed between the 101st and the people of Mosul was shattered in their absence. The peace that began to crumble in the fall of 2003 completely fell apart when the insurgency blitzed Mosul in full force shortly after the 101st redeployed.

Nineveh Governor Ghanim al-Basso, without his mentor, resigned months after the last 101st soldier left Iraq. In his place came Usama Kashmula, but he would only be in power for a very short time. On July 14, 2004, Kashmula's convoy traveling back home from Baghdad was ambushed with grenades and small arms fire. The governor and two men traveling with him were killed.

Kashmula's assassination would mark the beginning of many bloody months ahead in the streets of Mosul, for the citizens walking them and the soldiers patrolling them. The nadir came on December 22, the single bloodiest attack in Mosul of the Iraq war to date. At a camp used by the 2-44th Air Defense Artillery

Regiment across the street from the Mosul Airfield, a suicide bomber killed
fourteen U.S. soldiers, four U.S. civilian contractors, and three Iraqi soldiers sitting
down to eat their lunch.

But for the returning soldiers returning to Mosul, a city the division patrolled
from April of 2003 to February of 2004, the toughest heartbreak was reserved for
them. The city they held together for nearly a year had largely fallen apart in their
absence. The police force they built – a force that had initially performed well
after the 101st left Mosul to Brig. Gen. Carter Ham and his Stryker Brigade troops
– slowly collapsed in 2004 under an intense insurgent campaign to undo what the
101st and Petraeus had spent much of 2003 doing.

"Mosul's security forces weathered the outbreak of violence in Iraq better
than anyone else in the country except Basra, but it was already clear that the
insurgents were intent on using Mosul as a command point," Petraeus said. With
insurgent roots growing deeper into Mosul in the summer of 2004, Iraqi security
forces became increasingly intimidated. The intelligence that 101st officers had
depended on Iraqi police officers to relay from the field suddenly went silent.

In November of 2004, with Ham forced to detach a battalion of his already
stretched force to prepare for the battle to retake Fallujah, the police force the
101st built from the ground-up came crashing back down. Without a follow-on
force available to support the police force, the insurgent campaign to destroy the
Mosul police force did just that, destroying most of the city's police stations,
including the Mosul Police Academy and the main police station Anderson and
Brig. Gen. Frank Helmick opened eleven months earlier. Police Chief Mohammed
Barhowie ceded the city after all but about 800 of his policemen melted away
during the insurgent blitz.

Ham reconstructed the force before rotating back to the States, without the
police officers who fled the scene. The academy was rebuilt, as were the police
stations.

A similar story unfolded in Tal Afar, where insurgents had spent much of the
post-Petraeus era establishing enclaves in the city. Like Fallujah, Tal Afar also
needed to be repossessed from insurgent hands during raids in June and September
of 2005. Unlike Fallujah, the enemy the 3rd AD patrols found was predominately
foreign, Syrian. "There is certainly a sense that they could be doing more," Petraeus
said of Syrian government and their inability to stop the flow of insurgents from
their side of the border.

But through the struggles of 2004 and 2005 has come a largely quite 2006 in Nineveh. While daily bloodshed from Iraq dominates the American news, the violence has largely been kept out of the area the 101st patrolled three years ago. For a country with limitless economic potential – nearly $500 million in potential oil revenue, according to Petraeus – the advances of the Iraqi government could reverberate across the globe for generations. So too could fall of the Iraqi government to radical Islam. The former 101st commander is an optimist, but a realist. "Imagine if people weren't blowing themselves up everyday in Iraq."

It has been painful process, but the goal of Iraqification continues to move forward. On May 20, 2006, thirty-seven of forty members of new Prime Minister Nouri al-Maliki were sworn in, establishing an Iraqi government that united ministry chiefs from all three of Iraq's major sects. It was an accomplishment that American troops had sacrificed for with their lives, but one that the Bush Administration will foretell a future abatement in violence. Prime Minister Tony Blair, appearing in Baghdad days after the government was inaugurated, spoke to the people of Iraq in unusually blunt terms. "There is now no vestige of excuse for anyone to carry on with terrorism or bloodshed."

SOURCES

Interviews

Lt. Col. Curtis Craft, 431st Civil Affairs Battalion. Interview by Thomas L. Day. December 6, 2003. Civilian-Military Operations Center, Mosul, Iraq.

Lt. Col. Richard Ott, 926th Engineering Group commander. Interview by Thomas L. Day. December 6, 2003. Civilian Military Operations Center, Mosul, Iraq.

Lt. Col. Friedbert Humphrey, 431st Civil Affairs Battalion commander. Interview by Thomas L. Day. December 8, 2003. Civilian Military Operations Center, Mosul, Iraq.

Lt. Col. Richard Whitaker, 101st Airborne Division Staff Judge Advocate. Interview by Thomas L. Day. December 8, 2003. 101st Airborne Division Main Compound, Mosul, Iraq.

Phil Schreier, December 7, 2003, personal email.

Cpl. Nick Degreek, 101st Airborne Division. Interview by Thomas L. Day. December 9, 2003. 101st Airborne Division Main Compound, Mosul, Iraq.

Chap. (Lt. Col.) Chester C. Egert, 101st Airborne Division, Division Chaplin. Interview by Thomas L. Day. December 10, 2003. 101st Airborne Division Main Compound, Mosul, Iraq.

Capt. Wade Reeves, 431st Civil Affairs Detachment. Interview by Thomas L. Day. December 11, 2003. Civilian Military Operations Center, Mosul, Iraq.

Capt. John Gerald, 431st Civil Affairs Detachment. Interview by Thomas L. Day. December 11, 2003. Civilian Military Operations Center, Mosul, Iraq.

Secretary of Defense Donald Rumsfeld. Interview by Lesley Stahl for CBS's 60 Minutes. December 14, 2003. Washington, D.C.

Staff Sgt. William Staunaker, 101st Airborne Division Psychological Operations. Interview by Thomas L. Day. December 15, 2003. Quyarrah Airfield, Quyarrah, Iraq.

Capt. Richard Morgan, 2-327th Infantry Regiment, 101st Airborne Division. Interview by Thomas L. Day. December 16, 2003. Quyarrah Airfield, Quyarrah, Iraq.

Capt. Kellie Rourke, 101st Aviation Regiment. Interview by Thomas L. Day. December 17, 2003. Quyarrah Airfield, Quyarrah, Iraq.

Lt. Col. Donald Fryc, 2-44th Air Defense Artillery Regiment commander, 101st Airborne Division. Interview by Thomas L. Day. December 23, 2003. Camp Claiborne, Mosul, Iraq.

Capt. Michael Troxell, Headquarters and Headquarters Company commander, 159th Aviation Regiment. Interview by Thomas L. Day. January 2, 2004. Mosul Airfield, Mosul, Iraq.

Capt. Lester Centurion, 101st Airborne Division, Division Artillery (DIVARTY). Interview by Thomas L. Day. January 15, 2004. Camp Doha, Kuwait.

Capt. Monica Strye, 2-17th Cavalry Regiment. Interview by Thomas L. Day. January 16, 2004. Camp Doha, Kuwait.

Capt. Gary Lyke, 2-17th Cavalry Regiment. Interview by Thomas L. Day. January 17, 2004. Camp Doha, Kuwait.

Sgt. First Class Hector Jusino, 801st Main Support Group. Interview by Thomas L. Day. April 2, 2004. Clarksville, Tenn.

Mrs. Christina Jusino. Interview by Thomas L. Day. April 2, 2004. Clarksville, Tenn.

Sgt. First Class Pete Johanningsmeier, 3-187th Infantry Regiment. Interview by Thomas L. Day. April 5, 2004. Fort Campbell, Ky.

Ms. Rebecca Weiss. Interview by Thomas L. Day. Clarksville, Tenn. April 9, 2004.

Lt. Col. Christopher Hughes, 2-327th Infantry Regiment former commander. Interview by Thomas L. Day. April 21, 2004. Pentagon City, Va.

Spc. Pete Tenorio, 3-187th Infantry Regiment. Interview by Thomas L. Day. April 28, 2004. Fort Campbell, Ky.

Capt. Margaret Smith, 9-101st Aviation Regiment. Interview by Thomas L. Day (with supporting documents provided). May 3, 2004. Fort Campbell, Ky.

Maj. Gen. David H. Petraeus, 101st Airborne Division commanding general. Interview by Thomas L. Day. May 11, 2004. Fort Campbell, Ky.

Lt. Col. Laura Richardson, 5-101st Aviation Regiment commander. May 21, 2004. Fort Campbell, Ky.

Col. Michael Linnington, 187th Infantry Regiment commander. Interview by Thomas L. Day. May 24, 2004. Fort Campbell, Ky.

Col. James Laufenberg, 101st Airborne Division chief of staff. Interview by Thomas L. Day. May 24, 2004. Fort Campbell, Ky.

Maj. Dennis Smith, 187th Infantry Regiment. Interview by Thomas L. Day (phone interview). June 1, 2004. Fort Campbell, Ky.

Col. Joseph Anderson, 502nd Infantry Regiment commander. Interview by Thomas L. Day. June 3, 2004. Fort Campbell, Ky.

Col. Fredrick B. Hodges, 327th Infantry Regiment commander. Interview by Thomas L. Day. June 21, 2004. Fort Campbell, Ky.

Sgt. First Class Dennis Foley, 2-44th Air Defense Artillery. Interview by Thomas L. Day. June 22, 2004. Fort Campbell, Ky.

Col. Gregory Gass, 101st Aviation Regiment commander. Interview by Thomas L. Day. June 28, 2004. Fort Campbell, Ky.

Capt. Leo Barren, 327th Infantry Regiment. Interview by Thomas L. Day. July 12, 2004. Fort Campbell, Ky.

Sgt. First Class Joe Montoya, 187th Infantry Regiment. Interview by Thomas L. Day. July 13, 2004. Fort Campbell, Ky.

Capt. Marc Cloutier, 187th Infantry Regiment. Interview by Thomas L. Day. July 15, 2004. Fort Campbell, Ky.

Maj. Susan Arnold, 101st Airborne Division Office of the Staff Judge Advocate. Interview conducted by Thomas L. Day. Interview conducted on July 20, 2004.

Capt. Julie Simoni, 101st Airborne Division Office of the Staff Judge Advocate. Interview by Thomas L. Day. July 20, 2004. Fort Campbell, Ky.

Mr. Ted Sorensen, special council to Pres. John F. Kennedy. Interview by Thomas L. Day (phone interview). July 21, 2004. Fort Campbell, Ky.

Pfc. Alexis Jacquez, 2-502nd Infantry Regiment. Interview by Thomas L. Day. July 21, 2004. Fort Campbell, Ky.

Staff Sgt. Jeffery Stout, 2-502nd Infantry Regiment. Interview by Thomas L. Day. July 21, 2004. Fort Campbell, Ky.

Capt. Jon Boyer, 101st Office of the Staff Judge Advocate. Interview by Thomas L. Day. August 3, 2004. Fort Campbell, Ky.

Spec. Ryan Deckerd, 101st Office of the Staff Judge Advocate. Interview by Thomas L. Day. August 3, 2004. Fort Campbell, Ky.

Mrs. Pam Hayry. Interview by Thomas L. Day. August 12, 2004. Fort Campbell, Ky.

Capt. Mathew Konz, Air Assault School commander. Interview by Thomas L. Day. September 17, 2004. Fort Campbell, Ky.

Lt. Col. Christopher Pease, 2-187th Infantry Regiment commander. Interview by Thomas L. Day. September 28, 2004. Fort Campbell, Ky.

Phil Fulmer, head coach, University of Tennessee Football. Interview by Thomas L. Day. October 6, 2004. Fort Campbell, Ky.

Capt. Jamie Phillips, 502nd Infantry Regiment Staff Judge Advocate. Interview by Thomas L. Day. October 6, 2004. Fort Campbell, Ky.

First Sgt. Patrick Keough, Delta Company, 2-187 Infantry Regiment. Interview by Thomas L. Day. October 7, 2004. Fort Campbell, Ky.

Lt. Col. Darryl Reyes, 101st Airborne Division G-2. Interview by Thomas L. Day (email interview). October 7, 2004. Fort Campbell, Ky.

Lt. Gen. David H. Petraeus. Interview by Thomas L. Day. October 2, 2005. Fort Belvoir, Va.

Brig. Gen. Frank Helmick. Interview by Thomas L. Day. October 31, 2005. Arlington, Va. (The Pentagon).

Lt. Gen. David H. Petraeus. Interview by Thomas L. Day. December 22, 2005. Fort Leavenworth, Kan.

Sources

Jim Dwyer. Interview by Thomas L. Day. January 9, 2006. New York, New York.

Maj. Joseph Kuchan. "An Najaf." January 9, 2006. (Personal Email)

Capt. Maggie Smith. "Re: My Book." May 15, 2006. (Personal Email)

Rebecca Weiss. Interview by Thomas L. Day. May 17, 2006. (Personal Email)

Col. Christopher Hughes. "Re: Along the Tigris" May 21, 2006. (Personal Email)

Articles

Dwyer, Jim. 2003. A Ferocious Competitor Pushes His Soldiers, and Himself, Hard. *The New York Times,* 18 March, national edition.

Amanpour, Christiane, Jane Arraf, Ryan Chilcote, Bob Franken, Art Harris, Tom Mintier, Karl Penhaul, Nic Robertson, Walter Rodgers, Brent Sadler, Ben Wedeman, Barbara Starr, and Mike Mount. "Ground troops clash over Baghdad airport." CNN.com, April 4, 2003. <http://www.cnn.com/2003/WORLD/meast/04/03/sprj.irq.war.main/>

Dreazen, Yochi J. 2003. Army Orders Troops to Seize TV Station in Northwest Iraq: A Major Balks at Directive and Gets Relieved of Duty. *The Wall Street Journal,* 8 May, national edition.

Reeve, William., "Afghanistan's turbulent history." BBCNews. Sept. 28, 2001. <news.bbc.co.uk/1/hi/world/south_asia/1569826.stm>

Priest, Dana., Booth, William, and Schmidt, Susan. 2003. A Broken Body, a Broken Story, Pieced Together. *The Washington Post,* 17 June, national edition.

Gibbs, Nancy. "An American Family Goes to War." Time Magazine, March 24, 2003.

Gibbs, Nancy. "'Ladies and Gentlemen, We Got Him." Time Magazine, December 22, 2003. Pages 15-21.

Zucchino, David. 2003. Fewer than 1,000 troops were ordered to capture a city of 5 million Iraqis. *The Los Angeles Times,* 7 December, national edition.

"U.S. officials: Attempts to rescue downed pilots failed." CNN.com. Mar. 26, 2003. <http://edition.cnn.com/2003/WORLD/meast/03/26/sprj.irq.rescue.attempt>

Rather, Dan. "60 Minutes II: The Rescue – Former POWs tell their story." CBSNews.com. Sept. 17, 2003. <http://www.cbsnews.com/stories/2003/05/14/60II/main553850.shtml>

Cuadros, P., and Sieger, Maggie. "A Role Model for Baby Brother" Time Magazine, December 29, 2003. Page 66.

Booth Thomas, Cathy. "War Ages a Roguish Son." Time Magazine, December 29, 2003. Pages 60-61.

Ripley, Amanda. "For Those Left Behind, an Anxious Kinship." Time Magazine, December, 29, 2003. Page 62-63.

Ratnesar, R. and Weisskopf, Michael. "Portrait of a Platoon: How a Dozen Soldiers – Overworked, Under Fire, Nervous, Proud – Chase Insurgents and Try to Stay Alive in One of Baghdad's Nastiest Districts." *Time* Magazine, December 29, 2003. Pages 60-81.

Gibbs, Nancy. "Person of the Year: The American Soldier." Time Magazine, December 29, 2003. Pages 32-41.

Kelly, James. "What Happened That Day on Patrol." Time Magazine, December 29, 2003. Page 8.

Thompson, Mark. "Paul Wolfowitz: The Godfather of the Iraq War." Time Magazine, December 29, 2003. Page 91.

Malone, James. "Soldier slain in Iraq laid to rest: Officer's bravery remembered at Fort Campbell." Courier-journal.com. October 25, 2003. <www.courier-journal.com/localnews/2003/10/25ky/wir-front-funeral1025-9379.html>

Thomas, Evan, and Rob Nordland. "See How They Ran: They hoarded money, and the huddled in fear. Inside the path of Saddam's sons, the raid that grounded them – and the hunt for the Ace of Spades." Newsweek, August 5, 2003. Pages 22-29.

Van Marsh, Alphonso, Satinder Bindra, Jamie McIntyre, Jane Arraf, Nic Robertson, Christine Amanpour and Dana Bash. "Rumsfeld: In the end, Saddam 'not terribly brave." CNN.com. Dec. 14, 2003. <www.cnn.com/2003/WORLD/meast/12/14/sprj.irq.main>

"Profile: Muqtada al-Sadr." aljazeera.net. April 5, 2004. <http://english.aljazeera.net/NR/exeres/815FF50A-4D63-43CB-A404-84DF9E6CDF70.htm>

Duffy, Michael. "So Much for the WMD." *Time* Magazine. February 9, 2004. Pages 43-46.

Hersh, Seymour M. "Torture at Abu Ghraib: American soldiers brutalized Iraqis. How far up does the responsibility go?" *The New Yorker*, May 10, 2004.

Nordland, Rob. "Iraq's Repairman: Mission Impossible? David Petraeus is tasked with rebuilding Iraq's security forces. An up-close look at the only real exit plan the United States has – the man himself." *Newsweek*. July 5, 2004. Vol. CXLIV, No. 1. Pages 22-30.

Gass, Gregory. "The 101st Aviation Brigade in Iraq." *Rotor and Wing*. October and November, 2003.

Books

Atkinson, Rick. 2004. *In The Company Of Soldiers*. New York: Henry Holt and Company.

Atkinson, Rick. 1989. *The Long Gray Line*. New York: Henry Holt and Company.

Woodward, Bob. 2004. *Plan of Attack*. London: Simon and Schuster.

Woodward, Bob. 2002. *Bush at War*. New York: Simon and Schuster.

Murry, W., and Robert H. Scales, Jr. 2003. *The Iraq War*. Cambridge, Mass., and London: The Belknap Press of Harvard University Press.

Giuliani, Rudolph W. 2002. *Leadership*. New York: Miramax Books.

Rapport, Leanord and Norwood, A. 1948. *Rendezvous with Destiny*. Old Saybrook, Conn.: Konecky & Konecky.

Nagl, John. 2002. *Eating Soup with a Knife*. Chicago: University of Chicago Press.

Petraeus, David Howell, Ph.D. *The American military and the lessons of Vietnam: A study of military influence and the use of force in the post-Vietnam era*. Ann Arbor, Mich: UMI Dissertation Services.

Videos

The Road to Baghdad. Produced by Lori Butterfield. 115 min. National Geographic, 2003. DVD.

Other

Pelley, Scott. (2003). War and Peace. In 60 Minutes II. New York, N.Y.: CBS.

United States. U.S. European Command. Operation Enduring Freedom – One Year of Accomplishments (Press Release). 7 October 2002

U.S. Army. *Official Report on 507th Maintenance Co.: An Nasiriyah, Iraq*. March 23, 2003.

United States. U.S. Central Command. *Operation Soda Mountain Humanitarian Projects Help Iraqis* (Press Release). 18 July 2003.

101st Airborne Division, *101st Airborne Division (AASLT) OPERATION IRAQI FREEDOM Chronology and Operational Data Report*. Capt. James A. Page. June 14, 2004.

Iraqi Destiny

Petraeus, David. 2003. Eagle 6 wishes troops happy Thanksgiving. *Iraqi Destiny*. 27 Nov.

Petraeus, David. 2003. Eagle 6 sends. *Iraqi Destiny*. 21 June.

Bennett, David. 2003. Saddam captured: Search ends in Ironhorse AO. *Iraqi Destiny*. 18 Dec.

Hutcheson, Joshua. 2003. 101st and Mosul Olympic committee develop youth soccer program. *Iraqi Destiny*. 24 Jul.

Xenikakis, Mary Rose. 2003. 'Screaming Eagle' soccer team gets a new look courtesy of 101st. *Iraqi Destiny*. 21 Aug.

Day, Thomas. 2003. Anti-corruption commission established in Mosul. *Iraqi Destiny*. 11 Dec.

Day, Thomas. 2003. Iraqi firefighters complete training in Mosul. *Iraqi Destiny*. 6 Nov.

Jones, Christopher. 2003. 101st grieves the loss of 502nd CSM, driver. *Iraqi Destiny*. 27 Nov.

Day, Thomas. 2003. Americans, Iraqis secure border. *Iraqi Destiny*. 13 Nov.

Hutcheson, Joshua. 2004. 101st helps celebrate Iraqi Army birthday. *Iraqi Destiny*. 15 Jan.

Jones, Christopher. 2003. Screaming Eagles rebuild school in Kanash. *Iraqi Destiny*. 15 Jan.

Woodward, Robert. 2003. Memorial held for three MPs in Karbala. *Iraqi Destiny*. 23 Oct.

Jones, Christopher. 2003. Fallen MP commander honored, unit colors passed. *Iraqi Destiny*. 6 Nov.

Jones, Christopher. 2003. Currency exchange kicks off for Iraqi people. *Iraqi Destiny*. 23 Oct.

Day, Thomas. 2003. 101st, Mosul banks race to meet October 15 deadline. *Iraqi Destiny*. 25 Sept.

Jones, Christopher. 2003. Troops Celebrate Christmas in Iraq. *Iraqi Destiny*. 25 Dec.

Day, Thomas. 2003. "Operation Santa Strike" swarms Mosul homeless shelter. *Iraqi Destiny*. 25 Dec.

Day, Thomas. 2003. Mosul Area Houses of Warship Receive Heaters. *Iraqi Destiny*. 25 Dec.

Day, Thomas. 2003. "Strike" Brigade remembers two fallen soldiers. *Iraqi Destiny*. 18 Dec.

Day, Thomas. 2003. Clinics open with help of Bechtel funding. *Iraqi Destiny*. 6 Nov.

Day, Thomas. 2003. 101st remembers fallen Blackhawk crew. *Iraqi Destiny*. 13 Nov.

Xenikakis, Mary Rose. 2003. Adult education center helps brighten the north. Iraqi Destiny. 6 Nov.

Xenikakis, Mary Rose. 2003. Tal Afar police academy helps put trained force back on the streets. *Iraqi Destiny*. 2 Oct.

Kent, Blake. 2003. 326th Engineers pay tribute to slain officer. *Iraqi Destiny*. 13 Nov.

Bremer, Louis Paul III. 2003. Bremer urges understanding during Ramadan. *Iraqi Destiny*. 31 Oct.

Day, Thomas. 2003. Artillerymen pay tribute to slain NCO. *Iraqi Destiny*. 31 Oct.

Jones, Christopher. 2003. First Children's clinic north of Mosul opens. *Iraqi Destiny*. 31 Oct.

Xenikakis, Mary Rose. 2003. Badush hospital reopens : 2-44 ADA takes small steps in reconstruction of health clinic. *Iraqi Destiny*. 31 Oct.

Risner, Joshua. 2003. Weapons policy in effect for people of Ninevah. *Iraqi Destiny*. 3 Jun.

Risner, Joshua. 2003. Weapon search continues. *Iraqi Destiny*. 21 Jun.

Day, Thomas. 2003. Mosul Central Bank rebuilding project begins. *Iraqi Destiny*. 25 Dec.

Jones, Christopher. 2003. 101st donates more than 230 computers to City Hall. *Iraqi Destiny*. 18 Dec.

Jones, Christopher. 2003. Communication underway in Iraq. *Iraqi Destiny*. 18 Dec.

Jones, Christopher. 2003. Coalition-trained attorneys complete training. *Iraqi Destiny*. 6 Nov.

Day, Thomas. 2003. 101st, CPA detail local agricultural initiatives. *Iraqi Destiny*. 16 Oct.

Day, Thomas. 2003. Kisik Oil Refinery opens. *Iraqi Destiny*. 25 Sept.

Day, Thomas. 2003. 101st Airborne, Mosul police open new station. *Iraqi Destiny*. 25 Dec.

Matise, James. 2003. 101st celebrates 4th, CG reenlists 158. *Iraqi Destiny*. 8 July.

Matise, James. 2003. Iraq, Syria border opened. *Iraqi Destiny*. 15 May.

Woodward, Robert. 2003. Kurdish, Arab farmers agree. *Iraqi Destiny*. 15 May.

Talento, Catherine. 2003. Fallen soldier remembered. Iraqi Destiny. 13 June.

Risner, Joshua. 2003. Strike 6 surfs the radio waves in Mosul. *Iraqi Destiny*. 3 June.

Matise, James. 2003. Mosul Election: Interim government underway in Northern Iraq. *Iraqi Destiny*. 8 May.